Social Capital

Social Capital

Theory and Research

Nancy Lin
Karen Cook
Ronald S. Burt
editors

AldineTransaction
A Division of Transaction Publishers
New Brunswick (U.S.A.) and London (U.K.)

Fourth printing 2008
Copyright © 2001 by Transaction Publishers, New Brunswick, New Jersey.

This book is printed on acid-free paper that meets the American National Standard for Permanence of Paper for Printed Library Materials.

Library of Congress Catalog Number: 00-052396
ISBN: 978-0-202-30643-8 (cloth); 978-0-202-30644-5 (paper)
Printed in the United States of America

Library of Congress Cataloging-in-Publication Data

Social capital: theory and research / edited by Nan Lin, Karen Cook, Ronald S. Burt.
       p. cm.—(Sociology and economics)
  Includes bibliographical references and index.
  ISBN 0-202-30643-7 (cloth: alk. paper)—ISBN 0-202-30644-5 (pbk: alk. paper)
   1. Social networks. 2. Social structure. I. Lin, Nan, 1938-. II. Cook, Karen S. III. Burt, Ronald S. IV. Series.

HM741.S628 2001
306.3—dc2l   00-052396

CONTENTS

Part III: *Social Capital in Organizational, Community,*
and Institutional Settings

PREFACE

Social capital as both concept and theory has drawn much intellectual interest and research in the past two decades. The attraction of the notion is perhaps in part due to the common understanding that as a social element, it may capture the essence of many sociological concepts (e.g., social support, social integration, social cohesion, and even norms and values) and serve as an umbrella term that can easily be understood and transported across many disciplines. It may also be due to the appreciation that as capital, it shares commonalities with other forms of capital (notably human capital) in its focus on a payoff or utility. Intellectually and as a counterpoint theory to human capital, it excites scholars, especially sociologists, who have explored other useful concepts in capturing the elements or resources embedded in social structures and networks rather than in individuals. Since it shares human capital's utilitarian aspect (capital), these scholars see it as providing the necessary basis of a common language for analyzing capitalization (investment and production) of social- and individual-based resources for certain utilitarian outcomes. Still others, especially those engaged in policy analysis and decision making, find in social capital a potential policy leverage: if human capital can be manipulated for the good of individuals and society, perhaps social capital can be as well.

These attractions have also resulted in a multitude of perspectives (e.g., is social capital a collective or individual asset?), definitions (is it community participation, social networks, or trust?), theoretical propositions (are closed or open networks better?), and emphases (can social capital operate in economic activities and organizations? Can it work in different social and institutional contexts?). In fact, there is a looming danger that the free flow of understanding, application, and interpretation of social capital may soon reach a point where the term might be used in whatever way it suits the purpose at hand, and thus be rendered meaningless as a scientific concept that must meet the rigorous demands of theoretical and research validity and reliability. Without a shared perspective, systematic operationalization, and programmatic studies, social capital may be in danger of becoming one of many fads and fashions that come and go in sciences and social sciences, and ultimately be abandoned for its lack of distinctive features and contributions to the scientific knowledge.

To address some of these issues and exchange research information, we

organized an international conference on social capital held in October–
November 1998 at Duke University. We invited speakers who in our judgment were conducting significant work on social capital, and over 150
scholars and professionals participated in the three-day event. In the subsequent year and a half, we have asked a number of the presenters to re-
vise and update their presentations; the current volume is the outcome of
this collective effort.

This volume investigates social capital from a social-network perspective and provides a forum for ongoing research programs initiated by some
sociologists. These scholars and programs share certain understandings
and approaches in their analyses of social capital. First, they argue that social networks are the foundation of social capital. Social networks simultaneously capture individuals and social structure, thus serving as a vital
conceptual link between actions and structural constraints, between micro-
and macrolevel analyses, and between relational and collective dynamic
processes. Second, they are cognizant of the dual significance of the "structural" features of the social networks and the "resources" embedded in the
networks as defining elements of social capital. Trying to reflect these elements in the conceptualization and operationalization of social capital,
these scholars' work forms a common, although by no means uniform, basis for constructing and building knowledge about social capital. Third,
they analyze the precedents as well as consequences of social capital. For
them, social capital not only serves as an exogenous force, leading to certain outcomes, but more importantly is itself the consequence of other
exogenous and dynamic forces. Specifically, these scholars focus on structural features in the political economy, the society, the community, and the
organizations which may account for the formation and distribution of social capital. Fourth, these scholars share the commitment that research on
social capital must be a multimethod, multilevel, and multisite enterprise.
The variety of methodologies employed (ranging from case studies to multilevel analysis) and the global nature of the research enterprise (works
conducted in the United States, Canada, the Netherlands, Hungary, mainland China, and Taiwan) highlight the shared interest in and sensitivity to
the multimethod approach to validating hypotheses and in the contingent
nature of findings.

The volume is divided into three parts. Part I clarifies social capital as a
concept and explores its theoretical and operational bases. Lin, in the initial essay, provides a brief account that places the development of social
capital in the context of the family of capital theorists, and identifies some
critical but controversial perspectives and statements regarding social capital in the literature. It makes the argument for the network perspective:
why and how such a perspective can clarify controversies and advance our
understanding of a whole range of instrumental and expressive outcomes.

Burt tackles a major debate between two different conceptual perspectives on networks as social capital: an open network or a research focus on linkages with ties outside a social group, or a closed network emphasizing internal cohesion. Rather than seeing them as competing paradigms, Burt argues that they are in fact complementary. The open network argument, as exemplified in the analysis of structural holes, is the paradigm if ties to outside the group add value to the group or its members. On the other hand, the network closure argument seems to be useful when resources inside the group are sufficient and mobilized for group or individual members' gain. Thus, the chapter proposes an integration of the two models in a more general one in which holes and closure are contingency factors in the calculation of the value of the capital.

Lin, Fu, and Hsung, in the next chapter, take on the methodological issue of designing an appropriate measurement of social capital. Assuming that embedded resources in social connections characterize social capital, they demonstrate—with survey data from Taiwan—the utility of the position-generator methodology, which yields good psychometric properties and credible validity in a status-attainment model. The measurement is also sensitive in illustrating differential returns of social capital to men and women in different employment contexts (i.e., whether self-employed or working for others).

Part II reports on current efforts in the assessment of social capital's utility in the labor market, and how it operates from both the employer's and laborer's points of view. The labor market is a research arena where a substantial number of social-capital studies have been conducted. Job-search studies have clearly demonstrated the utility of social capital for job seekers to attain better occupations. Only recently, however, has attention turned to the utility of social capital from employers' perspective. The principal argument is that social capital should benefit both employers and employees. For employers, networks present an important avenue for enlarging application pools, providing additional or new information about applicants, and furnishing a social environment to induce employees to stay with the firm. More important, networks help employers match the requirements of certain jobs with applicants. In cases where jobs require external contacts or network skills, social connections facilitate the identification of applicants with the appropriate qualifications, especially those who have networks rich in resources or social skills for the specific jobs. Thus, it should be the case that social capital carries returns for both the employer and the employee, matching supply and demand for labor in a mutually beneficial way.

Fernandez focuses on employee referrals and calculates the returns or benefits in the use of interpersonal connections for both the employer and the employee. He and co-author Castilla investigate returns to employees who refer new recruits to jobs as customer service representatives. As they clearly show, the bonus incentive is the leading inducement to employees to engage in such actions. Further, those who are in structurally advantaged positions (they themselves had been referred or have served as customer service representatives) are more likely to take such actions. They thus demonstrate that social capital (evoking interpersonal ties) represents a purposive investment for those in a position to take advantage of incentives and results in monetary returns.

Marsden examines the utility of social capital from the employer's perspective. He argues that the use of network practices for recruiting new employees from outside as well as promoting or transferring current employees depends on costs, benefits, and constraints associated with its usage in different circumstances. Social capital tends to benefit simple, private-sector organizations, positions that require additional training, and jobs in managerial, professional/technical, or sales/service rather than un- or semiskilled occupations.

Erickson also focuses on the demand and supply of social capital and argues that employers define jobs in terms of human capital (education and experience) and social capital (networks rich in external contacts) requirements, and match employees who fit these requirements. For jobs that require social capital, occupants with such network resources are also better rewarded in terms of higher rank and pay beyond the contribution of human capital.

Flap and Boxman examine the question of why informal searches do not always yield better job outcomes for persons seeking jobs with a panel study of job applicants as well as a sample of the employers. In combining these data, they demonstrate: (1) that it is important to take both employer and applicant characteristics into account in determining whether social connections would be used in the matching process; (2) that in fact employer's requirements (e.g., minimizing damage or risk, and the potential for a commitment to develop a career with the firm) may be more important; and (3) that as a result of this two-way process, it cannot be expected that applicants using informal job search processes would automatically be better off (e.g., gain better jobs and income).

Part III examines how social capital operates in organizational, community, and institutional settings. Examining social capital with the network approach does not suggest that the larger social contexts are to be ignored; instead, it actually provides a foundation on which individual actions and societal constraints and opportunities can be better analyzed and understood. Thus, it is most advisable that social capital studies always concern themselves with larger social contexts. Essays in this section demonstrate how such designs and analyses can bear fruit. Lazega and Pattison use a case study approach to examine a law firm, where temporary task forces present occasions for possible status auctions and competitions. Use of p* models to study the multiplexity of resource (advice, friendship, and co-workers) exchanges in the substructural level finds that advice ties promote co-worker ties. It is therefore proposed that a multiplexity of resource exchanges may be seen as social capital that both promotes and softens status competition. Advice ties and friendships also show significant multiplexity and exchange effects. Thus, the authors suggest that friendship both directly and indirectly softens the status differences in advice ties.

Wellman and Frank address the issue by employing a multilevel methodology to demonstrate that social capital, as crystalized in social support, is facilitated by tie characteristics, and micro- and mesolevel variables, with both social support and tie characteristics simultaneously functions of the larger social networks. Thus, the presence of a larger percentage of parents and children in a network facilitates greater support behavior for parents and children. This strategy demonstrates the simultaneous significance of individual agency and dyadic relations, as well as network properties for the utility of social capital.

Examining the larger social contexts also allows us to test the boundaries and contingencies of the usual expectations of the utility of social capital as initially formulated in certain specific social and cultural environments. Are weaker or stronger ties better for accessing better resources? Is gender homogeneity or homophily more useful in accessing better resources? Hurlbert, Beggs, and Haines study some of these issues. Their research program examines the use of social networks and embedded resources in what they call "extreme environments" such as in the wake of a disaster (e.g., a hurricane) or life in a property-stricken community. Their findings challenge conventional expectations and suggest that networks and social capital useful in one social context may not work in another. Thus, different social groups (gender or poor / rich), for different purposes (formal or informal support), may or may not benefit from certain network characteristics (size, density, and homophily).

How does social capital operate in other cultures? Bian makes an attempt to analyze the notion of *guanxi*, a term commonly used to denote social connections among the Chinese. Bian suggests that in fact there are possibly three understandings or theories about *guanxi*, each emphasizing a certain feature of social connections: (1) it signifies and consolidates extended families, (2) it evokes instrumental use of connections, or (3) it performs asymmetric exchanges in order to expand the diversity of one's connections. Using banquet giving and attending as indicators of culturally important social occasions, he sets up hypotheses for testing these alternative theories. With panel data from urban China, Bian confirms the significance of *guanxi* as a means of network diversity.

The dynamic transformation of political and economic institutions experienced by a society provides another arena for examining the social context for social-capital dynamics. Angelusz and Tardos were able to conduct panel studies in Hungary before and after the collapse of the Communist regime (1987 and 1997). The question they posed is whether factors affecting social capital (resources embedded in social networks) changed during this transformation, and if so in what particular manner. Using four different methodologies to measure social capital (the name generator, the position generator, the sending of Christmas and New Year greeting cards, and membership in voluntary associations), they found that wealth became more significantly related to social capital after the collapse of the regime. Surprisingly, political involvement persisted in significance during the two periods, and education showed no substantial increase in significance over this period. The authors suspect that the transformation is still under way, and further observation will be needed to gain a better understanding of the social dynamics affecting the social capital distribution in Hungary.

This collection by no means claims to be representative of all significant work on social capital currently taking place around the world; nor is it our aim to settle all controversies and debates. Space limitations do not even allow us to include important research programs using the social-capital-network perspective to examine many other critical issues and outcomes, such as quality of life, health and mental health, and collective behaviors and actions. Excluded also is the arena of cyberspace, where rigorous and systematic examinations and presentations will showcase the creative construction and reconstruction of social capital in dynamic cybernetworks. Nevertheless, we hope that the volume serves as a focal reference demonstrating how social capital has been pursued as a theoretical concept guiding systematic research. These theoretical and research insights, both positive and negative, help form the bases for intellectual dialogue and research development when other topics and arenas are engaged.

Nan Lin
Karen Cook
Ronald S. Burt

Part I

Social Capital: Networks and Embedded Resources

1

Building a Network Theory
of Social Capital

Nan Lin

In the past two decades, social capital in its various forms and contexts has emerged as one of the most salient concepts in social sciences. While much excitement has been generated, divergent views, perspectives, and expectations have also raised the serious question: is it a fad or does it have enduring qualities that will herald a new intellectual enterprise? The purpose of this chapter is to review social capital as discussed in the literature, identify controversies and debates, consider some critical issues, and propose conceptual and research strategies for building a theory. I argue that such a theory and the research enterprise must be based on the fundamental understanding that social capital is captured from embedded resources in social networks. Deviations from this understanding in conceptualization and measurement lead to confusion in analyzing causal mechanisms in the macro- and microprocesses. It is precisely these mechanisms and processes, essential for a theory about interactions between structure and action, to which social capital promises to make contributions.

I begin by exploring the nature of capital and various theories of capital, so that social capital can be properly perceived and located. I then identify certain controversies which, unless clarified or resolved, will hinder the development of a theory and the research enterprise. By considering social capital as assets in networks, I discuss some issues in conceptualization, measurement, and causal mechanism (the factors leading to inequality of social capital and the returns following investments in social capital). A proposed model identifies the exogenous factors leading to the

3

acquisition (or the lack) of social capital as well as the expected returns of social capital.

WHAT IS CAPITAL?

To understand social capital, it is necessary to consider the family of capital theories and trace their historical and conceptual development. A more detailed explication of the concepts of capital and social capital is available elsewhere (Lin 2001). Suffice it here to present a summary of their historical development. The notion of capital can be traced to Marx (1933/1849, 1995/1867, 1885, 1894; Brewer 1984). In his conceptualization, capital is part of the surplus value captured by capitalists or the bourgeoisie, who control the means of production, in the circulation of commodities and monies between the production and consumption processes. In such circulation, laborers are paid for their labor (commodity) with a wage allowing them to purchase commodities (such as food, shelter, and clothing) to sustain their lives (exchange value). But the commodity processed and produced by the capitalists can be circulated to and sold in the consumption market at a higher price (user value). In this scheme of the capitalist society, capital represents two related but distinct elements. On the one hand, it is part of the *surplus value* generated and pocketed by the capitalists (and their "misers," presumably the traders and sellers). On the other hand, it represents an *investment* (in the production and circulation of commodities) on the part of the capitalists, with expected returns in a marketplace. Capital, as part of the surplus value, is a product of a process; capital is also an investment process in which the surplus value is produced and captured. It is also understood that the investment and its produced surplus value refer to a return/reproduction of the process of investment and of more surplus values. It is the dominant class that makes the investment and captures the surplus value. Thus, it is a theory based on the exploitative nature of social relations between two classes. I have called Marx's theory of capital the *classical theory of capital* (Lin 2001, Chapter 1).

Subsequent theoretical modifications and refinements have retained the basic elements of capital in the classical theory, as represented in Table 1. Fundamentally, capital remains a surplus value and represents an investment with expected returns. Human-capital theory (Johnson 1960; Schultz 1961; Becker 1964/1993), for example, also conceives of capital as investment (e.g., in education) with certain expected returns (earnings). Individual workers invest in technical skills and knowledge so that they can negotiate with those in control of the production process (firms and their agents) for payment of their labor-skill. This payment has value that may be more than what the purchase of subsisting commodities would require

Table 1. Theories of Capital[a]

	Explanation	Capital	Level of Analysis
The Classical Theory (Marx)	Social relations; Exploitation by the capitalists (bourgeoise) of the proletariat	A. Part of surplus value between the use value (in consumption market) and the exchange value (in production-labor market) of the commodity B. Investment in the production and circulation of commodities	Structural (classes)
The Neocapital Theories			
Human Capital (Schultz, Becker)	Accumulation of surplus value by laborer	Investment in technical skills and knowledge	Individual
Cultural Capital (Bourdieu)	Reproduction of dominant symbols and meanings (values)	Internalization or misrecognition of dominant values	Individual/class
Social Capital (Lin, Burt, Marsden, Flap, Coleman)	Social relations; Access to and use of resources embedded in social networks	Investment in social networks	Individual
(Bourdieu, Coleman, Putnam)	Solidarity and reproduction of group	Investment in mutual recognition and acknowledgment	Group/individual

aSummary of discussion from Lin (2001, Chapters 1 and 2).

and, thus, contain surplus value that in part can be spent for leisure and lifestyle needs and turned into capital. Likewise, cultural capital, as described by Bourdieu (Bourdieu 1990; Bourdieu & Passeron 1977), represents investments on the part of the dominant class in reproducing a set of symbols and meanings, which are misrecognized and internalized by the dominated class as their own. The investment, in this theory, is in the pedagogic actions of the reproduction process, such as education, the purpose of which is to indoctrinate the masses to internalize the values of these symbols and meanings. Cultural-capital theory also acknowledges that the masses (the dominated class) can invest and acquire these symbols and meanings, even if they misrecognize them as their own. The inference is that while cultural capital is mostly captured by the dominant class through intergenerational transmissions, even the masses (or at least some of them) may generate returns from such investment and acquisition.

However, these theories break significantly from the classical theory—that is, because the laborers, workers or masses can now invest, and thus acquire certain capital of their own (be they skills and knowledge in the case of human capital, or "misrecognized" but nevertheless internalized symbols and meanings), they (or some of them) can now generate surplus value in trading their labor or work in the production and consumption markets. The social relations between classes (capitalists and noncapitalists) become blurred. The image of the social structure is modified from one of dichotomized antagonistic struggle to one of layered or stratified negotiating discourses. I have called these the *neocapitalist theories* (Lin 2001, Chapter 1). The distinctive feature of these theories resides in the potential investment and capture of surplus value by the laborers or masses. Social capital, I argue, is another form of the neocapital theories.[1]

WHY DOES SOCIAL CAPITAL WORK?[2]

The premise behind the notion of social capital is rather simple and straightforward: *investment in social relations with expected returns* (Lin 2001, Chapter 2). This general definition is consistent with various renditions by scholars who have contributed to the discussion (Bourdieu 1980, 1983/1986; Burt 1992; Coleman 1988, 1990; Erickson 1995, 1996; Flap 1991, 1994; Lin 1982, 1995; Portes 1998; Putnam 1993, 1995a). Individuals engage in interactions and networking in order to produce profits. Generally, four explanations can be offered as to why embedded resources in social networks will enhance the outcomes of actions (Lin 2001, Chapter 2). For one, it facilitates the flow of *information*. In the usual imperfect market situations, social ties located in certain strategic locations and/or hierarchical positions (and thus better informed about market needs and demands) can provide an individual with useful information about opportunities and choices otherwise not available. Likewise, these ties (or their ties) may alert an organization (be it in the production or consumption market) and its agents, or even a community, about the availability and interest of an otherwise unrecognized individual. Such information would reduce the transaction cost for the organization to recruit "better" (be it skill, or technical or cultural knowledge) individuals and for individuals to find "better" organizations that can use their capital and provide appropriate rewards. Second, these social ties may exert *influence* on the agents (e.g., recruiters or supervisors of the organizations) who play a critical role in decisions (e.g., hiring or promotion) involving the actor. Some social ties, due to their strategic locations (e.g., structural holes) and positions (e.g., authority or supervisory capacities), also carry more valued resources and exercise greater power (e.g., greater asymmetry in dependence by these agents), in organizational agents' decision making. Thus, "putting in a word" carries a certain weight in the decision-making process regarding an individual. Third, social-tie resources, and their acknowledged relationships to the individual, may be conceived by the organization or its agents as certifications of the individual's *social credentials*, some of which reflect the individual's accessibility to resources through social networks and relations—his/her social capital. "Standing behind" the individual by these ties reassures the organization (and its agents) that the individual can provide "added" resources beyond his/her personal capital, some of which may be useful to the organization. Finally, social relations are expected to reinforce identity and recognition. Being assured of one's worthiness as an individual and a member of a social group sharing similar interests and resources not only provides emotional support but also public acknowledgment of one's claim to certain resources. These *reinforcements* are essential for the maintenance of mental health and the entitlement to resources. These four elements—*information, influence, social credentials,* and *reinforcement*—may explain why social capital works in instrumental and expressive actions not accounted for by forms of personal capital such as economic capital or human capital.[3]

PERSPECTIVES AND CONTROVERSIES IN SOCIAL CAPITAL

While the fundamental definition of social capital is in general agreed on, two perspectives can be identified relative to the level at which return or profit is conceived—whether the profit is accrued for the group or for individuals. In one perspective, the focus is on the use of social capital by individuals—how individuals access and use resources embedded in social networks to gain returns in instrumental actions (e.g., finding better jobs) e gains in expressive actions. Thus, at this relational level, social be seen as similar to human capital in that it is assumed that such investments can be made by individuals with expected return, some benefit or profit, to the individual. Aggregation of individual returns also benefits the collective. Nonetheless, the focal points for analysis in this perspective are (1) how individuals invest in social relations, and (2) how individuals capture the emebedded resources in the relations to generate a return. Representative works (see review in Lin 1999) can be found in Lin (Lin & Bian 1991; Lin & Dumin 1986; Lin, Ensel, & Vaughn 1981), Burt (1992, 1998, 1997), Marsden (Marsden & Hurlbert 1988; Campbell, Marsden, & Hurlbert 1986), Flap (Boxman, De Graaf, & Flap 1991; De Graaf & Flap 1988; Flap & De Graaf 1988; Flap 1991; Sprengers, Tazelaar, & Flap, 1988; Volker & Flap 1996), and Portes (Portes & Sensenbrenner 1993) as well as in discussions of social capital by Coleman (1990) and Bourdieu (1983/1986).

Another perspective has its focus on social capital at the group level, with discussions dwelling on (1) how certain groups develop and maintain more or less social capital as a collective asset, and (2) how such a collective asset enhances group members' life chances. Bourdieu (1983/1986, 1980) and Coleman (1988, 1990) have discussed this perspective extensively and Putnam's empirical work (1993, 1995a, 2000) is exemplary. While acknowledging the need for individuals to interact and network to develop payoffs of social capital, the central interest of this perspective is to explore the elements and processes in the production and maintenance of the collective asset. For example, dense or closed networks are seen as the means by which collective capital can be maintained and reproduction of the group can be achieved. Another major interest is how norms and trust, as well as other properties (e.g., sanctions, authority) of a group are essential in the production and maintenance of the collective asset.

Whether social capital is seen from the societal-group level or the relational level, all scholars remain committed to the view that it is the interacting members who make the maintenance and reproduction of this social asset possible. This consensual view puts social capital firmly in the neo-capital-theory camp.[4]

However, the divergence in analyzing social capital at different levels has created some theoretical and measurement confusion (Lin 2001, Chapter 2). Further confusion arises from the fact that some discussions have flowed freely between levels. For example, Bourdieu provides a structural view in pointing to the reproduction of the dominant class and nobility groups as the principal explanation of social capital, which is represented by aggregating (1) the size of the group or network and (2) the volume of capital possessed by members (Bourdieu 1983/1986, p. 248). This representation makes sense only when it is assumed that all members maintain strong and reciprocal relations (a completely dense or institutionalized network), so that the strength of relations does not enter into the calculus. Yet, Bourdieu also describes how individuals interact and reinforce mutual recognition and acknowledgment as members of a network or group. Coleman (1990, Chapter 12), while emphasizing how individuals can use sociostructural resources to obtain better outcomes in their (individual) actions, devotes much discussion to the collective nature of social capital in stressing trust, norms, sanctions, authority, and closure as part or forms of social capital. It is important to identify and sort through these confusions and reach some understanding before we can proceed to build a coherent theory of social capital. I have identified some of these issues in Table 2.

One major controversy generated from macro- versus relational-level perspectives is whether social capital is a collective or an individual good (see Portes' critique, 1998). Most scholars agree that it is both collective and individual; that is, institutionalized social relations with embedded resources are expected to benefit both the collective and the individuals in the collective. At the group level, social capital represents some aggregation of valued resources (such as economic, political, cultural, or social, as in social connections) of members interacting as a network or networks. The difficulty arises when social capital is discussed as a collective or even a public good, along with trust, norms, and other "collective" or public goods. What has resulted in the literature is that the terms have become alternative or substitutable terms or measurements. Divorced from its roots in individual interactions and networking, social capital becomes merely another trendy term to employ or deploy in the broad context of improving or building social integration and solidarity. In the following, I argue

Table 2. Controversies in Social Capital[a]

Issue	Contention	Problem
Collective or individual asset (Coleman, Putnam)	Social capital or collective asset	Confounding with norms, trust
Closure or open networks (Bourdieu, Coleman, Putnam)	Group should be closed or dense	Vision of class society and absence of mobility
Functional (Coleman)	Social capital is indicated by its effect in particular action	Tautology (cause is determined by effect)
Measurement (Coleman)	Not quantifiable	Heuristic, not falsifiable

[a]Adapted from Lin (2001, Chapter 2, Table 2.1).

that social capital, as a relational asset, must be distinguished from collective assets and goods such as culture, norms, trust, etc. Causal propositions may be formulated (e.g., that collective assets, such as trust, promote the relations and networks and enhance the utility of embedded resources, or vice versa), but it should not be assumed that they are all alternative forms of social capital or are defined by one another (e.g., trust is capital).

Another controversy, related to the focus on the collective aspect of social capital, is the assumed or expected requirement that there is closure or density in social relations and social networks (Bourdieu 1986; Coleman 1990; Putnam 1993, 1995a,b, 2000). Bourdieu, from his class perspective, sees social capital as the investment of the members in the dominant class (as a group or network) engaging in mutual recognition and acknowledgment so as to maintain and reproduce group solidarity and preserve the group's dominant position. Membership in the group is based on a clear demarcation (e.g., nobility, title, family) excluding outsiders. Closure of the group and density within the group are required. Coleman, of course, does not assume such a class vision of society. Yet, he also sees network closure as a distinctive advantage of social capital, because it is closure that maintains and enhances trust, norms, authority, sanctions, etc. These solidifying forces may ensure that individuals can mobilize network resources.

I believe that the linkage between network density or closure to the utility of social capital is too narrow and partial. Research in social networks has stressed the importance of bridges in networks (Granovetter 1973; Burt 1992) in facilitating information and influence flows. To argue that closure or density is a requirement for social capital is to deny the significance of bridges, structural holes, or weaker ties. The root of preferring a dense or closed network lies, rather, in certain outcomes of interest (Lin 1992a, 1986, 1990). For *preserving or maintaining resources* (i.e., expressive actions), denser networks may have a relative advantage. Thus, for the privileged class, it would be better to have a closed network so that the resources can be preserved and reproduced (e.g., Bourdieu 1986); or for a mother to move to a cohesive community so that her children's security and safety can be assured (Coleman 1990). On the other hand, for *searching for and obtaining resources* (i.e., instrumental actions), such as looking for a job or better job (Lin 1999; Marsden & Hurlbert 1988; De Graaf & Flap 1988; Burt 1992), accessing and extending bridges in the network should be more useful. Rather than assert that closed or open networks are required, it would be theoretically more viable to (1) conceptualize for what outcomes and under what conditions a denser or more sparse network might generate a better return, and (2) postulate deduced hypotheses (e.g., a denser network would be more likely to promote the sharing of resources which, in turn, maintain group or individual resources; or, an open network would be more likely to access advantaged positions and resources, which in turn enhance the opportunity to obtain additional resources) for empirical examination.

A third controversy that requires clarification is Coleman's statement that social capital is any "social-structural resource" that generates returns for an individual in a specific action. He remarks that "social capital is defined by its function" and "it is not a single entity, but a variety of different entities having two characteristics: They all consist of some aspect of a social structure, and they facilitate certain actions of individuals who are within the structure" (1990, p. 302). This "functional" view may be a tautology: social capital is identified when and if it works; the potential causal explanation of social capital can be captured only by its effect, or whether it is an investment depends on the return for a specific individual in a specific action. Thus, the causal factor is defined by the effect. Clearly, it would be impossible to build a theory where causal and effectual factors are folded into a singular function. This is not to deny that a functional relationship may be hypothesized (e.g., resources embedded in social networks enhances obtaining better jobs). But the two concepts must be treated as separate entities with independent measurements (e.g., social capital is the investment in social relations and better jobs are represented by occupational status or supervisory position). It would be incorrect to allow the outcome variables to dictate the specification of the causal variable (e.g., for actor X, kin ties are social capital because these ties channel X to get a better job, and for actor Y, kin ties are not social capital because these ties do not channel Y to get a better job). The hypothesized causal relationship may be conditioned by other factors (e.g., family characteristics may affect differential opportunities for building human and social capital) which need be specified in a more elaborate theory. A theory would lose parsimony quickly if the conditional factors become part of the definitions of the primary concepts. In fact, one would question whether it remains a theory if it is required to make a good prediction for every individual case and individual situation.

Perhaps related to this view of social capital as indistinguishable from its outcome—and perhaps given his view that social capital, as a collective good, can also be seen in many different forms such as trust, norms, sanctions, authority, etc.—Coleman questions "whether social capital will come to be as useful a quantitative concept in social science as are the concepts of financial capital, physical capital, and human capital; its current value lies primarily in its usefulness for qualitative analyses of social systems and for those quantitative analyses that employ qualitative indicators" (1990, pp. 304–5). Again, the confusion can be seen as resulting from extending the notion of social capital beyond its theoretical roots in social relations and social networks and the unattainable theoretical position that prediction holds for every individual case. Once these issues are resolved, social capital should and must be measurable.

CONCEPTUALIZING AND MEASURING SOCIAL CAPITAL

These debates and clarifications lead to the suggestion that social capital, as a concept, is rooted in social networks and social relations, and must be measured relative to its root. Therefore, social capital can be defined as *resources embedded in a social structure which are accessed and/or mobilized in purposive actions* (Lin 2001, Chapter 3). By this definition, the notion of social capital contains three ingredients: resources embedded in a social structure; accessibility to such social resources by individuals; and use or mobilization of such social resources by individuals in purposive actions. Thus conceived, social capital contains three elements intersecting structure and action: the structural (embeddedness), opportunity (accessibility) and action-oriented (use) aspects.

These elements have been mentioned by most scholars working on social capital. The social resources theory (Lin 1982) has specifically proposed that access to and use of social resources (resources embedded in social networks) can lead to better socioeconomic status. Further, the theory proposes that access to and use of social resources are in part determined by positions in the hierarchical structure (the strength of position proposition) and by the use of weaker ties (the strength of tie proposition). Bourdieu defines the volume of social capital as a function of the size of the network and the volume of capital (economic, cultural and symbolic) possessed by networked individuals. Burt (1992) postulates that certain network positions (structural holes and structural constraints) have effects on individuals getting better positions or rewards in organizations. Flap (1994) defines social capital as a combination of network size, relationship strength, and resources possessed by those in the network. Portes (1998) also advocates focusing on social relations and networks in the analysis of social capital.

Embedded Resources and Network Locations

Given the significance of resources and relations in social capital, it is not surprising that scholarly research has shown differential focus on one of the two elements. Some have chosen to focus on the location of individuals in a network as the key of social capital. Burt's work (1992) typifies this approach. By identifying the locations of individual nodes, it is possible to assess how close or how far the node is from a strategic location, such as a bridge, where the occupant has the competitive advantage in possible access to more, diverse, and valued information. Strength of ties (Granovetter 1973, 1974) is also a well-known, conceptually argued, network-location measurement of a bridge's usefulness. Other location measures are readily available in the literature, such as density, size, closeness, betweenness, and eigenvector (see review of such location measures in Borgatti, Jones, and Everett (1998)). Implicit in this approach is the argument that network location is the key element of identifying social capital.

Another approach focuses on embedded resources. In social-resource theory, valued resources in most societies are represented by wealth, power, and status (Lin 1982). Thus, social capital is analyzed by the amount or variety of such characteristics in others with whom an individual has direct or indirect ties. Measurement of social resources can be further specified as network resources and contact resources. Network resources refer to those embedded in one's ego-networks, whereas contact resources refer to those embedded in contacts used as helpers in an instrumental action, such as job searches. Thus, network resources represent accessible resources and contact resources represent mobilized resources in instrumental actions. For contact resources, the measurement is straightforward—the contact's wealth, power and/or status characteristics, typically reflected in the contact's occupation, authority position, industrial sector, or income.

There is little dispute that embedded resources are valid measures for social capital. There is some debate as to whether network locations are measures of social capital or precursors to social capital. My view is that if it is assumed that social capital attempts to capture valued resources in social relations, network locations should facilitate, but not necessarily determine, access to better embedded resources. What types of network locations evoke resources in order to generate returns depend on the type of returns one expects. In the Modeling Section below, I argue that two types of outcomes are possible as returns to social capital: instrumental and expressive. In the former, the return is the gaining of added resources, resources not possessed by ego; whereas in the latter, the return is the maintaining of possessed resources. For example, if we assume that bridges link to different information, the utility of that information depends on whether it concerns resources valued by the individual but not yet attained. If it does not, then the bridge serves little utility. If it does, the bridge is very useful. That is, not all bridges (or network locations) lead to better information, influence, social credentials or reinforcement. A bridge linking an individual looking for a job in a corporation to people occupying influential positions in large corporations will likely be of significantly more utility to that individual than a bridge that leads to others who are members of a health club. On the other hand, a mother with young children would prefer to live in a dense, cohesive community rather than one with a mobile population and open access to the external world. Likewise, a person facing personal stresses such as divorce might benefit from access to and interaction with others who have had similar stress and understand its psychological effects, rather than someone who is happily married. These are expressive actions and we should expect the benefit of a dense network and homogenous partners.

These considerations suggest that network locations should be treated as exogenous variables rather than endogenous variables of social capital itself. I will return to this topic in the Modeling section. Suffice it to conclude here that social capital is more than mere social relations and networks; it evokes the resources embedded and accessed. Nevertheless, such embedded resources cannot possibly be captured without identifying network characteristics and relations. Network locations are necessary conditions of embedded resources. In a given study, it is advisable to incorporate measures for both network locations and embedded resources.

Measuring Social Capital as Assets in Networks

Paralleling these two conceptual elements of social capital have been two principal approaches in measuring social capital as assets captured by individuals in social networks, as depicted in Table 3. The first approach is to measure embedded resources. Here, resources embedded in the social networks are seen as social capital's core element. Thus, measurements focus on the valued resources (e.g., wealth, power, and status) of others accessed by individuals in their networks and ties. Such measurements can

Table 3.   Social Capital as Assets in Network

Focus	Mesurements	Indicators
Embedded resources	Network resources	Range of resources, best resource, variety of resources, composition (average resources); contact resources
	Contact statuses	Contact's occupation, authority, sector
Network locations	Bridge or access to bridge	Structural hole, structural constraint
	Strength of tie	Network bridge, or intimacy, intensity, interaction, and reciprocity

be made relative to two frameworks: (1) network resources and (2) contact resources. The former tap resources represented in the network an individual has access to. Typically, they include (1) the range of resources among ties (or the "distance" between the highest and lowest valued resources), (2) the best possible resources in the networks or among ties (or upper "reachability" in the resource hierarchy), (3) the variety or heterogeneity of resources in the networks, and (4) the composition of resources (average or typical resources). Research indicates that these measures are highly correlated and tend to form a single factor, with the highest loading usually on the range or upper-reachability measures. Contact resources indicate the valued resources represented by contacts or helpers in specific actions. These measures, usually the valued resources (wealth, power, and status) of the contact(s), are applied in the context of specific actions, such as job searches. There is consistent, strong evidence that both network and contact resources positively affect the outcome of instrumental actions, such as job searching and job advances (Lin 1999).

Another prevailing measurement strategy focuses on network locations as measurements of social capital. A major perspective is the argument that bridges or access to bridges facilitates returns in actions. Granovetter's notion of bridges as expressed in the strength of weak ties (1973) was a preview of this argument, which is elaborated and formalized by Burt in his notions of structural holes and constraints (1992). Other measures of bridges (e.g., betweenness) would also be candidates for social capital, even though they are used less in the social-capital context.

There are many other measures, such as size, density, cohesion, and closeness of social networks which are candidates as measures for social capital (Burt & Minor 1982; Burt 1984; Borgatti, Jones, & Everett 1998). However, research evidence is much less clear as to their viability in a social-capital theory. Unless clear theoretical arguments are presented along with the use of any specific measures, as both measures of social resources and network locations have been, it would be ill-advised simply to use any network measure as an indicator of social capital.

Sampling Techniques

Three sampling techniques have been employed to construct measures of social capital, as can be seen in Table 4. The saturation sampling technique is useful when it is possible to map a definable social network. In such networks, data from all nodes are gathered and their relationships identified, and measurements of network locations can be developed. The advantage of this technique is that it allows detailed and complete analyses of every network location as well as embedded resources in each node. Because of the requirement that the network have a defined and manageable bound-

Table 4. Measurement Techniques

Technique	Advantages	Disadvantages
Saturation survey	Complete mapping of network	Limited to small networks
Name-generator	Customized content areas	Lack of sampling frame
	Ego-centered network mapping	Biased toward strong ties
Position-generator	Content free	Lack of specificity of
	Sampling of hierarchical	relations
	positions	
	Multiple "resources" mapped	
	Direct and indirect accesses	

ary, it is a technique most useful for studies of social capital within an organization or a small network among organizations.

For larger and less definable networks, ego-network sampling techniques are used. Typically, the name-generator (Laumann 1966; Wellman 1979; McCallister & Fischer 1978; Burt 1984; Marsden 1987) technique is employed. This measurement technique elicits a list of ties from ego, and the relationships between them as well as among them are identified. From these data, locations of ego as well as these ties, relative to one another, can be computed. Network resources can also be obtained from the name-generator technique. Measures such as composition (typical resource characteristics), heterogeneity (diversity of resources), and upper reachability (best possible resources) can be computed. The advantages of this approach include (1) the identification of specific content areas, relative to actions under investigations, as naming items, and (2) the mapping of ego-network locations and characteristics as well as social resources embedded in the ego-network. However, there are several serious shortcomings to this technique.

First, there is no theoretical or empirical framework that identifies the universe population from which the content areas to be studied can be sampled. While there may be a general understanding that certain instrumental and expressive dimensions might be involved (Lin 1986), no consensual knowledge is available as to what specific content areas under such dimensions constitute a set of elements in a content population for sampling. As a consequence, different content areas and wordings used make comparative analysis and validation impossible.

Second, the name-generator methodology tends to elicit stronger rather than weaker ties. Cognitively, names that come to mind first tend to be social ties with which ego is more intimate, more intensive in relations, more frequently interactive with, or more reciprocal in exchanges This bias may even be "beneficial" if the return or outcome concerns expressive or psychological consequences such as quality of life, health or mental health, as these returns are expected to be affected by strong-tie support or social integration (Lin 1986). If, however, the returns concern instrumental outcomes such as searching for better job or earnings, where theories have argued for the strength of weaker ties or bridges (Granovetter 1974; Lin 1982; Burt 1992), then the measure might miss the more critical social ties.

A third shortcoming of the name-generator methodology is that it identifies individual actors rather than social positions. When, as in many structural theories, the concerns focus on social positions (White, Boorman, & Breiger, 1976; White 1992; Cook 1982; Burt 1992), the name generator would not be appropriate.

While these shortcomings have been known, only recently has an alternative methodology emerged. The position-generator technique (Lin & Dumin 1986) samples positions in a given hierarchy representative of resources valued in the collective (e.g., occupational status or prestige, authority positions, sectors, etc.). In this technique, a sample of positions with identified valued resources (occupational status, authority positions, industrial sectors, etc.) is used and the respondent is asked to indicate if she / he knows anyone having that job or position. From the responses, it then becomes possible to construct network resource indexes such as extensity (number of positions accessed), range or heterogeneity (the "distance" between the "highest" and "lowest" positions accessed), and upper reachability ("highest" position accessed).

The position-generator methodology has several advantages: (1) it can be based on a representative sample of positions meaningful to a given society; (2) it can directly or indirectly identify linkages to such resource positions; and (3) it can be based on multiple resource criteria (e.g., occupation, authority, and industry). Studies in North America (Erickson 1996), as well as Europe (e.g., Flap & Boxman in the Netherlands: Boxman, De Graaf, & Flap 1988; Volker & Flap in East Germany:Volker & Flap 1996; Argelusz & Tardos in Hungary: Angelusz & Tardos 1991; Tardos 1996), have proven the utility of this theoretically derived methodology in the contact of social capital and instrumental action. It seems particularly useful if the valued resources are considered the core element of social capital. A sample of the position-generator instrument is presented in Table 5. A chapter in this volume (Lin, Fu, & Hsung) illustrates the utility of this methodology with data from Taiwan.

MODELING SOCIAL CAPITAL

To operationalize explicitly the critical elements, we may sharpen the definition of social capital to *investment in social relations by individuals through which they gain access to embedded resources to enhance expected returns of in-*

Table 5. Position Generator for Measuring Accessed Social Capital: An Example

Here is a list of jobs (show card). Would you please tell me if you happen to know someone (on a first-name basis) having each job?

Job	1. Do you know any-one having this job?[a] (If not, go to #7)	2. How long have you known this person (no. of years)	3. What is your relationship with this person?	4. How close are you with this person?	5. His/her gender	6. His/her job	7. Do you think you may find such a person through someone you know? (Person M)	8. Repeat #2–6 for Person M
Job A								
Job B								
Job C								
etc.								

[a]If you know more than one person, think of the one person whom you have known the longest (or the person who comes to mind first).

18

strumental or expressive actions. From this, three processes can be identified for modeling: (1) investment in social capital, (2) access to and mobilization of social capital, and (3) returns of social capital. While the above discussion clarifies social capital's definition, elements, and measurements, it is necessary to discuss briefly the types of outcomes that can be considered as expected returns. I propose two major types of outcomes: (1) returns to instrumental action, and (2) return to expressive action (Lin 1992, 1986, 1990). Instrumental action is taken to obtain resources not possessed by the actor, whereas expressive action is taken to maintain resources already possessed by the actor.

For instrumental action, we may identify three possible returns: economic, political, and social. Each can be seen as added capital. Economic return is straightforward. Political return is similarly straightforward, represented by hierarchical positions in a collective. Social gain needs some clarification. I have argued that reputation is an indication of social gain (Lin 2001, Chapter 9). Reputation can be defined as favorable/unfavorable opinions about an individual in a social network. A critical issue in social exchange where social capital is transacted is that the transaction may be asymmetric: a favor is given by the alter to ego. The ego's action is facilitated, but what is the gain for the alter, the giver of the favor? Unlike economic exchange, where reciprocal and symmetric transactions are expected in the short or long term, social exchange may not entail such expectation. What is expected is that the ego and the alter both acknowledge the asymmetric transactions that create the former's social debt to the latter, who accrues social credit. Social debt must be acknowledged in the public for the ego to maintain his/her relationship with the alter. Public recognition in the network spreads the reputation of the alter. The greater the debt, the larger the network, and the stronger the need for the ego and the alter to maintain the relationship; the greater the propensity to spread the word in the network and, thus, the greater the reputation gained by the alter. In this process, the alter is gratified by the reputation, which, along with material resources (such as wealth) and hierarchical positions (such as power) constitutes one of the three returns fundamental in instrumental actions. I have discussed this issue elsewhere (Lin 1998; 2001).

For expressive action, social capital is a means to consolidate resources and to defend against possible resource losses (Lin 1986, 1990). The principle is to access and mobilize others who share interest and control of similar resources so that embedded resources can be pooled and shared in order to preserve and protect existing resources. In this process, alters are willing to share their resources with egos because the preservation of the ego and its resources enhances and reinforce the legitimacy of alters' claim to like resources. Three types of return may be specified: physical health, mental health, and life satisfaction. Physical health involves maintenance of physical functional competence and freedom from diseases and injuries. Mental health reflects the capability to withstand stresses and the maintenance of cognitive and emotional balance. Life satisfaction indicates optimism and satisfaction with various life domains such as family, marriage, work, and community and neighborhood environments.

Oftentimes, returns to instrumental actions and expressive actions reinforce each other. Physical health offers the capacity to endure work load and may be responsible for attaining economic, political, and social status. Likewise, economic, political, or social status often offers resources to maintain physical health (exercise, diet, and health maintenance). Mental health and life satisfaction are likewise expected to have reciprocal effects on economic, political, and social gains. Factors leading to the instrumental and expressive returns, however, are expected to show differential patterns. As mentioned earlier, it may well be that open networks and relations are more likely to enable access to and use of bridges to reach to resources lacking in one's social circle and to enhance one's chances of gaining resources/instrumental returns. On the other hand, a denser network with more intimate and reciprocal relations among members may increase the likelihood of mobilizing others with shared interests and resources to defend and protect existing resources/expressive returns. Further, exogenous factors such as community and institutional arrangements and prescriptive versus competitive incentives may differentially contribute to the density and openness of networks and relations and the success of instrumental or expressive actions.

Having discussed the core elements of social capital, clarified some of the measurement and sampling issues, identified the types of returns, and briefly postulated differential patterns of causal effects, I would like to propose a model as an initial step of theorizing social capital. As can be seen in Figure 1, the model contains three blocks of variables in causal sequences. One block represents preconditions and precursors of social capital: the factors in the social structure and each individual's position in the social structure that facilitate or constrain the investment of social capital. Another block represents social capital elements, and a third block represents possible returns for social capital.

The process leading from the first to the second block describes the formation of the inequality of social capital: what structural and positional elements affect opportunities to construct and maintain social capital. It delineates patterns of differential distributions for social resources that are embedded, accessed, or mobilized. It should further demonstrate that there are social forces that determine such differential distributions. Thus, it is incumbent on a theory of social capital to delineate the patterns and determinants of the two ingredients of social capital or *the inequality of social capital* as accessible social resources and mobilized social resources (Lin

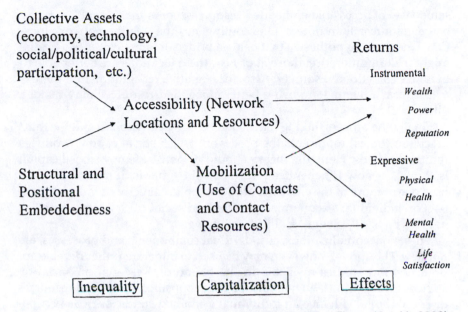

Collective Assets
(economy, technology,
social/political/cultural
participation, etc.)

Returns

Instrumental

Accessibility (Network
Locations and Resources)

Wealth

Power

Reputation

Structural and
Positional
Embeddedness

Mobilization
(Use of Contacts
and Contact
Resources)

Expressive

*Physical
Health*

*Mental
Health*

*Life
Satisfaction*

Inequality   Capitalization   Effects

Figure 1.   Modeling a theory of social capital (adapted from Figure 13.1, Lin 2000).

2000, 2001, Chapter 7). Two types of causation forces are of special interest
to scholars in the analysis of inequality of social capital: structural and positional variations. A structure may be characterized by many variations,
such as economy, technology, and participation in the social, cultural, and
political arenas. Within a structure, individuals may be described as occupying different positions in social, cultural, political, and economic strata.
These variations may be hypothesized to affect the richness or poorness of
various social ingredients.

Within the second block, there is a process linking two elements of social capital: access to and use of. The process linking the two elements
represents social-capital mobilization—that is, given the unequal distributions of social capital how would an individual be enabled or disabled to
mobilize such capital for specific actions? This is where the model, while
recognizing structural contributions to social capital, as captured in the inequality process, also emphasizes possible choice action in mobilization.

Third, the theory needs to demonstrate that the three ingredients are interconnected. Thus, it needs to propose a causal sequence in which embedded resources constrain and enable individual choices and actions. The
general expectation is that the better the accessible embedded resources,
the more embedded resources can and will be mobilized in purposive actions by an individual. The more intriguing question is why, given the

same level of accessible embedded resources, some individuals mobilize better resources than others. One contingency may be the network location. One could hypothesize that being a bridge or being closer to a bridge might make a difference: those at or near these locations are better able to mobilize embedded resources. Also, the cognitive recognition that there is a structural advantage to using better embedded resources may make a difference.

Finally, the process linking the second block (social capital) and the third block (outcomes) represents the process in which social capital produces returns or yields. Here, the theory should demonstrate how social capital is capital, or how it generates return or gain—that is, it should propose how one or more of the elements of social capital directly or indirectly impact an individual's economic, political, and social capital (resources), or her/his physical, mental, and life well-being.

These conceptualizations, as individual components and processes, are not new. This model, however, may be used to integrate rather diverse approaches and studies available in the literature. Research on social-resources theory (Lin 1999) has verified the proposition that social resources or social capital enhance an individual's attained status, such as occupational status, authority, and placement in certain industries. Through these attained positions, social capital enhances economic earnings as well. These relationships hold up after family background and education are taken into account. Burt (1997, 1998) and others (e.g., Podolny & Baron 1997) have shown that advances and economic rewards are also enhanced in organizations for individuals at strategic locations in the informal networks. Those closer to structural holes or bridges and, thus, under fewer structural constraints, seem to gain better returns, presumably because such locations give these individuals better opportunities to access certain capital in the organization. Research is progressing on how organizations use social capital to recruit and retain individuals. Fernandez and associates (Fernandez & Weinberg 1997) have shown that referrals increase applications, recruit better qualified candidates, and reduce costs in the screening process.

Some studies focus on collective assets. In Putnam's studies (1993, 1995a,b), this is indicated by participation in civic associations (e.g., churches, PTAs, Red Cross) and social groups (bowling leagues). Coleman (1990) provides examples of diffusion of information and mobilization through social circles among radical Korean students (i.e., network as capital), a mother moving from Detroit to Jerusalem in order to have her child walk to playground or school safely (norm as capital); and diamond traders in New York making trades through informal ties and informal agreements (network and trust as capital). Portes (1998) also specified "consummatory" and instrumental consequences of social capital (see Portes and Sensenbrenner 1993 for the consummatory consequences—solidarity and reciprocal support—of social capital for immigrant groups). While the primary focus for them is on the development, maintenance, or decline of collective assets, we need to be aware that not every member has an equal opportunity to access such assets. Thus, how these collective assets in conjunction with individuals' positions in these strata constitute precursors exogenous to the process of accessing or mobilizing social capital needs to be specified and demonstrated.

At the mesonetwork level, the focus shifts to how individuals have differential access to resources embedded in the collective. The question posed is why in a given collective certain individuals have better access to embedded resources than others. The nature of social networks and social ties becomes the focus of analysis. Granovetter (1973, 1974, 1982, 1985, 1995) proposes that bridges, usually reflected in weaker ties, provide better access to information. Burt (1992, 1997, 1998) sees that strategic locations in the networks, structural holes, or structural constraints imply better or worse access to information, influence, or control. Lin (1982, 1990, 1994a, 1995, 1999) has suggested that hierarchical positions as well as network locations facilitate or hinder access to embedded resources. Embedded resources are indicated by the wealth, status, and power of social ties.

At the microaction level, social capital is reflected in the actual linkage between the use of embedded resources in instrumental actions. For example, there is a substantial literature on how informal sources and their resources (contact resources) are mobilized in job searches and their effects on attained socioeconomic status (Lin, Ensel, & Vaughn 1981; De Graaf & Flap 1988; Marsden & Hurlbert 1988).

Research has also been extensive in the area of expressive actions' returns. Much is known about the indirect effects of networks on mental health and life satisfaction (Lin 1986; House et al. 1988; Berkman & Syme 1979; Berkman 1984; Hall & Wellman 1985; Wellman 1981; Kadushin 1983). In other words, network locations enhance the likelihood of accessing social support which, in turn, improves one's physical or mental well-being.

CONCLUDING REMARKS

Social networks scholarship has much to say about the development and future of social capital. Without anchoring the concept in social networks and embedded resources, chances are that social capital would fade away as an intellectual enterprise for the ever-broadening and -confounding definitions and almost utopian expectations of its practical applications. With ever-sharpening definitions and measurements, social-networks scholarship may have much to contribute to the sustained development of social capital as an intellectual enterprise.

NOTES

A portion of this chapter was presented as the Keynote Address at the XIX International Sunbelt Social Network Conference, Charleston, South Carolina, February 18–21, 1999, and appeared in *Connections*, 1999, 22–1: 28–51. I wish to thank Ronald S. Burt for reading and commenting on an earlier draft. I am, however, solely responsible for all the arguments presented here.

1. There is some ambiguity in Bourdieu's writings as to whether cultural capital should be seen as a structural theory or a theory that allows choice (Lin 2001, Chapter 1). He (Bourdieu 1990; Bourdieu & Passeron 1977) defines culture as a system of symbolism and meaning. The dominant class in the society imposes its culture by engaging in pedagogic action (e.g., education), which internalizes the dominant symbols and meanings in the next generation, thus, reproducing the salience of the dominant culture. The result is an internalized and durable training, *habitus*, in the reproduction of the culture. The masses are not cognitively aware of the imposition and take on the imposed culture as their own—misrecognition. This rendition of capital can trace its lineage to Marx. The social relations described by Marx are also assumed; there is a class, capitalists, who control the means of production—the process of pedagogic action or the educational institutions (in homes, schools, etc.). In the production (schooling) process, laborers (students or children) invest in the educational process and internalize the dominant class culture. Acquisition of this culture permits or licenses the laborers to enter the labor market, and earn money to support themselves. The capitalists, or the dominant class, gain cultural capital that supplements their economic capital and accumulate capital of both types in the circulation of the commodities (educated masses) and domination of the means of production (the educational institutions). However, there is a break from Marx, and it is important. Bourdieu does not assume perfect correspondence between the accumulation of economic and cultural capital. Some economic capitalists do not possess cultural capital and some cultural capitalists are not economically endowed. This less-than-perfect correspondence seems to open a possible path for some laborers, using their cultural habitus, to gain a foothold in the dominant class. It is conceivable that they become part of the educational institutions and gain returns in the labor market, due to their cultural capital. Bourdieu did not carry his analysis this far, but seems to leave open the process of social mobility and the possibility of agency.
2. This section is substantially extracted from Lin (2001, Chapter 2).
3. Another element, control, has also been mentioned for the usefulness of social capital. I consider control reflecting both the network location and the hierarchical position, central to the definition of social capital itself. Thus,

information, influence, social credentials, and reinforcement are all reasons why social capital works or controls.

4.   Two major and different theoretical positions distinguish scholars in the collective-asset camp. For Bourdieu, social capital represents a process by which individuals in the dominating class, by mutual recognition and acknowledgment, reinforce and reproduce a privileged group that holds various capital (economic, cultural and symbolic). Nobility and titles characterize such groups and their members. Thus, social capital is another way of maintaining and reproducing the dominant class. I would characterize this theoretical position as one that views social capital as class (privilege) goods. The other position on social capital as collective asset is represented by the works of Coleman and Putnam. Coleman, while defining social capital as consisting of any social-structural features or resources that are useful to individuals for specific actions, stresses social capital as a public good. These collective assets and features are available to all members of the group, be it a social group or community and regardless of which members actually promote, sustain, or contribute to such resources. Because social capital is a public good, it depends on the good will of the individual members to make such efforts and not to be free riders. Thus, norms, trust, sanctions, authority and other structural "features" become important in sustaining social capital. If one were forced to trace the theoretical lineage of these two explanatory schemes, one could argue that the privileged good view is principally an extension and elaboration of the social relations in the Marx' capital theory and that the public good view is primarily an extension and elaboration of the integrative or Durkheimian view of social relations.

REFERENCES

Angelusz, Robert, and Robert Tardos. 1991. "The Strength and Weakness of "Weak Ties." Pp. 7–23 in *Values, Networks and Cultural Reproduction in Hungary*, edited by P. Somlai. Budapest: The Coordinating Council of Programs.

Becker, Gary S. 1964/1993. *Human Capital*. Chicago, IL: University of Chicago Press.

Berkman, Lisa. 1984. "Assessing the Physical Health Effects of Social Networks and Social Support." *Annual Review of Public Health*. 5:413–32.

Berkman, Lisa F., and S. Leonard Syme. 1979. "Social Networks, Host Resistance, and Mortality: A Nine-Year Follow-Up Study of Alameda County Residents." *American Journal of Epidemiology* 109:186–284.

Borgatti, Stephen P., Candace Jones, and Martin G. Everett. 1998. "Network Measures of Social Capital." *Connections* 21(2):27–36, 2.

Bourdieu, Pierre. 1980. "Le Capital Social: Notes Provisoires." *Actes de la Recherche en Sciences Sociales* 3:2–3.

———. 1983/1986. "The Forms of Capital." Pp. 241–58 in *Handbook of Theory and Research for the Sociology of Education*, edited by John G. Richardson. Westport, CT: Greenwood Press.

————. 1990. *The Logic of Practice*. Cambridge, MA: Polity.

Bourdieu, Pierre, and Jean-Claude Passeron. 1977. *Reproduction in Education, Society, Culture*. Beverly Hills, CA: Sage.

Boxman, E. A. W., P. M. De Graaf, and Henk D. Flap. 1991. "The Impact of Social and Human Capital on the Income Attainment of Dutch Managers." *Social Networks* 13:51–73.

Breiger, Ronald L. 1981. "The Social Class Structure of Occupational Mobility." *American Journal of Sociology* 87(3):578–611.

Brewer, Anthony. 1984. *A Guide to Marx's Capital*. Cambridge, MA: Cambridge University Press.

Burt, Ronald S. 1984. "Network Items and the General Social Survey." *Social Networks* 6:293–339.

————. 1992. *Structural Holes: The Social Structure of Competition*. Cambridge, MA: Harvard University Press.

————. 1997. "The Contingent Value of Social Capital." *Administrative Science Quarterly* 42:339–65.

————. 1998. "The Gender of Social Capital." *Rationality and Society* 10(1):5–46, 1.

Burt, Ronald S., and M. J. Minor, eds. 1982. *Applied Network Analysis*. Beverly Hills, CA: Sage.

Campbell, Karen E., Peter V. Marsden, and Jeanne S. Hurlbert. 1986. "Social Resources and Socioeconomic Status." *Social Networks* 8(1), 1.

Coleman, James S. 1988. "Social Capital in the Creation of Human Capital." *American Journal of Sociology* 94:S95—S121.

————. 1990. *Foundations of Social Theory*. Cambridge, MA: Harvard University Press.

Cook, Karen S. 1982. "Network Structure from an Exchange Perspective." Pp. 177–99 in *Social Structure and Network Analysis*, edited by P. V. Marsden and N. Lin. Beverly Hills, CA: Sage.

De Graaf, Nan Dirk, and Hendrik Derk Flap. 1988. "With a Little Help from My Friends." *Social Forces* 67(2):452–72, 2.

Erickson, Bonnie H. 1995. "Networks, Success, and Class Structure: A Total View." Sunbelt Social Networks Conference. Charleston, SC, February.

————. 1996. "Culture, Class and Connections." *American Journal of Sociology* 102(1):217–51, 1.

Fernandez, Roberto M., and Nancy Weinberg. 1997. "Sifting and Sorting: Personal Contacts and Hiring in a Retail Bank." *American Sociological Review* 62:883–902.

Flap, Henk D. 1991. "Social Capital in the Reproduction of Inequality." *Comparative Sociology of Family, Health and Education* 20:6179–202.

————. 1994. "No Man Is An Island: The Research Program of a Social Capital Theory." World Congress of Sociology. Bielefeld, Germany, July.

Flap, Hendrik Derk, and Nan Dirk De Graaf. 1988. "Social Capital and Attained Occupational Status." *Netherlands Journal of Sociology*.

Granovetter, Mark. 1973. "The Strength of Weak Ties." *American Journal of Sociology* 78:1360–80.

————. 1974. *Getting a Job*. Cambridge, MA: Harvard University Press.

————. 1982. "The Strength of Weak Ties: A Network Theory Revisited." Pp. 105–

30 in *Social Structure and Network Analysis,* edited by Peter V. Marsden and Nan Lin. Beverly Hills, CA: Sage.

———. 1985. "Economic and Social Structure: The Problem of Embeddedness." *American Journal of Sociology* 91:481–510.

———. 1995. *Getting a Job (Revised Edition).* Chicago, IL: University of Chicago Press.

Hall, Alan, and Barry Wellman. 1985. "Social Networks and Social Support." Pp. 23–42 in *Social Support and Health,* edited by S. Cohen and S. L. Syme. Orlando, FL: Academic Press.

House, James, Debra Umberson, and K. R. Landis. 1988. "Structures and Processes of Social Support." *Annual Review of Sociology* 14:293–318.

Johnson, Harry G. 1960. "The Political Economy of Opulence." *Canadian Journal of Economics and Political Science* 26:552–64.

Kadushin, Charles. 1983. "Mental Health and the Interpersonal Environment: A Re-Examination of Some Effects of Social Structure on Mental Health." *American Sociological Review* 48:188–98.

Laumann, Edward O. 1966. *Prestige and Association in an Urban Community.* Indianapolis, IN: Bobbs-Merrill.

Lin, Nan. 1982. "Social Resources and Instrumental Action." Pp. 131–45 in *Social Structure and Network Analysis,* edited by Peter V. Marsden and Nan Lin. Beverly Hills, CA: Sage.

———. 1986. "Conceptualizing Social Support." Pp. 17–30 in *Social Support, Life Events, and Depression,* edited by Nan Lin, Alfred Dean and Walter Ensel. Orlando, FL: Academic Press.

———. 1990. "Social Resources and Social Mobility: A Structural Theory of Status Attainment." Pp. 247–171 in *Social Mobility and Social Structure,* edited by Ronald L. Breiger. New York: Cambridge University Press.

———. 1992. "Social Resources Theory." Pp. 1936–42 in *Encyclopedia of Sociology, Volume 4,* edited by Edgar F. Borgatta and Marie L. Borgatta. New York: Macmillan.

———. 1994. "Action, Social Resources, and the Emergence of Social Structure: A Rational Choice Theory." *Advances in Group Processes* 11:67–85.

———. 1995. "Les Ressources Sociales: Une Theorie Du Capital Social." *Revue Francaise de Sociologie* XXXVI(4):685–704, 4.

———. 1998. "Social Exchange: Its Rational Basis." World Congress of Sociology. Montreal, August.

———. 1999. "Social Networks and Status Attainment." *Annual Review of Sociology* 23.

———. 2000. "Inequality in Social Capital." *Contemporary Sociology* 29–6 (November):785–95.

———. 2001. *Social Capital: A Theory of Social Structure and Action.* New York: Cambridge University Press.

Lin, Nan, and Yanjie Bian. 1991. "Getting Ahead in Urban China." *American Journal of Sociology* 97(3):657–88, 3.

Lin, Nan, and Mary Dumin. 1986. "Access to Occupations Through Social Ties." *Social Networks* 8:365–85.

Lin, Nan, Walter M. Ensel, and John C. Vaughn. 1981. "Social Resources and Strength of Ties: Structural Factors in Occupational Status Attainment." *American Sociological Review* 46(4):393–405, 4.

Lin, Nan, Yang-chih Fu, and Ray-may Hsung. 1998. "Position Generator: A Measurement for Social Capital." Social Networks and Social Capital. Duke University, November.

Marsden, Peter V. 1987. "Core Discussion Networks of Americans." *American Sociological Review* 52:122–31.

Marsden, Peter V., and Jeanne S. Hurlbert. 1988. "Social Resources and Mobility Outcomes: A Replication and Extension." *Social Forces* 66(4):1038–59, 4.

Marx, Karl (David McLellan, editor). 1995 (1867, 1885, 1894). *Capital: A New Abridgement.* Oxford: Oxford University Press.

Marx, Karl. 1933 (1849). *Wage-Labour and Capital.* New York: International Publishers Co.

McCallister, L., and Claude S. Fischer. 1978. "A Procedure for Surveying Personal Networks." *Sociological Methods and Research* 7:131–48.

Podolny, Joel M., and James N. Baron. 1997. "Social Networks and Mobility." *American Sociological Review* 62:673–93.

Portes, Alejandro, and Julia Sensenbrenner. 1993. "Embeddedness and Immigration: Notes on the Social Determinants of Economic Action." *American Journal of Sociology* 98(6):1320–50, 6.

Portes, Alex. 1998. "Social Capital: Its Origins and Applications in Modern Sociology." *Annual Review of Sociology* 22:1–24.

Putnam, Robert D. 1993. *Making Democracy Work: Civic Traditions in Modern Italy.* Princeton, NJ: Princeton University Press.

———. 1995a. "Bowling Alone, Revisited." *The Responsive Community*, Spring, 18–33.

———. 1995b. "Tuning In, Tuning Out: The Strange Disappearance of Social Capital in America." The 1995 Itheiel de Sola Pool Lecture. American Political Science Association. September.

———. 2000. *Bowling Alone: The Collapse and Revival of American Community.* New York: Simon & Schuster.

Schultz, Theodore W. 1961. "Investment in Human Capital." *The American Economic Review* LI(1):1–17, 1.

Sprengers, Maarten, Fritz Tazelaar, and Hendrik Derk Flap. 1988. "Social Resources, Situational Constraints, and Reemployment." *Netherlands Journal of Sociology* 24.

Tardos, Robert. 1996. "Some Remarks on the Interpretation and Possible Uses of the "Social Capital" Concept with Special Regard to the Hungarian Case." *Bulletin de Methodologie Sociologique* 53:52–62, 53.

Volker, Beate, and Henk Flap. 1996. "Getting Ahead in the GDR: Human Capital and Social Capital in the Status Attainment Process Under Communism." Universiteit Utrecht, the Netherlands.

Wellman, Barry. 1979. "The Community Question: The Intimate Networks of East Yorkers." *American Journal of Sociology* 84:1201–31.

Wellman, Barry. 1981. "Applying Network Analysis to the Study of Social Support." Pp. 171–200 in *Social Networks and Social Support*, edited by B. H. Gottlieb. Beverly Hills, CA: Sage.

White, Harrison C. 1992. *Identity and Control. A Structural Theory of Social Action*. Princeton: Princeton University Press.

White, Harrison C., S. A. Boorman, and Ronald L. Breiger. 1976. "Social Structure from Multiple Networks: I. Blockmodels of Roles and Positions." *American Journal of Sociology* 81:730–80.

2

Structural Holes versus Network Closure as Social Capital

Ronald S. Burt

This chapter is about two network structures that have been argued to create social capital. The closure argument is that social capital is created by a network of strongly interconnected elements. The structural hole argument is that social capital is created by a network in which people can broker connections between otherwise disconnected segments. I draw from a comprehensive review elsewhere (Burt 2000) to support two points in this chapter: there is replicated empirical evidence on the social capital of structural holes, and the contradiction between network closure and structural holes can be resolved in a more general network model of social capital. Brokerage across structural holes is the source of value added, but closure can be critical to realizing the value buried in structural holes.

SOCIAL CAPITAL METAPHOR

The two arguments are grounded in the same social capital metaphor, so it is useful to begin with the metaphor as a frame of reference. Cast in diverse styles of argument (e.g., Coleman 1990; Bourdieu & Wacquant 1992; Burt 1992; Putnam 1993), social capital is a metaphor about advantage. Society can be viewed as a market in which people exchange all variety of goods and ideas in pursuit of their interests. Certain people, or certain groups of people, do better in the sense of receiving higher returns to their efforts. Some people enjoy higher incomes. Some more quickly become prominent. Some lead more important projects. The interests of some are better served than the interests of others. The human capital explanation of the inequality is that the people who do better are more able individuals; they are more intelligent, more attractive, more articulate, more skilled.

Social capital is the contextual complement to human capital. The social capital metaphor is that the people who do better are somehow better connected. Certain people or certain groups are connected to certain others, trusting certain others, obligated to support certain others, dependent on exchange with certain others. Holding a certain position in the structure of these exchanges can be an asset in its own right. That asset is social capital, in essence, a concept of location effects in differentiated markets. For example, Bourdieu is often quoted in defining social capital as the resources that result from social structure (Bourdieu & Wacquant 1992:119, expanded from Bourdieu 1980): "social capital is the sum of the resources, actual or virtual, that accrue to an individual or group by virtue of possessing a durable network of more or less institutionalized relationships of mutual acquaintance and recognition." Coleman, another often-cited source, defines social capital as a function of social structure producing advantage (Coleman 1990:302; from Coleman 1988:S98): "Social capital is defined by its function. It is not a single entity but a variety of different entities having two characteristics in common: They all consist of some aspect of a social structure, and they facilitate certain actions of individuals who are within the structure. Like other forms of capital, social capital is productive, making possible the achievement of certain ends that would not be attainable in its absence." Putnam (1993: 167) grounds his influential work in Coleman's metaphor, preserving the focus on action facilitated by social structure: "Social capital here refers to features of social organization, such as trust, norms, and networks, that can improve the efficiency of society by facilitating coordinated action." I echo the above with a social capital metaphor to begin my argument about the competitive advantage of structural holes (Burt 1992:8,45).

So there is a point of general agreement from which to begin a discussion of social capital. The cited perspectives on social capital are diverse in origin and style of accompanying evidence, but they agree on a social-capital metaphor in which social structure is a kind of capital that can create for certain individuals or groups a competitive advantage in pursuing their ends. Better connected people enjoy higher returns.

TWO NETWORK MECHANISMS

Disagreements begin when social capital as a metaphor is made concrete with network models of what it means to be "better" connected. Connec-

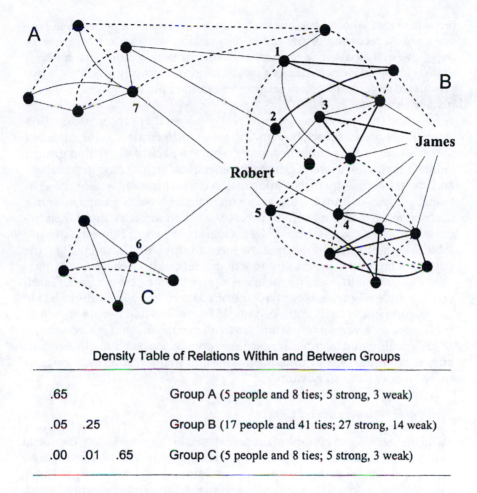

Density Table of Relations Within and Between Groups

.65			Group A (5 people and 8 ties; 5 strong, 3 weak)
.05	.25		Group B (17 people and 41 ties; 27 strong, 14 weak)
.00	.01	.65	Group C (5 people and 8 ties; 5 strong, 3 weak)

Figure 1.   Network around Robert and James.

tions are grounded in the history of a market. Certain people have met frequently. Certain people have sought one another out. Certain people have
completed exchanges with one another. There is at any moment a network,
as illustrated in Figure 1, in which individuals are variably connected to
one another as a function of prior contact, exchange, and attendant emotions. Figure 1 is a generic sociogram and density table description of a network. People are dots. Relationships are lines. Solid (dashed) lines connect
pairs of people who have a strong (weak) relationship.

In theory, the network residue from yesterday should be irrelevant to
market behavior tomorrow. I buy from the seller with the most attractive
offer. That seller may or may not be the seller I often see at the market, or

the seller from whom I bought yesterday. So viewed, the network in Figure 1 would recur tomorrow only if buyers and sellers come together as they have in the past. The recurrence of the network would have nothing to do with the prior network as a casual factor. Continuity would be a by-product of buyers and sellers seeking one another out as a function of supply and demand.

Selecting the best exchange, however, requires that I have information on available goods, sellers, buyers, and prices. Information can be expected to spread across the people in a market, but it will circulate within groups before it circulates between groups. A generic research finding in sociology and social psychology is that information circulates more within than between groups—within a work group more than between groups, within a division more than between divisions, within an industry more than between industries. For example, the sociogram in Figure 1 and the density table at the bottom of the figure show three groups (A,B,C), and the generic pattern of ingroup relations stronger than relations between groups (diagonal elements of the density table are higher than the off-diagonals, each cell of the density table is the average of relations between individuals in the row and individuals in the column). The result is that people are not simultaneously aware of opportunities in all groups. Even if information is of high quality, and eventually reaches everyone, the fact that diffusion occurs over an interval of time means that individuals informed early or more broadly have an advantage.

Structural Holes as Social Capital

Participation in, and control of, information diffusion underlies the social capital of structural holes (Burt 1992). The argument describes social capital as a function of brokerage opportunities, and draws on network concepts that emerged in sociology during the 1970s, most notably Granovetter (1973) on the strength of weak ties, Freeman (1977) on betweenness centrality, Cook and Emerson (1978) on the benefits of having exclusive exchange partners, and Burt (1980) on the structural autonomy created by complex networks. More generally, sociological ideas elaborated by Simmel (1955 [1922]) and Merton (1968 [1957]) on the autonomy generated by conflicting affiliations are mixed in the hole argument with traditional economic ideas of monopoly power and oligopoly to produce network models of competitive advantage.

The weaker connections between groups in Figure 1 are holes in the social structure of the market. These holes in social structure—or more simply, structural holes—create a competitive advantage for an individual whose relationships span the holes. The structural hole between two groups does not mean that people in the groups are unaware of one another. It only means that the people are focused on their own activities such that they do not attend to the activities of people in the other group. Holes are buffers, like an insulator in an electric circuit. People on either side of a structural hole circulate in different flows of information. Structural holes are thus an opportunity to broker the flow of *information* between people, and *control* the projects that bring together people from opposite sides of the hole.

Structural holes separate nonredundant sources of information, sources that are more additive than overlapping. There are two indicators of redundancy: cohesion and equivalence. Cohesive contacts (contacts strongly connected to each other) are likely to have similar information and therefore provide redundant information benefits. Structurally equivalent contacts (contacts who link a manager to the same third parties) have the same sources of information and therefore provide redundant information benefits.

Robert and James in Figure 1 have the same volume of connections, six strong ties and one weak tie, but Robert has something more. James is tied to people within group B, and through them to friends of friends all within group B, so James is well informed about cluster B activities. Robert is also tied through friends of friends to everyone within group B, but in addition, his strong relationship with person "7" is a conduit for information on group A, and his strong relationship with "6" is a conduit for information on group C. His relationship with 7 is for Robert a network bridge in that the relationship is his only direct connection with group A. His relationship with contact 6 meets the graph-theoretic definition of a network bridge. Break that relationship and there is no connection between groups B and C. More generally, Robert is a broker in the network. Network constraint is an index that measures the extent to which a person's contacts are redundant (Burt 1992). James has a constraint score twice Robert's (30.9 versus 14.8) and Robert is the least constrained of the people in Figure 1 (-1.4 Z-score). Network betweenness, proposed by Freeman (1977), is an index that measures the extent to which a person brokers indirect connections between all other people in a network. Robert's betweenness score of 47.0 shows that almost half of indirect connections run through him. His score is the highest score in Figure 1, well above average (47.0 is a 4.0 Z-score), and much higher than James's 5.2 score, which is below average.

Robert's bridge connections to other groups give him an advantage with respect to information access. He reaches a higher volume of information because he reaches more people indirectly. Further, the diversity of his contacts across the three separate groups means that his higher volume of information contains fewer redundant bits of information. Further still, Robert is positioned at the crossroads of social organization so he is early to learn about activities in the three groups. He corresponds to the "opinion leaders" proposed in the early diffusion literature as the individuals responsible for the spread of new ideas and behaviors (Burt 1999a,b). Moreover, Robert's more diverse contacts mean that he is more likely to be a candidate discussed for inclusion in new opportunities. These benefits are compounded by the fact that having a network that yields such benefits makes Robert more attractive to other people as a contact in their own networks.

There is also a control advantage. Robert is in a position to bring together otherwise disconnected contacts, which gives him a disproportionate say in whose interests are served when the contacts come together. Moreover, the holes between his contacts mean that he can broker communication while displaying different beliefs and identities to each contact ("robust action" in Padgett and Ansell 1993; see Brieger 1995 on the connection with structural holes). Simmel and Merton introduced the sociology of people who derive control benefits from structural holes: The ideal type is the *tertius gaudens* (literally, "the third who benefits"), a person who benefits from brokering the connection between others (see Burt 1992, 30–32, for review). Robert in Figure 1 is an entrepreneur in the literal sense of the word—a person who adds value by brokering the connection between others (Burt 1992, 34–36; see also Aldrich 1999, Chap. 4; Thornton 1999). There is a tension here, but not the hostility of combatants. It is merely uncertainty. In the swirling mix of preferences characteristic of social networks, where no demands have absolute authority, the *tertius* negotiates for favorable terms. Structural holes are the setting for *tertius* strategies, and information is the substance. Accurate, ambiguous, or distorted information is strategically moved between contacts by the *tertius*. The information and control benefits reinforce one another at any moment and cumulate together over time.

Thus, individuals with contact networks rich in structural holes are the individuals who know about, have a hand in, and exercise control over more rewarding opportunities. The behaviors by which they develop the opportunities are many and varied, but the opportunity itself is at all times defined by a hole in the social structure. In terms of the argument, networks rich in the entrepreneurial opportunities of structural holes are entrepreneurial networks, and entrepreneurs are people skilled in building the interpersonal bridges that span structural holes. They monitor information more effectively than bureaucratic control. They move information faster, and to more people, than memos. They are more responsive than a bureaucracy, easily shifting network time and energy from one solution to another (vividly illustrated in networks of drug traffic: Williams 1998; Morselli 2000; or health insurance fraud: Tillman & Indergaard 1999). More in control of their surroundings, brokers like Robert in Figure 1 can tailor solutions to the specific individuals being coordinated, replacing the boilerplate solutions of formal bureaucracy. To these benefits of faster, better solutions, add cost reductions; entrepreneurial managers offer inexpensive coordination relative to the bureaucratic alternative. Speeding the process toward equilibrium, individuals with networks rich in structural holes operate somewhere between the force of corporate authority and the dexterity of markets, building bridges between disconnected parts of a market where it is valuable to do so.

In sum, the hole prediction is that in comparisons between otherwise similar people like James and Robert in Figure 1, it is Robert who has more social capital. His network across structural holes give him broad, early access to, and entrepreneurial control over, information.

Network Closure as Social Capital

Coleman's (1988, 1990) view of social capital focuses on the risks associated with being a broker. I will refer to Coleman's view as a closure argument. The key idea is that networks with closure—that is to say, networks in which everyone is connected such that no one can escape the notice of others, which in operational terms usually means a dense network—are the source of social capital.

Network closure does two things for people in the closed network. First, it affects access to information (Coleman 1990:310; cf. 1988:S104): "An important form of social capital is the potential for information the inheres in social relations. . . . A person who is not greatly interested in current events but who is interested in being informed about important developments can save the time required to read a newspaper if he can get the information he wants from a friend who pays attention to such matters." For example, noting that information quality deteriorates as it moves from one person to the next in a chain of intermediaries, Baker (1984; Baker & Iyer 1992) argues that markets with networks of more direct connections improve communication between producers, which stabilizes prices, the central finding in Baker's (1984) analysis of a securities exchange.

Second, and this is the benefit more emphasized by Coleman, network closure facilitates sanctions that make it less risky for people in the network to trust one another. Illustrating the trust advantage with rotating-credit associations, Coleman (1988:S103; 1990:306–7; see Biggart 2000 for a closer look at how such associations operate) notes, "But without a high degree of trustworthiness among the members of the group, the institution could not exist—for a person who receives a payout early in the sequence of meetings could abscond and leave the others with a loss. For example, one could not imagine a rotating-credit association operating successfully in urban areas marked by a high degree of social disorganization—or, in other words, by a lack of social capital." With respect to norms and effective sanctions, Coleman (1990:310–11; cf. 1988:S104) says; "When an effective norm does exist, it constitutes a powerful, but sometimes fragile, form of social capital. . . . Norms in a community that support and provide effective rewards for high achievement in school greatly facilitate the school's task." Coleman (1988:S107–8) summarizes: "The consequence of this closure is, as in the case of the wholesale diamond market or in other similar communities, a set of effective sanctions that can monitor and guide behavior. Reputation cannot arise in an open structure, and collective sanctions that would ensure trustworthiness cannot be applied." He continues (1990:318); "The effect of closure can be seen especially well by considering a system involving parents and children. In a community where there is an extensive set of expectations and obligations connecting the adults, each adult can use his drawing account with other adults to help supervise and control his children."

Coleman's closure argument is prominent with respect to social capital, but it is not alone in predicting that dense networks facilitate trust and norms by facilitating effective sanctions. In sociology, Granovetter (1985, 1992:44) argues that the threat of sanctions makes trust more likely between people who have mutual friends (mutual friends being a condition of "structural embeddedness"): "My mortification at cheating a friend of long standing may be substantial even when undiscovered. It may increase when the friend becomes aware of it. But it may become even more unbearable when our mutual friends uncover the deceit and tell one another." There is an analogous argument in economics (the threat of sanctions creating a "reputation" effect, e.g., Tullock 1985; Greif 1989): Mutual acquaintances observing two people (a) make behavior between the two people public, which (b) increases the salience of reputation for entry to future relations with the mutual acquaintances, (c) making the two people more careful about the cooperative image they display, which (d) increases the confidence with which each can trust the other to cooperate. This chapter is about social capital, so I focus on Coleman's prediction that network closure creates social capital. I have elsewhere discussed the network structures that facilitate trust, showing that closure's association with distrust and character assassination is as strong as its association with trust (Burt 1999a, 2001).

The closure prediction, in sum, is that in comparisons between otherwise similar people like James and Robert in Figure 1, it is James who has more social capital. Strong relations among his contacts give James more reliable communication channels, and protect him from exploitation because he and his contacts are more able to act in concert against someone who violates their norms of conduct.

NETWORK EVIDENCE

Figure 2 contains graphs describing five study populations of managers. I focus on these managers because on them I have detailed and comparable network data. Managers in four of the Figure 2 populations completed network questionnaires in which they were asked to name (a) people with whom they most often discussed important personal matters, (b) the people with whom they most often spent free time, (c) the person to whom they report in the firm, (d) their most promising subordinate, (e) their most valued contacts in the firm, (f) essential sources of buy-in, (g) the contact most important for their continued success in the firm, (h) their most difficult contact, and (i) the people with whom they would discuss moving to a new job in another firm. After naming contacts, respondents were asked about their relation with each contact, and the strength of relations between contacts (see Burt 1992:121–25, 1997b; Burt, Hogarth, & Michaud, 2000, for item wording and scaling).

The horizontal axis of each graph in Figure 2 is a network constraint index, C, that measures social capital. Network constraint measures the extent to which a network is directly or indirectly concentrated in a single contact. Constraint varies with three dimensions of a network: size, density, and hierarchy (see Burt 1992:50ff., 1995, 1998, 2000). Constraint is low in large networks of disconnected contacts. Constraint is high in a small network of contacts who are close to one another (density), or strongly tied to one central contact (hierarchy). The index begins with a measure of the extent to which manager i's network is directly or indirectly invested in his or her relationship with contact j: $c_{ij} = (p_{ij} + \Sigma_q p_{iq} p_{qj})^2$, for $q \neq i,j$, where p_{ij} is the proportion of i's relations invested in contact j. The total in parentheses is the proportion of i's relations that are directly or indirectly invested in connection with contact j. The sum of squared proportions, $_j c_{ij}$, is the network constraint index C. I multiply scores by 100.

As a frame of reference, network constraint is 27.9 on average across the 841 observations in Figure 2, with a 10.5 standard deviation. The network around Robert in Figure 1 is less constrained than average (C = 15). Robert would appear to the far left in each Figure 2 graph. The network around James is slightly more constrained than average (C = 31).

Association between performance and network constraint is a critical test for the two leading network mechanisms argued to provide social capital. More constrained networks span fewer structural holes, which means less social capital according to the hole argument. *If networks that span structural holes are the source of social capital, then performance should have a negative association with network constraint.* More constraint means more network closure, and so more social capital according to the closure argu-

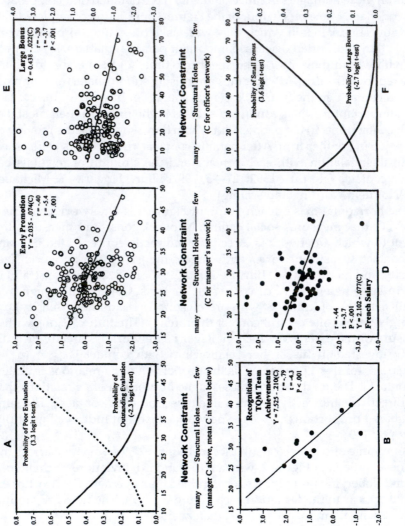

Figure 2. Social capital matters.

40

ment. *If network closure is the source of social capital, then performance should have a positive association with constraint.*

The vertical axes in Figure 2 measure performance (explained below for each study population). Each graph in Figure 2 shows a strong negative association, supporting the argument that structural holes are the source of social capital.

Performance Evaluations

Graphs A and B show a negative association between network constraint and performance evaluations. Figure 2A is based on a representative sample of staff officers within the several divisions of a large financial organization in 1996 (Burt, Jannotta, & Mahoney 1998). The dependent variable is job performance evaluation, taken from company personnel records. Employees are evaluated at the end of each year on an A, B, C scale of "outstanding" to "poor" with plus and minus used to distinguish higher from lower performances within categories. The evaluations stay with an employee over time to affect future compensation and promotion. Women are the majority of the several hundred employees in the staff function (76% of all officers within the function). Of 160 staff officers who returned network questionnaires, the majority are women (69%). The results in Figure 2 are for the women (see Burt 2000:Table 2, for the men). Graph A in Figure 2 shows how the probability of an "outstanding" and a "poor" evaluation changes with network constraint. The graph is based on a logit regression predicting the two extremes of evaluation with the middle category as a reference point. Evaluations are adjusted for the four management job ranks defined by the firm because more senior officers are more likely to be evaluated as "outstanding" (Burt, Jannotta, & Mahoney 1998: 84). Officers with less constrained networks, like Robert, have a significantly higher probability of receiving an outstanding evaluation (-2.3 t-test). The stronger effect is the tendency for officers living in the closeted world of a constrained network to receive a "poor" evaluation (3.3 t-test).

Figure 2B is taken from Rosenthal's (1996) dissertation research on the social capital of teams. Troubled by the variable success of total quality management (TQM) and inspired by Ancona and Caldwell's (1992a, 1992b) demonstration that networks beyond the team are associated with team performance, Rosenthal wanted to see whether the structure of external relationships for TQM teams had the effect predicted by the hole argument. She gained access to a midwest manufacturing firm in 1994 that was in the process of using TQM teams to improve quality in all of its functions in its several plants (a total of 165 teams). She observed operations in two plants, then asked the senior manager responsible for quality in each plant to evaluate the performance of each TQM team in his or her plant. Evaluations were standardized within plants, then compared across plants to identify functions in which team performance most varied. The study population was teams assigned to a function with high success in some plants and low success in other plants. Selecting two functions for study, Rosenthal sent to each employee on the selected teams a network questionnaire; the survey data were used to compute constraint in each person's network within and beyond the team.

The vertical axis in Figure 2B is the standardized team evaluation, and the horizontal axis is average constraint on people in the team. The association is as predicted by the hole argument, and quite striking ($-.79$ correlation). Teams composed of people whose networks extend beyond the team to span structural holes in the company are significantly more likely to be recognized as successful.

Promotions

Figure 2C shows a negative association between promotion and network constraint. The data are taken from a probability sample of senior managers in a large electronics manufacturer in 1989. Performance and network data on these managers have been discussed in detail elsewhere (Burt 1992, 1995, 1997a,b, 1998). Survey network data were obtained on diverse relationships using the questions described above. Performance and background data on each manager were taken from company personnel records. Company personnel records provided each manager's rank (four levels defined by the firm), date promoted to current rank, date entered the firm, functional area of responsibility (defined by the firm as sales, service, manufacturing, information systems, engineering, marketing, finance, and human resources), and the usual personnel-file variables such as gender, family, income, and so on.

Income in the study population was too closely tied to job rank to measure the relative success of individual managers. Time to rank was a better performance variable (Burt 1992:196–7). Whether promoted internally or hired from the outside, people promoted to senior rank in large organizations have several years of experience preceding their promotion. A period of time is expected to pass before people are ready for promotion to senior rank (see Merton 1984, on socially expected durations). How much time is an empirical question, the answer to which differs among individual managers. Some managers are promoted early. Early promotion is the difference between when a manager was promoted to his current rank and a human-capital baseline model predicting the age at which similar managers are promoted to the same rank to do the same work: E(age) – age. Expected age at promotion E(age), is the average age at which managers with specific personal backgrounds (education, race, gender, and seniority) have been promoted to a specific rank within a specific function (rank, function, and plant location). Expected age at promotion is 12% of the population variance in promotion age, and residuals are distributed in a bell curve around expected promotion age (Burt 1992:126–31; 1995). The criterion variable in Figure 2C is the early promotion variable standardized to zero mean and unit variance.

Figure 2C contains the 170 most senior men responding to the survey (see Burt 1998:14, for the senior women). The negative association between early promotion and constraint is statistically significant (−5.4 t-test). Men promoted early to their current senior rank tend to have low-constraint networks (left side of the graph), while those promoted late tend to have high-constraint networks (right side of the graph).

Compensation

Graphs D, E, and F show negative associations between compensation and network constraint. Figure 2D contains 60 people who were a representative sample of senior managers across functions in a division of a large French chemical and pharmaceuticals company in 1997 (Burt, Hogarth, & Michaud 2000). Again, survey network data were obtained on diverse relationships using the questions described above. Performance and background data on managers in the study population were taken from company personnel records. Seventy-two percent of the study-population variance in annual salaries can be predicted from a manager's job rank and age (salary slightly more associated with age than seniority). The residual 28% of salary variance defines the performance variable in Figure 2D. Relative salary is based on the difference between a manager's salary and the salary expected of someone in his rank at her age: salary − E(salary). Associations with other background factors are negligible with rank and age held constant (Burt, Hogarth, & Michaud 2000). Relative salary is standardized across all 85 managers in the study population to zero mean and unit variance (a score of 1.5, for example, means that the manager's salary is one and a half standard deviations higher than the salary typically paid to people in his rank at his age). The negative association between relative salary and network constraint is statistically significant (−3.7 t-test). The managers who enjoy salaries higher than expected from their rank and age tend to be managers with networks that span structural holes in the firm.

Figure 2E contains investment officers in a financial organization in 1993 (Burt 1997a). The study population includes bankers responsible for client relations, but also includes a large number of administrative and support people who participate in the bonus pool. Performance, background, and network data on the study population are taken from company records. Seventy-three percent of the variance in annual bonus compensation, which varies from zero to millions of dollars, can be predicted from job rank (dummy variables distinguishing ranks defined by the organization), and seniority with the firm (years with the firm, and years in current job). Salary is almost completely predictable from the same variables (95% of salary variance). With rank and seniority held constant, there are no significant bonus differences by officer gender, race, or other background factors on which the firm has data. The residual 27% of bonus variance defines the performance variable in Figure 2E. Relative bonus is based on the difference between the bonus an officer was paid and the bonus typical for someone in his rank, at her age, with his years of seniority at the firm: bonus − E(bonus). I standardized relative bonus across all officers in the study population to zero mean and unit variance (so a score of 1.5, for example, means that an officer's bonus is one and a half standard deviations higher than the bonus typically paid to people at his rank or her rank, age, and seniority). Figure 2E contains a random sample of 147 men analyzed for social capital (see Burt 2000:Table 2, for results on female bankers).

The work of this population requires flexible cooperation between colleagues. It is impossible to monitor their cooperation through bureaucratic chains of command because much of their interpersonal behavior is unknown to their immediate supervisor. The firm is typical of the industry in using peer evaluations to monitor employee cooperation. Each year, officers are asked to identify the people with whom they had substantial or frequent business dealings during the year and to indicate how productive it was to work with each person. The firm uses the average of these peer evaluations in bonus and promotion deliberations. The firm does not look beyond the average evaluations. However, there is a network structure in the evaluations that, according to social capital theory, has implications for an officer's performance, which in turn should affect his bonus (see Eccles & Crane 1988, Chapter 8). From peer evaluations by the investment officers and colleagues in other divisions of the firm, I identified the people cited as productive contacts by each of the officers, and looked at evaluations by each contact to see how contacts evaluated one another. I then computed network constraint from the network around each officer.

What makes the study population analytically valuable is the time order between the network and performance data. Social capital theory gives a causal role to social structure. Consistent with the argument, I assume the primacy of social structure for theoretical and heuristic purposes. I am limited to assuming the primacy of social structure because the data collected in the other Figure 2 study populations are cross-sectional and so offer no evidence of causation (see Burt 1992:173–80, for discussion). It is difficult to gather survey network data, wait for the relative success of managers to emerge over time, and then gather performance data. The network data on the investment officers were obtained in the routine of gathering peer evaluations to affect bonus compensation five months later.

There is a negative association in Figure 2E between bonus compensation and network constraint (-3.7 t-test). The managers who received bonuses higher than expected from their rank and seniority tend to have networks that span structural holes in the firm. The logit results in Figure 2F show that the association is even stronger than implied by the results in Figure 2E. There is a triangular pattern to the data in Figure 2E. On the right side of the graph, officers with the most constrained networks receive low bonuses. On the left, officers receiving larger bonuses than their peers tend to have low-constraint networks, but many officers with equally unconstrained networks receive small bonuses. I attribute this to annual data. The low-constraint networks that span structural holes provide better access to rewarding opportunities, but that is no guarantee of exceptional gains every year. There is a .47 partial correlation between bonus in the current year and bonus in the previous year (after rank and seniority are held constant). Even the most productive officers can see a lucrative year followed by a year of routine business. So, the logit results in Figure 2F more accurately describe the social-capital effect for the investment officers. I divided the officers into three bonus categories: large (bonus more than a standard deviation larger than expected from rank and seniority), medium, and small (bonus more than a standard deviation smaller than expected from rank and seniority). Network constraint this year significantly decreases the probability of a large bonus next year (-2.7 t-test), but the stronger effect is the increased probability of receiving a low bonus next year (3.6 t-test).

Other Evidence

Across the five study populations in Figure 2, social capital results from brokerage across structural holes, not from network closure. Elsewhere, I review research based on less detailed network data, but research on a broader diversity of substantive questions on a broader diversity of study populations (Burt 2000). The conclusion of the review is the same as here: closed networks—more specifically, networks of densely interconnected contacts—are systematically associated with substandard performance. For individuals and groups, networks that span structural holes are associated with creativity and innovation, positive evaluations, early promotion, high compensation and profits.

RETHINKING COLEMAN'S EVIDENCE

The most authoritative evidence in Coleman's argument for closure as a form of social capital comes from his studies of high-school students. He argues that closure explains why certain students are more likely to drop out of high school. When the adults in a child's life are more connected with one another, the closure argument predicts trust, norms, and effective sanctions more likely among the adults, which means that the adults can more effectively enforce their interest in having the child complete his or her education.

Coleman (1988, 1990:590–97) offers three bits of evidence to show that children living within closed networks of adults are less likely to drop out of high school: First, children in families with two parents and few children are less likely to drop out of high school (two parents living together can collaborate more effectively in the supervision of a child than two parents living apart). Second, children who have lived in the same neighborhood all their lives are less likely to drop out of high school (parents, teachers, and other people in the neighborhood are more likely to know one another and collaborate in the supervision of a child than can parents new to the neighborhood). Third, children in Catholic and other religious private schools are less likely to drop out (parent, teachers, and parents of the child's friends at the private schools are more likely—relative to adults in the same roles in a public school—to know one another and collaborate in the supervision of a child).

Two questions: First, is "not dropping out of school" a productive performance criterion for estimating social capital effects? Performance variation around "drop out" is probably driven by factors different from those that determine variation at the other end of the performance continuum, the "stay-in-school-and-do-well" end of the continuum. For example, analyzing data on mathematics achievement from the National Education Longitudinal Study survey of 9,241 students in 898 high schools, Morgan and Sørensen (1999a,b:674) raise questions about the value of network closure: "In contrast to [Coleman's] basic hypotheses, our findings lead us to conclude that the benefits offered by the typical network configurations of horizon-expanding schools outweigh those of norm-enforcing schools." Like Coleman before them, Morgan and Sørensen have limited network data available for their analysis,[1] but their two network variables do measure closure of a kind, so the negative association between math scores and "parents know parents" raises questions for scholars committed to the closure argument.

Second, the accumulating evidence of brokerage as social capital invites speculation about the role that brokerage could be playing in Coleman's evidence. Grant that children are less likely to drop out of school if they have a constrained network in which friends, teachers, and parents are all strongly connected to one another so as to eliminate opportunities for the child to play contacts against one another. Constraint from parents and teachers has positive long-term consequences for children, forcing them to focus on their education. But is this social capital of the child or its parents?

The evidence reviewed in this chapter is about the social capital of the person at the center of the network. The social capital associated with higher performance by adults comes from a network of disconnected contacts. At some point on the way to adulthood, the child shaped by the environment takes responsibility for shaping the environment, and is rewarded in proportion to the value he or she adds to the environment. Constraint, positive for the child, is detrimental to adults, particularly adults charged with managerial tasks at the top of their firm. Moreover, the parental network around their child defines only part of the social-capital effect on educational achievement. The complete story is about effective adult supervision (closure argument) combined with parental ability to wrestle resources out of society to support the child (hole argument). Whatever the effect of closure providing adult control over the child, how much greater is the effect of a parent network that spans structural holes at work such that the parents bring home earlier promotions and higher compensation as illustrated in Figure 2?

A POINT OF INTEGRATION

There remains an important role for closure. It can be critical to realizing the value buried in structural holes.

External and Internal Constraint

Begin with the table in Figure 3. Rows distinguish groups in terms of their external network. Groups can be distinguished on many criteria. I have in mind the two network criteria that define information redundancy (cohesion and structural equivalence), but it is just as well to have in mind a more routine group; a family, a team, a neighborhood, or some broader community such as an industry. Some groups are composed of individuals with many nonredundant contacts beyond the group—as illustrated by the three-person sociograms at the top of the table. People in each of the two groups have a total of six nonredundant contacts beyond the group. With respect to network measurement, nonredundant contacts mean a lack of external constraint on the group. The horizontal axis in Figure 2B, for example, measures the average network constraint on individuals in TQM teams. Low-constraint teams, to the left in the graph, were composed of employees with many nonredundant contacts beyond their team. In spanning structural holes beyond the team, their networks reached a diverse set of perspectives, skills, or resources. They were the high-performance teams. At the other extreme, to the right in Figure 2B, low-performance teams were composed of individuals with redundant contacts beyond the

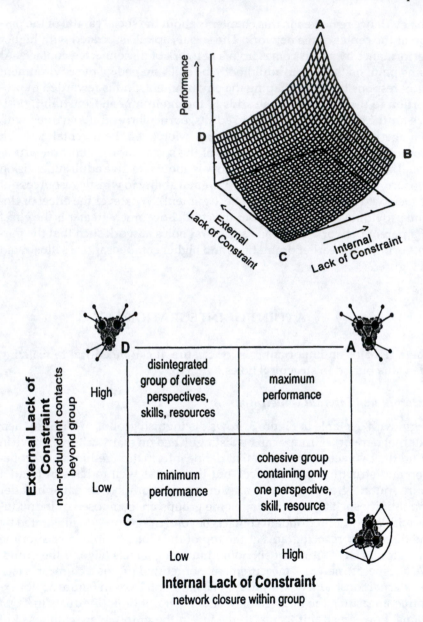

Figure 3.   Social capital matters.

team. The sociogram at the bottom of Figure 3 is an illustration. The group's four contacts beyond the team are interconnected, and so are redundant by cohesion. Such a team has access to a single set of perspectives, skills, or resources, and is expected not to see or successfully implement new solutions, as illustrated in Figure 2B by their poor performance with respect to TQM.

Columns distinguish groups in terms of network closure. Structural holes between people or organizations in a group weakens in-group communication and coordination, which weakens group ability to take advantage of brokerage beyond the group. Closure eliminates structural holes within the team, which improves communication and coordination within the team. The sociogram to the left of the table in Figure 3 shows a group with disconnected elements within it. The two sociograms to the right of the table show groups with all three elements connected. Density or hierarchy can provide network closure, though hierarchy seems to be the more potent form of closure (Burt 2000). A leader with strong relations to all members of the team improves communication and coordination despite coalitions or factions separated by holes within the team.

Performance Surface

The graph at the top of Figure 3 shows group performance across the cells of the table. Performance here is an undefined mixture of innovation, positive evaluation, early promotion, compensation, and profit. Points A, B, C, and D at the corners of the table in Figure 3 correspond to the same points in the graph.

Performance is highest at the back of the graph (quadrant A), where in-group closure is high (one clear leader, or a dense network connecting people in the group) and there are many nonredundant contacts beyond the group (member networks into the surrounding organization are rich in disconnected perspectives, skills, and resources). Performance is lowest at the front of the graph (quadrant C), where in-group closure is low (members spend their time bickering with one another about what to do and how to proceed) and there are few nonredundant contacts beyond the group (members are limited to similar perspectives, skills, and resources).

Figure 3 is my inference from three bits of evidence, all of which are reviewed in detail elsewhere (Burt 2000:Figure 5). In fact, the Figure 3 interaction between brokerage and closure is the concept of structural autonomy from which the hole argument emerged (Burt 1980, 1982, 1992: 38–45).

The first evidential bit comes from research with census data describing the association between industry profit margins and market structure. Industry profit margins increase with closure among industry producers and increase with the number of nonredundant suppliers and customer markets (Burt 1992, Chapter 3; 2000:Figure 6). Analogy with the market structure research is productive in two ways: The market results are based on a census of market conditions, so they include data on the performance-network association at extremes not present in most samples of managers. Second, the market results across a broader range of network conditions show a nonlinear form of returns to network structure. The strongest network effects occur with deviations from minimum network constraint. With respect to network structure within a group, in other words, performance should be weakened more by the first significant disconnection in the group than by one more disconnection within an already disorganized group. With respect to external structure, performance should be weakened more by the entry of one strong perspective, or skill, or resource in the surrounding organization than it is by the entry of another external pressure on a group already frozen by external pressures.

A second bit of evidence for the integration is Reagans and Zuckerman's (1999) study of performance in 223 corporate R&D units within 29 major American firms in eight industries. They report higher levels of output from units in which scientists were drawn from widely separate employee cohorts (implying that their networks reached diverse perspectives, skills, and resources outside the team) *and* there is a dense communication network within the unit. Tenure diversity (or other kinds of diversity, see Williams & O'Reilly 1998) can be disruptive because of the difficulties associated with communicating and coordinating across different perspectives, but when communication is successful (as implied by a dense communication network within the team), team performance is enhanced by the brokerage advantages of the team having access to more diverse information. Reagans and Zuckerman's finding is a segment somewhere between points A and C on the performance surface at the top of Figure 3.

A third bit of evidence for the integration comes from the contingent value of social capital to managers (Burt 1997a, 2000:Figure 6). Social capital is most valuable to managers who hold relatively unique jobs (such as CEO, divisional vice-president, or people managing ventures of a kind new to their organization). These are people who have the most to gain from the information and control benefits of social capital. The contingency argument is that numerous peers define a competitive frame of reference against which any one manager's performance can be calibrated, so managers doing similar work come to resemble one another in their efforts. Burt (1997a, 2000:Figure 6) shows a nonlinear decline in the value of social capital in proportion to the number of managers—peers—doing the same work. Assume that network closure among peers decreases with the number of peers; network closure among many people being more difficult to sustain than closure among a few people. Then the negative association between peers and the value of social capital is a negative association between closure and the value of social capital. The social capital of brokerage across structural holes is again more valuable to a group where there is network closure within the group—point A at the back of the graph in Figure 3. Along the axis from point C to D in the graph, low closure means poor communication and coordination within a group and such a group can be expected to perform poorly, benefiting from external networks only in the richest diversity of perspectives, skills, and resources.

Frame of Reference for Integrating
Research Results

Figure 3 can be a useful frame of reference for integrating research results across studies. A study can show exclusive evidence of social capital from network closure or structural holes without calling either argument into question.

For example, Greif (1989) argues that network closure was critical to the success of the medieval Maghribi traders in North Africa. Each trader ran a local business in his own city that depended on sales to distant cities. Network closure among the traders allowed them to coordinate so as to trust one another, and so profitably trade the products of their disparate business activities. The traders individually had networks rich in brokerage opportunities, but they needed closure with one another to take advantage of the opportunities. More generally, in an environment rich in diverse perspectives, skills, and resources, group performance depends on people overcoming their differences to operate as a group. Group performance will vary with in-group closure, not brokerage, because brokerage opportunities beyond the group are abundant for everyone (this is the Figure 3 surface from point A to point D).

Rosenthal's (1996) study of TQM teams illustrates the other extreme. People on the teams had been trained to act as a team and there was enthusiasm for quality management in the firm—so the teams did not differ greatly in their closure. Closure was high in all of them. Therefore, team performance varied as illustrated in Figure 2B with a team's external network. If a cohesive team can see a good idea, it can act on it. With all teams cohesive, those with numerous nonredundant contacts beyond the team had the advantage of access to a broader diversity of perspectives, skills, and resources. Several recent studies report high performance from groups with external networks that span structural holes (see Burt 2000 for review): Geletkanycz and Hambrick (1997) on higher company performance when top managers have boundary-spanning relationships beyond their firm and beyond their industry; Ahuja (1998) on the higher patent output of organizations that hold broker positions in the network of joint ventures or alliances at the top of their industry; Pennings, Lee, and Witteloostuijn (1998) on the survival of accounting firms as a function of strong partner ties to client sectors; Stuart and Podolny (1999) on the higher probability of innovation from semiconductor firms that establish alliances with firms outside their own technological area; McEvily and Zaheer (1999) on the greater access to competitive ideas enjoyed by small job manufacturers with more nonredundant sources of advice beyond the firm; Sørensen (1999) on the negative effect on firm growth of redundant networks beyond the firm; Hansen, Podolny, and Pfeffer (2000) on computer new-product teams completing their task more quickly when the team is composed of people with more nonredundant contacts beyond the team; Baum, Calabrese, and Silverman (2000) on the faster revenue growth and more patents granted to biotechnology companies that have multiple kinds of alliance partners at start-up; Koput and Powell (2000) on the higher earnings and survival chances of biotechnology firms with more kinds of activities in alliances with more kinds of partner firms; and Podolny (2000) on the higher probability of early-stage investments surviving to IPO for venture-capital firms with joint-investment networks of otherwise disconnected partners. With Figure 3 in mind, these studies tell me not that the closure argument is in error so much as that closure within business groups is less often problematic than brokerage beyond the group. More generally, the relative performance of cohesive groups will vary with the extent to which a group is composed of people with networks rich in structural holes, not network closure, because closure is high for all of the groups (this is the Figure 3 surface from point A to point B, illustrated in Figure 2B).

In short, structural holes and network closure can be brought together in a productive way. The integration is only with respect to empirical evidence. The mechanisms remain distinct. Closure describes how dense or hierarchical networks lower the risk associated with transaction and trust, which can be associated with performance. The hole argument describes how structural holes are opportunities to add value with brokerage across the holes, which is associated with performance. The empirical evidence reviewed supports the hole argument over closure. However, my summary conclusion illustrated in Figure 3 is that while brokerage across structural holes is the source of added value, closure can be critical to realizing the value buried in the structural holes.

NOTE

1. For example, the "density of student friendship networks" to which they refer in their conclusion is not a network density measure; it is a count of a

student's closest friends named in an interview with the student's parent (0 to 5, "friends in school" variable in Morgan and Sørensen, 1999a:666–67). "Friends in school" is an indicator of intergenerational network closure, and, consistent with the closure argument, has a positive association with a student's gain in math scores to 12th grade (primarily for students averaged across schools; Morgan and Sørensen, 1999a:669, 1999b:698; Carbonaro 1999:684–85). The "density of parental networks" in Morgan and Sørensen's conclusion is also a count. It is the number of the named close friends for whom the interviewed parent claims to know one or both of the friend's parents ("parents know parents" variable). "Parents know parents" is another measure of intergenerational network closure, but in contradiction to the closure argument, has a negative association with a student's gain in math scores (again primarily for students averaged across schools, Morgan and Sørensen, 1999a:669, 1999b:698). Inferences are complicated by the fact that "friends in school" is of course strongly correlated (.58) with "parents know parents." More consequential, Morgan and Sørensen's network variables are enumerations by the parent, not the student. The student need not agree with the parent's selection of best friends, and the student's network can extend well beyond the view of his or her parents (recall that these are high school students; see Hirschi 1972 on the significance for delinquent behavior of a boy's friends unknown to his father).

REFERENCES

Ahuja, Gautam. 1998. Collaboration networks, structural holes, and innovation: a longitudinal study. Paper presented at the annual meetings of the Academy of Management.

Aldrich, Howard E. 1999. *Organizations Evolving.* Thousand Oaks, CA: Sage.

Ancona, Deborah G., and David F. Caldwell. 1992a. Demography and design: Predictors of new product team performance. *Organization Science* 3:321–41

———. 1992b. Bridging the boundary: External activity and performance in organizational teams. *Administrative Science Quarterly* 37:634–65.

Baker, Wayne E. 1984. The social structure of a national securities market. *American Journal of Sociology* 89:775–811.

Baker, Wayne E., and Ananth Iyer 1992. Information networks and market behavior. *Journal of Mathematical Sociology* 16:305–32.

Baum, Joel A. C., Tony Calabrese, and Brian S. Silverman. 2000. "Don't go it alone: Alliance network composition and startups' performance in Canadian biotechnology." *Strategic Management Journal* 21:267–94.

Biggart, Nicole Woolsey. 2000. Banking on each other: The situational logic of rotating savings and credit associations. Paper presented at the 2000 Organization Science Winter Conference.

Bourdieu, Piere. 1980. Le capital social: Notes provisoires. *Actes de la Recherche en Sciences Sociales* 3:2–3.

Bourdieu, Pierre, and Loïc J. D. Wacquant. 1992. *An Invitation to Reflexive Sociology.* Chicago, IL: University of Chicago Press.

Brieger, Ronald L. 1995. Socioeconomic achievement and the phenomenology of achievement. *Annual Review of Sociology* 21:115–36.

Burt, Ronald S. 1980. Autonomy in a social topology. *American Journal of Sociology* 85:892–925.

———. 1982. *Toward a Structural Theory of Action*. New York: Academic Press.

———. 1992. *Structural Holes*. Cambridge, MA: Harvard University Press.

———. 1995. Le capital social, les trous structuraux, et l'entrepreneur translated by Emmanuel Lazega.. *Revue Française de Sociologie* 36:599–628.

———.1997a. The contingent value of social capital. *Administrative Science Quarterly* 42:339–65.

———. 1997b. A note on social capital and network content. *Social Networks* 19:355–73.

———. 1998. The gender of social capital. *Rationality and Society* 10:5–46.

———. 1999a. Entrepreneurs, distrust, and third parties. Pp. 213–243 in *Shared Cognition in Organizations*, edited by Leigh L. Thompson, John M. Levine, and David M. Messick. Hillsdale, NJ: Lawrence Erlbaum.

———. 1999b. The social capital of opinion leaders. *Annals* 566:37–54.

———. 2000. The network structure of social capital. Pp. 345–423 in *Research in Organizational Behavior*, edited by Robert I. Sutton and Barry M. Staw. Greenwich, CT: JAI Press.

———. 2001. Bandwidth and echo: Trust, information, and gossip in social networks. In *Networks and Markets*, edited by Alessandra Casella and James E. Rauch. New York: Russell Sage Foundation.

Burt, Ronald S., Joseph E. Jannotta, and James T. Mahoney. 1998. Personality correlates of structural holes. *Social Networks* 20:63–87.

Burt, Ronald S., Robin M. Hogarth, and Claude Michaud. 2000. The social capital of French and American managers. *Organization Science* 11:123–47.

Carbonaro, William J. 1999. "Openning the debate on closure and schooling outcomes." *American Sociological Review* 64:682–86.

Coleman, James S. 1988. Social capital in the creation of human capital. *American Journal of Sociology* 94:S95—S120.

———. 1990. *Foundations of Social Theory*. Cambridge, MA: Harvard University Press.

Cook, Karen S., and Richard M. Emerson. 1978. Power, equity and commitment in exchange networks. *American Sociological Review* 43:712–39.

Eccles, Robert G., and Dwight B. Crane. 1988. *Doing Deals*. Boston, MA: Harvard Business School Press.

Freeman, Linton C. 1977. A set of measures of centrality based on betweenness. *Sociometry* 40:35–40.

Geletkanycz, Marta A., and Donald C. Hambrick. 1997. The external ties of top executives: implications for strategic choice and performance. *Administrative Science Quarterly* 42:654–81.

Granovetter, Mark S. 1973. The strength of weak ties. *American Journal of Sociology* 78:1360–80.

———. 1985. Economic action, social structure, and embeddedness. *American Journal of Sociology* 91:481–510.

———. 1992. Problems of explanation in economic sociology. Pp. 29–56 in *Networks and Organization*, edited by Nitin Nohria and Robert G. Eccles. Boston, MA: Harvard Business School Press.

Greif, Avner. 1989. Reputation and coalition in medieval trade: evidence on the Maghribi traders. *Journal of Economic History* 49:857–82.

Hansen, Morten T., Joel M. Podolny, and Jeffrey Pfeffer. 2000. So many ties, so little time: a task contingency perspective on the value of social capital in organizations. Paper presented at the 2000 Organization Science Winter Conference.

Hirschi, Travis. 1972. *Causes of Delinquency*. Berkeley, CA: University of California Press.

Koput, Kenneth, and Walter W. Powell. 2000. Not your stepping stone: collaboration and the dynamics of industry evolution in biotechnology. Paper presented at the 2000 Organization Science Winter Conference.

McEvily, Bill, and Akbar Zaheer. 1999. Bridging ties: a source of firm heterogeneity in competitive capabilities. *Strategic Management Journal* 20:1133–56.

Merton, Robert K. (1957) 1968. Continuities in the theory of reference group behavior. Pp. 335–440 in *Social Theory and Social Structure*. New York: Free Press.

———. 1984. Socially expected durations: a case study of concept formation in sociology. Pp. 262–83 in *Conflict and Consensus* edited by Walter W. Powell and Richard Robbins. New York: Free Press.

Morgan, Stephen L. and Aage B. Sørensen. 1999a. "A test of Coleman's social capital explanation of school effects." *American Sociological Review* 64:661–81.

———. 1999b. "Theory, measurement, and specification issues in models of network effects on learning." *American Sociological Review* 64:694–700.

Morselli, Carlo. 2000. "Structuring Mr. Nice: entrepreneurial opportunities and brokerage positioning in the cannabis trade." *Crime, Law and Social Change* 33: In Press.

Padgett, John F., and Christopher K. Ansell. 1993. Robust action and the rise of the Medici, 1400–1434. *American Journal of Sociology* 98:1259–1319.

Pennings, Johannes M., Kyungmook Lee, and Arjen van Witteloostuijn. 1998. Human capital, social capital, and firm dissolution. *Academy of Management Journal* 41:425–40.

Podolny, Joel M. 2000. "Networks as the pipes and prisms of the market." Graduate School of Business, Stanford University.

Putnam, Robert D. 1993. *Making Democracy Work*. Princeton, NJ: Princeton University Press.

Reagans, Ray, and Ezra W. Zuckerman. 1999. Networks, diversity, and performance: the social capital of corporate R&D units. Graduate School of Industrial Administration, Carnegie Mellon University.

Rosenthal, Elizabeth A. 1996. *Social Networks and Team Performance*. Ph.D. Dissertation, Graduate School of Business, University of Chicago.

Simmel, Georg. [1922] 1955. *Conflict and the Web of Group Affiliations* (translated by Kurt H. Wolff and Reinhard Bendix). New York: Free Press.

Sørensen, Jesper B. 1999. Executive migration and interorganizational competition. *Social Science Research* 28:289–315.

Stuart, Toby E., and Joel M. Podolny. 1999. Positional causes and correlates of strategic alliances in the semiconductor industry. Pp. 161–82 in *Research in the Soci-*

ology of Organizations, edited by Steven Andrews and David Knoke. Greenwich, CT: JAI Press.

Thornton, Patricia H. 1999. The sociology of entrepreneurship. *Annual Review of Sociology* 25:19–46.

Tillman, Robert, and Michael Indergaard. 1999. Field of schemes: health insurance
fraud in the small business sector. *Social Problems* 46:572–90.

Tullock, Gordon. 1985. Adam Smith and the prisoners' dilemma. *Quarterly Journal
of Economics* 100:1073–81.

Williams, Katherine Y., and Charles A. O'Reilly III. 1998. Demography and diversity in organizations: a review of 40 years of research. Pp. 77–140 in *Research
in Organizational Behavior*, edited by Barry M. Staw and L. L. Cummings.
Greenwich, CT: JAI Press.

Williams, Phil. 1998. The nature of drug-trafficking networks. *Current History*
97:154–59.

3

The Position Generator: Measurement Techniques for Investigations of Social Capital

Nan Lin, Yang-chih Fu, and Ray-May Hsung

As social capital gains currency in the social sciences (Bourdieu 1980, 1983/1986; Coleman 1988, 1990; Putnam 1993, 1995a, 1995b; Lin 1995; Burt 1997, 1998; Portes & Sensenbrenner 1993; Portes 1998), it also increasingly faces divergence in conceptualization and measurement. The proliferation of meanings attached to the concept has broadened its appeal to an ever larger community of scholars and audience, yet also has threatened its integrity. Serious questions have been raised about the concept's rigor and its utility in scientific theory. We argue that the scientific viability of the notion of social capital depends on the development of an approach that integrates theory and measurement of the concept. Without a clear conceptualization, social capital may soon become a catch-all term broadly used in reference to anything that is "social." Without a clear measurement, it will be impossible to verify propositions or to accumulate knowledge.

The purposes of this paper are fourfold. First, it will evaluate the conceptualization of social capital. Second, it will provide a report on the development of a particular measurement methodology—the position generator—as guided by one specific conceptualization. The third purpose is to demonstrate the measurement's utility in testing specific propositions regarding the function of social capital in one instrumental context—stratification and mobility in one society (Taiwan). The final goal is to propose further refinements of the measurement methodology in advancing the concept of social capital.

TOWARD A THEORY OF SOCIAL CAPITAL

Social capital can be defined as resources embedded in a social structure that are accessed and/or mobilized in purposive actions (Lin 1982, 2001; also see Chapter 1 of this book). By this definition, the notion of social capital contains three ingredients: resources embedded in a social structure; accessibility to these social resources by individuals; and use or mobilization of them by individuals engaged in purposive action. Thus conceived, social capital contains both structural (accessibility) and action-oriented (mobilization or use) elements. The two ingredients also reflect differential levels of analysis, as diagramed in Figure 1. At the mesostructural level, social capital captures the extent to which individuals have differential accessibility to collective resources. At the microaction level, social capital captures how accessed resources are differentially mobilized by individuals in conjunction with specific actions.

This conceptual framework suggests three types of research tasks for building a theory of social capital. These tasks are also illustrated in Figure 1. First, the theory should be expected to delineate patterns of differential distributions for social resources that are accessed or mobilized. It should further demonstrate that there are social forces that determine such differential distributions. Thus, it is incumbent on a theory of social capital to

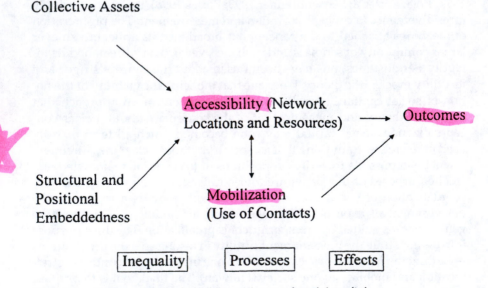

Figure 1.   Research tasks in building a theory of social capital.

delineate the patterns and determinants of the two ingredients of social capital or *the inequality of social capital* as accessible social resources and mobilized social resources. Two types of causation forces are of special interest to scholars in the analysis of the inequality in social capital: structural and positional variations. A structure may be characterized in many ways such as diversity in culture and ideology, level of industrialization and technology, level of education, extent of physical and natural resources, economic productivity, etc. (see Chapter 1 of this book). Within a structure, individuals may be described as occupying different positions in social, cultural, political, and economic strata. These variations may be hypothesized to affect the richness or poorness of various social ingredients.

Second, the theory should demonstrate how social capital is capital, or how it generates return or gain. That is, it should propose how one or more of the ingredients directly or indirectly impact an individual's well-being. In propositional terms, these are termed effect hypotheses and can be stated as follows:

Effect Hypothesis 1: The greater the embedded resources accessible by an individual, the better the individual's well-being.

Effect Hypothesis 2: The better embedded resources mobilized by an individual, the better the outcome of an individual's purposive action.

Third, the theory needs to demonstrate that the two ingredients are interconnected. Thus, it needs to propose a causal sequence in which embedded resources constrain and enable individual choices and actions. These propositions can be termed process hypotheses and stated as follows:

Process Hypothesis: The better the accessible embedded resources, the better embedded resources can and will be mobilized in purposive actions by an individual.

It is this conceptual framework and its propositions that should guide research programs as well as evaluations of the extent to which each program is successful. There is significant space left for research entrepreneurship. For example, the outcome variables for each hypothesis remain to be conceptualized and operationalized, and may range from group solidarity to individual job attainment or life satisfaction (see Chapter 1). Nevertheless, these conceptual analyses should help assess how each research program contributes to the building of a theory of social capital.

Different research programs may choose to focus on one or more ingredients and on one or more of the tasks. One program, for example, may focus on the documentation of the distribution of resources in a social structure, with the purpose of describing the relative distribution of resources as a collective asset in the structure. Putnam's (1993, 1995a, 1995b) work is exemplary in this regard, as he has chosen to focus on the distribution of collective assets in a social structure, as reflected in the prevalence of and participation in voluntary organizations or social groups, for example. In this research program, the richness or poorness of collective assets, over historical periods or across societies, is the focus of analysis, and its beneficial or detrimental effects for the structure or participating individuals are benchmarked in time or space.

Another research program may choose to focus on accessibility to embedded resources. Burt's efforts (1997, 1998), for example, have demonstrated the strategic advantages of certain network locations as reflected in relative profits for the occupants of a firm. In this program, researchers consider strategic locations (i.e., structural holes and structural constraints) as indicating social capital itself or assume that the locations have differential accessibility to embedded resources. The program of research proceeds to verify the linkages between strategic locations and certain structural or organizational consequences (e.g., better-than-expected promotions or bonuses).

Still a third type of research program may choose to focus on the use or mobilization of embedded resources. An illustration is Coleman's study (1990) of how a mother with a child moved from Detroit to Jerusalem in order to take advantage of social norms and sanctions that would provide better security for the child to go to the playground or school. In this analysis, richness/poorness of social capital is assumed as given, and the focus is on the choice made by the mother in mobilizing richer social capital by moving the family to Jerusalem. Likewise, Portes' description (Portes & Sensenbrenner 1993) of how some ethnic immigrants in New York City sought help from compatriots for a legal defense fund assumes that the ethnic community is the structure containing collective capital and focuses on the actions of individual immigrants who need to mobilize resources from that structure.

Some research programs have sought to examine several of these ingredients simultaneously. The social resource research tradition (Lin 1982; Marsden & Hurlbert 1988; De Graaf & Flap 1988; Flap & De Graaf 1988; Erickson 1996) seeks to describe how individuals access and use embedded resources to achieve instrumental goals, such as attaining better socioeconomic status. In this research program, social capital is captured either as (1) the accessed embedded resources by individuals, and/or (2) embedded resources actually used or mobilized in the analysis of their effects on outcomes in the status-attainment process such as occupational status, authority positions, or an advantaged or disadvantaged industrial sector.

ACCESS TO EMBEDDED RESOURCES: A PIVOTAL POINT
FOR RESEARCH

While the general conceptual framework and different propositions suggested here provide an elastic range of research enterprises, most researchers working on social capital probably agree that the significance of a theory of social capital lies in its intended demonstration that structure and action interact in a meaningful way. Ideally, research programs should seek to clarify simultaneously how individuals are afforded and constrained by their relative accessibility to resources embedded in the social structure, and how they take actions to mobilize the embedded and accessible social resources to generate returns for their own well-being. Thus, a social capital theory must contain and demonstrate the meso-micro linkage and the dynamic interactive effects between structure and action. Based on this analysis, it can be argued that a critical aspect of research is the point where individuals intersect with structure—which embedded resources are accessible to whom. At this level of analysis, there are two critical research questions: (1) inequality of access in the social structure (who has better or worse access to the embedded resources); and (2) the return of unequal access for individual well-being.

A further important theoretical advantage of this ground-up approach to studying social capital is that it enables the term "social capital" to be used parallel to other related terms, such as "human capital" and "cultural capital," in the general theory group that can be identified as the neocapital theory group (Lin 2001). Unlike the classic theory of capital (Marx 1933), where capital is a term associated with classes and therefore subject to macroanalysis, neocapital theories concern the investment and return of capital at the individual level. For human capital (Schultz 1961; Becker 1964, 1993), which is central to neoclassical economics, research tends to measure human capital as individual assets—education, on-the-job training, job experiences, etc. The notion has been extended to almost anything that improves individual skills and knowledge (e.g., health, family support: Becker 1981, 1991, 1964/93). But the major theoretical argument and most research enterprises are built on the notion and measurement of human capital as individual assets. Likewise, cultural capital, as explicated by Bourdieu (Bourdieu 1972, 1997; Bourdieu & Passeron 1977), is the "misrecognition" and absorption of individuals with the values and ideologies espoused by the dominant class. In each case, capital can eventually be transformed from individual to collective assets, but the point of departure in the conceptual analysis and research efforts are firmly rooted at the point where individuals are shown to intersect with the structure.

It is this arena in which we wish to make a contribution. Specifically, building on the growing research literature regarding the analysis of access to social resources, we hope to demonstrate that a particular measurement methodology promises to yield theoretical and empirical insights demonstrating the utility of social capital in the context of structured action, using data from a particular society, Taiwan.

MEASURING ACCESSIBILITY: THE POSITION GENERATOR

There are two methodologies commonly used to measure access to social capital: name generators and position generators. The name generator is the more common methodology and has been used extensively in the network literature. The general technique is to pose one or more questions about the ego's contacts ("names") in certain social contexts or situations which may range from role or content (neighbors, important family or work matters) to closeness (confidences, intimacy, etc.), geographic limits, or for specific periods of time. Such questions generate a list of contacts ranging from three to five or as many as volunteered by ego. This approach was pioneered by Laumann (1966), Wellman (1979), and Fischer and his associates (Fischer 1977, 1982), and standardized in other community studies (Hall & Wellman 1985; Wellman 1981; Lin, Dean, & Ensel 1986) and national samples (Burt 1984; Marsden 1987). Numerous studies have adopted this approach in identifying ego-centric networks.

This methodology has been adapted to measure social capital in three different but related ways. In one approach, the network characteristics are taken as indicators of social capital, either as collective social capital or as access to social capital. Collective social capital is summarized in terms of density or sparseness of relationships among social ties (ego and alters), for example. Or, the location of an ego relative to alters in this network is used to indicate the relative advantage in the access to social capital (the bridge, or near a bridge, structural holes or structural constraints). Burt's (1992, 1997, 1998) conceptualization of social capital utilizes this network-as-capital approach and argues that theoretically and empirically, the location-as-capital measurement is superior to the dispersion-as-capital measurement. In another approach, compositions of alter characteristics are constructed to indicate social capital (Campbell, Marsden, & Hurlbert 1986). Again, two types of measures have been devised . One constructs a composition of the collective resources possessed by the alters (mean education, occupational prestige, or income; or range, diversity and heterogeneity of education, occupational prestige, or income as well as gender, age, and other characteristics). Another measure assesses the best-possible resources (the highest education, occupational prestige, or income) characterizing alters. Many researchers have adopted this approach in examining social resources or social capital, as exemplified by Campbell,

Marsden, and Hurlbert (1986), Sprengers, Tazelaar, and Flap (1988), Boxman, De Graaf, and Flap (1991), and Boxman and Flap (1990).

There are a number of problems associated with the use of the name generators to measure social capital (see Chapter 1). In short, it tends (1) to be bound with specified content areas (the generating items), (2) to elicit stronger rather than weaker ties, and (3) to locate access to individuals rather than social positions.[1] More importantly, we argue, name generators fall short on two sampling issues important to the development of social capital as a theory. For one, by definition, these generators are content bound. Unless there is information about the population or universe of the contents (roles, intimacy, geography, etc.), there is no possibility of systematically sampling elements or contents. A hit-or-miss approach thus ensues—contents are selected by individual researchers who make judgment calls, or use "conventional" wisdom and practice. Moreover, if weaker ties, bridges, structural holes, or absence of structural constraints are theoretically expected to have a certain instrumental utility for accessing better information and resources (Granovetter 1974; Burt 1992), then name-generators fall far short of assuring that such ties will be evoked. These concerns lead us to suggest that greater research attention should be given to another measurement technique: the position generator.

Position generators, first proposed by Lin and associates (Lin & Dumin 1986), use a sample of ordered structural positions salient in a society (occupations, authorities, work units, class or sector) and ask respondents to indicate contacts (e.g., those known on a first-name basis), if any, in each of the positions. From the responses, it becomes possible to construct measures of (1) *range* of accessibility to different hierarchical positions in the society (e.g., the distance between the highest and lowest accessed positions); (2) *extensity* or heterogeneity of accessibility to different positions (e.g., number of positions accessed); and (3) *upper reachability* of accessed social capital (e.g., prestige or status of the highest position accessed). Further, relationships (either direct or indirect) between the ego and contact for each position can be identified. Such quarry may yield information regarding strength of ties, or the possible use of bridges.

We should note that the position generator derives from certain theoretical decisions. For example, it chooses to sample positions in a hierarchical structure, rather than sampling ego-centered interpersonal ties. To the extent that social capital reflects embedded resources in the structure, then this approach should yield meaningful information regarding ego's access to such structurally embedded resources. The measurement is also deliberately content-free and role/location-neutral. Only after accessibility to a position is ascertained can the actual relationship or its content between ego and the contact be assessed. Conceivably, the generator casts a wide net over a range of relationships. It may well be that social capital, in its capacity to affect many aspects of well-being, should also contain social resources scattered throughout the continuum of relationships' strength or intensity. As a measurement tool, it does not preclude such linkages from presenting themselves in the data.

A concrete example of this approach may illustrate how it is devised and used. Lin and Dumin (1986) analyzed the data from an Albany study in which 20 occupations were sampled from the U.S. 1960 census listing, with all occupations ranked according to job prestige scores. At equal intervals on these scaled scores, occupations were identified. From the group of occupations at the sampled interval, the most popular (frequency of occupants) occupation was selected. Each respondent was asked if he / she had any contact (on a first-name basis) with a person in each of the positions.[2] For each accessed position, the respondent identified the contact's relationship (relative, friend, or acquaintance). From the data matrix, Lin and Dumin constructed two social resources access measures: the highest status accessible (the position accessed with the highest prestige score), and the range of statuses accessed (the difference between the highest and lowest accessed statuses). Analyses showed that the two measures were positively and significantly related to current occupational status. Further analysis showed that respondents' original positions (father's occupational prestige scores, or white-blue and high-low occupational groupings, or those associated with the respondents' first jobs) and these two measures were positive and significant. When Lin and Dumin analyzed the relationships between the three types of ties (relatives, friends, acquaintances) and the access variables, they found that friends as well as acquaintances provided the best access to both the highest-status positions and the range of accessed statuses. Thus, they concluded that the position generator yields measures of accessed social resources that exerted returns on attained status, and that such accessibility is in part contingent on the original structural position of ego as well as ego's wider networks.

Usage of the position-generator approach has yielded similar findings for different political economies (e.g., capitalist and socialist) and populations (e.g., normal labor force, unemployed, new workers, particular industries) (Hsung & Hwang 1992; Volker & Flap 1996; Angelusz & Tardos 1991; Erickson 1998). Erickson (1995, 1996) expanded this approach by using Wright's (1979) class dimensions (control of property, control of organizations, and control of skill) to select nineteen job positions in her study of the private security industry in Canada, with equal success.

In the remainder of this chapter, we wish to illustrate the utility of the position-generator methodology with data from an island-wide survey of employed labor forces in Taiwan. We focus our attention on three topics. First, we wish to examine how access to social capital is contingent on a number of structural positions (gender, marital status, education and employment) and social contacts (daily contacts and familiarity with the contacts), as well as with specific relationships (kin versus nonkin) evoking such access. Second, further analyses will be conducted to ascertain how access to social capital generates differential returns in terms of job prestige and income. Particular attention will be given to differential returns to males and females. Finally, we will further assess how access to social capital contributes to the income of entrepreneurs (those who form their own firms and businesses) and whether such a contribution is similar or different for male and female entrepreneurs.

THE TAIWAN SOCIAL NETWORKS STUDY

An island-wide survey of adults was conducted in Taiwan in February 1997. The survey, designed by a team of sociologists, was first examined and discussed with a focus group of ten persons from a wide range of social strata and then subjected to a pretest with 400 respondents. The finalized instrument was administered in interpersonal interviews with respondents in an island-wide stratified (levels of urbanization) probability (by district and household) sample of adults aged 20–74. A total of 2,835 sampled respondents completed the surveys. The sample consisted of nearly an equal number of males and females whose mean age was 42, with slightly more than half (53 percent) having received education at or above the high school level; a comparison shows that female respondents received less education than males. About three-quarters (72 percent) of the respondents were married. A summary of respondent characteristics is shown in Table 1.

Table 1.   Summary of Sample Characteristics (N = 2,835)

Variable	Percent or Mean			Gender Significance
	Sample	Males	Females	
Gender—males	50.9%			
Age	41.6	41.9	41.3	
Education				.00
Less than high school	47.4%	43.7%	51.4%	
High school	28.5	29.5	27.5	
College or more	24.0	26.8	21.1	
Marital status				
Single	21.1%	25.2%	16.8%	.00
Married	71.8	70.4	73.3	.08
Divorced or widowed	7.1	4.4	9.8	.09/.00

Table 2. Summary of Position-Generated Variables

Variable	Sample	Males	Females	Gender Significance
		Mean or Percent		
Extensity (number of positions accessed)	6.5	7.0	6.1	.00
Upper reachablity (prestige of highest accessed position)	69.4	69.3	69.6	.43
Range of prestige (difference between highest/lowest positions accessed)	39.6	39.8	39.4	.55
Accessed positions (prestige score)				
Physician (78)	50.3%	49.2%	51.4%	.23
Lawyer (73)	23.9	26.0	21.8	.01
Owner of large factory/firm (70)	34.2	40.1	28.2	.00
Assemblymen/women (69)	31.0	35.6	26.2	.00
Manager of large factory/firm (62)	42.8	49.7	35.7	.00
High School teachers (60)	59.9	61.1	58.6	.17
Division head (55)	20.6	24.2	16.8	.00
Reporter (55)	21.2	24.5	17.7	.00
Nurse (54)	53.5	47.6	59.7	.00
Owner of small factory/firm (48)	68.1	71.8	64.3	.00
Police (40)	55.6	59.4	51.5	.00
Electrician (36)	70.1	76.0	64.0	.00
Truck driver (31)	51.6	59.8	43.2	.00
Office workman/guard (26)	43.3	47.6	38.8	.00
Housemaid, cleaning worker (22)	29.5	28.4	30.6	.21

THE POSITION GENERATOR AND DATA

The generating question was: "Among your relatives, friends, or acquaintances, are there people who have the following jobs? If so, what is his/her relationship to you? If you don't know anyone with these jobs, and if you need to find such a person for private help or to ask about some problems, whom among those you know would you go through to find such a person? Who would he/she be to you? What job does he/she do?" Following these questions were fifteen "job" positions sampled from two structural dimensions: occupational prestige and class. For occupational prestige, we followed the prestige ratings constructed by Hwang (1998) for Taiwan occupations. The instrument is translated and reproduced in Appendix A. The sampled positions have prestige scores ranging from 78 (physician) to 22 (housemaid, cleaning worker) and can be roughly grouped into three "classes": the upper class (consisting of high-status professionals such as physician and lawyers, owners of large factories, county-level legislators), the middle class (middle-level professionals such as high school teachers, reporters and nurses, managers of large factories/firms, middle-level administrators and division heads, and owners of small factories and firms), and the lower class (police, electricians, truck drivers, office workmen and guards, and housemaids and workers). These positions and their relative rankings are displayed in Table 2.

Three indexes were constructed from the position-generator items: (1) extensity: number of positions accessed; (2) upper reachability: the prestige score of the highest position accessed; and (3) range of prestige scores of the highest and lowest positions accessed. As can be seen in Table 2, on average, the respondents accessed between six and seven sampled positions, with the highest prestige score among accessed positions being 69 and the average range of prestige scores between the lowest and highest accessed positions about 40 points. A comparison between males and females shows that while males tended to access more positions, there was no significant difference between males and females in terms of upper reachability (the highest prestige score) or the range of scores. Why both males and females accessed a similar range or upper reachability requires further analysis.

We then examined the detailed data on accessibility to each of the sampled positions. As shown in Table 2, the positions were rearranged in descending order in accordance with their prestige scores. The most accessible positions, by more than half of the respondents, included physicians, high school teachers, owners of small factories/firms, the police, electricians, and truck drivers. The least accessible positions (cited by less than a third of the respondents) included lawyers, assemblymen/women, division heads, reporters, and housemaids and workers. Comparing data from male and female respondents shows that males are more likely to access all sampled positions, except physicians, high school teachers, nurses, and housemaids and workers. A discernable pattern thus emerges. While females have equal or better access to positions related to the spheres of education, health, and household activities, males have the overall advantage in accessing more positions in the structure. Because of the high prestige of physicians and the low prestige of housemaids and workers, access to which seems to be equal for both males and females, there are no differences between males and females on upper reachability and range.

We conclude that the structure of social capital, while showing superficial similarities, is essentially different for males and females. Females are generally disadvantaged in accessing many of the positions, but probably compensate by the roles they play relative to household well-being, such as education for children, health care for family members, and household maintenance. Such roles and the social resources they access may be useful for maintaining some sense of well-being; however, these social resources may not be as useful when such access is seen as social capital for gains in the labor force. Thus, all subsequent analyses are conducted separately for males and females.

Because the three measures of position data (extensity, upper reachabil-

Table 3.   Factor Structures of Access to Social Capital

	Sample (N = 2,693)	Males (N = 1,394)	Females (N = 1,299)
Factor eigenvalues			
I	2.25	2.31	2.19
II	0.03	0.02	0.03
III	−0.11	−0.11	−0.13
Factor loading on Factor I[a]			
Extensity	0.80	0.82	0.78
Range	0.94	0.95	0.94
Upper reachability	0.85	0.87	0.84
Factor scoring on Factor I[a]			
Extensity	0.15	0.15	0.15
Range	0.65	0.65	0.64
Highest prestige	0.21	0.20	0.21

[a]Principal component, minimal eigenvalue of 1, and varimax rotation.

ity, and the range) were highly correlated, we proceeded to construct a composite variable. A factor analysis, as presented in Table 3 (with principal component methodology, varimax rotation, and a criterion of an eigenvalue equal to or greater than 1), yielded a single factor solution and almost identical patterns and coefficients for the male and female sub-samples. A factor score was computed for both male and female respondents as a weighed sum of the three measures (.15 extensity + .65 range + .21 upper reachability). The range variable carried at least three times more weight than the other two variables; thus, this composite variable, called "access to social capital," more heavily reflects the range of positions accessed.

INEQUALITY IN ACCESS TO SOCIAL CAPITAL AND ITS DIFFERENTIAL RETURNS

The next research task is to assess the differential access to social capital: what characteristics would enhance or hinder access to social capital? We identified three groups of structural variables. The first group reflects household compositions. The analysis above suggests that females' access may be affected by family-domain activities. We do not have actual data on the use of doctors and nurses, school-age children, or employment of housemaids, so we used two measures—household size (logged) and presence of grandchildren in the household—on the assumption that larger households might increase the likelihood of having school-age children and the need for health and household services. Using the presence of grandchildren is a conservative estimate of the number of school-age children, and may also reflect the respondent's relative age (a correlation of .40). The expectation is that these variables are more likely to affect females' access to social capital than males' access.

The second group of variables taps the respondent's social status, specifically education and employment. These reflect possible avenues of extending one's social networks, and both variables indicate the broadening of one's social contacts. Especially in Taiwan, identification with school is very strong; alumni groups are usually active as a social network. Employment reflects the opportunities for further social contacts in the labor force. Since education is universal up to the completion of junior high school, we expected education to benefit both males and females in their access to social capital. However, participation in the labor force may not reflect equal standing in it; thus, we expected that employment should benefit males more than females.

The third group of variables measures extensity of social contacts. In the questionnaire, each respondent was asked to estimate the size of daily contacts ("In an ordinary day, how many people are you roughly in contact with? 1. 0–4 persons; 2. 5–9 persons; 3. 10–19 persons; 4. 20–49 persons; 5. 50–99 persons; 6. 100 or more). It was followed with the question, "How well do you know these persons? (1. Know almost all of them; 2. Know most of them; 3. About half and half; 4. Don't know most of them; 5. Know almost none of them). The score was reversed, so that the higher the score, the less familiar each respondent is with his/her daily contacts. The expectation was that the size of daily contacts would benefit both males and females. Familiarity with contacts was used to estimate the strength of ties with daily contacts. Here, we were uncertain what to expect. The hypothesis of the strength of weak ties (Granovetter 1974) might suggest that extensive, less-familiar contacts should extend one's networks and provide access to better social capital. However, data from Singapore (Bian & Ang 1997) and mainland China (Bian 1997) suggest that, at least in these societies, contact with total strangers yields no benefit, and extended family in these societies, as well as in Taiwan (Hsung 1992), continues to play a critical role in one's linkage with the larger society. Thus, stronger ties may in fact serve as important bridges extending one's networks. We simply let the data speak on the two alternative hypotheses.

Finally, we incorporated information on whether each access was to kin or nonkin. Informed by the significance of family in Chinese societies as well as the persistent significance of kinship in North America (Wellman 1990), we wished to examine whether the kin versus nonkin distinction makes a difference in degrees of access to various positions and, therefore, social capital. Again, we let data inform us whether stronger (kin) or weaker (nonkin) ties were more beneficial. Table 4 presents the basic data on access to each position through kin ties. In general, males tended to use more nonkin ties in accessing various positions, with the exception of

Table 4.　Access to Social Capital by Kin

| Accessed Positions (prestige score) | Percent Using Kin Ties | | | Gender Significance |
	Sample	Males	Females	
Physician (78)	22.8	23.0	22.5	.82
Lawyer (73)	18.6	17.9	19.6	.57
Owner of large factory/firm (70)	15.8	13.7	18.8	.03
Assemblymen/women (69)	15.5	12.5	19.8	.00
manager of large factory/firm (62)	16.4	11.9	22.8	.00
High school teacher (60)	36.9	34.7	39.3	.05
Division head (55)	22.5	19.8	26.6	.05
Reporter (55)	14.2	13.6	15.1	.61
Nurse (54)	37.8	37.8	37.9	.97
Owner of small factory/firm (48)	23.9	17.9	30.8	.00
Police (40)	32.6	30.4	35.3	.04
Electrician (36)	24.4	21.7	27.8	.00
Truck driver (31)	24.6	18.1	34.0	.00
Office workman/guard (26)	10.1	8.6	12.1	.05
Housemaid, cleaning worker (22)	13.7	13.5	14.0	.83
Association between				
Extensity	−0.21	−0.19	−0.21	
Range of prestige scores	−0.21	−0.20	−0.21	
Upper reachability	−0.15	−0.13	−0.18	

physicians, lawyers, nurses, police, office workmen/guards, and house-maids, for whom males and females seemed to have equal access. We computed a variable representing the percentage of a respondent's access to various positions that is mediated by kin ties and correlated it with the three access variables. The results, also presented in Table 4, suggest that the associations tend to be negative: nonkin ties yield better access to social capital.

We regressed the composite access to social capital variable on the other variables described above. The results of regression analyses, controlling for age and being married, are presented in the first two columns in Table 5. In the first equations (Model 1), we included all exogenous variables, except percentage of access through kin ties. For both males and females, access to social capital was contingent on being married, education level, and extensity of daily contacts. Males and females did differ on two factors relating to access to social capital. Males benefitted from being in the labor force, while females did not, suggesting that work-related networks facilitated males' access to social capital. Also, females were further hindered by having grandchildren in the household. It is worth noting that females, in contrast, rely more on education than males in gaining better access to social capital.

Table 5. Determinants of Access to Social Capital[a]

Exogenous Variable	Access to Social Capital			
	Model 1		Model 2	
	Males (N = 1,386)	Females (N = 1,293)	Males (N = 1,386)	Females (N = 1,293)
Age	-0.07	0.08*	-0.05	0.09**
	(-0.07)	(0.08)	(-0.06)	(0.09)
Married	4.58***	2.89***	4.93***	3.04***
	(0.16)	(0.09)	(0.17)	(0.19)
Household size (log)	-1.40	-0.56	-1.21	-0.47
	(-0.05)	(-0.02)	(0.06)	(-0.02)
Grandchildren in house	0.71	-1.18**	0.81	-1.00
	(0.05)	(-0.08)	(0.06)	(-0.07)
Education	0.45***	1.24***	0.44***	1.19***
	(0.15)	(0.33)	(0.14)	(0.32)
Employed	4.50***	-0.00	1.87*	-0.20
	(0.13)	(-0.00)	(0.05)	(-0.01)
Size of daily contacts	2.33***	1.72***	2.30***	1.62***
	(0.24)	(0.17)	(0.23)	(0.16)
Familiarity with contacts	0.86*	0.98*	-0.75	-0.98*
	(0.06)	(0.07)	(-0.05)	(-0.07)
Percent accesses thru kin			-8.58***	-6.97***
			(-0.17)	(-0.14)
Intercept	30.88	25.52	32.67	27.67
R^2	0.12	0.14	0.15	0.17

*$p < .05$.
**$p < .01$.
***$p < .001$.
[a]Partial regression coefficients; standardized coefficients in parentheses.

Familiarity with contacts has a positive, though modest, effect on access to social capital. Thus, it lends some support to the notion that a useful social network should contain strong as well as weak ties. Having more familiar ties in one's contact networks does not, however, exclude the utility of "weaker" ties in accessing specific social capital. Therefore, in the next equations (Model 2) we added the percentage of access through kin ties to the estimations As can be seen in Table 5, the negative and significant coefficients for both males and females provided tangible evidence that social ties outside one's extended family are helpful in accessing social capital. These effects are additional benefits, beyond those already accounted for by all the variables entered in Model 1. We hasten to add that this is not a direct test of the strength of the weak-ties hypothesis, since kin versus nonkin ties cannot be equated with strong versus weak ties. It is quite clear, however, that in Taiwanese society, social ties beyond one's extended family are useful channels for reaching better resources.

If the nature of access to social capital is different for males and females, with advantages going to the males, then we would expect that the benefit or return from access to social capital should be greater for males than females, especially if the return is assessed by gains in the labor force. To examine this hypothesis, we determined the effect of access to social capital on current job prestige and income. For effects on job prestige, all exogenous variables for access to social capital were used as exogenous variables or potential determinants. Since these analyses were conducted only for those who were employed, the variable of employment was eliminated. The age variable was also eliminated, as it was highly correlated with education (-0.38 for males and -0.53 for females), being married (0.48 for males and 0.19 for females), and having grandchildren (0.40 for males and 0.41 for females).[3] Results for job prestige are shown in the first two columns in Table 6. Education, as expected, was a major determinant

Table 6. Determinants of Job Prestige and Income[a]

Exogenous Variable	Job Prestige		Monthly Income (logged)	
	Males (N = 1,209)	Females (N = 755)	Males (N = 1,145)	Females (N = 722)
Married	0.31	0.96	0.13***	0.08*
	(0.01)	(0.04)	(0.09)	(0.07)
Household size (log)	−1.85**	−1.18	ne[b]	ne
	(−0.09)	(−0.05)		
Grandchildren in house	−0.06	0.18	−0.16***	−0.08***
	(−0.00)	(0.01)	(−0.21)	(−0.12)
Education	0.96***	1.89***	0.02***	0.04***
	(0.40)	(0.62)	(0.18)	(0.27)
Size of daily contacts	0.23	0.57*	0.10***	0.05***
	(0.03)	(0.07)	(0.20)	(0.13)
Familiarity with contacts	0.02	−0.14	0.01	0.02
	(0.00)	(−0.01)	(0.02)	(0.04)
Access to social capital	0.14***	0.01	0.01***	0.00*
	(0.17)	(0.01)	(0.16)	(0.07)
Percent access thru kin	−3.31**	0.89	−0.17***	−0.18***
	(−0.08)	(0.02)	(−0.07)	(−0.04)
Job prestige			0.01***	0.01***
			(0.14)	(0.16)
Intercept	28.56	25.07	0.38	0.47
R²	0.26	0.40	0.31	0.30

*$p < .05$.
**$p < .01$.
***$p < .001$.
[a]Partial regression coefficients; standardized coefficients in parentheses.
[b]ne, not entered.

of job prestige. Access to social capital, however, benefitted males and not females. Accessing these positions through nonkin also produced greater benefit for males than for females.

Finally, we estimated the effects of access to social capital on income. The measure of income was derived from the question, "Including year-end bonuses, may we ask what your average monthly income is?" and twenty-three response categories of grouped interval brackets ranging up to NT300,000 or more (equivalent to about U.S. $940 in 1997). We used the log of this measure as the income variable. As presented in the last two columns in Table 6, access to social capital is highly significant in association with monthly income for males, and not for females. Again, females tend to benefit more from education than males in income attainment.

A general pattern has emerged. While social capital, in general, generates returns in job prestige and income, it is the males who generate more returns from social capital than do females. Females, rather, have to rely on human capital (education) more for their job and economic attainments.

ACCESS TO SOCIAL CAPITAL AND ENTREPRENEURSHIP

Job prestige as usually used in Western countries, however, is not the only meaningful measure of job returns in Taiwan. The occupational structure is such that a significant portion of the labor force is self-employed or employed in family enterprises. It has been documented that self-employment provides an important and meaningful alternative to being employed by others, especially in the private sector (Shieh 1989, 1990, 1993; Ke 1993; Hsung & Hwang 1992; Stites 1982, 1985). For these entrepreneurs, access to social capital, along with extensive social contacts, should provide vital resources. But would such benefits also accrue to female entrepreneurs as well as to male entrepreneurs? We proceed to explore this question.

In the questionnaire, each respondent was asked, "May we ask where you work now, or work for whom?" About 29 percent indicated that they worked for themselves (self-employed), and another 8 percent worked for family-owned firms (employed by family), whereas the remainder (63 percent) worked for others (employed by others). Self-employed entrepreneurs have previously been found to be less educated and from less advantaged (lower parental job status) or self-employed (parents had own businesses) families. They may not be in the upper levels of the occupational structure, but they perform reasonably well in earnings.

The question for us is whether or not these entrepreneurs benefit from access to social capital, and whether such benefits are again unequal between male and female entrepreneurs. Analyses for income were therefore

Table 7. Return on Access to Social Capital to Income for Self-Employed Males[a]

Exogenous Variable	Self-Employed		Employed by Others		Employed by Family	
	Males (N = 361)	Females (N = 130)	Males (N = 652)	Females (N = 492)	Males (N = 42)	Females (N = 74)
Married	0.02 (0.01)	0.01 (0.01)	0.18*** (0.21)	0.10*** (0.12)	0.21 (0.19)	0.02 (0.01)
Household size (log)	0.21** (0.16)	0.02 (0.02)	0.01 (0.02)	0.13*** (-0.14)	0.08 (0.06)	0.03 (-0.02)
Grandchildren in house	-0.13*** (-0.19)	-0.09 (-0.13)	-0.07** (-0.09)	0.04 (0.05)	-0.11 (-0.16)	-0.11 (-0.16)
Education	0.07*** (0.33)	0.02 (0.14)	0.01*** (0.12)	0.04*** (0.38)	0.07 (0.37)	0.00 (0.01)
Size of daily contacts	0.08*** (0.16)	0.01 (0.01)	0.03** (0.10)	0.03* (0.08)	0.07 (0.20)	0.03 (0.08)
Familiarity with contacts	-0.01 (-.02)	0.07 (0.14)	-0.01 (-0.03)	0.01 (0.01)	-0.00 (-0.01)	0.07 (0.08)
Access to social capital	0.01** (0.14)	0.01 (0.13)	0.00*** (0.11)	0.00 (0.06)	0.00 (0.00)	0.00 (0.07)
Percent of access through kin	-0.01 (-0.00)	-0.1 (-0.00)	-0.13*** (-0.08)	-0.14** (-0.09)	-0.03 (-0.01)	-0.62* (-0.27)
Job prestige	0.01** (0.13)	0.01** (0.25)	0.01*** (0.35)	0.01*** (0.22)	0.01 (0.18)	0.01 (0.19)
Firm size	0.00** (0.11)	0.02 (0.15)				
Intercept	0.08	0.45	0.75	0.79	0.14	0.40
R^2	0.37	0.23	0.34	0.39	0.35	0.24

* $p < .05$.
** $p < .01$.
*** $p < .001$.
[a] Partial regression coefficients; standardized coefficients in parentheses.

conducted separately for the self-employed, those employed by others, and those employed by their own families. The results are presented in Table 7.

Since the group "employed by family" consists of small numbers of respondents, we will focus our attention on a comparison between the self-employed and those employed by others. The data for those employed by others and for both males and females (columns three and four in Table 7) fairly duplicate the general results provided in Table 6 (last two columns). For both male and female entrepreneurs, accessing social capital through kin ties does not decrease economic benefits. These patterns suggest that entrepreneurs need to use both kin and nonkin contacts to locate beneficial social capital. The benefit of relying on nonkin for those employed by others has largely disappeared. When firm size is taken into account, these relationships remain the same. We take these findings as important clues suggesting that there is indeed a social basis for the notion of family enterprises in Taiwan as well as in other East Asian countries. Family enterprises may not be the only avenue for entrepreneurship, but they are a very important segment of it.[4]

DISCUSSION

The position-generator methodology has yielded informative findings from surveys conducted in Taiwan. It demonstrates gender-based inequality in access to social capital largely based on the advantage of being in the labor force for males and the disadvantage of being tied down with household obligations for females. The data further show differential returns of access to social capital for males and females. Males benefit much more from access to social capital and nonkin relations in getting more prestigious jobs and higher incomes than females do. Females, in contrast, rely more on human capital (education) to gain job prestige and higher income. The relative utility of human capital and social capital is a matter of degree rather than dichotomy, however. As demonstrated clearly by the analyses, each form of capital generates returns and most individuals benefit from having both. Yet, as distinct segments of a population differentially benefit from each, research will help to identify the sources of variations in access to different types of capital and delineate the social dynamics involved in the creation and utility of capital in a given social structure.

The position-generator methodology also sheds light on the debate concerning whether the extensity of social contacts or the strength of ties generates better access to social capital. As it turns out, both arguments receive support. The data clearly show that the extensity of daily contacts, rather than whether such contacts tend to be close or not, facilitates access to better social capital in general. However, when it comes to accessing specific social capital—for example, a particular position in the social structure—nonkin and perhaps weaker ties are useful. Thus, extensity of social contacts affords the range of possible ties within which the search for specific social capital is likely to be more successful.

This analysis also suggests avenues for integrating two approaches to the measurement of social capital: network location and social resource. To the extent that extensity of daily contacts reflects relative locations in social networks, there is a clear association between the two: better network locations increase the likelihood of reaching better social resources. It remains unclear whether it is advantageous to view both network locations and social resources as indicators of social capital or to postulate network locations as a precursor of social capital, the social resources accessed. Our current inclination is to consider network locations as a precursor to social capital, for the simple reason that the relationship between the two should be a proposition to be examined rather than assumed. However, we are open to possible alternative integrations of these two types of measurement. The ultimate choice should be determined by the relative theoretical advantage and empirical meaningfulness each choice lends in advancing a theory of social capital.

Finally, the measurement of social capital by the position-generator technique helps clarify the linkage between social institutions and social stratification. The measurement is flexible enough to sample a population of positions meaningful in a social stratification system, be they occupations, incomes, authority positions, and/or types of employment. Such flexibility in sampling lends itself to the analysis of how social institutions are tied to social capital. In our data, the examination of family enterprises, favored by a significant segment of the labor force in Taiwan, clarifies conditions under which strong ties or weak ties may be useful in the construction and utility of social capital.

In conclusion, the position-generator methodology has yielded consistent findings across a wide spectrum of societies (North America, Asia, and Europe), populations (communities, new laborers, unemployed laborers, members of different industries or social organizations), and political economies (socialist states such as China and preliberation East Germany and Hungary, and capitalist states). Yet, much work remains to be done to examine the dynamics of social capital, as outlined in the beginning of our chapter. The interconnections between the various ingredients of social capital have seldom been studied or verified, and work on the inequality of social capital seems to be just commencing. Outcomes of social capital are being extended to many other areas of well-being, ranging from group cohesion and solidarity to life satisfaction and mental distress. Moreover, knowledge about access to social capital in and across firms and organizations has barely begun to accumulate. With a standardized measurement, we are encouraged that intellectual enterprises may yet validate and build coherent theories of social capital.

APPENDIX A: THE POSITION GENERATOR USED IN THE 1997 TAIWAN STUDY

Q1. Among your relatives, friends, or acquaintances, are there people who have the following jobs?

Q2. If so, what is his/her relationship to you?

Q3. If you don't know anyone with these jobs, and if you need to find such a person for private help or to ask about some problems, who among those you know would you go through to find such a person? Who would he/she be to you?

Q4. What job does he/she do?

Item	Q1	Q2	Q3	Q4
Responses	1. Yes	see list	see list	see list
	2. No	below	below	below
	(Skip to Q 3)			119 No contact
				111 Direct contact

a. High school teacher
b. Electrician
c. Owner of small factory/firm
d. Nurse
e. Assemblymen/women at
   provincial or city/county level
f. Truck driver
g. Physician
h. Manager of large factory/firm
i. Police (regular policeman)
j. Head of division, county/city government
k. Housemaid or cleaning worker
l. Reporter
m. Owner of big factory/firm
n. Lawyer
o. Office workman or guard

NOTES

An earlier version of this chapter was presented at the Social Networks and Social Capital Conference, October 30—November 1, 1998, Duke University. We wish to thank Karen Cook for her helpful editorial comments.

1. Variations in network structures, locations of egos, and distributions of re-
    sources as captured in name generators are significantly contingent on the
    specific wording, content, or role in name-generating questions and, to a
    lesser extent, on the number of names generated. In addition, the data gen-
    erated tend to reflect relations and resources of stronger ties, stronger role
    relations, or ties in close geographic limits. Campbell and Lee (1991) com-
    pared four studies (Fischer's Northern California study, Wellman's York
    study, the 1985 GSS survey, and their own Nashville study) and showed that
    network size was affected by procedures, heterogeneity on age and school-
    ing varied, and traits of relationships (duration, frequency of contact, etc.)
    also varied.
2. If a respondent indicated that he/she knew more than one contact for a po-
    sition, he/she was instructed to focus on the first contact that came to mind.
3. When age was incorporated into the equations, presented in Table 6, the co-
    efficients for the key variables—household size, education, access to social
    capital, percentage accesses through kin, and job prestige—remain stable,
    while coefficients for being married and having grandchildren showed
    distortions.
4. The self-employed groups in columns 1 and 2 show some differences
    between males and females. For male entrepreneurs, extensity of daily con-
    tacts continues to be beneficial, but this is not the case for female entrepre-
    neurs. To further understand the difference between the male and female
    entrepreneurs (self-employed), we analyzed if they employed others. Thirty-
    eight percent of the male entrepreneurs answered in the affirmative (158 of
    417), as did 32 percent among the female entrepreneurs (48 of 152). How-
    ever, the number of employees hired shows a significant difference: male en-
    trepreneurs hired an average of 11 employees, and female entrepreneurs
    only 4. Just over a quarter (26 percent) of the male entrepreneurs hired 10 or
    more employees, whereas only 10 percent of the female entrepreneurs did.
    This difference cannot be accounted for by different patterns in family en-
    terprises. Both male and female entrepreneurs are equally likely to hire
    nonkin (65 percent of the male entrepreneurs hired most or all employees
    outside their kin, compared to 60 percent of the female entrepreneurs).
    Thus, we conclude that the scope of the enterprises that male entrepreneurs
    tend to engage in accounts for the greater extent of their daily contacts.

REFERENCES

Angelusz, Robert, and Robert Tardos. 1991. "The Strength and Weakness of 'Weak
    Ties.'" Pp. 7–23 in *Values, Networks and Cultural Reproduction in Hungary*, edited
    by P. Somlai. Budapest: Coordinating Council of Programs.
Becker, Gary S. 1964/1993. *Human Capital*. Chicago: University of Chicago Press.
———. 1981/1991. *A Treatise on the Family (Enlarged Edition)*. Cambridge, MA: Har-
    vard University Press.
Bian, Yanjie. 1997. "Bringing Strong Ties Back In: Indirect Connection, Bridges, and
    Job Search in China." *American Sociological Review* 62(3):36–385, 3.

Bian, Yanjie, and Soon Ang. 1997. "Guanxi Networks and Job Mobility in China and Singapore." *Social Forces* 75:981–1006.

Bourdieu, Pierre. 1972/1977. *Outline of a Theory of Practice*. Cambridge: Cambridge University Press.

———. 1980. "Le Capital Social: Notes Provisoires." *Actes de la Recherche en Sciences Sociales* 3:2–3.

———. 1983/1986. "The Forms of Capital." Pp. 241–58 in *Handbook of Theory and Research for the Sociology of Education*, edited by John G. Richardson. Westport, CT: Greenwood Press.

Bourdieu, Pierre and Jean-Claude Passeron. 1977. *Reproduction in Education, Society, Culture*. Beverly Hills, CA: Sage.

Boxman, E. A. W., P. M. De Graaf, and Henk D. Flap. 1991. "The Impact of Social and Human Capital on the Income Attainment of Dutch Managers." *Social Networks* 13:51–73.

Boxman, E. A. W., and Hendrik Derk Flap. 1990. "Social Capital and Occupational Chances." Presented at the The International Sociological Association XII World Congress of Sociology, July, Madrid.

Burt, Ronald S. 1984. "Network Items and the General Social Survey." *Social Networks* 6:293–339.

———. 1992. *Structural Holes: The Social Structure of Competition*. Cambridge, MA: Harvard University Press.

———. 1997. "The Contingent Value of Social Capital." *Administrative Science Quarterly* 42:339–65.

———. 1998. "The Gender of Social Capital." *Rationality and Society* 10(1):5–46, 1.

Campbell, Karen E., Peter V. Marsden, and Jeanne S. Hurlbert. 1986. "Social Resources and Socioeconomic Status." *Social Networks* 8(1), 1.

Coleman, James S. 1988. "Social Capital in the Creation of Human Capital." *American Journal of Sociology* 94:S95—S121.

———. 1990. *Foundations of Social Theory*. Cambridge, MA: Harvard University Press.

De Graaf, Nan Dirk, and Hendrik Derk Flap. 1988. "With a Little Help from My Friends." *Social Forces* 67(2):452–72, 2.

Erickson, Bonnie H. 1995. "Networks, Success, and Class Structure: A Total View." Sunbelt Social Networks Conference. Charleston, SC, February.

———. 1996. "Culture, Class and Connections." *American Journal of Sociology* 102(1):217–51, 1.

———. 1998. "Social Capital and Its Profits, Local and Global." The Sunbelt XVIII and 5th European International Conference on Social Networks. Sitges, Spain, May 27–31.

Fischer, Claude S. 1977. *Networks and Places*. New York: Free Press.

———. 1982. *To Dwell Among Friends: Personal Networks in Town and City*. Chicago: University of Chicago Press.

Flap, Hendrik Derk, and Nan Dirk De Graaf. 1988. "Social Capital and Attained Occupational Status." *Netherlands Journal of Sociology*.

Granovetter, Mark. 1974. *Getting a Job*. Cambridge, MA: Harvard University Press.

Hall, Alan, and Barry Wellman. 1985. "Social Networks and Social Support." Pp. 23–42 in *Social Support and Health*, edited by Sheldon Cohen and S. Leonard Syme. Orlando: Academic Press.

Hsung, Ray-May. 1992. "Social Resources and Petite Bourgeoisie." *Journal of the Chinese Sociological Association* 16:107–38.

Hsung, Ray-May, and Yih-Jyh Hwang. 1992. "Job Mobility In Taiwan: Job Search Methods and Contacts Status." The XII International Sunbelt Social Network Conference. San Diego, February.

Ke, Chih-ming. 1993. *Market, Social Networks, and the Production Organization of Small-Scale Industry in Taiwan: The Garment Industries in Wufenpu.* Taiwan: Institute of Ethnology, Academia Sinica.

Laumann, Edward O. 1966. *Prestige and Association in an Urban Community.* Indianapolis: Bobbs-Merrill.

Lin, Nan. 1982. "Social Resources and Instrumental Action." Pp. 131–45 in *Social Structure and Network Analysis*, edited by Peter V. Marsden and Nan Lin. Beverly Hills, CA: Sage.

———. 1995. "Les Ressources Sociales: Une Theorie Du Capital Social." *Revue Francaise de Sociologie* XXXVI(4):685–704, 4.

———. 2001. *Social Capital: A Theory of Social Structure and Action.* London and New York: Cambridge University Press.

Lin, Nan, and Mary Dumin. 1986. "Access to Occupations Through Social Ties." *Social Networks* 8:365–85.

Lin, Nan, Al Dean, and Walter Ensl. 1986. *Social Support, Life Events, and Depression.* Orlando, FL: Academic Press.

Marsden, Peter V. 1987. "Core Discussion Networks of Americans." *American Sociological Review* 52:122–31.

Marsden, Peter V., and Jeanne S. Hurlbert. 1988. "Social Resources and Mobility Outcomes: A Replication and Extension." *Social Forces* 66(4):1038–59, 4.

Marx, Karl. 1933 (1849). *Wage-Labour and Capital.* New York: International Publishers Co.

Portes, Alejandro, and Julia Sensenbrenner. 1993. "Embeddedness and Immigration: Notes on the Social Determinants of Economic Action." *American Journal of Sociology* 98(6):1320–50, 6.

Portes, Alex. 1998. "Social Capital: Its Origins and Applications in Modern Sociology." *Annual Review of Sociology* 22:1–24.

Putnam, Robert D. 1993. *Making Democracy Work: Civic Traditions in Modern Italy.* Princeton, NJ: Princeton University Press.

———. 1995a. "Bowling Alone, Revisited." *The Responsive Community*, Spring, 18–33.

———. 1995b. "Tuning In, Tuning Out: The Strange Disappearance of Social Capital in America." The 1995 Itheiel de Sola Pool Lecture. American Political Science Association. September.

Schultz, Theodore W. 1961. "Investment in Human Capital." *The American Economic Review* LI(1):1–17, 1.

Shieh, Guo-shiung. 1989. "From Dark Hands to Boss." *Taiwan Sociological Research Quarterly* 2(2), 11–54.

———. 1991. "The Network Labor Process: The Subcontracting Networks in the Manufacturing Industries of Taiwan." *Bulletin of the Institute of Ethnology Journal* 71:161–82.

———. 1992. *"Boss" Island: Subcontracting Networks and Micro-Entrepreneurship in Taiwan's Development.* New York: Peter Lang.

———. 1993. "Dynamics of Working, Bossing and Entrepreneuring: Research on the Founding and Surviving of the Small Manufacturing Units in Taiwan." *Taiwan Sociological Research Quarterly* 15:93–130.

Sprengers, Maarten, Fritz Tazelaar, and Henk Derk Flap. 1988. "Social Resources, Situational Constraints, and Reemployment." *Netherlands Journal of Sociology* 24:98–116.

Stites, R. 1982. "Small-scale Industry in Yingge, Taiwan." *Modern China* 8(2): 247–79

———. 1985. "Industrial Work as an Entrepreneurial Strategy." *Modern China* 11(2); 227–46.

Volker, Beate, and Henk Flap. 1996. "Getting Ahead in the GDR: Human Capital and Social Capital in the Status Attainment Process Under Communism." Universiteit Utrecht, The Netherlands.

Wellman, Barry. 1981. "Applying Network Analysis to the Study of Social Support." Pp. 171–200 in *Social Networks and Social Support*, edited by Benjamin H. Gottlieb. Beverly Hills, CA: Sage.

———. 1979. "The Community Question: The Intimate Networks of East Yorkers." *American Journal of Sociology 84:* 1201–31.

———. 1990. "The Place of Kinfolk in Personal Community Networks." *Marriage and Family Review* 15:195–227.

Part II

Social Capital in the Labor Market

4

How Much Is That Network Worth?
Social Capital in Employee
Referral Networks

Roberto M. Fernandez and Emilio J. Castilla

The notion of social capital has been applied to disparate phenomena rang-ing from job search (Flap & Boxman 1999) to economic development (Woolcock 1998). Perhaps inevitably, the concept has taken on a number of disparate meanings over the years (for recent reviews, see Adler & Kwon 1999; Burt 1998). Several scholars (e.g., Adler & Kwon 1999; Baron & Han-nan 1994:1122–24) have questioned the utility of continuing with such a catholic approach in this area. In our research, we focus on one particularly important feature of the concept of social capital, the notion that it can yield returns on investment. We argue that if the term "social capital" is to mean anything more than "networks have value," then we will need to demon-strate key features of the analogy to "real" capital. If "social" capital is like "real" capital, we should be able to isolate the value of the investment, the rates of return, and the means by which returns are realized.

We argue that a common organizational practice—hiring new workers via employee referrals—provides key insights into the notion of social cap-ital. In our research (Fernandez et al. 2000), we examined social-capital in-vestments and returns from the perspective of the employer. We argued that employers who use such hiring methods are quintessential "social capitalists," viewing workers' social connections as resources in which they can invest and gain returns in the form of improved hiring outcomes. The investment took the form of a referral bonus paid to employees who refer workers who are subsequently hired; the returns are measured in real dollar impacts on hiring outcomes (savings on recruitment costs and lower turnover for referred than nonreferred hires).

In this chapter, we shift our focus to the *employee's* social-capital investment. Just as employers might reap benefits from workers' networks, individual workers might view their own networks as a source of instrumental value. This is especially likely to be the case for workers employed at a firm that offers referral bonuses for recruiting applicants. From the individual worker's perspective, the social capital investment takes the form of time and energy expended in referring candidates for employment, while the referral bonus constitutes the return on this investment. We examine data on all workers who were eligible to make referrals over the period of the study, and examine the determinants of referring. In order to assess the returns on referring, we use the referral bonus to calculate the expected value of referring. Although our measures of investment are indirect, we develop a model of workers' referring behavior in order to shed light on the nature of workers' investments in referral recruitment.

We begin by summarizing the results of the firm's social-capital investment in its referral program. We then shift to the perspective of the employee and discuss the value of the referral bonus for prospective referrers. We then turn to the empirical data to estimate predictive models of who participates in the referral program. We conclude with a discussion of the implications of the model for our understanding of social capital.

THE FIRM'S INVESTMENT

In Fernandez et al. (2000), we studied hiring for entry-level customer service representatives at a telephone call center of a large financial services institution.[1] We used unique company data on the dollar costs of screening, hiring, and training of referrals and nonreferrals to identify the dollar investments and returns that the firm made by using referrals in their hiring process. We identified three mechanisms by which the firm could reap returns on these investments—i.e., the referrals produce a "richer pool" of applicants interpretation; the referrals are "better matched" argument, which is common within economics; and the referrals benefit from "social enrichment" of the workplace mechanisms, which is emphasized by sociologists.

To the extent that referred applicants constitute a richer hiring pool than nonreferrals, this suggests that it would take fewer screens to hire appropriate people from among a pool of referral applicants than it would nonreferral applicants. Thus, economizing on screening costs is one mechanism by which employers can realize returns from using the social capital of their employees during recruitment. In order to address the "richer pool" argument, we used data on the pool of applicants to entry-level jobs to test whether referrals show evidence of being more appropriate for the job at the application stage.

The "better match" theory posits a second mechanism by which employers may realize returns to their social capital investment: savings due to referrals' lower turnover. Here, the argument is that referrals should be better informed than nonreferrals about the more informal characteristics of the job. Since referrals would have a better sense of what the job entailed than nonreferrals, fewer referrals than nonreferrals would conclude upon experiencing the job that it is not for them and leave. We tested the "better match" interpretation of referral hiring by comparing the posthire turnover data for referrals and nonreferrals, and looking for evidence that referrals provide a conduit for information between the employer and the applicant.

Finally, the "social enrichment" explanation of recruitment via referrals argues that the connection between the new hire and the job is enriched by the existence of a prior friend or acquaintance that might ease the transition to a new job setting. This can increase workers' attachment to the firm, thereby lowering turnover and economizing on the costs associated with the training of replacements. We tested the "social enrichment" argument by examining data on interdependence between referrals and referrers on posthire attachment to the firm.

We found evidence of both the "richer pool" and "social enrichment" processes, but very little evidence of the posthire "better match" explanation of referral hiring. Moreover, we gauged the firms' dollar returns associated with the referral program. Using their internal accounting data on the dollar costs of screening, hiring, and training, we identified the dollar investments that the firm made by hiring referrals and partitioned the dollar returns across the three mechanisms.

Table 1 summarizes the return on investment calculations we made with respect to the referral program. The firm invests $10 for each referral who is interviewed, and $250 for each referral who is hired and remains with the firm 30 days. Each applicant screen (paper screening plus short telephone interview) cost $7.00. On a per-hire basis, screening costs for referrals are $63.33, interview costs are $701.75, and offer costs are $212.87, for a total of $977.95 per hire. The corresponding figures for nonreferrals are $117.15, $1,055.29, and $221.94, for a total cost per hire of $1,394.37. The total difference between referrals and nonreferrals is $416.43 per hire; 85 percent of the savings are associated with the interview stage. The $416.43 difference yields a 66.6 percent return on the firm's $250 incremental out-

Table 1. Per-Hire Dollar Savings Associated with Hiring Referrals via the "Richer Pool" Mechanism for Each Stage of the Hiring Process

Application Screening Stage	Referrals		Nonreferrals		Referral's
	Screens per Hire	Cost per Hire	Screens per Hire	Cost Per Hire	Savings Per Hire
Cost: $7.00 per screen	9.043 @ $7.00 = $63.33		16.735 @ $7.00 = $117.15		$53.82
Interview Stage	Interviews Per Hire	Cost Per Hire	Interviews Per Hire	Cost Per Hire	Savings Per Hire
Cost: $120 (referrals) $110 (nonreferrals) Per interview	5.846 @ $120.00 = $701.75		9.596 @ $110.00 = $1055.29		$355.54
Offer Stage	Offers Per Hire	Cost Per HirePer	Offers Per Hire	Cost Per Hire	Savings Per Hire
Cost: $200.00 per offer	1.064 @ $200.00 = $212.87		1.110 @ $200.00 = $221.94		$9.07
Total costs per hire		$977.95		$1394.37	$416.43
Referral bonus (investment)		$250.00			
Total costs		$1227.95		$1394.37	$166.43

Net benefit: $166.43, or 66.6 percent return on investment

lay in the form of the referral bonus. Thus, we found that the firm's social capital investment was justified based on the prehire "richer pool" process (for details of the cost accounting, see Fernandez et al. 2000).

We also considered the posthire "better match" and "social enrichment" processes. To the extent that there were returns associated with these mechanisms, they should have manifested themselves in referrals showing lower turnover rates. However, our analyses of turnover differences associated with recruitment source showed no practical or statistically reliable return on the $250 investment vis-à-vis the "better match" mechanism. We did find evidence of the social enrichment process. The firm, however, did not reap any financial benefits via this mechanism. Overall, referrals did not differ from nonreferrals in turnover, but there was significant heterogeneity among referrals in turnover depending on the behavior of their referrer. Referrals whose referrer leaves showed an annual replacement cost of $3,129, not including the cost of replacing the referrer. Referrals whose referrer stays had an annual replacement cost of $1,633. Thus, if a new hire were to be converted from the "referrer leaves" to a "referrer stays" category, the bank would save $1,496 in replacement costs. When considered in relation to the investment of $250, these savings in replacement costs would indicate very large returns. However, because the firm did not make any attempt to manage the social enrichment process (e.g., by attempting to break the relationship between referrers who are likely to leave and their referrals), the $1,496 figure represents *potential* savings that the firm does not currently realize (for further details, see Fernandez et al. 2000).

THE REFERRER'S PERSPECTIVE

Just as the referral program may be seen as an investment that yields returns for the firm by saving on hiring costs, the referral program may also be analyzed as a social capital investment from the point of view of a person employed at the phone center. From the referrer's perspective, the referral bonus can be seen as returns (compensation) for the referrer's use of his/her social capital (i.e., network of acquaintances) on behalf of the firm.

The management at the phone center offered bonuses to employees who referred friends or acquaintances for customer-service representative positions. The firm pays the employee $10 for suggesting a candidate who is interviewed, and $250 if the candidate is hired and stays with the company 30 days.[2] Table 2 reports information on the rate at which the firm paid out these bonuses over the two-year period of our study. The top panel shows that nearly 65 percent of applicants who are referred are granted interviews (for details of the analyses, see Fernandez et al. 2000). Thus at the interview phase, the expected value for employees' referring is $6.48. However, the bottom panel shows that a much lower percentage of referral attempts pay off in the $250 bonus: only 10.9 percent of referred applicants are hired and last the required 30 days. Ninety-four percent of those

Table 2. Expected Value Payoffs for Referring Applicants to Firm

	Bonus (If Applicant Is Successful)	Probability of Applicant Success	Expected Value
1. Interview bonus			
(Interview|Application)	$10	.648	$6.48
2. Hire and 30 day bonus			
(Offer|application)		.119	
(Hire|offer)		.940	
(30 days|hire)		.971	
(30 days|application)	$250	.109	$27.14
Total	$260		$33.62

who are offered jobs are hired, and 97.1 percent of hires stay with the firm 30 days; however, only 11.9 percent of referred applicants are initially offered jobs. From the referring employee's perspective, the firm's second bonus program yields an expected value of $27.14. Thus, the total value of the programs to an employee who refers a successful candidate (i.e., *ex post*) is $260; the *ex ante* value of the program to a referring employee is $33.62.

Of course, these are average payoffs, and there is certain to be variation in the chances of receiving the payoff. Indeed, the structure of the program creates an incentive for referrers to "game" the bonus system. While management's and referrer's incentives may be aligned in some cases (e.g., by referrers attempting to influence the referral, thereby raising the probability that the referral will accept the job), this is not necessarily the case. If, in pursuit of the bonus, referrers attempt to influence recruiters' screening decisions (interview or offer) such that recruiters are passing unqualified people on (who would otherwise be rejected), then the firm might be suffering adversely from the effects of the bonus program. Indeed, one of the firm's recruiters expressed just such a concern in an interview with us.[3] Similarly, referrers who attempt to influence the propensity of the referral to stay at least 30 days are well aligned with management's interests, as long as the attempt is not to get the referral to delay his/her departure until the thirty-first day.

We examined the data for evidence of such gaming behavior. Despite the fact that recruiters seem to prefer referral to nonreferral candidates, we know that recruiters do not communicate with referrers while screening applicants for interviews or offers (see Fernandez et al. 2000). At least with respect to influences on the recruiters, we find no evidence of such attempts. Regarding the later phases (offer acceptance and turnover) of the bonus payout criteria, we think the available evidence casts doubt on this too. Neither the acceptance rate of job offers nor the percent of hires staying 30 days differs significantly for nonreferrals and referrals (90.1 vs. 94 percent for job offers and 98.1 vs. 97.1 percent of hires staying 30 days; see Fernandez et al. 2000). If there are attempts to influence the referral in order to reap the bonus, they appear to have failed in this context.

Our analyses thus far have identified a total potential return for referring of $260. In order to reap this payoff, however, referrers need to invest time and energy in recruiting customer-service representative candidates. We are limited in our ability to measure the degree of investment since our dataset does not contain direct measures of the amount of time and resources that referrers expend in recruiting referrals. We gain some insight into the nature of this investment, however, by studying the determinants of referring behavior. To our knowledge, these data are unique in their ability to address factors that distinguish employees who refer from those who do not refer applicants.

Who Refers?

As we showed in Table 2, the referral program in this context is structured in such a way that the expected value of referring applicants is $33.62. However, the vast majority of employees at the phone center passed up the opportunity to claim the referral bonus: 70.3 percent (2,891 of 4,114) of the people employed at the phone center did not refer anyone during the period of the study. What distinguishes those who refer from those who do not?

If referring behavior is understandable as a type of investment, we conjecture that the cost of recruiting applicants is likely to be an important determinant of referring.[4] The most important cost in this setting is likely to be the time needed to identify recruits and convince them to apply. Economists typically measure the value of time by an individual's wage rate (Winship 1983). Wages might also index structural accessibility to appropriate candidates since high-wage workers might be less likely to know people who would be interested in applying for a low-wage, entry-level job. Indeed, the evidence we found showing homophily between referrers' wages and applicants' wages on their last job (Fernandez et al. 2000) supports this inference. Thus, both these arguments would predict that high-wage employees would be less likely to refer applicants than low-wage workers.[5]

In addition to low wages, in this setting, structural accessibility to potentially fruitful referrals is likely to be associated with two others factors. First, workers who themselves had been hired as a referral are likely to have better access to appropriate job candidates. Because these workers have been recruited as referrals themselves, the referral program is likely to be more salient to such workers, and should better understand the nature of the referral recruitment process than nonreferrals. Also, such workers are more likely to be embedded in referral networks, and thus better positioned to suggest applicants.

The second factor affecting access is whether or not the person had ever worked as a telephone customer service representative for the bank is also likely to predispose workers to referring candidates to the CSR position. There is clear evidence that people tend to refer people like themselves in this setting (Fernandez et al. 2000); thus, former customer service representatives should be more likely to know people who might be interested in CSR positions. In addition, having done the job themselves, such workers should be better able to explain the job to potential candidates.[6]

Unlike the time-value rationale discussed above, we think that having been a referral or a CSR are unlikely to be conscious investments in social capital. This does not mean, however, that such statuses do not yield value for the employee in this setting. While we think it is implausible that the prospect of garnering a referral bonus would play a large role in employees' *choosing* these statuses, it is possible that workers consider the chances of winning a referral bonus as a kind of fringe benefit when deciding between jobs at different firms. Irrespective of how calculated the choice of these statuses has been, once workers are in these positions, they are much better positioned to refer others and pursue referral bonuses.

Thus far, the arguments suggest that the effects of wages and structural access on referring will be analytically separate. While the time costs of seeking out appropriate people are likely to be greater for people who are structurally less well-connected, for a given time cost (wage), the rate of referring should be higher for people who are more likely to be connected to appropriate applicants (i.e., referrals and former CSRs). This relationship between wages and referral and CSR statuses is important because it gives us a way of estimating the social capital value of structural access in this setting (see below).

It is also plausible, however, that the effects of accessibility and wages will combine as determinants of referring. Because access can shorten the time requirements for recruiting referrals, structural access could *substitute* for time in producing referrals, yielding a negative interaction between wages and access. Thus, the effect of wages on referring will depend on the level of structural access: As wages decrease, the payoff in terms of the referring rate will be much greater for structurally connected than disconnected individuals. While this predicted interaction complicates the analyses we present below, it allows us to address the contingent nature of the social capital value of structural access in this setting.

Data and Measures

In order to test these predictions, we assembled a time-varying data file for all workers at risk of referring an applicant to a telephone customer-service representative job over the period of the study. We were successful in coding data for 96.4 percent (3,968 of 4,114) of the workers employed at the phone center. There were no limits on the number of applicants a person could refer,[7] and the number of referrals per referrer varied between 1 and 6 (although 79.7 percent referred only one, and 15.8 percent referred two applicants). A total of 1,546 referral applications were produced over the two-year period under study, and we were able to locate the identity of the referrer and the date of the referral for 90.2 percent (1,395) of the referral applications.

We estimated Weibull event history models treating the dependent variable—making a referral—as a repeated event.[8] We included three sets of variables among the predictors in these models. First, we measured worker's hourly wages. As we discussed above, wages might index both time-value and structural access. Since wages varied over the two-year period of the study, we coded hourly wage as a time-varying covariate. Second, we coded two measures of individual's structural access to hirable applicants. We coded a dummy variable for whether the worker had him- or herself been hired as a referral. The second structural-access variable we use is a dummy variable for whether or not the person had ever worked as a telephone customer-service representative for the bank.

The last set of factors we included in the model for referring were control variables for individual background characteristics. We distinguished gender with a dummy variable (1 = female), and coded the individual's age at the earliest time that he/she appeared within the two-year observation window. We also measured minority status as a dummy variable, coded 1 for African Americans, Hispanics, Native Americans, or Asians, and 0 otherwise. Marital status at time of hire was coded as a dummy variable 1 = married, and 0 otherwise. Finally, we measured education with two dummy variables, the first for whether the person has a Bachelors' degree (1 = BA and 0 otherwise), and a second dummy variable for 2 years of college (1 = 2 years of college, 0 otherwise).[9]

Results

Model 1 of Table 3 presents a simple repeated event Weibull model predicting referring, ignoring potential interaction effects. While we did not present hypotheses about their effects, the control variables show several interesting relationships with referring. Controlling other factors, we find that minorities are more likely to refer candidates than nonminorities. Minorities might be using the referral program to increase their representation in the company. We cannot be sure of this, however, since applicants do not list their race or ethnic background on the applications, and so we cannot tell whether minorities' referrals are homophilous with respect to race (i.e., whether minority employees are more likely to refer minority than nonminority candidates).[10]

We also found that married workers are more likely to refer than those who are not married. Here, too, since applicants do not list their marital status on the application form, we cannot be sure whether this pattern is due to a tendency for workers to refer people like themselves. The coefficient for age, however, shows that older workers are *less* likely to refer applicants than are younger workers. This is consistent with the general tendency for network size to decrease with age (see Burt 1991). It might,

Table 3. Weibull ModelsPredicting Referring as a Repeated Event[a] (Standard errors in parentheses).

	1	2
Gender	.092	.105
(1 = female)	(.084)	(.084)
Age (in years)	−.039*	−.037*
	(.005)	(.005)
Minority status	.417*	.393*
(1 = minority)	(.166)	(.164)
Marital status	.128*	.123*
(1 = married)	(.072)	(.072)
Education	−.039	−.037
(1 = BA)	(.127)	(.126)
Education	−.099*	−.153
(1 = AA)	(.213)	(.215)
Hourly wage[b]	−.099	−.078*
	(.019)	(.017)
Referral	1.451*	2.079*
	(.102)	(.419)
Customer service	.324*	2.094*
representative	(.071)	(.364)
Hourly wage[b]		−.078*
× referral		(.046)
Hourly wage[b]		−.181*
× cust. serv. rep.		(.037)
Constant	−3.821*	−4.215*
	(.278)	(.293)
Weibull	1.127*	1.152*
rho parameter	(.035)	(.035)
χ^2	535.710	622.180
d.f.	9	11
p	<.00001	<.00001
N	3,946	3,946
Referrals made	1,391	1,391

*$p < .05$, one-tailed test.
[a]Standard errors in parentheses.
[b]Time-varying covariate.

however, also be due to the fact that the customer-service representative position is an entry-level job. Regardless of network size, young people are likely to have an edge in knowing people who are specifically seeking such jobs.

Turning to the main variables of interests, we find that, controlling other factors, high-wage workers are significantly less likely to refer people than are low-wage workers. This result plausibly reflects two distinct tendencies. First, it could be that high-wage workers are simply less likely to know people who might be interested in an entry-level job in their network. Second, the value of time for high-wage workers is greater than for low-wage workers, so the incentive level of the referral program (*ex ante* $33.62, and *ex post* $260) is likely to be too low to encourage high-wage workers to search very much for new candidates.

Consistent with our predictions with respect to structural availability, Model 1 also shows that having been hired as a referral and having worked as a CSR are both positively associated with referring. This supports the idea (discussed above) that a favorable structural position dramatically lowers the costs of proposing referral candidates. Finally, the *rho* parameter is significantly greater than 1, implying that the baseline hazard of referring is increasing with increased exposure, i.e., the longer people are employed at the phone center.

We examined the data for evidence that structural availability can act as a substitute for wage in producing referrals. In Model 2, we added interaction terms for the access variables (referral and CSR) with wage to the regressors. A chi-square test of the contrast between Models 1 and 2 shows a significant improvement in fit (LL chi-square 86.47, with 2 d.f.). Moreover, both interaction terms are in the predicted direction (i.e., negative) and individually statistically significant ($p < .05$, one-tailed test). The pattern of effects for the control variables does not change with the introduction of the interaction terms. However, the interactions substantially alter our interpretation of the impact of wage on the propensity to refer. Model 2 shows that low-wage workers who are not themselves referrals or present or former CSRs are significantly more likely to refer people than similarly disconnected high-wage workers (main effect of wage −.078). The propensity to refer, however, is much stronger for low-wage referrals (double, in fact; the main effect of −.078 + referral by wage interaction of −.078) and low-wage CSRs (main effect −.078 + CSR by wage interaction of −.181). The intercept shifts for referral and CSR greatly increase over those in Model 1. When considered in combination with the interaction terms, these patterns suggest that the chances of referring are highest for low-wage referrals who are also CSRs, and that as wages increase, referring falls off at a steeper rate for referrals who are CSRs than for nonreferral, non-CSR employees.

In order to explore the implications of these results, and to get a better sense of the magnitudes of the effects implied by the model, we plotted the predicted probabilities of referring at least once (recall that referring is a repeated event) based on Model 2 (see Figure 1).[11] We plotted wage-referring profiles for four groups based on their levels of structural access to candidates: (1) referral, CSR; (2) referral, non-CSR; (3) nonreferral, CSR; (4) nonreferral, non-CSR. Wages at the phone center ranged from a low of $5.25 to $100 per hour, although the distribution is very skewed to the left, with a

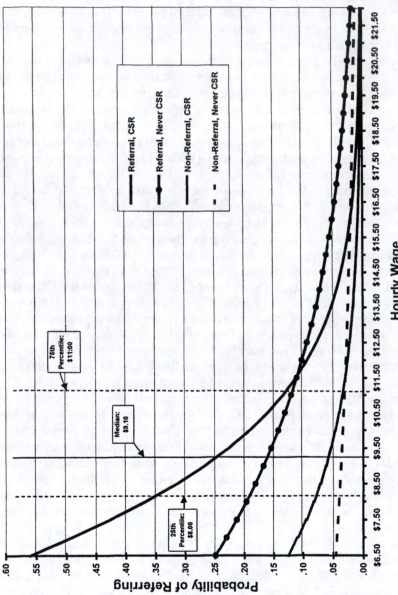

Figure 1.   Predicted probability of referring by hourly wage (Table 3, Model 2).

96

median wage of just $9.10. We plotted the model predictions for wages from the 5th percentile ($6.50) to the 95th percentile ($22.00), indicating on the x-axis of Figure 1 where the 25th, 50th, and 75th percentiles fall.

The first thing to notice is that curves for all four groups are downwardly sloping with increasing wages. As we argued above, this could be due to a rational calculus with respect to time investment due to an increasing opportunity cost of time, and / or the lower levels of access that high-wage workers may have to appropriate candidates. The second obvious pattern is that the curves start from dramatically different points, and show very different rates of decline as wages increase. Those with the most access to potential hires—referrals who have been CSRs—are most responsive to the effects of wages on referring, while those in the least favorable structural position—nonreferral, non-CSRs—are least responsive to changing wages.

Further examining Figure 1, we see that differences in referring associated with CSR status virtually disappear by the 75th percentile of the wage distribution. For referrals, the curve for CSRs starts at about 56 percent, and declines to about 14 percent by the 75th percentile of the wage distribution, while the non-CSR curve begins lower (25 percent) and declines more slowly, crossing the 75th percentile of the wage distribution at about 12 percent. For nonreferrals, the CSR curve starts at about 12 percent, declining to 3 percent by the 75th percentile, while the non-CSR curve begins at 4.6 percent and declines to about 3 percent at the 75th percentile. In contrast, referral / nonreferral differences in referring are even larger at the beginning (56 vs. 12 percent for CSRs and 25 vs. 4.6 percent for non-CSRs), and remain substantial at the 75th percentile of wages (14 vs. 3 percent for CSRs and 12 vs. 3 percent for non-CSRs).

These findings have important implications with respect to workers' social capital investments and rates of return. Since, in the limit, the chances of receiving the referral bonuses are nil for people who do not know anyone to refer, the incentive argument would suggest that we should see a flat relationship between wages and referring as we approach this limit. Consistent with this argument, the chances of referring are indeed quite low for low-wage, nonreferral, non-CSRs (i.e., 4.6 percent for workers earning $6.50 per hour), and the wage-referring profile stays relatively flat as wages increase. While we cannot in the present study separate the accessibility and incentive components of wages (see note 5), these findings are consistent with a central implication of a social capital approach to referring, i.e., at least some part of the wage effects reflect people's responses to monetary incentives for referring.[12] To the extent that monetary incentives are a determinant of referring, they appear to be more important for referrals than nonreferrals.

These findings also suggest that differences in the effects of wages between referrals and nonreferrals and CSRs and non-CSRs also translate into variation in rates of return to social capital investments in this setting. Since we did not find individual differences in the *benefits* of referring (the numerator in a rate-of-return calculation; see note 4), the differences in the effects of wages across these various groups reflect variation in the underlying *costs* of referring (the denominator). Without direct measures of time invested in referring, we cannot offer precise estimates of rates of return. We can, however, use the model to make some educated guesses with respect to the relative value of referral and CSR status under differing assumptions about the meaning of the wage effect.

Whether wages are indexing time-value, class-based access to eligible others, or both, the value of referral and CSR statuses appear to be substantial. Assuming for the moment that all of the wage effects reflect differences in time-value, then the differences in referring rates between referral, CSRs and nonreferral, non-CSRs suggest that the former group can produce a referral at much faster rates than can the latter group. At a time-value of $6.50 per hour, it is rational to invest a little over 5 hours (Expected value of $33.62 / $6.50 per hour = 5.17 hours) to searching for a referral. At a wage of $6.50, however, referral, CSRs produce referrals at over 12 times the rate of nonreferral, non-CSRs (referral rates of 56 percent vs. 4.6 percent). Even at higher wages, the difference in referring rates remains substantial. For example, at $11.00 (i.e., the 75th percentile of the wage distribution) the referring rate of referral, CSRs is 4.4 times that of nonreferral, non-CSRs (13.3 vs. 3.0 percent). Only above the 90th percentile of wage distribution (i.e., $16.10) do the differences in referring rates between these groups wholly disappear. These results suggest that referral, CSRs are much more time-efficient in their search for referrals than are nonreferral, non-CSRs.[13]

On the other hand, if wages were to measure only access to candidates interested in an entry-level job, we can use the hourly wage metric to measure the implied value of referral and CSRs statuses. In this case, levels of access associated with wages appear to extend to much-better-paid referral, CSRs than nonreferral, non-CSRs. We take the act of referring someone as evidence of access to appropriate people. Using the referring rate of nonreferral, non-CSRs as the threshold for evidence of access (i.e., 4.6 percent referring rate), we find that referral, CSRs show the same level of access at relatively high wages ($13.75, or the 86th percentile of the wage distribution) that nonreferral, non-CSRs do at quite low wages ($6.50, or the 5th percentile). Nonreferral, CSRs, show a 4.6 percent referring rate at a somewhat lower wage of $10.00 per hour (i.e., the 64th percentile). Thus, if high wages are cutting off people from social circles containing potential entry-level employees, the isolating effects of wages are very different for nonreferrals than referrals, and CSRs than non-CSRs. Setting the threshold for evidence of access lower (e.g., a referring rate 3.0 percent) narrows the wage gaps for the various groups,[14] but it is safe to conclude that any wage-based isolation from networks of potentially hirable candidates is considerably tempered by having been a referral or a CSR.

SUMMARY AND CONCLUSION

We have argued that a common organizational practice—hiring new workers via employee referrals—provides key insights into the notion of social capital. Employers who use such hiring methods are quintessential "social capitalists," viewing workers' social connections as resources in which they can invest, in order to gain economic returns in the form of better hiring outcomes. Similarly, employees referring potential hires may also be regarded as attempting to garner social capital returns from connections. We began by summarizing our analyses of the employer's social-capital investment and returns (Fernandez et al. 2000). We identified three ways through which such returns might be realized: the "richer pool," the "better match," and the "social enrichment" mechanisms. Using unique data on hiring from a bank's credit-card phone center, we found support for the "richer pool" process. Conversely, we found scant evidence for the posthire "better match" theory. We did, however, find evidence supporting the "social enrichment" process. Consistent with our prediction, we observed interdependence of turnover between referrers and referrals, a process that is not predicted by the socially atomistic "better match" theory.

We employed company data on the dollar costs of screening, hiring, and training to estimate the firm's investment and returns in the social capital of its employees. We found that the referral program yields significant economic returns for the company. These returns are realized by savings in screening costs due to referrals being more appropriate for the job at application (i.e., the "richer pool" mechanism). The firm's $250 investment (in the form of a referral bonus) yields a return of $416 in reduced recruiting costs, a rate of return of 67 percent. While there is a clear evidence of a net benefit to the firm in recruiting referrals via the "richer pool" process, we found that the "better match" process does not produce significant returns to the firm's social-capital investment. While we did find evidence of the social-enrichment process at work in the phone center, the firm was not managed in such a way as to reap any financial benefits via this mechanism.

We then turned to the employee's perspective. We first assessed the pay-offs associated with referring. We estimated the probabilities of receiving the referral bonuses ($10 for candidates who are interviewed, $250 for hires who remain with the company at least 30 days) to calculate the expected values of referring candidates to the customer-service representative position. The expected value of the interview-based bonus is $6.48, and the expected value of the posthire bonus is $27.14. Thus, the *ex ante* value of the referral program to potential referrers is $33.62, while successful referrers receive a total bonus of $260.

We then addressed the issue of the investment required to obtain these benefits. Although we do not have direct measures of time and effort expended in searching for referral candidates, we gained insight into the nature of the investment by studying the determinants of referring. We assembled data on all workers who were eligible to make referrals over a two-year period, and develop an event history model of referring, treating referring as a repeated event. We found that *ceteris paribus* low-wage employees—who would find the bonuses most valuable—are more likely to refer than high-wage employees. However, this wage effect was much stronger for those in better positions to refer appropriate applicants, i.e., those who had themselves been hired as a referral or worked as a CSR. Low-wage employees lacking these characteristics refer others at very low rates, and decrease their referral rates very slowly as wages increase. Such a pattern—low rates of participation for low-wage workers and a lack of sensitivity to increasing wages—is consistent with the idea that at least part of the motivation for referring is a response to the incentives offered by the referral bonuses. Even though the value of low-wage workers' time is quite low, and would therefore justify more hours of search for referral candidates, the incentive effects of the referral bonus are nil for nonreferral, non-CSR workers since they are poorly positioned to suggest appropriate candidates.

If we are correct that at least some of the referring behavior we observe can be understood in instrumental terms, then we may draw some tentative conclusions with respect to workers' investments in social capital. First, if the use of one's social network for the company is motivated by the pursuit of the referral bonus, then our results suggest that the incentive effects of the bonus are highly contingent. At least in this setting, investment—and returns—to social capital vary dramatically for people in different structural positions. This finding might be seen as an illustration of a more general principle deriving from expectancy theories of motivation: If you don't think you have a chance to get a reward, then the reward is not motivating (Lawler 1973).

These analyses also showed that occupancy of favorable structural positions (in this case, referral and CSR statuses) yields great value for their incumbents, although occupancy of these positions is not likely to have been produced by the conscious pursuit of the referral bonus. We have noted that the use of the term "social capital" in connection with social network processes focuses attention on notions of investment and return, i.e., on the instrumental uses of social relationships. In this case, however, value (in terms of improved chances of receiving the referral bonus) is apparently accruing to well-positioned individuals, without such people having instrumentally chosen those positions. Most likely, these people have discovered the instrumental value vis-à-vis the referral bonus after they found themselves in these positions. Absent the instrumental pursuit of these positions, we think it is misleading to think of occupancy of these positions as *investments*, and any advantages accruing to their incumbents as *returns* attributable to the positions themselves.

We do, however, think it is reasonable to regard the *effort expended in the search* for a referral candidate as a social capital investment to the extent that such search behavior is driven by the pursuit of the referral bonus. This distinction is not merely semantic. As we have previously argued (Fernandez et al. 2000), in order to avoid the confusion that has resulted from the casual use of the concept of social capital, researchers using the term should specify the investment and the mechanisms by which social actors realize returns. In this setting, it was possible that people in referral and CSR positions might have received higher returns by using their positions to raise their chances of receiving the bonus, thus raising the numerator of the rate of return calculation. While we found no evidence of this having occurred, we argue that it would be the purposive action of influencing the bonus system that should be thought of as the investment. In this setting, we think that referrers achieve returns by a different mechanism. Occupancy of referral and CSR positions serves to facilitate search, resulting in a greater return for the incumbents of these positions by lowering the denominator (search costs) in the rate of return calculation.

In conclusion, these findings illustrate something quite general about the nature of social networks as social capital. While network phenomena may invoke a variety of forms of social action (see e.g., Blau 1964), a hallmark of social capital is the mean-ends rationality that Weber (1978 [1922]) identified as associated with action in markets. We suggest that the benefits of applying the term social capital to network-related processes are most likely to outweigh the costs of using the term the more clearly the analysis addresses "investment for return" phenomena. We think our analysis of the firm's and referrer's sides of referral hiring provides an excellent example of one such instance.

NOTES

1.   We refer the reader to Fernandez et al. (2000) for the details of the data collected for this project. In brief, we collected data on over 4,100 external ap-

plications for telephone customer-service jobs over a two-year period (January 1995 through December 1996) and tracked turnover for 325 people hired during this time frame. Over 1,500 of the applications were referrals, and we know the identity of the referrer for a very high percentage of the referral applications. Most important for this study, we also collected data on all workers employed at the site over the period of the study, and identify whether they participated in the company's referral program for customer service representatives.

2.   Note that applicants cannot be hired without an interview.

3.   This recruiter was concerned that referrals from referrers who are just doing it for the money would be worse than nonreferral applications. In her words: "I know people who would refer their dog if they can get a $250 bonus."

4.   While we focus on the *costs* of referring in the analyses that follow, it is also theoretically possible for there to be individual differences in the *benefits* of referring; i.e., for the same costs of referring, individuals might differ in their chances of receiving the referral bonus. We found no evidence of systematic variation in the extent to which individuals receive the referral bonus once they have referred someone (see the discussion above regarding "gaming"). Moreover, we found no evidence that referrer's characteristics were significantly related to success at the interview and offer stages (Fernandez et al. 2000). In light of these findings, we feel confident that referring is largely determined by costs in this setting.

5.   Ideally, we would like to separate the time-value and structural-accessibility effects of wages by observing the intensity of the search for referrals by employees with different wage rates (for a given wage, individuals who are structurally disconnected should devote fewer hours to search). However, we do not directly observe search effort, and thus cannot separate these two effects of wages in this study. Note, however, that the distinction between these two components of wages is less important from the firm's perspective. For either reason, the firm can expect that high-wage employees will be less likely to produce good referral candidates.

6.   While this latter point seems plausible, we found scant evidence that referrers were explaining anything to referrals in this context. Referrals were no better informed than nonreferrals about key features of the job (e.g., starting wages and schedules) than nonreferrals (Fernandez et al. 2000).

7.   While the referral bonus program was widely available to workers working at the firm, fewer than 10 of the 4,114 people employed at the phone were barred from participating in the program. Managers who have hiring authority cannot claim a referral bonus for someone who winds up working for them (they could, however, refer people to other shifts). Second, human-resources personnel who screen applicants for the job cannot participate in the referral program. Due to data limitations, we could not identify these workers in order to exclude them from the set of people at risk for referring. In light of their small numbers (less than 0.2 percent), we ignore this limitation of the data in the models we present below.

8.   We also experimented with Cox regression models (with repeated events)

which, unlike Weibull models, make no assumptions about the time pattern of the hazard rates. Those analyses yield very similar results to those we present here. We present the Weibull models here because, unlike the Cox model, we can use the parameters of the Weibull model to generate predicted values (see note 11).

9. The tendency to associate with others like one's self (i.e., the homophily principle) suggests that all of these background characteristics might influence structural availability. Likewise, these variables may also affect individuals' time-value calculations (e.g., leisure time may be more important to married people). We explored the possibility of interactions between the background control variables and our measures of time-costs and structural availability in preliminary analyses. At least with respect to referring behavior, we find little evidence of significant interactions; consequently, we have used a simple linear specification for the effects of these variables.

10. We did, however, find evidence of racial homophily between referrers and those who were ultimately hired in this setting, as well as another unit of the bank (see Neckerman & Fernandez 1998).

11. Note that the model is highly nonlinear. In order to generate these predictions, we evaluated the model at the mean for age (i.e., 33.1 years), and the modal categories for the dummy independent variables (i.e., males, who are nonminority, married, but without a BA or AA degree). We set the time multiplier (*rho*) to the length of the observation window for our data, i.e., 24 months.

12. On the other hand, we still cannot be sure that the wage effects reflect *only* monetary incentives. Although the curve for nonreferral, non-CSRs is *relatively* flat, it still shows a declining pattern with wage (see the main effect of wage in Model 2).

13. Of course, it is also possible that, despite having equivalent wages, referral, CSRs value their time at much lower rates than nonreferral, non-CSRs. While we cannot rule out this possibility without data on actual search activity for referrals, we think that time efficiency is a much more plausible interpretation of these differences.

14. A higher threshold for evidence of access would, of course, widen these differences. Note, however, that this would involve using wage rates that are lower than those observed in our data for nonreferral, non-CSRs.

REFERENCES

Adler, Paul S., and Seok-Woo Kwon. 1999. "Social Capital: The Good, the Bad, and the Ugly." Unpublished manuscript. Department of Management and Organization, University of Southern California.

Baron, James N., and Michael T. Hannan. 1994. "The Impact of Economics on Contemporary Sociology." *Journal of Economic Literature* 32:1111–46.

Blau, Peter. 1964. *Exchange and Power in Social Life*. New York: John Wiley.

Burt, Ronald S. 1991. "Measuring Age as a Structural Concept." *Social Networks* 13:1–34.

————. 1998. "The Network Structure of Social Capital." Paper presented at a conference "Social Networks and Social Capital," Duke University, October 13, 1998.

Fernandez, Roberto M., Emilio J. Castilla, and Paul Moore. 2000. "Social Capital at Work: Networks and Employment at a Phone Center." *American Journal of Sociology* 105(5):1288–1356.

Fernandez, Roberto M., and Nancy Weinberg. 1997. "Sifting and Sorting: Personal Contacts and Hiring in a Retail Bank." *American Sociological Review* 62:883–902.

Flap, Henk, and Ed Boxman. 1999. "Getting a Job as a Manager." Pp. 197–216 in *Corporate Social Capital and Liability*, edited by Roger Th. A. J. Leenders and Shaul M. Gabbay. Boston, MA: Kluwer.

Lawler, E. E. 1973. *Motivation in Work Organizations*. Belmont, CA: Brooks/Cole.

Neckerman, Kathryn, and Roberto M. Fernandez. 1998. "Keeping a Job: Network Hiring and Turnover in a Retail Bank." Unpublished manuscript. Columbia University, Department of Sociology.

Weber, Max. 1978 [1922]. *Economy and Society*. Translated by Gunther Roth and Claus Wittich. Berkeley, CA: University of California Press.

Winship, Christopher. 1983. "The Allocation of Time Among Individuals." *Sociological Methodology*.

Woolcock, Michael. 1998. "Social Capital and Economic Development: Toward a Theoretical Synthesis and Policy Framework." *Theory and Society* 27(2):151–208.

5

Interpersonal Ties, Social Capital, and Employer Staffing Practices

Peter V. Marsden

Linkages between individual social networks and labor market outcomes command substantial scholarly attention (see reviews in Lin 1999; Marsden & Gorman forthcoming). Important elements of this body of research include Granovetter's (1974) findings that persons with wide-ranging networks are more likely to be approached by potential employers (rather than actively searching for work) and tend to locate better jobs, and studies by Lin and colleagues associating access to high-status contacts with more favorable attainments (Lin, Ensel, & Vaughn 1981; Lin 1999). Importantly, it is not the "use of contacts" per se that appears to be advantageous, but instead having networks with certain types and configurations of contacts (Marsden & Gorman forthcoming).

Most studies focus on the individual rather than the employer. This chapter considers the job-matching process from the employer's side, examining the use of social networks in both recruitment from the external labor market and intraorganizational promotion and transfer processes. Individuals can succeed by drawing on the social capital that resides in their networks only if employer staffing processes encourage, or at least permit, the dissemination of information and influence via interpersonal social ties.

Extending previous analyses by Kalleberg, Knoke, Marsden, and Spaeth (1996: chapter 7) and Marsden and Gorman (1999), this chapter examines recruitment sources involving interpersonal contacts across many organizations. Such a view of staffing practices complements that provided by focused studies of recruiting by single employers (Fernandez & Weinberg 1997; Fernandez, Castilla, & Moore 2000; Petersen, Saporta, & Seidel forthcoming). Patterns in the use of interpersonal recruiting channels are anticipated by arguments about the presumed information benefits, costs, and constraints associated with them. Referrals from employees and referrals from business and professional contacts are used for recruiting into different kinds of jobs, however. Business/professional sources are most likely to be activated for recruitment into higher-status positions, while employee referrals are much less often used for recruitment into managerial work. This may reflect the more heterogeneous information apt to flow through employee networks, together with differing information requirements of recruitment for occupations of different kinds.

The next section of the chapter reviews the information benefits and costs associated with interpersonal recruiting sources, as well as constraints surrounding their use. These considerations imply that such methods will be used more frequently in recruiting at certain types of workplaces, and for certain types of positions and occupations. The National Organizations Study (NOS) and its measures of recruitment methods are next introduced. After results of multivariate analyses are presented, the final section summarizes and interprets the findings.

RECRUITING THROUGH SOCIAL TIES: BENEFITS, COSTS, AND CONSTRAINTS

Barber (1998) dissects the employer's side of the staffing process into three temporally ordered stages: (1) generating applicants through the choice of a target population and a recruiting source or mode; (2) maintaining the interest of applicants in potential employment while the organization gathers information and evaluates candidates through interviewing and other selection activities; and (3) influencing the applicant's decision to accept employment, once the employer has offered the position to a prospect. The first stage, generation of applicants, corresponds to "extensive search" in the job search literature (Rees 1966), while the second encompasses "intensive search" activities. As Barber notes, the organization's discretion is limited in the third stage, where the applicant/potential employee is the principal actor.[1]

This chapter considers Barber's first stage, applicant generation or recruitment. Here, the organization must assemble a "useful" pool, i.e., a sufficiently large set of "hireable" applicants. The organization's hiring standards (Cohen & Pfeffer 1986) affect its threshold for what applicants are "good enough to hire," and therefore its information needs. The sufficiency of a pool is also shaped by the likelihood that applicants will accept employment if offered it, and by their expected tenure with the organization.

Other things being equal, larger pools are apt to be more useful. Applicant pools can be too large, however, in at least two distinct ways that pose potential screening costs. If the employer's quality threshold for new hires is modest, such that many applicants exceed it, larger pools will require substantial winnowing. And if a recruitment source generates large numbers of inappropriate applicants who lie beneath a quality threshold, extensive selection efforts are required to identify the minority of applicants in which the employer has a genuine interest.

Applicant quality usually involves the appropriateness of training, qualifications and experience, but also extends to "soft skills" such as comportment, demeanor, and punctuality. A small pool of applicants may prove extremely useful if it is composed principally of above-threshold applicants having a good fit with the organization's staffing needs, especially if they are apt to accept positions if offered them. Indeed, by virtue of the lower associated costs of selection and screening, such a pool is in many ways superior to a larger pool of persons having more heterogeneous qualifications.

Many arguments set forth on behalf of network recruitment rest on the presumably superior quality of information that flows through interpersonal ties. Such sources may also be less costly. Formal methods such as newspaper advertising or job posting generate more standardized and less nuanced information about each applicant, but compensate by generating larger pools.[2] Organizational environments also present incentives toward and constraints against the use of particular recruiting sources. The following sections discuss these considerations in more detail, pointing to organizational and occupational conditions under which particular factors may be especially salient.

Information Benefits

Network ties can be conduits for several distinct kinds of job-relevant information. The most elementary of these is information about vacancies at an employer, or about the mere existence of nominally qualified candidates who might fill them; in tight labor markets even this spare knowledge may be useful to employers. Social ties may also convey information about amounts of experience and credentials such as education, though more formal channels can transmit these sorts of data equally well. More unique is the capacity of interpersonal networks to provide situated data about the nature of a candidate's performance on past jobs, and context-specific judgments about her or his likely performance if hired by the employer in question. In some cases social ties yield information about the candidate's employment alternatives and likelihood of accepting a prospective offer.

Referrals conveying these forms of information can serve to reduce considerably the uncertainty that an employer faces when adding a new person to an organization. Employers should be especially concerned with high-quality information under several conditions: when performance and skills are difficult to observe, when staffing strategy is flexible, when the use of networks is a central component of performance, and when selection errors are costly. In general, these considerations suggest that employers should tend to use interpersonal recruiting strategies for higher-status positions.

The information provided by referrals through networks should be of special value when skills cannot be assessed readily using objective measures. This assumes particular importance if the position to be filled involves the exercise of substantial discretion, or if the skills at issue are interpersonal rather than technical. Under these circumstances, subjective evaluations obtained through social networks may provide the best available information about a candidate's potential (Pfeffer 1977). This suggests that referrals should be used heavily in hiring into well-paid, autonomous occupations such as managerial, professional, and skilled-craft positions.

In flexible organizations with staffing strategies that adapt goals and objectives to the capabilities of their personnel, rather than seeking people who fit the requirements of standardized jobs, there is also a premium on specific information about a potential addition. In such organizations, staffing is equivalent to strategy formation (Snow & Snell 1993); they make less use of formal job descriptions and written rules, substituting mutual adjustment via social networks as a coordination mechanism. Interpersonal skills and the capacity to operate within networks are vital in such systems; such employers should, therefore, have relatively high needs for information when making staffing decisions. Thus, organizations without formal job descriptions should make greater use of interpersonal contacts in recruiting.

Interpersonal skills and the ability to form and maneuver within networks of contacts are also central components of effective performance in jobs that involve frequent communication with clients or customers. For example, investment banks rely on their employees' networks of external ties to attract new business and maintain client relationships (Eccles & Crane 1988). Here, recruiting through informal networks serves as a test or selection device as well as a mode of locating available candidates: the fact that an employer becomes aware of a candidate through a network channel may be a revealing signal of her or his capacity to invest in and draw on interpersonal social capital, and thereby to succeed in the position in question. This implies greater use of interpersonal staffing methods for certain professional, sales, and service occupations.

When selection errors are costly, employers should be disposed to seek out higher-quality information available through social ties. Risk increases to the extent that the performance of a given employee affects organizational performance. Costs of hiring mistakes also rise if the employer invests in training the newly hired or promoted employee, because such investments are lost if the individual's subsequent performance is subpar or if s/he departs for another opportunity. Similarly, it is costly to erroneously place a person on a multiple-level job ladder, since incumbents in such positions may have long tenures in the organization. Due process guarantees may make it difficult to discharge them, and selection into one position on a ladder may enhance formal eligibility for upward moves, irrespective of performance. Thus, there should be more use of social ties in recruitment when those in a position are to receive formal training, or when their positions lie on multiple-level ladders.

Beyond informing employers about qualifications and performance, interpersonal channels may yield information about the prospect that a candidate will accept a job offer, and about the likelihood that she or he will remain with the employer. Recruitment through social contacts—by comparison to "broadcast" methods such as advertisements, signs, or job postings—makes use of interactive channels. As such, interpersonal ties have the capacity to improve the fit between individual and organization by offering informal versions of "realistic job previews" (Wanous & Colella 1989). Individuals who learn about an employer through network contacts can make more informed decisions about whether to seek employment there, or to remain under consideration at later stages of the staffing process. These properties of interpersonal channels seem rather generic, and do not imply greater or lesser reliance on network recruiting for particular types of organizations or positions.

Costs

The intrinsic costs of administering recruiting procedures drawing on interpersonal contacts are low. Such methods do not require specialized staffing personnel; they need not involve monetary outlays, as advertisements and the use of employment agencies do; and if used passively, they may not make extensive demands on managerial time. If current employees serve as recruiters by recommending appropriate associates from outside the organization, the employer can realize substantial savings in both recruiting and screening costs. For internal actions, substantial information is acquired in the course of undertaking other tasks, and the direct marginal costs of recruiting via contacts approach zero. Even when invoked actively, using such methods may involve little more than picking up the telephone or wandering down the hall to discuss a candidate.

There are, of course, conditions under which costs of using interpersonal contacts can be appreciable. For example, there are monetary costs to "bounty" systems in which employers give bonuses to current employees who refer successful applicants (Fernandez et al. 2000).[3] To the extent that such incentive programs generate too many applicants or encourage employees to refer inappropriate candidates, they can increase screening time as well. Costs can also be substantial when interpersonal ties are invoked proactively by the employer. Activation of ties to well-informed work/professional "market mavens" who can provide in-depth information about candidates involves costs in terms of access time; it also retires "information debts" that may have been accumulated in past transactions. These costs of gaining access and obtaining data may be especially notable for closely held information or confidential matters.

One reason for relying on relatively low-cost recruitment methods that involve interpersonal ties is that alternatives are too expensive. It may not be cost-effective for small, single-site organizations to incur the overhead costs of administering formal staffing procedures, for example. Establishments within multisite organizational systems are, however, often required to use centrally prescribed formal approaches to staffing, and hence less apt to use methods that involve social networks.

Because the range of candidates that can be identified using interpersonal ties is limited to those who can be tapped through current employees, selecting officials, or their work-related contacts, a potential cost of using such methods is the foregone opportunity of considering talented candidates outside of those networks. Pools of external applicants tend to be smaller when formal methods are not used (see above, note 2). Also, the homophily that typifies interpersonal networks (Marsden 1988) means that the sociodemographic composition of an applicant pool recruited through interpersonal channels tends to resemble that of the set of persons currently employed. Underrepresented groups are thus likely to remain underrepresented if establishments emphasize interpersonal recruiting sources (Reskin & McBrier 2000).

The opportunity costs of using interpersonal channels in internal recruiting within small, single-site establishments should be low, because selecting officials are apt to have direct or indirect social ties to most or all employees. In larger establishments and establishments within multisite organizations, on the other hand, the pools of internal candidates that can be defined on the basis of social ties will usually include much smaller fractions of the potentially eligible workforce, and thus a greater opportunity cost. Accordingly, such procedures should be used less often in large or multiple-site establishments.

Equity Pressures and Other Constraints

Constituencies both internal and external to organizations exert pressures on them to allocate rewards in an equitable and procedurally rational manner. Charges of prejudice and favoritism are more readily raised when recruiting methods draw on interpersonal contacts than when they rely on objective, universalistic criteria. In comparison with formalized staffing methods, "network hiring" is also less consistent with norms of rationality and bureaucratization, which many see as institutionalized myths or societal values that infuse organizations (Meyer & Rowan 1977; Bridges & Villemez 1991; Baron, Dobbin, & Jennings 1986).

External pressures emanate from unions and regulatory bodies. Numerous scholars have documented differences in personnel practices between unionized and nonunion workplaces (e.g., Jacoby 1985; Baron et al. 1986; Dobbin, Edelman, Meyer, Scott, & Swidler 1988). Cohen and Pfeffer (1986), for example, argue that unions advocate formalized approaches to internal staffing because such procedures can prevent employers from penalizing employees with prounion attitudes. Institutional arguments hold that exposure to the public sphere places organizations under special pressure to conform to evolving norms about legitimate employment practices (Dobbin et al. 1988). Larger establishments and establishments within multisite organizations are more visible to regulators, and consequently such establishments should be more reluctant to use staffing procedures that involve interpersonal ties. Public-sector establishments, in particular, must demonstrate high levels of fairness, objectivity, and openness in their employment practices; they are also subject to civil service laws and regulations that mandate the use of certain formal procedures (DiPrete 1989; Tolbert & Zucker 1983). Thus, public-sector establishments should be especially likely to avoid the selection of personnel via interpersonal networks.

Internally, personnel departments are likely to advocate formal methods of identifying and selecting promotion candidates. Personnel professionals are especially aware of the constraints and sensitivities of external constituencies (Jacoby 1985); they also enhance their intraorganizational power through the possession of specialized knowledge about how to conduct personnel actions (Pfeffer & Cohen 1984). Hence establishments with personnel departments should make less extensive use of staffing procedures involving contacts.

THE NATIONAL ORGANIZATIONS STUDY

The data examined in this chapter are drawn from the National Organizations Study (NOS), conducted during 1991. Telephone interviews were completed with informants for a multiplicity sample (see Parcel, Kaufman, & Jolly 1991) representative of U.S. work establishments.[4] When contacting establishments, NOS interviewers were instructed to speak with "the

head of the personnel department or the person responsible for hiring."
Overall, the NOS attempted to contact informants for 1,067 establishments;
it successfully conducted interviews with 688 of them, a completion rate of
64.5 percent.[5] For additional details about field procedures used in the
NOS, see Spaeth and O'Rourke (1994) or Kalleberg et al. (1996:Chapter 2).

To take into account possible between-occupation, within-establish-
ment variation, the NOS interview schedule repeated several question sequences, including those on staffing, for up to three different occupations
in each establishment. One of these was the job title of the employees "most
directly involved" with the main product or service provided by the establishment; this is called the "core" occupation. A second was the occupation of the General Social Survey (GSS) respondent who provided the
name of the establishment. Finally, questions were also posed about "managers or other administrators." This multiple-occupation design permits
the separation of establishment- and occupation-level influences on several NOS outcome variables.

MEASURING STAFFING METHODS

The NOS interview schedule included separate sets of questions about external and internal staffing. The frequency with which an establishment
used network-related methods of external recruitment for a particular occupation was measured using the following items:

How often do you use each of the following methods to find [cores/
GSSs/managers or administrators]? What about

• Referrals from current employees?
• Referrals from business or professional contacts?
• Unsolicited inquiries by telephone, mail, or in person?

Unsolicited inquiries are included among methods involving interpersonal ties since some (e.g. Manwaring 1984; Fevre 1989; Wial 1991) suggest
that passive recruitment may represent "unofficial" network staffing, as
direct applicants learn about openings through contacts already employed
at a workplace. The NOS also posed questions about formal methods, such
as newspaper advertisements and employment agencies. The informant
for the establishment was asked to say whether each method was used
"frequently," "sometimes," or "never." Informants answered these questions only when there had been external hiring into the occupation in question within the past two years.

The use of internal staffing methods drawing on social ties was assessed
using a similar sequence of questions:

When you fill this job with a person already in the organization, how often do you

- Ask the person leaving the job to recommend other current employees?
- Ask others at your workplace for recommendations?
- Go directly to specific employees and encourage them to apply?

The internal staffing sequence also included questions about seniority and job posting. The sequence was administered if an informant said that the establishment ever fills vacancies in a given occupation with current employees.[6] Response options were the same as those for the questions about external recruitment.

Table 1 presents the percentages of informants who answered "frequently" to the questions about staffing methods, separately for the three occupations studied in the NOS. There is substantial use of interpersonal methods by U.S. employers. The unweighted percentages, which reflect the experience of the typical employee (see note 4) show that employee referrals are used frequently in hiring into more than a third of "core" positions, while business and professional sources of advice are often used in locating employees for more than a fifth of such positions. Employee referrals are used somewhat less commonly—and business or professional contacts more often—for managerial positions than for core ones. Unsolicited inquiries are frequently used for staffing about a third of core and GSS positions, but only about a fifth of managerial ones.

Job posting is the most common method for notifying current employees about promotion and transfer opportunities, but there is likewise widespread use of social ties in internal staffing actions. Previous occupants of positions to be filled internally are "frequently" asked for recommendations in only about a tenth of the cases, but referrals from others in the workplace are often obtained for about a quarter of the occupations studied; these percentages are similar for managerial and core positions. Those in charge of staffing often approach candidates directly for about a fifth of positions filled from within the organization; this is somewhat more common for managerial than for core work. At least one of these three internal approaches involving contacts is used frequently for 35 percent of the core occupations, and over 40 percent of managerial ones.

The prevalence of interpersonal staffing channels is even more notable when external and internal hiring are considered together. Figures not displayed in Table 1 reveal that one or more of the interpersonal staffing methods was used frequently in more than 45 percent of the organization-occupation cases included in the NOS. Informants said that their establishments "never" used any such channels in less than one case out of ten.[7]

Table 1. Recruitment Methods in NOS Establishments

	Percent of Employees in Establishments Using Method "Frequently" (N)[a]			Percent of Establishments Using Method "Frequently"[a]		
	Core	GSS	Manager	Core	GSS	Manager
External Recruitment						
Newspaper advertisements	40.8 (468)	48.0 (196)	50.2 (269)	36.1	34.4	32.2
Signs posted	13.1 (467)	7.7 (196)	10.1 (267)	14.6	3.7	7.1
Employee referrals	36.7 (469)	28.6 (196)	22.2 (266)	36.7	21.0	26.2
Business/professional referrals	20.7 (469)	19.9 (196)	27.1 (266)	23.3	30.3	29.8
Employment agencies	18.9 (470)	17.3 (196)	17.2 (267)	12.7	15.0	20.3
Unsolicited inquiries	33.0 (469)	35.7 (196)	22.0 (268)	23.7	15.9	18.9
Internal Recruitment						
Seniority lists	38.5 (387)	34.4 (221)	18.4 (446)	26.9	39.0	29.8
Job posting	67.8 (388)	64.7 (221)	59.5 (449)	42.2	45.3	41.6
Referrals from incumbent	8.1 (382)	8.3 (218)	12.4 (442)	12.7	12.8	11.7
Referrals from others	24.1 (386)	16.9 (219)	25.2 (445)	25.0	22.6	22.4
Direct approaches	19.4 (386)	16.4 (219)	28.4 (447)	24.1	25.6	33.1
Any informal method	34.8 (388)	29.0 (221)	43.0 (449)	38.1	34.0	41.1

Source: 1991 National Organizations Study.

Note: Questions about external recruitment were asked only when a given type of employee had been hired from outside within the preceding two years. Questions about internal recruitment were asked only when informants stated that current employees were "sometimes" promoted or transferred to fill vacancies in a given occupation.

[a] "Employee" percentages are for the "unweighted" NOS sample (see note 4). "Establishment" percentages (for the "weighted" NOS sample) were derived by weighting employee percentages inversely proportional to establishment size. Hence Ns for establishment percentages are the same as those presented for employee percentages.

The weighted and unweighted percentages shown in Table 1 do not differ greatly from one another, which means that the distributions of staffing methods are similar whether viewed from the standpoint of employees or from that of establishments (see note 4). When there are differences, weighted percentages for interpersonal methods (excepting unsolicited inquiries) tend to be larger than the corresponding unweighted figures. Smaller establishments, then, make somewhat greater use of interpersonal contacts in staffing, though differences by establishment size are modest overall.

ORGANIZATIONAL AND OCCUPATIONAL CORRELATES OF INTERPERSONAL STAFFING

The discussion above posited that staffing methods in general, and methods drawing on interpersonal ties in particular, are chosen in light of the benefits, costs, and constraints associated with their use. The mix of benefits, costs, and constraints linked to contacts varies across organizations and occupations. At the establishment level, the frequency of network recruitment should differ by establishment size, affiliation with a larger organization, auspices (public, nonprofit, or private-sector), presence of unions, presence of a personnel department, and the existence of formalized job descriptions. Likewise, approaches to staffing should vary across jobs. There should be more use of interpersonal staffing if a position is part of a multiple-level job ladder, if it involves formal training, or if it is well paid. Moreover, there should be differences in the use of such methods across major occupational categories, with more network recruiting for higher-status positions.

Table 2 presents results of multivariate analyses that reveal organizational and occupational differences in the use of interpersonal staffing methods; measures of explanatory variables are described in the appendix. Estimates presented are based on ordinal logistic regression, including a random organization-level effect because of the nesting of occupational observations within establishments (Goldstein 1995:108–9). Separate equations were estimated for the three external staffing methods measured. Findings for recruiting for internal promotions and transfers, however, refer to a composite indicator giving the maximum frequency with which any of the three interpersonal methods was used; similar factors predict use of the three internal methods (Marsden & Gorman 1999), and establishments using one of them also tend to use the others.

Findings for the use of external business/professional referrals and the use of informal methods in internal recruitment are highly consistent with the expectations outlined above. Occupational differences are especially

Table 2. Correlates of Informal Recruitment Methods (Ordinal Logistic Regression Coefficients)

Explanatory Variable	External Referrals from Employees	External Referrals from Business/Professionals	Walk-in or Unsolicited Applicants	Informal Internal Staffing
Establishment size (log)	0.050 (0.058)	−0.007 (0.059)	**0.168** (0.059)	−0.015 (0.059)
Multisite organization	−0.045 (0.163)	**−0.400** (0.167)	−0.213 (0.167)	**−0.383** (0.168)
Public sector	**−0.634** (0.196)	**−0.502** (0.198)	0.125 (0.197)	**−0.527** (0.182)
Nonprofit sector	−0.256 (0.284)	**−0.645** (0.289)	0.169 (0.289)	−0.240 (0.285)
Union presence scale	**0.350** (0.141)	0.128 (0.143)	−0.056 (0.143)	−0.035 (0.135)
Personnel department	0.208 (0.215)	0.170 (0.219)	0.119 (0.219)	−0.296 (0.214)
Formal job descriptions	−0.196 (0.237)	0.194 (0.241)	0.043 (0.241)	−0.141 (0.246)
Formal training	0.064 (0.187)	0.223 (0.190)	0.127 (0.188)	**0.465** (0.186)
Multiple levels in job	0.037 (0.160)	−0.123 (0.162)	0.025 (0.159)	−0.215 (0.156)
Managerial job	**−0.578** (0.230)	**0.814** (0.234)	−0.361 (0.227)	**0.993** (0.224)
Professional job	0.237 (0.250)	**1.040** (0.256)	**0.416** (0.249)	**0.729** (0.266)
Sales/service job	0.012 (0.251)	**0.515** (0.256)	0.149 (0.250)	**0.683** (0.283)
Administrative support job	−0.468 (0.287)	0.580 (0.291)	−0.188 (0.285)	0.160 (0.293)
Craft job	−0.019 (0.461)	0.209 (0.469)	−0.547 (0.460)	0.472 (0.420)
Log average pay in job	−0.245 (0.152)	**0.390** (0.155)	**−0.315** (0.154)	−0.092 (0.170)
First threshold	1.330 (1.461)	**−5.945** (1.497)	1.473 (1.472)	0.343 (1.626)
Second threshold	**3.975** (1.467)	**−3.181** (1.486)	**3.692** (1.477)	2.804 (1.629)
Establishment variance	**0.647** (0.171)	**0.689** (0.177)	**0.834** (0.178)	**0.931** (0.176)
(N)	(893)	(892)	(895)	(1010)

Source: 1991 National Organizations Study.

a**Bold** coefficients are more than twice their standard errors.

116

marked. Table 2 shows that employers are much more apt to use business/ professional contacts when recruiting for managerial, professional, or sales/service positions than for the reference category of semi- or unskilled occupations. Business contacts are used significantly more often in external recruiting for better-paid positions. Similar occupational differences are found for the activation of networks in internal staffing processes. Such recruiting methods are also used more often when those in an occupation are to receive training. These findings are as anticipated by the above reasoning about information benefits and risks of foregoing training investments.

Recruiting methods involving interpersonal ties—both external and internal—are consistently less used by public-sector establishments than by workplaces in the private, for-profit sector. Regression coefficients indicate that nonprofit establishments, too, make lower use of interpersonal staffing than do those in the private sector, but this difference is statistically significant only for external referrals from business and professional contacts. Constraints related to sectoral location appear to place strong limits on the use of social capital by those seeking jobs or promotions.

NOS establishments that are part of multisite organizations are generally less apt to rely on interpersonal methods of staffing, especially external referrals from business/professional contacts and internal recruiting via networks. These differences likely reflect centrally prescribed bureaucratic routine, the greater opportunity costs associated with network hiring in such settings, and lower per-event costs of maintaining formal structures for staffing.

Several implications of the logic outlined above were not confirmed by the findings, however. Net of adjustments for other factors, the use of most staffing methods does not vary with establishment size, the presence of a personnel department, or whether a position is part of a multiple-level ladder. As anticipated by a "flexible staffing" logic, interpersonal staffing is sometimes negatively associated—in this sample—with the presence of formalized job descriptions, but no regression coefficient for the presence of job descriptions is statistically significant.

Contrary to expectations, reliance on interpersonal staffing methods did not prove to be inversely related to the presence of unions. The one statistically significant difference found, in fact, was that union presence is *positively* associated with using external referrals from employees. This may indicate that the union itself constitutes a structure facilitating referrals. Employers may choose voluntarily to locate new employees through the pertinent union, or contractual or noncontractual understandings may oblige them to do so.

The discussion of information benefits of referrals concluded that interpersonal sources should be more prominent in staffing actions for higher-status positions. As noted, the regression coefficients in Table 2 are consistent with this expectation for external business/professional referrals and internal staffing actions. Observe, however, in the first column of Table 2 that the pattern of occupational differences is quite different—indeed almost opposite—for external recruiting via the social networks of current employees. Here, we see that employers are just as likely to emphasize employee referrals for recruitment into professional/technical, sales/service, and craft occupations as for unskilled occupations. In contrast to the findings for the other interpersonal methods, though, they are much *less* likely to use such referrals when filling managerial positions. These findings are discussed further in the conclusion.

Few of the predictor variables introduced here are associated with the widespread use of unsolicited applications as a mode of staffing. Larger workplaces more often use such applications, presumably because they receive more of them by virtue of their size (Marsden & Campbell 1990). Unsolicited inquiries are used significantly more in staffing positions that are less well paid; this might reflect relatively lower quality thresholds for hiring in such positions which—in turn—imply less incentive for employers to assemble extensive information. If direct applications to employers depend on information flows from current employees, these flows follow a pattern different from that for other types of network hiring. Many direct applicants may well be true "cold callers."

SUMMARY AND DISCUSSION

The findings presented above reveal the organizational and occupational conditions that most welcome the use of individual social capital in socioeconomic attainment. Among these circumstances are private-sector location and a comparative lack of organizational complexity—in particular, single-site organizations tend to make greater use of interpersonal staffing. It is also evident that staffing methods drawing on social contacts are more likely to be involved in hiring and promotions/transfers for comparatively complex work. There is more room for network capital to be useful to a job seeker or employee when seeking a managerial, professional, or sales/ service job than an unskilled one, especially if the position will require training investments on the part of the employer. These occupational differences are highly consistent with Burt's (1997:351–59) observations about the conditions under which social capital is more and less valuable to individuals. By and large, the differences reported fit expectations about conditions under which benefits, costs, and constraints of network staffing differ across employers and kinds of work.

Employers use referrals from employees in a fashion that differs from the pattern for other interpersonal methods. Indeed, the finding that employee referrals are more frequently used in the private sector is their only commonality with the other methods studied here. Employee referrals are used less, rather than more, for recruitment into managerial work, and they are used significantly more in unionized settings. None of the other interpersonal methods studied tends to be frequent under similar conditions.

The distinctiveness of occupational differences for referrals from current employees reminds us that not all referrals are alike. Contacts differ in what they know about a prospective employee; some may know only of a person's availability, while others may possess the full range of detailed data discussed above. Those making referrals also differ in credibility; the nature of a contact's prior relationship to the candidate may color the usefulness of the information that she or he provides to the employer. Business or professional contacts who can assess applicants from a relatively detached vantage point provide maximally useful referrals. Those connected to an applicant through family or communal ties, on the other hand, may be seen as agents for the prospective employee; they also may lack specific knowledge of the applicant's specific capacities and prior work performance.

Employee social networks are composed of a mixture of contacts drawn from multiple settings, including work, family, community, and associations. In general, employees tend to know, and therefore to be in a position to refer, others having occupations and skill levels similar to their own (Laumann 1973: Chapter 4). Given the pyramidal structures typical of work organizations, this implies that employees will be most able to tell employers about persons who can fill positions requiring modest qualifications. They may be able to provide very good information about those in their work-related networks (both within and outside of the organization), especially if they are members of work-related groups such as unions or professional associations. Employee referrals of persons known in more communally-based contexts of activity (e.g. family or neighborhood) are apt to be both less knowledgeable and less credible with respect to specific information.

Thus, referrals from employees are likely to be quite heterogeneous in terms of information quality. This need not deter employers from using such social ties to locate prospective employees, if quality thresholds are modest. In light of such considerations, though, it is hardly surprising that recruiting through networks of current employees is less common for managerial positions than for semi- or unskilled ones.

External business or professional sources, by contrast, are likely to know the candidates they refer in a work-related context that enables them to provide an employer with high-quality and credible information. Professionals, in particular, tend to have extra-organizational ties to one another through participation in professional associations and experience in professional schools. Managers, too, are likely to have developed cross-organizational ties as a result of previous positions, boundary-spanning work, or participation in industry associations and conferences. Unions may likewise serve as a locus of work-related ties. Business and professional sources, then, are likely to yield high-quality information, and organizations should tend to activate them when filling high-status positions having high quality thresholds.

Similarly, social ties used to form pools of candidates for internal promotion or transfer are, almost by definition, channels that have substantial work-related content. Those making such recommendations often will be former supervisors or coworkers of those referred. As such they will have been in a position to observe a referral's work—frequently over a protracted period—and to have participated in ongoing workplace networks that convey information about reputation and subtleties of performance. Such channels should thus carry relatively rich information flows of the kind that an employer will seek out when promoting or transferring people into unique, high-responsibility positions.

The different patterns of occupational differences displayed in Table 2 are consistent with these observations, which also aid in the interpretation of other findings presented—such as the positive link between union presence and recruiting via current employees. The referral potential of networks within professional associations may account for the fact that employee referrals are used to locate professionals at least as often as for unskilled workers—rather than much *less* often, as for managerial positions.[8]

APPENDIX: MEASUREMENT OF EXPLANATORY VARIABLES

This appendix describes the measurements of independent variables that appear in Table 2. Descriptive statistics reported are for 1,620 organization-occupation observations in the NOS. Analyses in this chapter examine subsets of these in which there had been external hiring within the two years prior to the survey, or in which vacancies were ever filled using current employees. More details on measures in the NOS appear in Kalleberg et al. (1996).

Size. Natural logarithm of the number of full-time employees in the establishment (mean, 4.31; standard deviation, 2.17).

Multisite organization. Dummy variable identifying the 57% of observations from establishments that are part of larger, multiple-establishment organizations.

Personnel department. Dummy variable identifying the 38% of observations from establishments that have a separate department or section responsible for personnel and / or labor relations.

Job descriptions. Dummy variable identifying the 78% of observations from establishments in which there are written job descriptions for most jobs.

Union presence. Scale combining four items indicative of the presence of unions (mean, 1.41; standard deviation, 0.60).

Public sector. Dummy variable identifying the 28% of observations from establishments operated by federal, state, or local governments.

Nonprofit sector. Dummy variable identifying the 8% of observations from private, not-for-profit establishments.

Training. Dummy variable identifying the 66% of observations in which those in an occupation had received formal training within the past two years.

Multiple levels. Dummy variable identifying the 57% of observations in which an occupation has more than one level.

Occupational categories. Core and GSS occupations were classified into three-digit 1980 Census codes by the NOS, and were subsequently grouped into the six broader classes used in this chapter. No specific occupational title was used by the NOS when asking about "managers and administrators," so all observations for these occupations are in the "managerial" group. Overall, 43% of observations are managerial, 15% are professional, 14% are in sales or service occupations, 9% are in administrative support occupations, 3% are in craft occupations, and 17% are in semi- or unskilled occupations.

Average pay in job. Natural logarithm of informant's report of the typical earnings of an employee in an occupation. Findings in Kalleberg and Van Buren (1996) were used in regression-imputing some missing data (mean, 10.10; standard deviation, 0.63).

NOTES

A previous version of this chapter was presented at a conference on Social Networks and Social Capital held at Duke University, Durham, NC, October 30–November 1, 1998. Data collection and writing were supported by National Science Foundation awards SES-8911696 and SBR-9511715. I am indebted to Elizabeth H. Gorman for discussions and assistance, and to Ronald S. Burt for helpful comments.

1. While Barber's three stages are an extremely useful heuristic device for conceptualizing the staffing process, in practical situations the stages may be blurred or folded onto one another. Many searches to fill academic positions

correspond rather closely to Barber's model. At the other extreme are situations such as "spot" hiring for daywork or temporary work (e.g. McAllister 1998; Henson 1996), in which recruitment, selection, and choice take place almost simultaneously. Moreover, Barber's three-stage model is most suitable for "needs-driven" staffing in which recruitment activity is initiated by the departure of a previous employee or a decision to expand. Some staffing activity is instead more opportunistic: the decision to create a position occurs after the employer becomes aware of someone who might fill it (Granovetter 1974: Chapter 4; Snow & Snell 1993). In opportunistic staffing, some stages (e.g. applicant generation) of Barber's model may be omitted, and the temporal ordering of others may be inverted.

2. This is evident in data from the study analyzed below. The typical number of external applicants considered for a position was significantly larger if the establishment relied on newspaper advertisements, the posting of signs, employment agencies or placement services, or unsolicited inquiries as recruiting sources. Estimates are that using advertisements "frequently" rather than "never" increases the size of a pool by a factor of about 1.8, controlling for establishment size, occupation, and the use of other sources. By contrast, the size of an applicant pool did not vary significantly with reliance on employee or business/professional referrals; the sign of the regression coefficient for the latter type of referral was, however, negative.

3. Such systems often specify that referrals must accept positions and remain in them for a specified length of time before the referring employee receives the bounty or bonus.

4. A work establishment refers to a specific geographic site or address. Some establishments lie within larger, multisite firms or organizations. The sample of establishments was drawn as part of a topical module on "Organizations and Work" included in the 1991 General Social Survey (GSS; see Davis & Smith 1996). In 1991, the GSS interviewed a random sample of 1531 English-speaking U.S. adults. At the end of the interview, each employed respondent was asked to give the name, address, and telephone number of her/his workplace; married respondents were asked to provide the same information about the workplaces of their employed spouses. This generated a multiplicity sample in which work establishments have known, but unequal, probabilities of inclusion; the probability that an establishment is included in the NOS is proportional to its number of employees. Thus, there are more large establishments in the NOS than would appear if workplaces were to be drawn at random from some listing of establishments. The unweighted NOS sample describes work settings from the standpoint of a typical U.S. employee, since it gives each GSS respondent equal weight. To describe instead the population of U.S. work establishments, the data must be weighted inversely to workplace size. Most figures presented here are for the unweighted sample; see Winship and Radbill (1994) for recommendations concerning the use of sampling weights in regression analysis.

5. Owing largely to the clustering entailed in the area probability design of the GSS, some establishments were sampled more than once. The data reported in this chapter include only one record for such duplicated cases. Including

duplicate nominations, there were 1,127 interview attempts and 727 completions.

6. Because different filter questions precede the sequences about external and internal staffing, responses to the NOS staffing items refer to different sets of occupations. Typically, NOS occupations were filled through both external and internal recruitment. Those occupations most likely to be filled internally, but not externally, were managerial. By contrast, there was a tendency for professional, sales/service, and lower blue-collar positions to be filled via external hiring, but not internal promotion or transfer.

7. For occupations in which there was both internal and external hiring—and in which, therefore, informants were asked to respond to all staffing questions—the figures are even more extreme. In 55 percent of those cases, at least one informal method was used frequently; and all interpersonal methods were "never" part of the establishment's hiring practices in less than four percent of those occupations.

8. At least one important issue about social capital has not been addressed in this chapter. The analyses examined the organizational and occupational circumstances that invite individuals to draw on their social capital—not organizational social capital per se. How "organizational" social capital is to be conceptualized or measured with respect to recruitment processes is not self-evident. Some aggregation across the individual networks maintained by employees, especially those responsible for making staffing decisions, would seem to be involved, however. The findings here do make it clear that organizational social capital is probably not unitary—instead, employers must maintain different sets of interpersonal contacts for the distinct occupational labor markets on which they draw. An intriguing selection problem for future research is whether employers having better organization-level social capital are more apt to rely on interpersonal methods as a recruitment source.

REFERENCES

Barber, Alison E. 1998. *Recruiting Employees: Individual and Organizational Perspectives.* Thousand Oaks, CA: Sage Publications.

Baron, James N., Frank Dobbin, and P. Devereaux Jennings. 1986. "War and Peace: The Evolution of Modern Personnel Administration in U.S. Industry." *American Journal of Sociology* 92:350–83.

Bridges, William P., and Wayne J. Villemez. 1991. "Employment Relations and the Labor Market: Integrating Institutional and Market Perspectives." *American Sociological Review* 56:748–64.

Burt, Ronald S. 1997. "The Contingent Value of Social Capital." *Administrative Science Quarterly* 42:339–65.

Cohen, Yinon, and Jeffrey Pfeffer. 1986. "Organizational Hiring Standards." *Administrative Science Quarterly* 31:1–24.

Davis, James A., and Tom W. Smith. 1996. *General Social Surveys, 1972–1996: Cumulative Codebook.* Storrs, CT: Roper Center for Public Opinion Research.

DiPrete, Thomas A. 1989. *The Bureaucratic Labor Market: The Case of the Federal Civil Service.* New York: Plenum Press.

Dobbin, Frank, L. Edelman, John W. Meyer, W. Richard Scott, and Ann Swidler. 1988. "The Expansion of Due Process in Organizations." Pp. 71–98 in *Institutional Patterns and Organizations: Culture and Environment,* edited by Lynne G. Zucker. Cambridge, MA: Ballinger.

Eccles, Robert, and Dwight Crane. 1988. *Doing Deals: Investment Banks at Work.* Boston, MA: Harvard Business School Press.

Fernandez, Roberto M., Emilio Castilla, and Paul Moore. 2000. "Social Capital at Work: Networks and Hiring at a Phone Center." *American Journal of Sociology* 105:1288–1356.

Fernandez, Roberto M., and Nancy Weinberg. 1997. "Sifting and Sorting: Personal Contacts and Hiring in a Retail Bank." *American Sociological Review* 62:883–902.

Fevre, Ralph. 1989. "Informal Practices, Flexible Firms, and Private Labour Markets." *Sociology* 23:91–109.

Goldstein, Harvey. 1995. *Multilevel Statistical Models.* Second Edition. London: Edward Arnold.

Granovetter, Mark S. 1974. *Getting a Job: A Study of Contacts and Careers.* Cambridge, MA: Harvard University Press.

Henson, Kevin D. 1996. *Just a Temp.* Philadelphia: Temple University Press.

Jacoby, Sanford. 1985. *Employing Bureaucracy: Managers, Unions, and the Transformation of Work in American Industry, 1900–1945.* New York: Columbia University Press.

Kalleberg, Arne L., David Knoke, Peter V. Marsden, and Joe L. Spaeth. 1996. *Organizations in America: Analyzing Their Structures and Human Resource Practices.* Newbury Park, CA: Sage Publications.

Kalleberg, Arne L., and Mark E. Van Buren. 1996. "Is Bigger Better? Explaining the Relationship between Organization Size and Job Rewards." *American Sociological Review* 61:47–66.

Laumann, Edward O. 1973. *Bonds of Pluralism: The Form and Substance of Urban Social Networks.* New York: Wiley Interscience.

Lin, Nan. 1999. "Social Networks and Status Attainment." *Annual Review of Sociology* 25:467–88.

Lin, Nan, Walter M. Ensel, and John C. Vaughn. 1981. "Social Resources and Strength of Ties: Structural Factors in Occupational Status Attainment." *American Sociological Review* 46:393–405.

Manwaring, Tony. 1984. "The Extended Internal Labour Market." *Cambridge Journal of Economics* 8:161–87.

Marsden, Peter V. 1988. "Homogeneity in Confiding Relations." *Social Networks* 10:57–76.

Marsden, Peter V., and Karen E. Campbell. 1990. "Recruitment and Selection Processes: The Organizational Side of Job Searches." Pp. 59–79 in *Social Mobility and Social Structure,* edited by Ronald L. Breiger. New York: Cambridge University Press.

Marsden, Peter V., and Elizabeth H. Gorman. 1999. "Social Capital in Internal Staffing Practices." Pp. 180–96 in *Corporate Social Capital and Liability,* edited by Roger T. A. J. Leenders and Shaul M. Gabbay. Amsterdam: Kluwer Academic Publishers.

———. Forthcoming. "Social Networks, Job Changes, and Recruitment." In *Sourcebook on Labor Markets: Evolving Structures and Processes*, edited by Ivar Berg and Arne L. Kalleberg. New York: Plenum.

McAllister, Jean. 1998. "Sisyphus at Work in the Warehouse: Temporary Employment in Greenville, South Carolina." Pp. 221–42 in *Contingent Work: American Employment Relations in Transition*, edited by Kathleen Barker and Kathleen Christensen. Ithaca, NY: ILR Press.

Meyer, John W., and Brian Rowan. 1977. "Institutionalized Organizations: Formal Structure as Myth and Ceremony." *American Journal of Sociology* 83:340–63.

Parcel, Toby L., Robert L. Kaufman, and Leeann Jolly. 1991. "Going Up the Ladder: Multiplicity Sampling to Create Linked Macro-to-Micro Organizational Samples." Pp. 43–79 in *Sociological Methodology 1991*, edited by Peter V. Marsden. Oxford, U.K.: Basil Blackwell, Ltd.

Petersen, Trond, Ishak Saporta, and Marc-David L. Seidel. Forthcoming. "Offering a Job: Meritocracy and Social Networks." *American Journal of Sociology*.

Pfeffer, Jeffrey. 1977. "Toward an Examination of Stratification in Organizations." *Administrative Science Quarterly* 22:553–67.

Pfeffer, Jeffrey, and Yinon Cohen. 1984. "Determinants of Internal Labor Markets in Organizations." *Administrative Science Quarterly* 29:550–72.

Rees, Albert J. 1966. "Information Networks in Labor Markets." *American Economic Review* 56:559–66.

Reskin, Barbara F., and Debra Branch McBrier. 2000. "Why Not Ascription? Organizations' Employment of Male and Female Managers." *American Sociological Review* 65:210–33.

Snow, Charles C., and Scott A. Snell. 1993. "Staffing as Strategy." Pp. 448–78 in *Personnel Selection in Organizations*, by Neal Schmitt, Walter C. Borman, and Associates. San Francisco: Jossey-Bass.

Spaeth, Joe L., and Diane P. O'Rourke. 1994. "Design and Implementation of a National Sample of Work Establishments." *American Behavioral Scientist* 37: 872–90.

Tolbert, Pamela S., and Lynne G. Zucker. 1983. "Institutional Sources of Change in the Formal Structure of Organizations: The Diffusion of Civil Service Reform, 1880–1935." *Administrative Science Quarterly* 28:22–39.

Wanous, John P., and Adrienne Colella. 1989. "Organizational Entry Research: Current Status and Future Directions." Pp. 59–120 in *Research in Personnel and Human Resources Management*, volume 7, edited by Kendrith M. Rowland and Gerald R. Ferris. Greenwich, CT: JAI Press.

Wial, Howard. 1991. "Getting a Good Job: Mobility in a Segmented Labor Market." *Industrial Relations* 30:396–416.

Winship, Christopher, and Larry Radbill. 1994. "Sampling Weights and Regression Analysis." *Sociological Methods and Research* 23:230–57.

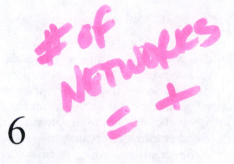

6

Good Networks and Good Jobs: The Value of Social Capital to Employers and Employees

Bonnie H. Erickson

Like other chapters in this volume, this paper defines social capital in the widest sense as the useful aspects of social networks. This general definition must be specified, however, since social networks have many aspects whose usefulness varies depending on the kind of outcome and the kind of context we are interested in (Erickson 2000). I argue that network variety, or the number of different kinds of people that someone knows, is a form of social capital valuable to both employers and employees in the hiring process. Network variety is social "capital" in the same sense that education and work experience are human "capital": all these forms of capital yield returns in the form of greater employee productivity.

Since hiring is a necessarily dual process matching the supply side (employees) with the demand side (employers), social capital is also dual. On the demand side, employers value potential employees with social capital because employers can convert individual social capital into organizational social capital by hiring the individual and mobilizing his or her contacts for organizational goals. Varied contacts are productive in the pursuit of goals concerning critical connections with a firm's environment, such as consequential relationships with current and potential clients or suppliers, ties to other powerful outside actors, channels to key information sources, or scanning developments in the firm's industry. Thus social capital is useful for precisely those goals pursued by employees at higher levels. It is managers and other higher-level employees, not those at the bottom of the ladder, who deal with people outside the organization in consequential ways. For example, lower-level employees may provide routine services to clients, but do not usually recruit them or make deals with them. Hence, social capital is a job qualification for many higher-level jobs, but not for lower-level ones. On the supply side, then, good networks are valuable to potential employees because they increase chances of getting a better job.

Using positive-seeming terms such as "value" and "productivity" should not mislead the reader into thinking that social capital's role in the hiring process is entirely benign. To the contrary: part of the purpose of this paper is to expose the important role social capital plays in exploitation and inequality. Marxians have long argued that employers appropriate and exploit the labor power of workers; here I point out that employers appropriate the power of employee connections as well as the power of their work. Wright (1985) argues that employees benefit unequally from their unequal control of key assets (including skills and organizational position); here I point out that employees also benefit unequally from their unequal social capital.

The research reported below makes a unique contribution in several ways. First, it examines social capital as something valuable *in itself*. Most past work on networks in the hiring process is devoted to the role of hiring through personal contacts: when do people get jobs, or employers seek employees, through personal referrals instead of impersonal means such as advertising? What difference does personal versus impersonal hiring make? (See Fernandez & Castilla, and Marsden in this volume). Often such research provides almost no information at all on social capital, since the only social relationship examined is the one that led to a job, and this only for those jobs found through personal means. Some research does measure social capital, but only considers its value as a route to effective personal hiring: people with better networks are more likely to be able to draw on a contact that can lead to a good job (see Flap & Boxman in this volume, and Lai, Lin, & Leung 1998). Attention has been limited to hiring *through* networks, not hiring *for* networks. Yet results below show that employers prefer to hire people with greater social capital for many upper-level jobs, and that employees with greater social capital get better jobs whether they were hired through personal contacts or not.

Second, this chapter clarifies the connections among different forms of capital in the hiring process. One possibility is that people with better social capital get better jobs, but the effect is spurious, because people with better human capital get both better jobs and greater network diversity. This possibility needs to be examined, given that abundant earlier research shows strong links between networks and both education and occupation. But results below show that social capital goes with better jobs and incomes even with good controls for education and relevant forms of work experience. The evidence favors an alternate conjecture from earlier network research: it is the effects of human capital, not social capital, that have been overestimated. Education and work experience predict job outcomes not only because they have market value in their own right, but at least in part because they lead to greater network diversity, so that controlling for social capital reduces (and explains) part of the apparent effect of human capital. In the study reported here, this is especially clear for work experience, which seems useful in part because of the valuable contacts developed.

Third, this research looks at the dual hiring process from both sides. Most studies examine employees or employers, but not both; welcome exceptions include chapters in this volume (Fernandez & Castilla, and Flap & Boxman). This chapter gives particularly novel attention to employer strategies concerning the positions for which they require human and social capital and their reasons for doing so. Oddly enough, previous research on employers has never directly asked them about social capital as a job qualification, though some has asked about use of personal recruitment, and a good deal has asked about the role of human capital. Analyzing both employer reports and employee outcomes provides two viewpoints on the same process. The two are remarkably consistent concerning capital: education, experience, and network diversity are all important for higher-level jobs. Comparing the two views also yields an interesting though not surprising discrepancy: gender and race have more to do with job outcomes than employer reports would lead one to expect.

Fourth, this research examines an industry of particular interest, private security in Toronto. This industry provides guard services, private investigation, and physical security systems such as burglar alarms and surveillance cameras. It is an industry in which networks should play a lively and revealing role, in part because firms tend to be smaller, single-site firms whose lower level of bureaucratization calls for network solutions to organizational problems such as a greater use of personal hiring (see Marsden in this volume). Further, the industry has negligible professionalization or government regulation; it operates with freewheeling capitalist competition reminiscent of the early capitalism in a Charles Dickens novel. Lacking formal ways to certify the value of their services, or to assess the value of supplies, access information, or perform other essential functions, firms must often rely on networks. Thus the value of social capital is extensive enough to provide a valuable first look at this neglected topic. Any investigation of the hiring process must be located within one or more specific industries, given that there is no single process: hiring processes vary from industry to industry, as earlier work on both the supply and the demand sides has shown.

I begin with a review of the two largely separate literatures on employer hiring practices and on the role of networks in getting a job, and use these reviews to help develop more specific hypotheses about the role of social capital. Since employers generally have more power to shape hiring processes, I begin with their side.

EARLIER RESEARCH

Employer Hiring Requirements

Partly in response to Granovetter (1974, 1995), research on employers' hiring requirements has revived recently. Bills (1992) provides a useful recent review. Work on employer standards routinely does *not* mention social networks. Researchers usually ask about education, experience, and other personal attributes (Bills 1992) or about formal screening devices such as reference checks and tests (Marsden 1994b). Even when researchers give employers open-ended probes, employers still reply in terms of education, experience, job history, and personality (Bills 1988:80–81). When networks are mentioned at all, it is not as a job qualification but as part of the recruitment process (e.g., Bills 1992:17, Marsden 1994a).

This lack of mention need not mean that networks do not in fact count as qualifications. Employers are typically inarticulate about how they hire and why (Bills 1992:23), and may not mention networks because no one has asked about them. Further, many employer surveys focus on lower-level jobs, which are just the kinds of jobs for which networks are not seen as assets. Yet some studies of high-level management show that the networks of higher-level employees can make a serious difference to a firm. For example, Geletkanyczm and Hambrick (1997) show that both company strategy and company performance respond to the ties that top executives have to people outside their firms. Moreover, the effects depend on the type of industry, consistent with Granovetter's insistence on the importance of studying one structural location at a time.

Thus, earlier work hints that networks may be a part of upper-level employee productivity, and hence valuable enough to be worth hiring for at such high levels, but available material is quite thin. What, then, is the value of networks, and for what kinds of work? Some jobs include responsibility for negotiating and maintaining important social relationships across the boundary between a firm and its environment. Company representatives recruit clients, work with existing clients, negotiate with suppliers, monitor markets, seek useful information, and deal with important outside organizations, such as governments. People are better equipped to do such work if they have a wide variety of contacts that give them access to people and social locations with resources that are useful to their firms. Thus network variety is social capital in this context, because network variety predicts wide-ranging access to external resources valuable to employing firms. This general conceptualization fits nicely with Lin's position generator, or, asking respondents whether they know anyone in each of a variety of occupations (see Lin, Hsung, & Fu in this volume). Lin's classic measure uses occupations ranging from high to low in prestige, a useful indicator of the overall variety of ties and of their access to varied resources differentially available up and down the ladder of prestige. It is a measure like a Swiss Army knife, fairly good for a wide range of work in different settings, and hence useful in studying a mix of industries as in a sample of people in a city or nation. But such an all-purpose tool is not ideal for specific settings within which particular kinds of ties will be the more powerful tools. For example, general network variety would be of little use to a newly minted sociologist looking for a job; he or she would be better off with contacts in a variety of sociology departments. Thus I developed a measure of varied contacts especially useful in the security industry, using key informant inputs. I also asked employers to explain what contacts they wanted in employees, and why such contacts were useful, material that underlines the appropriateness of the specific social capital measure used here.

Important external relationships have serious effects on firm fortunes, so such activities are typically defined as important work suitable for higher-level positions. Thus a good network is an asset for some kinds of good jobs. Good external networks are not prerequisites for *all* good jobs; for example, some management jobs, such as accounting, have primarily internal, not external responsibilities. The point is rather that good networks are an asset for many better jobs and very few worse ones. Some lower-level jobs also include working with outsiders, but in more narrowly defined ways that do not call on the worker's network as a resource. For example, retail sales clerks serve many customers but do not usually milk their networks to provide new customers (it is management's job to draw the customers) nor engage in the kind of extensive and discretionary interaction that could draw on social skills that a rich network can help to teach. Thus employers want good contacts for many higher-level jobs and few if any lower-level ones.

So far, I have argued as though there were only two choices for employers: to require social capital for jobs in which it would be useful and to ignore social capital for other jobs. But this is not quite the whole story. Social capital may be desirable, irrelevant, *or* undesirable and even repressed. As Portes and Landolt (1996) remind us, social capital has a down side even though it is usually discussed in terms of its considerable benefits. In competitive situations, one person's social capital advantage may mean another person's loss. From an employer's point of view, employee social capital can be an asset if used for the firm but a threat if used by the employee to set up another rival firm, or used by the employee after defecting to another firm. Some employers, as shown below, are leery of such threats and actively try to prevent them. Burt (1992) argues that well-structured networks give information and control benefits that enhance individual careers, and entrepreneurial people both benefit from entrepreneurial networks and try to enhance the structural value of their networks. Here I add that the people best able to enhance their network competitiveness are precisely those at the top of a firm, since they have the power to define work and networking opportunities for potential rivals below them, and top-level people sometimes try to enhance their own networks' value by limiting the networks of others. Employers also limit the networking opportunities of lower-level employees in a less deliberate manner, by defining their jobs in ways that limit the scope of employee interactions with outsiders.

Thus employers (1) need to meet a variety of important goals in connecting to the external environment, (2) see that they can mobilize employee networks to meet such goals, (3) hence want employees with varied contacts to meet varied objectives, and (4) define such goals as important enough to be the work of upper-level employees, hence (5) make good contacts a job requirement for some externally oriented upper jobs, while (6) ignoring contacts in hiring lower-level people who have limited external responsibilities—and even seek to contain lower-level employee networks, since these are of no great value to the firm but could become a threat if employees set up rival firms or defect to other firms with their social capital.

Employees and Their Networks

A quarter of a century ago, Granovetter (1974) launched a major research area concerning the use of personal contacts in getting a job. His original work showed that male professional, technical, and managerial workers used contacts often and profitably. Recently, in the second edition of his influential book, Granovetter (1995) gave a thoughtful review of the many studies that followed his. Research has found great variation in how much personal contacts are used to get jobs and in how jobs found through contacts differ from those found by other means. Granovetter traces the variations to differences in (1) people's networks, which vary in the number and type of useful contacts they include, (2) employer strategies, which vary in emphasis on personal or impersonal methods of recruiting labor, and (3) the wider institutional and historical context within which people seek jobs and employers seek labor. Thus, from the employee's point of view as well as from the employer's, it is essential to locate research within specific settings rather than combining many different labor markets within which networks will work differently.

Voluminous, intricate, and useful though this research tradition is, it has one astonishing gap: social networks. Very few studies include any information on people's networks; most studies record the type of tie used to get a job, *if* a tie was used, and the rest of a person's network is a mystery. The few studies that do include wider network information are primarily concerned with networks as potential sources of contacts leading to jobs. Yet, as argued above, the worker's network can be an asset in itself, as a whole, quite apart from its ability to provide a job lead.

Of the relatively few studies that include social capital, Lai, Lin, and Leung (1998) is the most recent and the most similar in approach to the study reported in this paper. (Lin 1999 provides a recent review of social capital and status attainment). Lai, Lin, and Leung (1998) show that people with greater social capital find jobs through contacts with higher status, and higher-status contacts produce higher-status jobs. While this is a valuable addition both to the status-attainment literature and to work on getting a job through personal means, the study is not concerned with the possible role of social capital as a job qualification in itself. Thus Lai, Lin, and Leung did not attempt to identify jobs for which employers might require good networks, but instead used occupational prestige as their outcome variable. Jobs of similar prestige can vary widely in their specific requirements, so it is not surprising that they found no effect of social capital on status attainment for people who did not use a contact to find their jobs. The negative finding is also related to the fact that Lai, Lin, and Leung were interested in the overall status-attainment process rather than with specific labor markets and hence worked with a general measure of social capital. Though this measure is very similar in structure to the one used here, and indeed an earlier report on it (Lin & Dumin 1986) was a model for the measure used here, their measure is not as tailored to the kinds of contacts that employers in a specific industry might want for a specific set of jobs. Differences in scope (a community survey for them, and industry study here), in measures of social capital (global for them, more industry-specific here), and in the job outcome (general occupational status for them, industry-specific job level and income here) all contribute to a striking contrast of results that makes a good deal of sense. Blending different types of social capital, jobs, and labor markets, they find that social capital leads to a better job only for those who get a job through a contact, and leads to a better job by leading to a higher-status contact. Working in a specific setting, the work reported below shows that social capital leads to better jobs and better pay *whether these jobs are found through personal contacts or not.*

Looking at the social and human capital that workers have, and the level and income of the jobs they have, will show whether good networks make their own contribution to getting a better job. It will also help to clarify some of the interconnections among these forms of capital. Notably, controlling for work experience often erases the apparent effect of using contacts on job quality, but work experience may be valuable in part because it allows people to build up better networks, so controlling for experience may control away network effects (Bridges & Villemez 1986). The work reported below shows that work experience does indeed have some of its effects through the network diversity that greater experience helps to bring.

METHODS

The Toronto Security Industry and Our Sample

Consistent with the arguments above, which call for setting-specific analysis of both employer requirements and the value of social capital to employees, this study examines one industry in one large market: the private security industry in Toronto. The industry includes hundreds of firms and thousands of workers in distinctly different jobs of varying type and desirability, important forms of variation for the theoretical issues in this paper. The research includes both interviews with employers about their hiring requirements and interviews with people these employers have hired into the jobs the employers describe, so that both sides of the hiring process can be directly compared for the same labor market.

The research team developed a list of security companies from the Yellow Pages, a list of licensed guard and investigation firms, and preliminary telephone checks. Of the firms still in business at the time of our survey, 161 companies, or just over 50 percent, cooperated with the research. Graduate-student research assistants conducted interviews with employers and most employees, and collected self-completed questionnaires from some employees, May 1991 to January 1992.

With a response rate of 50 percent, our data on employers compare favorably to other samples of employers, who are notoriously hard to reach; credit belongs to the energetic assistants, who took turns making up to a dozen call-backs to companies. The sample of employees is more haphazard since we were dependent on employers to provide access. Some companies refused, some let us approach employees at work, some let us solicit volunteers through notices, and some let us take random samples from personnel lists. The final sample of 281 employees is thus not random, but it is reasonably representative. The sample includes employees well distributed across the major occupations in this industry (see the Ns in Table 1 below) and the major kinds of employing firms (employees described the

Table 1. Good and Bad Jobs in the Security Industry

Job	Income	Autonomy	Routinization	N
Manager	8.4	14.3	2.1	79
Salesperson	7.8	14.5	2.4	50
Investigator	6.1	13.2	2.2	33
Supervisor	5.8	13.0	2.8	46
Hardware	7.0	13.6	2.3	36
Clerical	5.5	13.0	2.8	29
Guard	4.5	11.9	3.2	89

Note: Cell entries are mean values for scales described in the text. Some people contribute to more than one row (see discussion in text); the number of unique respondents is 281.

work done by their firms; 44 percent reported alarm installation, 42 percent reported guard work, and 36 percent reported investigation, with figures adding up to more than 100 percent because some firms offer multiple services). For guards and investigators, we can compare the sample to results from the 1991 census (Campbell & Reinhard 1994); see Appendix 1. Census and sample groups are similar in gender composition, rate of doing part time work, percentage of high school graduates, and mean yearly income. The sample may have somewhat higher incomes and somewhat more highly educated guards, but overall the similarities are strong considering that the comparison is unavoidably imperfect: the sample comes from the Toronto area, while the census results are national, and the sample includes only workers in the private security industry while the census includes guards and investigators in government organizations or in-house security services.

Since this was a one-shot survey, causal order is unavoidably more ambiguous than in longitudinal studies such as Flap and Boxman or Fernandez and Castells in this volume. Since the survey is limited to those already working in the industry, I cannot compare those who got jobs to those who did not, but can only compare better and worse job outcomes within the industry. A variety of selection effects may well be hidden.

MEASUREMENTS

I first describe the major kinds of jobs in the security industry, including their work, their desirability as better or worse jobs, and their networking responsibilities. Next I explain how we observed employer hiring requirements for these jobs, and last, employee capitals and control variables.

Good Jobs and Bad

We asked employers about eight jobs that are important in security work and that vary greatly in their desirability and tasks: managers, salespeople, consultants, investigators, supervisors, hardware workers, clerical workers, and guards. We also asked employees to report their jobs and job characteristics. In practice, it turned out, there is little distinction between consulting and selling: although a very few firms specialized in advice and referrals while doing no direct security work themselves, consulting usually meant advising the client on which of the firm's services to buy and how to make best use of them. Thus there is no useful employee reporting on consulting work as such. Job categories often overlap; for example, a member of a small investigation firm may do both management and investigation work. Since overlap is a real and extensive part of security work, I include employees under each kind of job they report doing when giving simple descriptive tables for jobs, even though this means that job categories are not mutually exclusive and statistical tests must be foregone (though tests will appear in the multivariate analyses of employee level and income, for which they are appropriate). I do define clerical workers as those who report doing *only* clerical work because office workers differ in important ways from other security workers. Much of their work is not specific to security as such but is generic office work, and clerical work is the only job category filled mainly by women. Clerical workers in this sample are 89 percent women, while workers in other job categories range from 69 percent men (for supervisors) to 92 percent men (for hardware workers).

Table 1, discussed below, summarizes employee reports of key indicators of job desirability for the seven jobs other than consulting. *Income* is personal income before taxes, measured on a 14 level scale from under $5,000 to $135,000 or more. *Autonomy* is the sum of four items asking whether people made decisions on their own, whether their supervisors decided what they did and how they did it, whether they controlled the speed at which they worked, and whether they had freedom to decide how to do their work; for each item, four response categories ranged from "never" to "almost always," and were recoded as needed so that higher numbers indicate higher autonomy. Possible values range from 4 to 16. Cronbach's alpha, .71, indicates good reliability. Work *routinization* is a single item asking how often the worker does the same thing over and over, with responses again ranging from "never" (1) to "almost always" (4). In the text of the job descriptions below, I also report occupational prestige scores when available in an updated internationally comparable version of the Treiman scale (Ganzeboom & Trieman 1996).

Managers have very high levels of income and autonomy and low levels of routinization (Table 1). The appropriate prestige scores are variable, from 52 for the general manager of a small business service firm to 70 for the head of a large company; 60, a reasonable overall value, is higher than the scores for every other job except investigator (also 60). As in other industries, security managers have high levels of variety and responsibility and their duties can include high-level negotiations with important outsiders.

Salespersons report the highest levels of autonomy and are second only to managers in income and absence of routinization. Salespersons interact with clients in consequential ways, most often on the client's turf, so sellers can and must work independently. (Much the same is true of consultants.) Prestige scores are not available.

Investigators have work more specific to security than the more generic work in management and selling. Investigators check up on people who may have made fraudulent insurance claims, or "floor walk" in a store pretending to be a customer while really looking for shoplifters, or work undercover as a company employee while detecting possible employee thefts, or trace missing persons, or serve documents, and so on. Investigators may or may not have much role in negotiations with clients or suppliers, but they often work independently in jobs that call for adept people handling and creative problem solving on the spot, and they often seek information from people outside their firm. Their pay and autonomy are moderate, and their work is little routinized.

Supervisors are usually promoted from the ranks of their own or a similar company, have only a little more power than the people they supervise, and often share in the same work as those they supervise. Thus they are only a little better off than clerical workers and guards in their income, autonomy, and routinization. Supervisors have primarily internal responsibilities such as assigning guards to shifts, and their contacts with outsiders are at most limited.

Hardware workers install or service security devices from simple home alarms to complex computer-controlled security systems. Most of their work is done on the client's premises and requires discretion and judgment in dealing with the client and adapting hardware to the client's needs. The work also calls for blue-collar skills such as electronics (an essential aspect of any alarm) and construction (since many alarms are installed in the fabric of buildings); these skills are well paid outside security. Thus hardware workers are quite high in income and autonomy (behind only salespeople and managers), and their work is as little routinized as that of managers or investigators. Though in these respects hardware jobs are good jobs, they are very much good blue-collar jobs, and fieldwork observations suggest that such jobs lack the prestige and status of nonmanual work. While alarm workers have no prestige scoring of their own, their prestige levels probably resemble those of blue-collar workers with similar skills, such as construction and electronics, which have prestige scores of 34 and 38 respectively.

Clerical workers do typical office work and, like their equivalents in other industries, report signs of a bad job: relatively low income and autonomy, relatively high routinization. Though worse off than hardware workers in these features of work, clerical workers are comparable or better off in prestige. Clerical work in general has a prestige score of 37, though prestige rises as high as 53 for a secretary. Office workers have little to do with outsiders beyond such trivial matters as preparing correspondence with them or greeting them when they call.

Guards clearly have the worst jobs in the industry, with the worst income, lowest autonomy, and greatest routinization. Guards typically go to a post, follow a simple set of unvarying procedures such as patrolling a building, make a report, and then do the same thing the next day. Their prestige score (30) is the lowest in the industry. Though guards often interact with outsiders, they are limited to narrow tasks. A guard may greet the residents of a condominium and assist them with small services such as looking after parcels, or direct shoppers in a mall to the washrooms.

Table 1 and prestige scores show that security jobs vary considerably in how desirable they are. The job descriptions above show that more desirable jobs tend to include more responsibility for relatively demanding and consequential forms of work with people outside the firm.

Hiring Requirements

To assess employer hiring requirements, interviewers asked a senior company representative (the owner or a top manager) to describe these for each of eight important jobs in the industry. Since employers tend to be inarticulate and need to be pressed for information on hiring (Bills 1992:23) the question wording is important. In this study we asked employers equally probing questions for all three forms of capital:

> We are interested in the qualifications that your company requires for employees of various types. Do you have minimum standards of education for these jobs? If so, how much education, and what type?
> Does your company require specific kinds of prior work experience for these positions? If so, please briefly describe your requirements.
> Does your company require that employees for these positions have good contacts? For those where you do require contacts, what kind are useful?

Though 161 company representatives gave interviews, they described only hiring requirements for jobs their company would hire for, so the number of respondents for each type of job varies from 53 for guard jobs to 116 for manager jobs.

Employee Social Capital

Using a format similar to that of Lin and Dumin (1986) I measure social capital in terms of the variety of different social locations in which a person has a contact. Interviewers asked:

> Now I am going to ask you whether you know anyone in a certain line of work at all, in the Toronto area—for example, whether you know any lawyers. Please count anyone you know well enough to talk to even if you are not close to them.

The measure includes nineteen categories: business owners outside your own company, business managers who run an establishment other than your own company, supervisors, lawyers, doctors, engineers, professors, school teachers, bankers, insurance brokers, accountants, carpenters, electricians, locksmiths, plumbers, and four ranks of police (constable, sergeant, detective, inspector). Social capital is the simple count of the number of different categories in which the respondent reported knowing someone.

The categories are quite varied in general ways, so the measure can be read as a measure of access to positions ranging in occupational prestige, like the measures used in Lin and Dumin (1986) and Lai, Lin, and Leung (1998). An alternative general interpretation is that the categories represent different classes and class fractions defined by control of company ownership, company management, professional skills, semiprofessional skills, and blue-collar skills (Wright 1985). But it is important to note that these general conceptions of network variety have been given specific indicators for access to information, resources, and skills especially valuable in the security industry. Business owners and managers, and many professionals, are valuable potential clients for company or office security contracts. Any of the categories could provide clients for home alarms, especially since the categories emphasize the higher-class and higher-income groups that most often buy home security (Hagan 1992.) Blue-collar workers have skills necessary for security hardware, while the police and several of the professionals and semiprofessionals can provide information invaluable for / to investigation work. Thus this is a measure of social capital, both in the general sense of access to a wide range of useful resources, and also (and even more) in the sense of access to resources useful in the industry within which employees work.

Employee Human Capital

Human capital includes both education and work experience. The general measure of education is years of formal schooling completed. Respondents also reported whether or not they had each of three kinds of vocational training potentially relevant to security work: law enforcement (useful for guards or investigators), electronics (useful for hardware workers), and business (useful for managers and office workers). Unlike many, if not most measures of work experience, the measures here used are not limited to overly general ones such as years in the labor force. Instead, the general measures are years of experience in the security industry before starting one's current job, and years of tenure in one's current job. Respondents also reported whether or not they had experience in specific kinds of work relevant to some security jobs: prior experience in management, and any experience in sales, police, electronics, and computers.

Other Employee Characteristics

When predicting employee level and income I will include three important control variables: age (in years), gender (1 = male, 0 = female), and race (respondents were coded 1 = nonwhite if the ethnic group they felt most a part of was Chinese, Japanese, Native Canadian, West Indian, African, Korean, Vietnamese, East Indian, or Pakistani, and otherwise coded 0 = white).

Getting a Job

Respondents reported how they got their current positions; they were coded as using a personal contact if they reported that there was anyone who helped in any way to get the job.

RESULTS

What Employers Want: Hiring Requirements for Security Jobs

Table 2 shows how often employers reported requiring each possible combination of contacts, experience, and education for each of the eight jobs they were asked about. For example, the first row shows that 116 firm representatives reported their firms' hiring requirements for managers: 33 percent of the employers reported requiring contacts, experience, and education; 9 percent reported requiring contacts, experience, but not education; 1 percent reported requiring contacts, education, but not experience; and so on.

To analyze hiring requirements we need to know both which kinds of jobs have more or less similar requirements *and* which combinations of requirements go together in specifications for similar jobs, since we are interested both in differences among jobs and in ways that different kinds of

Table 2. Employer Hiring Requirements

Row		Column								Row N
		1	2	3	4	5	6	7	8	
	CONTACTS	Y	Y	Y	Y	N	N	N	N	
	EXPERIENCE	Y	Y	N	N	Y	Y	N	N	
	EDUCATION	Y	N	Y	N	Y	N	Y	N	
1	Managers	33	9	1	1	22	21	3	10	116
2	Salespeople	26	23	5	8	7	16	3	11	87
3	Consultants	20	20	2	5	20	16	2	15	55
4	Investigators	14	13	6	7	26	12	7	14	69
5	Supervisors	11	6	0	0	39	21	6	16	80
6	Hardware	9	5	0	3	36	20	14	14	66
7	Clerical	2	4	2	1	36	24	12	23	110
8	Guards	0	2	0	6	21	8	26	38	53
	Column N	99	63	12	22	164	115	54	107	636

Note: Entries are row percentages, showing how often each possible combination of three possible requirements (contacts, experience, and education) was reported as required, for each of eight jobs. Y = required; N = not required. For further explanation see text.

capitals get packaged together in employer practices. Fortunately Breiger (1994) has developed an appropriate procedure, COMBINE. Briefly, COMBINE starts from a crosstabulation of counts (here, the raw data underlying Table 2) and combines rows with similar distributions and columns with similar distributions. COMBINE merges the pair of rows with most similar distributions first, then the most similar pair of rows in the new table, and so forth until all the remaining rows in the collapsed table are statistically different and hence should not be combined. COMBINE does the same for columns, and finally finds the best collapsing of both rows and columns. We can thus see both which sets of rows and columns have significantly different distributions and which of the differences are more significant. (For a more detailed description of COMBINE, see Beiger 1994; for statistical details of the analysis of Table 2, contact the author).

Table 2 summarizes the COMBINE results visually. The wide shaded horizontal bar between rows 4 and 5 shows the divide between jobs with the most distinct patterns of hiring requirements, rows 1–4 versus 5–8; within this major division, the narrower shaded horizontal bars divide jobs that have somewhat less different, but still significantly different patterns of hiring requirements (row 1 versus rows 2–4, and rows 5–7 versus 8); and rows not divided by a bar have similar patterns of hiring requirements. It is easy to see these row similarities and differences in Table 2, since more similar rows are put closer to each other, and the table reports row percentages. Similarly, Table 2 uses a thick shaded vertical bar to indicate combinations of hiring requirements that have the most different distribution over jobs (columns 1–4 versus 5–8) and thinner bars to indicate combinations somewhat less distinct (column 1 versus 2–4, and columns 5 and 6 versus 7 and 8).

Overall, Table 2 shows, social capital is quite often a job requirement though not as often as the more familiar human-capital components. Of all the 636 descriptions of job requirements, 31 percent included contacts, 52 percent included education, and 69 percent included experience. Though it is striking and important that fully a third of job requirements include contacts, Table 2 shows something far more profound: social capital is the most important form of capital in terms of the dual structure of jobs and requirements. The wide vertical shaded line in Table 2 divides the most different requirement bundles, which are just those that do or do not include social capital. This deep structural split interlocks with the split between the two sets of jobs most different in their hiring requirements: managers, salespeople, consultants, and investigators compared to supervisors, hardware workers, clerical workers, and guards. This is a split between good white-collar jobs and other jobs. It is pretty much a split between good jobs and bad, except for hardware workers, who have good but blue-collar jobs. The deep split interlock between jobs and requirements is simple:

employers often require contacts for good upper-level jobs and rarely require contacts for other jobs. The frequency with which employers require contacts (with or without human capital) is 44 percent for managers, 62 percent for salespeople, 47 percent for consultants, and 40 percent for investigators, contrasted with 17 percent for supervisors, 17 percent for hardware workers, 11 percent for clerical workers, and 8 percent for guards.

Thus employers seemed to want contacts for higher-level people whose work included consequential forms of the company's external affairs. This interpretation is bolstered by the more detailed comments employers made on the kinds of contacts they wanted, and why they wanted them. They wanted contacts in order to monitor the environment in general ("your job is to be constantly around what is happening in the environment, so you can attack it and address it" [#136]); to monitor the security industry in particular ("to hear what's going on in the industry" [#306]); to gain access to services and resources (for example, through ties "such that favors are owed" [#102]); to recruit new customers ("for new business" [#306]) as well as keeping the loyalty of old ones; to collect information generally ("to get information you usually won't get or have to pay for through the nose" [#364]); and to maintain good relationships with powerful external organizations ("a good rapport with police and the local authorities" [#141]).

The seriousness of contact requirements was clear from their frequency, from their close link to jobs with important external responsibilities, and from the care with which employers went on to describe the particular kinds of contacts they sought (Table 3). Contacts for managers and salespeople seemed to be especially important, since employers described these in detail most often (57 described valued contacts for managers, 40 for salespeople). Employers report wanting managers with a wide range of specific contacts including ties to the security industry, clients, suppliers, police, and government. Moreover, some employers want diversity as such. Some want to target any organization that might have a security need ("senior management contacts is really what it comes down to; memberships at golf clubs would be very handy" [#19]). Five percent of the mentions explicitly included variety, for example "all available" [366]. Thus social capital in the form of a diversified network is an asset for many management positions. Salespeople are expected to focus more on current and prospective clients, but also need a wide range of ties to do so. Much the same is true of consultants (who are often salespeople as well) except that they sometimes need ties to suppliers (especially suppliers of security hardware). For investigators, most of the required ties are channels for access to crucial information: ties to police, government, or various other sources. Though the particular form of useful variety varies, network variety is an asset for all of these relatively good jobs.

Table 3. The Kinds of Contacts Employers Want

	Security Industry	Current Clients	Potential Clients	Suppliers	Police	Governments	Informants	Varied Ties	Own Firm	N
Managers	25	16	21	11	18	5	0	5	0	57
Salespeople	15	25	48	8	5	0	0	0	0	40
Consultants	14	14	43	21	7	0	0	0	0	14
Investigators	7	0	13	0	27	13	13	27	0	15
Supervisors	14	29	0	29	0	0	0	0	29	7
Hardware	33	0	0	67	0	0	0	0	0	6
Clerical	0	0	0	0	0	0	0	0	100	1
Guards	0	0	0	0	0	0	0	0	0	0

Note: Except for the row Ns in the last column, entries are row percentages.

In striking contrast, employers had little to say about the kinds of contacts required for other jobs and some of what they did say concerned ties *inside* their own firms such as learning from coworkers: "saying 'how did you do this job?' or things like that so that you can share information" [#136]. Examples of external ties were often low-level matters such as routine ordering of supplies. Several employers explained why they did not require contacts for the lower-level positions: the work includes meeting outsiders in only very limited ways. For example, hardware workers "contact the customer, but they don't deal with them in terms of sales or that sort of basis. They go, they meet them, they go to the job and do the work"[#13].

Some employers not only see no need for their lower employees to have contacts, but actually want to limit their contacts. One reason is security. In undercover work, a widely know investigator cannot easily pretend to be someone else, and cannot easily avoid reprisals from people he or she has sent to jail. Even apparently innocuous jobs like monitoring alarm signals can arouse concern ("they shouldn't let anyone know where they work . . . who knows who's going to try to break in, try to do some wonderful stuff to the employees" [#136]). But another reason is protection of the employer's own interests against the potential threat of competition. Employers constantly face the possibility that employees may learn the business, make contacts, and go into business ("one of the biggest problems in this business is taking two years to train someone and having them start a small company out of their trucks" [#142]). If employers can keep employee contacts limited, they maintain a structural hole (Burt 1992) such that employees cannot develop the contact base needed to become rivals, and clients cannot recruit employees to provide services at reduced rates. Some employers even deny the value of contacts for higher-levels jobs, arguing that they themselves supply all useful contacts ("I've got contacts" [#15]); whether or not such employers are deliberately restricting the employees' contacts, their strategy will have that effect.

To see the role of human-capital requirements and how they combine with social-capital requirements, we must turn to the less significant divisions in Table 2. Let us begin with the upper-left hand quadrant of Table 2, the region of externally oriented jobs (rows 1–4) and job requirements, including social capital (columns 1–4). Within this region we see the interlock of the significant difference between managers and other upper-level jobs (row 1 versus 2–4), and between requiring all three forms of capital or not (column 1 versus 2–4). The defining difference here is that employers most often want it all for managers (33 percent of the time, employers require contacts *and* experience *and* education) while they often skip the education component for salespeople, consultants, or investigators. Table 2 as a whole shows that education is required most often for managers. Thus education may be a valuable form of human capital for manager-level jobs only. Further, one thing that all four of the upper-level jobs have in common, and one thing that distinguishes them from other jobs, is that they not only often require contacts but almost always require contacts in combination with experience (compare the moderately high percentages in columns 1 and 2 to the small ones in columns 3 and 4). This implies that employers are looking not only for contacts, but for the specifically useful contacts that experience is likely to provide. Thus part of the value of experience is just its ability to generate contacts, especially for higher-level jobs.

Continuing with the four higher-level jobs, the upper-right quadrant of Table 2 shows results for hiring requirements that do not include social capital. Many employers did not report requiring contacts, presumably because their upper-level jobs had limited external responsibilities; again, social capital is an asset for some, not all, upper-level jobs. Combining the upper-left and -right quadrants, we can see that employers very often required experience for upper-level jobs, but only sometimes added education requirements as well, suggesting that employers value experience more than education. I return to this below, when describing the specific types of education and experience employers report wanting.

The lower-left quadrant of Table 2 is another reflection of an earlier point: employers almost never require contacts for lower-level jobs. Interesting differences among lower-level jobs show up in the lower-right quadrant, where we see that employers more often than not want experience for lower-level jobs—except for security guards, for whom they require little. Most security guard work is easy to learn and poorly rewarded, so employers neither see a need for extensive qualifications of any kind nor are willing to pay for them. Indeed the modal requirement bundle for guards (given over a third of the time) is none of contacts, education, or experience. But employers consider supervisory, hardware, and clerical jobs to have higher skill requirements. For these jobs, a majority of employers report requiring experience. As for upper-level jobs, education is a less common requirement and is rarely required on its own without experience, suggesting again that experience is more valued.

Given the evident importance of experience, it is important to consider the specific kinds of experience employers sought, and later below to compare such requirements to the actual outcomes for employees. Employer comments on experience centered on whether they sought experience in their own security industry and whether they sought specific vocational skills available from experience outside the industry. Overall, employers felt that security-specific experience was important: useful skills come from "experience on the job" (#136) "in their respective fields" (#143). But some skills are seen as more transferable between industries than others. Clerical skills are seen as generic office skills available anywhere, and almost all (26/27) employers would accept clerical experience outside their industry for clerical jobs. Selling is also often seen as a generic skill, though specific knowledge of security products and markets can be valuable, so half (15/30) the employers accept selling experience outside security. A strong majority (79 percent to 88 percent) wanted security experience for managers (38/45), supervisors (23/26), and hardware workers (15/19). Where outside experience was acceptable it was because managerial skills or the core blue-collar skills involved in hardware are seen as generic, attainable outside security through other experience with management, electronics, or computers. There is no real external equivalent to investigation, though some employers see police experience as a rough start, and all (14/14) employers wanted security-specific experience for investigators. Overall, security employers take experience seriously. Employers want experience often, and carefully distinguish the kinds of experience they want for different jobs.

What is striking about the last of the three requirements, education, is that Table 2 implies employers do *not* take it seriously for jobs below management level. Except for the secondary split between managers and other upper-level jobs, education plays no part in the table's structure. Where combinations of hiring requirements are distinct, they differ in the presence or absence of contacts and/or experience, not the presence or absence of education. This may seem strange: education is generally important in contemporary labor markets and security employers often claim to require it. But when employers went on to discuss education in more detail, their lack of seriousness became plain. Some who say they have educational requirements go on to describe fuzzy ones (at least 15 reported that a certain level of education was "preferred" or "nice to see" but not in fact strictly required). Some set the standards so low that few applicants could be excluded. Only 13 employers require university-level training for any positions, including just four who require it for managers. High school or high school plus vocational training are the most popular choices overall, and requirements are similarly modest for all jobs except security guard. For guards the bar is set even lower, amounting to little more than a request for basic literacy: one employer required elementary school, six required grade 10, three high school, and one community college. Many employers explained that formal education does not teach skills useful in security work; experience is either a better teacher or the only teacher. Some employers do not even value the few programs designed for the industry: "young people are often enrolled in programs and courses for the security industry that have no real value; they are wasting their time and money" [#328]. Employers gave the most positive comments on specific vocational training useful for particular jobs, such as electronics or computers for hardware work.

So, what do employers want? They initially claim to want, but in fact do not very seriously want, education (as is true in many other industries; Bills 1988, 1992); only for managers do educational requirements seem important. For upper-level jobs with serious external responsibilities, employers often want a combination of experience and the useful contacts experience can help to bring. For lower-level jobs without such external scope they almost never require contacts, but often do want experience and the skills that they believe come from experience instead of education. For the lowest of jobs, security guard, they want very little of anything. Social capital plays a deep structural role. The presence or absence of social-capital hiring requirements marks the line between jobs with and without consequential external functions. This is also much the same as the line between better and worse jobs. From the employer's point of view, education is valuable capital sometimes for managers and not often for others; experience is valuable capital for all but the lowly guard jobs, especially valuable if it is directly relevant to the job, and often valuable because it leads to useful contacts; and social capital is valuable for jobs with consequential extra-firm responsibilities, as is often the case for upper-level jobs.

What Employers Get: The Actual Social and
Human Capital Reported by Employees

If human and social capital is important to employers as described above, then employers should pay corresponding attention to both in hiring, thus leading to predictable differences in the distribution of capitals among employees. In this section I consider univariate results for network variety and the specific kinds of education and work experience employers report valuing, later turning to multivariate results assessing the impact of capitals on employee access to better jobs and incomes.

According to employer accounts, social capital is useful only for higher-level jobs with serious external scope. Table 4 shows that network diversity is higher for managers, salespeople, and investigators, just the positions for which employers often require good contacts. People in such higher-level jobs know someone in about 13 different lines of work on average, while supervisors and hardware workers know someone in 10, and clerical workers and guards know someone in about 9. Given that the total number of kinds of work asked about was 19, there seems to be a sizable difference in the extent to which employees at different levels can access information and resources from a wide variety of social locations.

Employers report wanting security experience least often for clerks (for whom outside office experience is fine) and guards (for whom almost nothing is required); Table 5 shows that these employees have the shortest

Table 4.   Actual Employee Resources: Social Capital:
The Mean Number of Occupations in Which Employees
Know Someone

Employee's Job	Mean Network Diversity
Managers	13.1
Salespeople	13.5
Investigators	12.8
Supervisors	10.4
Hardware	11.1
Clerical	9.0
Guards	9.2

Note: See note to Table 1.

security industry experience. Although employers sometimes say that selling experience outside the industry is useful, and say that investigation experience inside security is essential, results do not support these nuances.
Instead, the higher the level of the job the greater the employee experience
within security. Employers also wanted experience specific to the particular field in which employees work; and managers have the highest rate of
management experience, salespeople the highest rate of sales experience,
investigators have one of the two highest rates of police experience, while
hardware workers lead in electronics and computer experience.

Employers often said they required education, but detailed analysis
suggested this was not a serious demand. Table 6 shows that employees in
all seven jobs have quite similar, modest levels of formal schooling, averaging 13 to 14 years, about equivalent to a high school degree (high school
ended with Grade 13 in Ontario when this research was conducted). Some

Table 5.   Actual Employee Resources: Work Experience

Employee's Job	Mean Years in Security Industry	Proportion with Experience in				
		Managing	Sales	Police	Electronics	Computers
Managers	10.0	.76	.73	.20	.33	.47
Salespeople	8.4	.67	.90	.22	.45	.43
Investigators	6.2	.50	.50	.21	.19	.34
Supervisors	4.4	.36	.57	.02	.30	.42
Hardware	5.0	.50	.71	.08	.74	.65
Clerical	3.8	.26	.41	.00	.07	.56
Guards	2.8	.33	.56	.07	.23	.30

Note: See note to Table 1.

Table 6.   Actual Employee Resources: Education

| | | Proportion with Vocational Training | | |
Employee's Job	Mean Years of Education	Law Enforcement	Electronics	Business
Managers	14.7	.25	.31	.80
Salespeople	14.5	.42	.21	.83
Investigators	14.1	.71	.05	.62
Supervisors	13.1	.36	.18	.61
Hardware	14.8	.18	.50	.45
Clerical	13.3	.15	.00	.60
Guards	13.9	.44	.07	.44

Note: See note to Table 1.

employers had a few good words for specific vocational training, and Table 6 also shows a match between some jobs and directly relevant training: investigators and guards have the highest rates of law-enforcement training, hardware workers lead in electronics, managers and salespeople in business training. Employers did seem to be serious about education for managers, so it is at first surprising to see that managers have a level of schooling similar to that for people in other jobs. But the role of education is masked by age, since managers tend to be older than other workers and hence come from cohorts with lower average levels of education. The multivariate results below will show that managers do have higher education net of other factors, including age.

Overall, employee capital distributions indicate that each kind of capital is valuable to employers much as employers claim when discussing their hiring requirements. Next I turn to a multivariate analysis of the impact of employee human and social capital on getting a better job or better incomes.

Social Capital, Human Capital, and Employee Success

To assess the multivariate effects of capitals and control variables on the level of position that employees have reached, I compare those who have or have not reached the level of management. Management jobs have the highest authority level and are also high in income and autonomy while low in routinization (Table 1). Moreover, management is the only kind of work for which employers show a serious interest in education (Table 2), so a focus on management gives the greatest scope to the traditional human-capital variables and makes a relatively conservative test of the possible independent contribution of social capital. Human capital here includes years of formal schooling and both the forms of experience that the work above showed are relevant for managers, that is, years of experience in the security industry and having any prior management experience. Table 7 shows logistic regressions predicting management level. In Tables 7 and 8, some variables are transformed to correct skew (age and job tenure square rooted, prior security experience logged) and some (age, network diversity, and whether or not a person got a job with someone's help) are centered to prevent multicollinearity problems with quadratic or interactive terms.

Model 1 of Table 7 shows controls and human capital, without social capital. All the human-capital variables increase the chances of being a manager: years of formal schooling, experience in security before one's current job, and prior management experience all go with greater chances of being at management level. Although employers had little to say about age, race, and gender, all of these are also important. The chances of being a manager rise with age until the mid-thirties and then level off. White people have a better chance to become managers than have nonwhites, and men are more likely to be managers than are women.

Model 2 shows that social capital, in the form of network diversity, also goes with management positions. Introducing social capital reduces the

Table 7. Capitals and Positions: Logistic Regressions Predicting Which Employees Are Managers

Predictors	Model 1	Model 2	Model 3
Age	.78**	.86**	.86**
Age squared	−.57**	−.60**	−.60**
Nonwhite	−1.27*	−1.07+	−1.07+
Male gender	1.16*	1.24*	1.24*
Education	.28**	.28**	.28**
Prior security experience	.97**	.76+	.76*
Prior management experience	1.15**	.85**	.85*
Network diversity		.14**	.14**
Got job through a contact			.01
(Diversity) × (Contact)			−.01
Constant	−6.34**	−6.12**	−7.77**
Model chi-square	87.51**	96.03**	96.04**
N	237	237	237

**$p < .01$.
*$p < .05$.
+$p < .10$.

Note: (Diversity) × (Contact) = interaction term for network diversity times a dummy variable indicating whether or not the respondent found the current job with the help of a personal contact.

Table 8.   Capitals and Income: Standardized Multiple Regressions

Predictors	Model 1	Model 2	Model 3
Age	.19**	.20**	.20**
Age squared	−.32**	−.33**	−.32**
Nonwhite	−.09	−.08	−.08
Male	.13*	.14*	.14*
Education	.14*	.13*	.14*
Prior security experience	.16**	.12+	.12+
Job tenure	.22**	.20**	.20**
Network diversity		.14**	.15*
Got job through a contact			−.04
(Diversity) × (Contact)			−.06
Adjusted R²	.312**	.327**	.325**
N	237	237	237

**p < .01.
*p < .05.
+p < .10.
Note: (Diversity) × (Contact) = interaction term for network diversity times a dummy variable indicating whether or not the respondent found the current job with the help of a personal contact.

coefficients for both the experience variables, consistent with the view that employees value experience in part for the useful contacts that experience brings. To get a sense of the relative impact of the various forms of capital, we can compare the exponentiated coefficients to see how much the odds of being a manager grow with a unit change in a variable. For social capital, knowing someone in one additional line of work multiplies the odds of being a manager by 1.15. Knowing someone in two additional lines of work multiplies the odds of management by 1.32, which is essentially the same as the impact of having one additional year of education (1.33). Knowing someone in six additional lines of work multiplies the odds by 2.26, nearly the same effect as having prior management experience, which multiplies the odds of being a manager in one's current job by 2.34. Thus the impact of social capital is substantial, even after carefully appropriate controls for human capital and age, race, and gender.

Model 3 adds whether or not respondents reported getting their jobs with the help of some other person and the interaction between using a contact and social capital. Both these new terms are nowhere near significance. Using a contact is no help in rising to management level; people in all sorts of security jobs often got those jobs through contacts. More important here, the nonsignificant interaction shows that social capital goes with greater odds of management position *whether someone used a contact or not*. Thus network diversity in and of itself helps people rise up employee ranks; it is not just that people with better networks have a better chance of using a contact and hence getting a better job. This is consistent with the earlier results showing the employers often want managers with good networks to help manage the external affairs of their companies.

Table 8 turns from whether or not an employee is a manager to how high an employee's income is. The appropriate experience variables change, from length of security-industry experience before the current job plus prior experience as a manager (for predicting management status) to prior industry experience plus length of tenure in the current job (for predicting income). There is no significant effect of being nonwhite, but other results are very similar to those for management position. Income rises with age, most rapidly for younger workers; men make more than women; and all forms of human and social capital are rewarded with higher income. It is interesting that education goes with higher income, despite the lack of employer attention to education in hiring. Even though employers do not often seek or reward education as such in this industry, they may well value some resources that education helps to build, resources such as verbal skills, cultural capital, personal autonomy, and so forth.

The effect of social capital on income is about as strong as the effect of education, prior industry experience, or tenure in one's current job. To assess the value of social capital to employees in dollars, consider the unstandardized coefficient, .08. Most employees earn incomes in the middle range of our income scale, where each level has a range of $10,000, so employees earn an additional $800 for every additional occupation within which they know someone. To give context to this number, consider that managers on average have contacts in four more occupations than do guards (Table 4) which corresponds to a social-capital-based income advantage of 4 × $800 = $3200, or about one tenth of the difference in the mean income of managers ($55,260) and guards ($25,194). Thus social capital has a substantial effect on employee incomes, as well as on their chances of holding management positions. This effect is not just a result of network-based hiring, but a reward to social capital as such, since social capital goes with higher income whether or not a person reported getting the current job with someone's help (see Model 3 in Table 8).

Thus, whether we consider job level or job pay, social capital is an asset distinct from, and comparable to the more familiar human-capital assets from the worker's point of view. Some of the well-documented value of human capital is in fact its contribution to social capital, especially the ability of industry-specific work experience to generate contacts useful in the industry.

DISCUSSION

The findings above suggest a banquet of important problems for future research. Granted that social capital plays an important part in hiring and rewards for some jobs, we need to know more about process (just how does social capital work) and labor market variability (how does social capital work in different industries).

Process questions include network probing and signaling in hiring. When employers hire for jobs with external contact requirements, how do they check on these, and what strategies do potential employees use to show off their social capital? People in any industry may use a direct approach (as in "what new clients might you be able to bring to this firm?"), but industries will also have their own culturally specific scripts for information exchange. Probably one popular form is the good story, a narrative that is compelling in terms of local culture but also rich in opportunities to mention contacts as actors in the drama recounted. In the security industry I have observed the use of "war stories" in a management-level hiring interview and in industry conference hallway conversations. People in investigation or guard work trade stories of the risks they have survived, the serious crimes they have investigated, the big arrests they have made. Not only does this establish their personal credentials of courage, experience and so forth, but it is a way to drop names while telling a good tale. People in hardware talk more about technically challenging alarm problems or difficult working conditions, but also use stories to establish the kinds of people they have worked with and know. A narrative is a yarn, and a good yarn snugly interweaves many strands, including the narrator's network strands.

Once hired, how do workers actually use social capital to further their own careers and the fortunes of their firms? Though we have a growing body of evidence that good networks do make a difference for many high-level workers, there is relatively little work on how the difference gets made. Just what aspects of networks work, and just how do they do their work? A diverse network may be valuable because it includes ties to people with usefully varied resources, such as potential clients or information sources. This is the use most prominent in employer accounts, and the use most emphasized in this paper. But network variety can also be a proxy for network structure. If a worker knows people in many quite different social locations, these people will tend to be structurally separated from each other and linked only through the worker, giving him or her a strong brokerage position, or social capital in Burt's (1992, 1997a) sense. And some of the value of a diverse network lies not just in the ties themselves, but also in their useful byproducts. For example people with more varied networks have more varied cultural repertoires, which help them to build smoother working relationships with a wider variety of other people, including those at different levels in their own firm (Erickson 1996). We need some intensive fieldwork on how the many different useful aspects of a useful network get put into play as people work.

The more we think about just what social capital does, the more we will also refine our ideas about how to conceptualize and measure it. For example, in this paper I use a measure of the number of different social locations to which a person has any access at all. This is the most critical single question to ask; there is a world of difference between having some access and having none. But if social capital is used for (say) enriching the client base, then the amount of access also counts; a salesperson in an investigation firm specializing in insurance frauds will surely benefit from knowing an insurance broker, but would also benefit even more from knowing thirty brokers. Whatever the most useful form of social capital may be for a particular kind of job, how does the potential value of social capital get transformed into actual returns? Few studies include both evidence that some kinds of networks work, and the detailed ethnographic study to show how they work, as in Uzzi's (1996) analysis of the social capital of garment firms.

Further, how do the nature and workings of useful social capital vary among different kinds of jobs, and what kinds of "kinds" of jobs does such a question reveal? We know that any one kind of social capital has varying value, varying, for example, between industries (Geletkanycz & Hambrick 1997) and between different management jobs in the same firm (Burt 1997a). On the one hand we need to enrich our portrait of such variations and theorize the conditions for the relevance of different interpretations of social capital. On the other hand, this will lead us to novel kinds of job typologies including a job's social location in the web of working relationships inside and outside the firm. For this chapter I have used a broad contrast between jobs with and without strategically important kinds of external relational duties, but this is a mere beginning. Even in this study of one industry, we have seen some variation in the requirements for externally oriented jobs in terms of network structure (e.g., managers need the most network variety), the kinds of people that a network should reach, and in the content of external ties (e.g., whether focused on client needs or on gaining investigative information). Some good jobs are more internally than externally oriented, and for them the most relevant form of social capital must be strategic location within the firm's own networks rather than diverse ties to the outer world. Some jobs straddle the boundary between inside and outside in ways that require a strategic blend of internal and external ties, and some data hint that a double-strength network of internal and external ties may be the most profitable for a manager (Burt 1997).

The final process question to work on is the enormous question of order and causality. How do social capital, human capital, and other interrelated variables affect each other over time? Like any one-shot survey, the study reported here cannot really address these critical issues. For example, it is hard to tell whether security managers have better social capital because they were hired in part for their social capital or because they have made useful contacts as managers; probably both things are true to some unknown extent. It is also impossible to tell whether managers have better social capital than those who aspired to be managers but were not hired. We need longitudinal studies, including ones that follow a pool of potential workers through their work trajectories, to sort out vital questions of this kind.

Finally, how does the general role of human and social capital vary across labor markets? We already know that the details vary greatly. Labor markets vary in whether or not they reward some combination of education, experience, and networks, in the particular kinds of capital they reward, in hiring strategies, and in the mix of jobs available. But some things, I argue, will prove to be more general. The value of social capital in the sense of far-flung diversity will always depend on the extent to which a job is part of a firm's unofficial department of external affairs, and hence the extent to which a rich network of external ties is a hiring requirement. Since external affairs can be consequential for the firm, jobs that call for external social capital will tend to be good jobs, though there will also be other good jobs that call for a more internally oriented network. Thus given a definition of a "good" network that suits a particular industry, and remembering that some internally oriented good jobs do not require extensive external networks, good networks help people to get good jobs.

APPENDIX 1: THE 1991 CENSUS AND THE RESEARCH SAMPLE

	1991 Census of Canada	Toronto Sample
Male (%)		
Investigators	77	84
Guards	76	76
Part-time workers (%)		
Investigators	14	7
Guards	26	25
High school graduates (%)		
Investigators	81	82
Guards	66	88
Mean annual income		
Investigators	33,530	48,940
Guards	21,263	25,194

REFERENCES

Bills, David B. 1988. "Educational Credentials and Hiring Decisions: What Employers Look for in New Employees." *Research in Social Stratification and Mobility* 7:71–97.

———. 1992. "A Survey of Employer Surveys: What We Know about Labor Markets from Talking to Bosses." *Research in Social Stratification and Mobility* 11:3–31.

Bridges, William, and Wayne Villemez. 1986. "Informal Hiring and Income in the Labor Market." *American Sociological Review* 51:574–82.

Breiger, Ronald L. 1994. "Dual Aggregation on the Basis of Relational Homogeneity." Paper presented at the International Social Networks Conference, New Orleans, February 17–20, 1994.

Burt, Ronald S. 1997a. "The Contingent Value of Social Capital." *Administrative Science Quarterly* 42: 339–65.

———. 1997b. "A Note on Social Capital and Network Contents." *Social Networks* 19:355–73.

———. 1992. *Structural Holes.* Cambridge, MA: Harvard University Press.

Campbell, Gayle, and Bryan Reinhard. 1994. "Private Security and Public Policing in Canada." Canadian Centre for Justice Statistics Juristat Service Bulleting vol. 14 no. 10 (March 1994), pp. 1–19.

Erickson, Bonnie H. 1996. "Culture, Class, and Connections." *American Journal of Sociology* 102:217–51.

———. 2000. "Social Networks." In Judith R. Blau (ed.), *The Blackwell Companion to Sociology.*

Ganzeboom, Harry B., and Donald J. Treiman. 1996. "Internationally Comparable Measures of Occupational Status for the 1988 International Standard Classification of Occupations." *Social Science Research* 25:201–39.

Geletkanycz, Marta A., and Donald C. Hambrick. 1997. "The External Ties of Top Executives: Implications for Strategic Choice and Performance." *Administrative Science Quarterly* 42:654–81.

Granovetter, Mark. 1974. *Getting a Job: A Study of Contacts and Careers.* Chicago: University of Chicago Press.

———. 1995. *Getting a Job: A Study of Contacts and Careers. Second Edition.* Chicago: University of Chicago Press.

Hagan, John. 1992. "Class Fortification against Crime in Canada." *Canadian Review of Sociology and Anthropology* 29:126–39.

Lai, Gina, Nan Lin, and Shu-Yin Leung. 1998. "Network Resources, Contact Resources, and Status Attainment." *Social Networks* 20:159–78.

Lin, Nan. 1999. "Social Networks and Status Attainment." *Annual Review of Sociology* 25:467–87.

Lin, Nan, and Mary Dumin. 1986. "Access to Occupations Through Social Ties." *Social Networks* 8:365–85.

Marsden, Peter V. 1994a. "The Hiring Process: Recruitment Methods." *American Behavioral Scientist* 37:979–91.

———. 1994b. "Selection Methods in U. S. Establishments." *Acta Sociologica* 37:287–301.

Portes, Alejandro, and Patricia Landolt. 1996. "The Downside of Social Capital."
 The American Prospect 26:18–21.
Uzzi, Brian. 1996. "The Sources and Consequences of Embeddedness for the Eco-
 nomic Performance of Organizations: The Network Effect." *American Sociolog-
 ical Review* 61:674–98.
Wright, Eric Olin. 1985. *Classes.* London: Verso Editions.

7

Getting Started: The Influence of Social Capital on the Start of the Occupational Career

Henk Flap and Ed Boxman

Public opinion thinks highly of the usefulness of networks as a key to occupational success. "Networking" has become a verb, it is "the art of talking to as many people as you can without directly asking anyone for a job" (*New York Times* 1991). Yet the quote also echoes an official universalistic ideology that forbids the use of personal contact to get ahead.

At least since the fifties it has been widely accepted in the social sciences that many persons find a job through some kind of informal relationship (e.g., Lipset, Bendix, & Malm 1955), but the full implications were not immediately realized. Economic job-search theory gave the finding a theoretical meaning. Information is a good that can be bought at a price, the price of search. Since informal search saves on search costs compared to making use of formal channels, it contributes to job-finding (Stigler 1961, 1962). The original assumption that people are fully informed has been dropped, since that is too strong, at least in the labor market.

It is not so much the difficulty of locating each other, but of establishing the quality of an offer. Informal channels provide both: extensive information on many offers and intensive information on a particular offer (Rees 1966). But does networking work? Economists have not conducted much empirical research on the precise role of informal social relations in the job finding process (Devine & Kiefer 1991).

The discussion was given a new twist by sociologists, who conducted more detailed studies of the role of networks in the labor market. They replicated earlier findings on the importance of personal relations in the labor market. Many a person does indeed find his job through informal channels. In 1981, 34 percent of Dutch male employees had found their first job through informal channels, as 32 percent did for their last or current job, numbers that increased to 45 percent and 52 percent in 1991 (De Graaf & Flap 1988; Moerbeek, Flap, & Ultee 1995). About the same percentages are found for other western industrial societies (Granovetter 1974/1995:140). Granovetter (1974/1995), Lin, Vaughn, and Ensel (1981), and Burt (1992) used such findings to sociologize our view of the labor market by stressing the embeddedness of search and hiring in social networks. They claim that all markets are socially organized by particularistic ties.

This sociological research also showed that networks do not function as job-search theory predicts. For example, there is a sizable amount of research indicating that informal search does not always bring a better job. Furthermore, large networks do not always lead to more informal searching, nor does a larger network guarantee that people will find a better job (for reviews see Flap 1991 and Lin 1999).

The issue is to come to a better understanding of the effects of networks of personal relations on labor-market outcomes. To this end we add two types of theoretical assumptions to job-search theory. First, we specify the influence of personal relations on job search and labor-market outcomes, by conceiving of personal relationships and the resources they give access to as social capital that is instrumental in goal attainment, such as getting a job. We take into account the multidimensional character of the concept of social capital, and that receiving information or help incurs reciprocity costs. Second, we argue the major social condition that complicates the use of social networks in the job-search process will be the selection behavior of employers, or better, the conditions that induce them to search for in-depth information. Yet, existing research on networks and labor-market outcomes concentrates mainly on the supply side of the labor market.

To inquire more deeply into the job-finding process we used a kind of panel design. Although the size of our sample is not that large, the design is strong. Data were collected on the job-entry process of a group of young people who at time t_1 had almost finished their higher vocational training. At time t_2 the majority of them had entered occupational life. We created a multiactor data set by interviewing the employers of the organizations they started to work with and the possible contact person as well (cf. Parcel, Kaufman, & Jolly 1991).

THEORETICAL MODEL

We base our explanation of job search, selection behavior, and the outcome of their match on a loosely conceived rational-choice model that includes auxiliary assumptions on how the relative attractiveness of each action depends on the social conditions in which the prospective job candidate or employer finds himself. These auxiliary assumptions on the expected costs and benefits of alternative actions are based on the relevant research literature. We draw freely on a range of insights taken from job-search theory (e.g., McKenna 1985), status-attainment research (e.g., Ganzeboom, Treiman, & Ultee 1991) and new structuralism within stratification research (e.g., Farkas & England 1994), social-network research, and add a few assumptions of our own. We use this rational-choice sociological model to formulate hypotheses and to organize our argument. The auxiliary assumptions are tested indirectly by looking at the predicted outcomes.

The Employees

We start with the people who are searching for a job. For the sake of simplicity we assume that in searching they have but two alternatives: use either formal channels only or informal channels as well. We assume that the direct costs of an informal search are very low, so they are not taken into account. We also assume, however, that an informal search does bring reciprocity costs (Grieco 1987). By asking for help, an actor incurs debts to be repaid as future services.

The social capital idea helps to specify the influence of social relations while searching for a job. Social networks are social capital because they are instrumental in goal attainment, e.g., in getting a job. Social capital is the resultant of the size of the network, the structure of the network, the investments in network members, and the resources of these network members (Burt 1992, 2000; Flap 1999, 2001). Prospective job seekers will be more inclined to venture on an informal search if they have social capital. Earlier research (Lin et al. 1981; De Graaf & Flap 1988; Marsden & Hurlbert 1988) consistently shows that a contact person with a higher status improves one's chances of finding a better job. Social capital is also a characteristic of the structure of ego's personal network: if ego has exclusive relations with his alters (ego is in between his alters and they have no alternative relationships), they will be more prepared to provide information or other help. The stronger the relationship is and the more the exchange rate favors the focal actor, the lower the reciprocity costs that someone incurs by asking for help will be.

Several labor-market characteristics may be expected to influence the decision to engage in informal job search, such as, e.g., the degree of closure in the particular job market in which the person is trying to locate a job. If there are relatively many inside promotions within work organizations in that market, it will be difficult for an outsider to find a job other than through informal means. Moreover, a greater labor supply within the sector in which someone is looking will make it more difficult to make one's qualities visible. Mobilization of network members will draw attention from a larger circle of persons to one's qualities. A greater number of personal social contacts between people in different organizations within the sector market should also make it easier to find a job through informal search. Finally, if it is known that an employer recruits through informal channels, those who are looking for a job will adapt by looking through informal contacts because that enhances their chances of finding a job.

Function characteristics like the difficulty with which function requirements can be measured and the necessity of company-specific skills will make it difficult for a candidate to convince an employer of his capacities all on his own or by showing his diplomas. Without a sponsor it will be difficult establish confidence with an employer that the person has the capacities needed for the job.

The personal situation will affect the extent of informal job search in a number of ways. One could assume, e.g., that a younger person will value a job relatively higher, because he still has a whole working life in front of him. His lifetime income depends on having a good start in his working career. Being a man or a woman might also be a consideration that propels actors to opt for informal search. Although research on the effect of gender on work commitment is not equivocal (Bielby 1992), it is sometimes assumed that women value the worth of a job somewhat lower than males because they can also find satisfaction and social approval in being a good mother and a homemaker. A person's financial situation might influence the value of having a job, e.g., having a partner without a job and children who depend on ego's earning power for a living puts a greater value on having a job. The human capital people enjoy also might affect the value they place on a job. Those with more human capital value having a job somewhat higher because a job brings them relatively more income and other rewards. Finally, social skills will enlarge the chances of getting a job through informal search.

Employers

Sometimes an employer makes a distinction between two consecutive phases, recruitment and selection. We concentrate on the selection phase, as the number of candidates generally was not the issue in West European labor markets at the time we conducted our research. Not too much should be made of this distinction, however, because it is not that easy to separate the two in reality, and methods employed in both phases are rather similar, that is, informal ways of recruitment often entail informal ways of selection (Windolf & Wood 1988).

Employers who want to select a good candidate have but two alternatives: selecting candidates on formal criteria—e.g., on education only—or making an extra effort by collecting in-depth information on the candidate—e.g., on his capabilities and trustworthiness—through informal relationships or psychological tests. If employers are insecure about the quality of an offer, they look for proxies that signal quality, as is argued by signalling theory, a later development of search-costs theory (Spence 1974, Rosenbaum, Kariya, Settersten, & Maier 1990). Several social conditions are expected to influence the attractiveness for employers of in-depth search.

An employer with many contacts with other organizations, particularly with persons in positions similar to his own, will more readily employ these contacts to gather intensive information on potential job candidates. If an employer knows many people from associations and clubs he belongs to or visits, and if he has many friends, acquaintances, and family members in positions similar to his own, he also has better access to in-depth information on potential candidates.

For some functions firm-specific human capital is of major importance. Educational certificates do not provide the needed information. Furthermore, employers will place a higher value on finding a good candidate if the productivity of an employee in a particular function is hard to measure. Training costs are another relevant factor, but since we do not have a measurement of these costs, we cannot analyse their influence. A good candidate is of great importance to an employer in functions with career tracks, with a prospect of reaching higher senior positions. Such functions are scarce and it is important to employers that they be filled by persons with growth potential. In all these cases in-depth information would reduce the risk of a wrong hiring (Windolf & Wood 1988).

A condition of great importance is the damage potential of a wrong hiring—when an employee in a particular position can do a lot of harm to the organization. The potential for doing damage to the work organization (Jacobs 1981) is great if an employee (a) can make costly errors because, e.g., the production technology is not robust enough; (b) does not reveal his true qualities and after being hired, turns out to be not as adequate as initially thought, but is hard to fire; or (c) acts opportunistically and employs the company's resources for his own private goals at the peril of the company and the task he is being paid for. The latter two problems are known in principal-agent literature as hidden information and hidden action (Petersen 1995). An employer could also try to diminish the risk of damage by an incentive structure such that employees will "spontaneously" act according to his plans and wishes. An internal labor market with job ladders and payment schedules is such a device. Since we have but one straightforward indicator of internal labor markets, however, i.e., the proportion of internal promotions in work organizations within a particular sector market, we will only touch upon the issue.

Now we consider the influence of organizational characteristics. Existing research suggests that this influence will not be great. Firms usually use a mix of hiring methods that is to a large extent firm-specific, in the sense that each firm has certain methods it uses in hiring for all its vacancies (Marsden 1994a). Organizations differ in the way they have organized their personnel department. Especially in small firms, human-resources management is in the hands of one person only. If organizations grow, frequently specific persons are appointed to select and hire personnel, for policy making, job classification, or training and education. Organizations with a personnel department are often better able to search intensively, to ask for and check up on referrals or test candidates themselves (Marsden & Campbell 1990:64, Marsden & Gorman 1999:194). Larger organizations have more financial means and other overhead to conduct in-depth searches. One might also argue that large organizations can afford to select candidates that turn out not to be so good after all, because they have more alternative functions and others can compensate for a wrong hiring.

Moreover, if an organization has decentralized its work activities into separate divisions, the personnel tasks probably will be less formalized. Moreover, within the divisions the chances will be greater for employees to know each other. This increases the chances of someone being around who is able to provide an accurate assessment of a candidate from within or outside the organization. A central position within the network of organizations will also make it easier to acquire in-depth information through informal channels.

Furthermore, to the extent that an organization has formal rules on selection and hiring, it will be more costly to obtain in-depth information through informal channels. A similar argument can be made for the influence of positive-action regulations on behalf of minority groups or women (see Marsden 1994b:293). Selecting on the basis of in-depth information is easier for organizations that have personnel for a temporary period, e.g., as a trainee. The candidate shows his capacities and character in that initial phase.

If there is an ample supply of labor, employers will prefer to amass information through informal channels, though mainly to restrict the number of applicants.

The Match

Finally, the match: when do better social networks and informal search produce a better job? The returns on social capital in the job search process are conditional upon whether the employer needs intensive information on available candidates. The match (from the perspective of a job-searcher) will be better if (a) the person looking for a job has much social capital, particularly if he also has much human capital to make productive; (b) the person looking for a job not only has much social capital, but also puts his social capital into action—that is, if he mobilizes his network members; (c) the employer selects through in-depth information, particularly if the job searcher has much social capital; (d) the contact person has many resources, particularly if he was mobilized through informal search activities by the prospective employee; (e) the contact person puts in a good word for the job searcher, particularly if the contact person has many resources; and (f) the relationship of the contact person with the employer or employees in the organization where a person applies for a job is strong.

DESIGN, DATA, AND MEASUREMENTS

Design and Data

In order to probe the causal relationship between social networks and labor-market positions and test the implications of the above-mentioned hypotheses, a longitudinal study was conducted in which the social networks and job-search behavior of persons who were in the process of finishing their higher vocational training were measured. In addition, recruitment procedures and support of persons with whom job seekers had contacts were investigated.

Our two-wave panel study was started in May 1989. At the first moment of measurement (t_1: May 1989), the social networks of 365 persons (197 men [54 percent] and 168 women [46 percent]) who were about to finish their higher vocational training (economics, engineering, and teacher training for elementary education) were charted. The distribution with regard to the sex of the respondents is skewed. Among the respondents with technical training only 6 percent are female, while 80 percent of the respondents who had been educated as teachers are female. One year later (t_2: May 1990), 303 of them were reinterviewed about their labor-market participation, the type of the job they had obtained, and the role of their personal social networks in the job-finding process.

In June 1990 we also investigated the employers' recruitment methods by a mail survey. It concerned the employers the prospective employees worked for or had contact with before they took on their present job ($N = 139$). Furthermore, in September 1990 we studied the nature and purposes of help, including information supplied by contact persons ($N = 88$), again by a mail survey. Finally, in May 1991 experts on labor markets ($N = 14$), either working as a manager of a regional job center, as human resources manager of a large Dutch company, or as job recruiter for a commercial placement service, scaled 68 jobs that had been obtained by our respondents according to four job characteristics.

We decided upon this design because (a) it enabled us to examine both network characteristics and labor-market behavior of job seekers, employers, and contact persons in one project; (b) there was no problem as to how to decide on causal order (e.g., do contacts lead to jobs or jobs to contacts?); (c) the duration of schooling of the job seekers (as an indicator for human capital) was the same for all; (d) the job of entrance (first job) explains a large part of the variance, statistically spoken, in the position ultimately achieved, as is shown in existing research; (e) in contrast to most existing research, not only persons who succeed in getting a job were studied, but also those who did not find a job; (f) the population of job seekers was located in the same geographically circumscribed labor market (same moment of measurement, same region); (g) objections against retrospective questions, especially with regard to the measurement of network characteristics (Bernard et al. 1984), were less severe in this design.

The response rate for the interviews on t_1 was 78 percent and on t_2 83 percent (not interviewed on t_2 were those who did not finish their vocational training and persons who were not, for other reasons, available for the labor market). Both interviews lasted about one hour and a half.

We used three methods to identify the social capital of the respondents. First, we used the position generator developed by Lin and Dumin (1986), in which respondents were asked whether they knew persons in certain occupations, and if so, whether a person named was a friend, an acquaintance, or a relative. These (40) occupations reflect the whole range of the occupational prestige scale for the Netherlands (Sixma & Ultee 1984). This method provides an indicator of the socioeconomic prestige of someone's personal network. Second, we used Fischer's "name-generator" approach (McCallister & Fischer 1978), which starts with name-generating questions that produce names of network members. Several questions were posed about these persons to interpret the names. We obtained information on 2,150 network members. Third, the role approach was used to identify family members and ego's partner if present ($N = 1,009$ persons). For the network members who were identified through the last two approaches, we collected data on their personal characteristics, the nature of the tie with the respondent, and data on the interconnectedness of ego's personal network. In total, we were able to obtain information on 3,159 network members.

At t_2 we asked the respondents about their job search, whether they had found a job, qualities of the job, and if their network members helped them in searching. Also, we obtained the names of 338 employers from the respondents. They were asked to name the first employer to which they applied for a job without success, as well as the name of their present employer. These employers were sent questionnaires to find out about their recruitment and selection behavior (response rate 41 percent, $N = 139$). The questionnaire concerns 103 employers with whom the respondents succeeded in getting a job and 36 employers where the respondents applied for a job without success. Of course the sample of employers is selective in that only employers responded who were named by respondents with a higher vocational training in the field of economics, engineering, and teacher training for elementary education. Furthermore, there is an over-representation of employers who are directors of schools for elementary education. This lack of representativeness of the population is less important here, however, because our primary goal was to test our theoretical assumptions. Finally, in the second interview we also asked our subjects about their contact persons, who acted as a relay or go-between ($N = 125$). These contact persons received a short questionnaire. The response rate of the contact persons was 58 percent ($N = 88$).

Measurements

The key concepts that we used in the description and the testing of the models (see next section) were measured in the following ways:

Job Searchers. Informal search was measured by the frequency (average per month) and the length (average in minutes) of the conversations with other persons about vacancies from the time they left school to the time they succeeded (or did not succeed) in finding a job. We took the product of these (normalized) continuous variables—which thus is also a continuous variable—to be an indicator for the length of time an aspiring job searcher did search informally. Furthermore, the respondents were asked about their various formal and informal job-search channels and which of them they used over the last 10 months.

As noted, to characterize a respondent's social capital relevant for locating a good job, we used both a position- and a name-generator procedure. As to the latter, we asked our respondents (at t_1) to mention names of relevant alters in six name-generator questions, e.g., the names of persons they talked to about vacancies or personal problems. We collected information on six of these persons and on their parents, eldest brother and sister, and partner, if not already mentioned, on their occupation, education, and their relationship with the respondent. In all we had this information on 3159 network members, with a maximum of 11 network members per respondent.

If we want to take seriously the notion that social capital is a multidimensional concept, we also need a multidimensional measurement instrument (Flap 1999; Snijders 1999). We used to three measurements of social capital. The first is a combination of the number of persons prepared to help, the extent to which they are prepared to help, and their resources (De Graaf & Flap 1988). As indicators of the willingness of network members to provide support, we used four indicators: (a) the length of time (in years) the respondent and the network member were acquainted; (b) the frequency of contact with the network member; (c) the intensity of the contact; and (d) the frequency with which the respondent provided services to the network member. These four variables were approximately one-dimensional (Cronbach's alpha = .76). We therefore took the unweighted sum of the four variables as an indicator for the strength of the relation with the network member. Moreover, we took this to be an indicator of the extent to which he was prepared to help ego. Resources of network persons (alters) were estimated using the scores of the occupations of the network members on the Ultee and Sixma (1984) occupational prestige scale for the Netherlands, a scale ranging from 13.4 to 89.1. From our measures of the strength of ties and the resources available through the ties we define our measure of social capital as the product of (1) the strength of the tie and (2) the resources of alter, summed over all network members. With regard to the multiplication we transformed the scale values of our measurements of the strength of the tie and the resources of alter to values between 0 and 1.

The second measurement of social capital also includes the structure of ego's network, i.e., his or her structural autonomy in his/her own network. As stated above, we gathered extensive data, at t_1, on six persons mentioned in the "Fischer questions." Also, we asked the respondents whether or not these persons knew each other and to what extent. We got 365 ego-centered networks. Using "STRUCTURE" (Burt 1989), we computed the relative autonomy of a respondent within his network ("1 minus network constraint"). Our second measure of social capital is analogous to the first, with the difference that the strength of a tie is mediated by a person's autonomy.

We also employed Lin and Dumin's position generator which is another multidimensional measure for social capital that provides information on the three fundamental dimensions of social capital. Results were rather similar while using this measure in the analyses instead of the measure that is based on Fischer's way of generating names. Moreover, our measure of social capital that includes autonomy and that represents best social capital's multidimensional nature could only be constructed as an extension of our "Fischer" measure.

In the mail survey on the recruitment methods of employers they were asked to estimate the percentage of higher employees within their organization who got their job via an internal appointment. The closure of the sector markets distinguished was estimated as the percentage of internal appointments averaged over the employers within such a market. We distinguished 24 sectors in total: apart from agriculture there were 4 in manufacturing, 10 in the commercial-service industry, and 9 in other types of services, mainly government. If a prospective employee searched in more than one market, we took the average closure of these markets. In our sample of employers, some sectors were not represented, although some (11 percent) of our sample of employees had found a job in such a sector. For those employees we assumed them to be in a sector market with a closure that is the average for all sectors, that is 37 percent internal appointments.

The respondent's estimation of the number of competitors for a vacancy he aspires to is taken as an indicator of the labor supply within a sector. It is plausible that in choosing a search strategy a job searcher reckons with this perceived labor supply and not with the actual labor supply.

The extent to which there are social relationships between employers or organizations in a sector was estimated with information from the employers' survey. First we asked in how many organizations the employers knew particular persons who could be contacted for referrals on suitable candidates for a vacancy. Next they were asked if there were personal contacts between—a maximum of four of—the organizations mentioned. To construct an indicator of the number of contacts between organizations in a sector we limited ourselves to these four organizations. Thus an employer can have a maximum number of contacts with four organizations and a minimum of none. The four organizations can be interrelated by a maximum of six relations and a minimum of none. We computed the average number of relationships for all the employers within our sample who were within a labor-market sector and attached these scores to the sectors where the job seekers had searched. When they searched for a job in more than one sector, we again took the average value of these sectors.

Job characteristics such as damage potential, measurement of job requirements, company-specific skills, and career potential were measured in a small study among 14 specialists of labor markets, such as directors of labor exchanges and personnel managers. Sixty-eight different functions were found by the job searchers. The four characteristics of these 68 jobs were scaled on five-point scales by the 14 specialists. The reliability of the four scales is respectively 0.92, 0.86, 0.87, and 0.93 (Cronbach's alpha). A factor analysis of the four job characteristics resulted in two factors that together explain most of the variance in the data. Company-specific skills required, and measurability of job qualifications load high on the first factor (both 0.91), and damage potential and career perspective do so on the second factor (0.94 and 0.75). Using these factors in the analysis did not result in findings that are different from those reported in the next section.

Concerning the personal situation: the measurement of age and sex does not need further explication. The financial situation of a prospective employee was indicated by the fact whether the respondent had a partner with an income of his or her own. Although we know this is an imperfect indicator, we did not have further information on the financial situation, such as the exact size of the household.

Human capital, indicated by the number of years of training, was nearly the same for all of the respondents. Still, respondents differ in skills and intelligence. As an indicator for these differences we used the average grade with which the students finished their higher vocational training. Differences between types of education were taken into account only in one analysis, in which using dummies for technical education or other, and economic education or other. Furthermore, if a respondent had a job on the side while being a student, had experience on the board of a voluntary organization, or was a trainee, these were taken (in months) as indicators of human capital too.

To measure the respondent's social skills we used a scale based on two questions and three judgment questions answered by the interviewers. The scores on these questions met the criteria of a Mokken-scale (H = 0.45, rho = .79).

Employers. The extent to which the employers used additional methods to select candidates on the basis of in-depth information (a continuous variable) was indicated by four questions. The first question was: "When you recruit personnel, do you use a psychological test?" Thirty-three percent of the employers did sometimes use this method and 9 percent usually did. Concerning concrete vacancies, employers were asked whether they had used one or more of the following informal methods in the last twelve months: (1) ask candidates for names of persons who could give referrals; (2) ask referents for actual information on candidates; and (3) take into account information provided by referents. The dichotomized scores on these four items (yes, sometimes, and often = 1; never, and not applying to = 0) form a one-dimensional scale "selection on the basis of in-depth information" (Cronbach's alpha = 0.78; N = 103).

As an indicator of the size of the employer's personal network we added up his memberships in clubs and voluntary associations. His professional network was estimated by the number of work organizations in which the employer knew persons he could call upon for referrals on candidates. The size of the company was asked directly. As an indicator of the number of temporary contracts and trainees within the work organization we took the number of higher-vocational trainees the employers contracted in a year relative to the total work force of the organization. The extent to which personnel functions were differentiated within the organization was indicated by the size of its personnel department. Formalization of recruitment procedures was indicated by the presence of a policy on affirmative action for women. Centrality of personnel functions within an organization was approximated by whether the organization was part of a larger firm, the assumption being that there would be less centrality within an organization when it is separate. Centrality of the work organization within the network of organizations was measured with a question on the existence of personal ties between persons within other organizations whom the employer could call upon for referrals on job candidates. The maximum number of organizations that could be mentioned was four. Moreover, for our measure we selected only organizations that were in the same market sector as the employer's own organization. Analogous to the analysis of the networks of the job searchers we computed the centrality of the employer's organization. Finally, answers to the question how many persons on average apply for a vacancy for which higher vocational training is the norm were taken as an indicator for the supply of labor an employer can choose from.

Contact Persons.   Whether a contact person put in a good word or provided references was taken as an indicator for the sort of help given. The occupational prestige of the contact was indicated by the score on the Ultee and Sixma prestige scale. The strength of the tie between a contact person and the employer was indicated by whether the contact person was a friend or relative of the employer, or something else. All this information was based on answers provided by the prospective employees.

Outcomes.   Income was indicated by gross monthly income in Dutch guilders (fringe benefits not included). Occupational prestige is measured as the average prestige score of the occupations mentioned on the Ultee and Sixma prestige scale.

Since the number of missing values on variables was relatively low, the missing values were replaced in the analyses by the average score of the variables concerned. (Using list-wise deletion of missing cases did not greatly affect the results.)

ANALYSIS AND RESULTS

Job Searchers

In this section we test the explanatory model of job-search behavior. Three quarters of the respondents used one or more formal channels (between t_1 and t_2). A similar percentage (70 percent) did use informal channels. So, when the questions are asked directly, there is no real confirmation of our assumption that job searchers always use formal channels. But we are less wide of the mark when we examine the answers on another question: 92 percent of the respondents did read advertisements on vacancies between t_1 and t_2.

We tested the explanatory model of job-search behavior with a standard

Table 1. Results of Regression Analyses of Informal Job Search by Prospective Employees (*N* = 303)

Variable	M1 β	M2 β	M3 β
Aspects of social capital			
Social capital (version 1)	.24***		.24***
Social capital (version 2)		.24***	
Labor-market characteristics			
Closure of sector market	.18**	.19**	.18**
Number of applicants	.23***	.22***	.24***
Number of contacts within sector market	.13*	.12*	.14*
Selection on in-depth information	.13	.12	.15*
Job characteristics			
Measurement of job requirements	−.07	−.01	
Company-specific skills	.05	.05	
Personal situation			
Age	.03	.04	
Sex	.00	−.00	
Financial situation (partner with income)	−.05	−.02	
Human capital (grade)	.21***	.21***	.21***
Social skills	.07	.07	
R^2	.25	.25	.24
F-value	8.03***	8.11***	15.61***

*$p < .05$.
**$p < .01$.
***$p < .001$.

model: linear regression-analysis. Table 1 contains the estimations of three models. Models M1 and M2 predict the probability of searching informally with all variables that are implied by the theoretical model for job-search behavior. The models differ only in the measurement of social capital. Model 3 is obtained via a standard "forward" selection procedure. Results with a "backward" selection procedure are exactly the same.

The results of Table 1 lead to the following conclusions. Persons more often search informally when they possess more social capital. It does not make a difference whether we use the one or the other of our two measurements of social capital. So, also taking structural autonomy into account on top of the strength of the ties and the social resources of the alters does not affect the previous results. Employers' selection behavior influences the search behavior of the job seekers; selection on intensive behavior by the former does promote informal searching by the latter. There are no indications that the characteristics of functions influence the search behavior of job seekers. Even with functions from which we expect that employers will select and hire new persons very carefully—for example, jobs with relatively high company-specific skills and jobs for which it is difficult to establish whether a candidate meets the job requirements—we did not find that job searchers use informal contacts more often. Furthermore, the higher the closure of the sector market and the more applicants one has to compete with, the more informal job searching there is. The latter is also true if organizations within the sector market where someone is looking for a job are more connected via personal contacts.

There is only limited support for our hypotheses on the influence of a personal situation on the frequency of use of informal search. Contrary to the predictions, older people do not search more informally than younger ones. Men also do not search more informally than women, nor do persons with a partner with a paid job. Persons with more human capital do not search more informally. Finally, there is no confirmation for the idea that persons with many social skills will search more informally. There is, however, a statistically significant positive relationship between social skills and social capital of .13.

Employers

An OLS-regression analysis was performed to test the extent to which the effects of the choice of the employer on how to select job candidates turned out as predicted. The same was done for the choice of the prospective employee.

In the first model of Table 2 the probability of selection on the basis of in-depth information was predicted by all of the conditions included in the theoretical model, except the training costs of a function, for which we had no measurement instrument. Models M2 and M3 were obtained via standard sequential selection procedures, respectively backward and forward selection.

None of the network characteristics of the employers has an effect on the employer's selection behavior, as was predicted. Job characteristics, on the other hand, do have the expected effects. Agency problems resulting from the character of the jobs induce employers to use additional selection methods. Which of the four job characteristics considered is most important is hard to decide, because there is a strong correlation among these characteristics. Measurement of job requirements and necessary company-specific skills appear—not in the complete analysis of the model but in a bivariate analysis—to have an effect on informal methods of intensive selection.

Internal labor markets, as indicated by the extent of internal promotions, do not function as equivalents for intensive selection procedures. Note, however, that the sign of the effect is indeed negative as the hypoth-

Table 2. Results of Regression Analyses of Selection on the Basis of In-depth Information by Employers ($N = 103$)

Variable	M1 β	M2 β	M3 β
Characteristics of network and network members			
Number of contacts with colleague employers	.05		
Size of network (number of memberships)	.02		
Job characteristics			
Company-specific skills	.24	.20*	
Measurement of job requirements	−.08		
Damage potential	.28*	.27**	
Career potential	−.05		.34***
Organization characteristics			
Size	−.01		
Number of trainees	−.03		
Differentiation of personel functions	.34*	.36***	.24**
Formalization of selection procedures	−.19	−.18	
Centrality within organization	−.03		
Centrality within network of organizations	.07		
Labor-market characteristics			
Number of applicants	.22*	.21*	.21*
Closure of sector market	.05		
R^2	.37	.36	.31
F-value	3.74***	10.98***	14.86***

*$p < .05$.
**$p < .01$.
***$p < .001$.

esis would predict. Whether the recruiting organization is an establishment of a larger organization with multiple sites does not have an effect. Organizations with differentiated personnel functions do appear to use more intensive methods. There is, however, a strong relationship between the size of an organization and the presence of a separate personnel division ($r = .66$). Therefore, these characteristics, when both are included in the analysis simultaneously, do not have an independent effect, as predicted.

The Match

When will the match of the search and selection processes be optimal for a job searcher? Or put another way, under what conditions will a job searcher succeed in finding a job with a high income and high occupational status? In this section we analyze the predictions on the importance of the different conditions mentioned above.

When we combine the different job-finding methods into formal and informal channels, 125 (44 percent) of the 284 respondents found a job through an informal channel. With respect to this there are no significant differences between the types of higher vocational training the respondents received. Nor did we find a significant difference between men and women.

In order to test the assumed effects on income and occupational prestige of different ways in which a match could occur we used OLS-regression. Table 3 presents the results on the predicted effects of human capital, personal situation, informal aspects, and selection behavior of the employers, and of characteristics of functions, organizations, and labor markets on income and status. It shows, while adding the variables to the analysis step by step, that sex, social capital, and job characteristics do have a significant effect on income. Note that the effect of the employer's selection behavior does disappear when job characteristics are included in model I3 of the analysis. The positive effects of a technical or economic education on income also disappear as soon as job characteristics are included in the analysis.

With regard to the assumed effects on occupational prestige, effects of status of informal search do remain significant, also when job characteristics are added. Having a contact person of high prestige again is an asset with regard to the prestige attained. Putting in a good word does—instead of what was expected—have a perverse, negative effect on the prestige of the job attained, which effect is even amplified if the good word is passed by a high-prestige contact person (interaction terms were established by multiplying the z-scores of the variables in question). Selection on the basis of in-depth information does not have an independent effect on occupational prestige.

We do not interpret the separate effects of the four job characteristics (career perspective, company specific skills required, difficulty of measuring job qualifications, and damage potential) on income and status because these characteristics are highly intercorrelated. This means that they explain the same variation in the dependent variable. A strong effect of career perspective on income or status, for example, does not mean very much in itself because the effects of the other job characteristics are partly hidden in this effect and the other way round.

CONCLUSION AND DISCUSSION

Our study demonstrates that (1) it is important to take into account both employer and applicant characteristics in determining whether social capital will be used in the matching process; (2) returns of social capital vary with the kind of job; (3) the explanation for this variation lies on the em-

Table 3. Results of Regression Analyses on Employee's Income and Occupational Prestige of His Human Capital, Personal Situation, Search Behavior, Employer's Selection Behavior, and Characteristics of Functions, Organizations (N = 284)

Dependent Variable	Income			Occupational Prestige		
	I1 β	I2 β	I3 β	P1 β	P2 β	P3 β
Education/human capital						
Economic education	.47***	.40***	.12	-.00	-.06	-.27*
Technical education	.42***	.38***	.02	.12	.10	-.21
Grade	.08	.08	.08	.05	.07	.06
Number of months trainee	.04	-.00	-.04	.06	-.00	-.03
Sideline	-.05	-.02	-.02	-.06	-.03	-.02
Number of committee memberships	.04	.04	.03	.11	.12*	.12*
Personal situation						
Sex (man = 1)	.17**	.13*	.18**	-.00	.00	-.04
Occupational prestige father	.02	-.00	-.01	-.00	-.01	.01
Informal aspects/selection-behavior employer						
Social capital		.16**	.12*		.12	.08
Social capital × human capital		-.00	.02		-.10	-.05
Informal job search		-.12	-.11		-.00	.03
Informal search × social capital		.10	.07		.07	.07
Occupational prestige contact person		.06	.01		.20**	.14*

Good word contact person	−.13*	−.13*		−.06	−.07	
Informal search × prestige contact person	−.02	−.07		−.02	−.03	
Good word × prestige contact person	−.16**	−.14*		.03	.04	
References × prestige contact person	.14**	.13*		−.01	−.03	
Selection on in-depth info	.00	.05		.14	.16*	
Selection on in-depth info × informal search	−.04	−.05		−.05	−.09	
Contact's relationship with employer	.04	.07		.09	.12	
Characteristics functions/organizations/labor markets						
Damage potential	.09			.04		
Career perspective	.61***			.26*		
Measurement	.07			.10		
Company-specific skills	−.21			.22*		
Closure of sector market	−.11			−.11		
Number of applicants	−.08			−.08		
Number of contacts within sector market	.12			.09		
Size of organization	.04			.00		
R^2	.35	.17	.05	.47	.38	.31
F-value	4.90***	2.61***	1.69	8.14***	7.95***	15.70***

*$p < .05$.
**$p < .01$.
***$p < .001$.

177

ployer side of the employee-employer match, as the employer tries to minimize risk and damage potential and promote commitment to develop a career with the firm by hiring through informal channels; and (4) as a result of this two-way process it is not wise to expect that those applicants who use informal job processes would automatically be better off, e.g., get better jobs and incomes.

Although the design of our study was quite strong, it left some wishes unfulfilled. We mention two points. To start with, we neglected the possible self-selection by our prospective employees for specific jobs and job markets that might have biased our conclusions. We simply assumed that people with a certain type of education would search for jobs in which candidates with their qualifications are sought.

Furthermore, we do not have extensive information on incentive structures within organizations that could be used by employers to guarantee that employees fulfill contracts. Incentives, such as close supervision, efficiency wages, or a high-trust personal relation with the employer may reduce the need for in-depth information on candidates.

Our study also suggests a number of lines for research. The study concentrated on social capital in the first phase of someone's career. Other research deals with social capital in later job transitions (Lin 1999) and, lately, there also is a growing body of research on the effects of social capital on mobility within organizations (e.g., Podolny & Baron 1997; for a review see Burt 2000). It would be interesting to combine these literatures, especially in light of a number of findings. For example, the largest steps in someone's career are taken if a person leaves one organization for another, and not one job for another within the same organization (Blossfeld & Mayer 1988). Moreover, during one's occupational career one's network becomes less ascribed and more achieved, i.e., family relations become less important than work contacts and acquaintances (Moerbeek et al. 1995). Finally, later on in someone's occupational career—when an individual has built up a network and earned a certain degree of labor experience—the interaction between human and social capital seems to become more important (this study, and Boxman, De Graaf, & Flap 1991).

Furthermore, contact persons should be integrated explicitly into theory and research on networks and labor-market outcomes. Contact persons do not pass on information indiscriminately and without further thought to whoever they are in touch with; they see the provision of information or any other help as an investment, or as the payment of an outstanding debt (Grieco 1987:41–49). Moreover, they will be made accountable to a certain degree for the persons they referred to an employer and who were hired. Employers trust information about a candidate's dependable quality that is provided by referrals from their own sitting personnel (Fernandez & Weinberg 1997; Marsden & Gorman 1999). Weak ties work only if there is an acute labor shortage and in sectors where training is linked with formal credentials (cf. Völker & Flap 1999). Research is hampered by the difficulty of getting a complete data-set on triads of employees, possible contact persons, and employers. For example, although we did our best, because of nonresponse by one or two of the other parties, we succeeded in completing only 20 percent of the triads that were successfully mobilized by our sample of prospective employees.

A major implication of our study is that particularism is here to stay. Technological developments, growing division of labor, increasing team production, shorter product cycles, more autonomous jobs, less-formal hierarchy, and the like, force people to cooperate more with others. These processes create tighter couplings between different pieces of technology and employees which makes it harder to establish the quality of a person's performance as well as enlarging the damage potential of a wrong hiring. Our research suggests that present-day particularism in labor markets serves to facilitate information on the quality of available candidates, and not to do favors to a prospective employee or a third person. Putting in a good word was shown to be counterproductive in that one can get a job but not a good one. Particularistic ties are used to further the universalistic goal of finding the best job or candidate available.

NOTE

We gratefully acknowledge the contribution of Reinhard Wippler and Jeroen Weesie to our research, which was made possible by a grant of the Dutch Science Foundation to the first author.

REFERENCES

Bernard, H. R., P. D. Killworth, D. Kronenfeld, and L. Sailer. 1984. The problem of informant accuracy: The validity of retrospective data. *Annual Review of Anthropology* 13:495–517.

Bielby, D. D. 1992. Commitment to work and family. *Annual Review of Sociology* 18:281–302.

Blossfeld, H. P., and K. U. Mayer. 1988. Labour market segmentation in the Federal Republic of Germany: An empirical study of segmentation theories from a life course perspective. *European Sociological Review* 4:123–40.

Boxman, E. A. W., H. D. Flap, and P. M. De Graaf. 1991. The impact of social and human capital on the income attainment of Dutch managers. *Social Networks* 13:51–73.

Burt, R. S. 1989. *Structure, Version 4.1.* New York: Center for the Social Sciences. Columbia University Press.

————. 1992. *Structural Holes. The Social Structure of Competition.* Cambridge: Harvard University Press.

————. 2000. The network structure of social capital. In B. M. Staw and Sutton, eds., *Research in Organizational Behavior* 20 (forthcoming).

De Graaf, N. D., and H. D. Flap. 1988. "With a little help from my friends." Social resources as an explanation of occupational status and income in the Netherlands, the United States and West Germany. *Social Forces* 67:453–72.

Devine, T. J., and N. M. Kiefer. 1991. *Empirical Labor Economics. The Search Approach.* New York: Oxford University Press.

Farkas, G., and P. England. 1994 (first ed. 1988). *Industries, Firms, and Jobs. Sociological and Economic Approaches.* New York: Plenum Press.

Fernandez, R. M., and N. Weinberg. 1997. Sifting and sorting: personal contacts and hiring in a retail bank. *American Sociological Review* 62:883–902.

Flap, H. D. 1991. Social capital in the reproduction of inequality, a review. *Comparative Sociology of Family, Health and Education* 20:6179–6202.

————. 1999. Creation and returns of social capital. *La Revue Tocqueville* 20:5–26.

————. 2001. No man is an island. Forthcoming in E. Lazega and O. Favereau, eds., *Markets and Organizations.* Oxford: Oxford University Press.

Ganzeboom, H. B. G., D J. Treiman, and W. C. Ultee. 1991. Comparative intergenerational stratification research: Three generations and beyond. *Annual Review of Sociology* 17:277–302.

Granovetter, M. S. 1974/1995 (2nd ed.). *Getting a Job.* Cambridge: Harvard University Press.

Grieco, M. 1987. *Keeping it in the Family: Social Networks and Employment Chance.* London: Tavistock.

Jacobs, D. 1981. Toward a theory of mobility and behavior in organizations. *American Journal of Sociology* 87:684–707.

Lin, N. 1999. Social networks and status attainment. *Annual Review of Sociology* 25:467–87.

Lin, N., and M. Dumin. 1986. Access to occupations through social ties. *Social Networks* 8:365–85.

Lin, N., J. C. Vaughn, and W. M. Ensel. 1981. Social resources and occupational status attainment. *Social Forces* 59:1163–81.

Lipset, S. M., R. Bendix, and T. Malm. 1955. Job plans and entry into the labor market. *Social Forces* 33:224–32.

Marsden, P. V. 1994a. The hiring process. Recruitment methods. *American Behavioral Scientist* 37:979–91.

————. 1994b. Selection methods in U.S. establishments. *Acta Sociologica* 37:287–301.

Marsden, P. V., and K. E. Campbell. 1990. Recruitment and selection processes: the organizational side to job searches. Pp. 59–79 in R. Breiger, ed., *Social Mobility and Social Structure.* Cambridge: Cambridge University Press.

Marsden, P. V., and J. S. Hurlbert. 1988. Social resources and mobility outcomes. *Social Forces* 66:1038–1959.

Marsden, P. V. and E. H. Gorman. 1999. Social capital in internal staffing practices. Pp. 180–1996 in R. Th. A. J. Leenders & S. M. Gabbay, eds., *Corporate Social Capital and Liability.* Boston: Kluwer

McCallister, L., and C. S. Fischer. 1978. A procedure for surveying personal networks. *Sociological Methods & Research* 7:131–48.

McKenna, C. J. 1985. *Uncertainty and the Labor Market: Recent Developments in the Job-Search Theory.* Brighton, Wheatsheaf Books

Moerbeek, H., H. Flap, and W. Ultee. 1995. "That's what friends are for." Ascribed and achieved social capital in the occupational career. Paper presented at the European Social Network Conference, July 6–10, London.

Parcel, T. L., R. L. Kaufman and L. Jolly. 1991. Going up the ladder: Multiplicity sampling to create linked macro-to-micro organizational samples. *Sociological Methodology* 2:43–79.

Petersen, T. 1995. The principal-agent relationship in organizations. Pp. 187–212 in P. Foss, ed., *Economic Approaches to Organizations and Institutions.* Dartmouth: Dartmouth Publishing Company.

Podolny, J. M., and J. N. Baron. 1997. Resources and relationships: social networks and mobility in the workplace. *American Sociological Review* 62:673–93.

Rees, A. 1966. Labor economics: Effects of more knowledge, information networks in labor markets. *American Economic Review* 56:559–66.

Rosenbaum, J. E., T. Kariya, R. Settersten, and T. Maier. 1990. Market and network theories of the transitions from high school to work: Their application to industrialized societies. *Annual Review in Sociology* 16:263–99.

Sixma, H., and W. C. Ultee. 1984. An occupational prestige scale for the Netherlands in the eighties. Pp. 29–39 in B. F. M. Bakker, J. Dronkers, and H. B. G. Ganzeboom, eds., *Social Stratification and Mobility in the Netherlands.* Amsterdam: Siswo.

Snijders, T. A. B. 1999. Prologue to the measurement of social capital. *La Revue Tocqueville* 20:27–44.

Spence, A. M. 1974. *Market Signalling: Informational Transfer in Hiring and Related Screening Processes.* Cambridge: Harvard University Press.

Stigler, G. J. 1961. The economics of information. *Journal of Political Economy* 69:213–25.

———. 1962. Information in the labor market. *Journal of Political Economy* 70:94–105.

Völker, B., and H. Flap. 1999. Getting ahead in the GDR. *Acta Sociologica* 37:17–34.

Windolf, P., and S. Wood. 1988. *Recruitment and selection in the labour market: a comparative study of Britain and West Germany.* Avebury: Aldershot.

Part III

Social Capital in Organizational, Community, and Institutional Settings

8

Social Capital as Social Mechanisms and Collective Assets: The Example of Status Auctions among Colleagues

Emmanuel Lazega and Philippa E. Pattison

This chapter describes the way in which the intersection of networks can be a social and informal mechanism that contributes to organizational governance. Specifically, it is about a mechanism that helps the organization deal with potentially negative effects of status competition between members. We identify our main contribution as twofold. First, status competition is examined as an "unbounded" status auction process. Sutton and Hargadon (1996) provided rich descriptions of "bounded" or "segregated"[1] status auctions in design firms; the status auction they describe is confined to the brainstorming room and designated brainstorming sessions. Here, we look at "unbounded" and diffuse status auction in which status displays and challenges occur throughout the organization. When status auctions cannot be confined or segregated from day-to-day operations, they need to be governed in some other way. We report how intersecting kinds of relationships serve that end. In other words, we describe how a specific kind of multiplexity in members' networks provides the social mechanism that helps to deal with the potentially negative effects of such auctions. Second, we use a specific data analysis method that is important to reconstitute this informal governance mechanism, especially because it helps to analyze the substructures of multiplex ties between members on which this mechanism is based.

In organized settings, participation in collective action—for example, team production, regulatory activity, or enforcement of previous agreements—requires cooperation with others, expressed through routine transfers or exchanges of various kinds of resources (Crozier & Friedberg 1977). These resources include information, coworkers' goodwill, advice, sometimes emotional support, and many other means that serve individual and collective ends. From a structural perspective, this means that specific local (uniplex or multiplex) substructures of social ties must be organized so that members can cooperate and exchange on an ongoing basis in the context of wider collective actors such as organizations.

These various kinds of resources and social ties have often been seen as constituting individual social capital for individual attainment. In this chapter, we do not focus on measuring the relative contribution of such social ties (and their structure) to maximization of individual performance in competitive arenas (Burt 1992). We are instead largely concerned with how members manage their social resources in order to fulfill their commitment to a broadly understood labor contract. This requires an understanding of the concept of social capital as a *collective asset*, encompassing any social mechanism that can characterize and help a corporate actor solve governance problems.

Citing Stinchcombe (1991:367), Hedstrom and Swedberg (1998) provide the following definition of a social mechanism: "Mechanisms in a theory are defined as bits of theory about entities at a different level (e.g., individuals) than the main entities being theorized about (e.g., groups), which help to make the higher-level theory more supple, more accurate, or more general." A social mechanism is thus intrinsically multilevel. Following this definition, we also believe that, like in the now well-established network approach to social capital, such mechanisms can be observed only through an analysis of social networks of members' ties within organizations. Recurring structural and substructural patterns of uniplex or multiplex ties are assumed to be beneficial to collective action because they solve problems of coordination, as well as problems of individual action (for instance, by reducing individual transaction costs or improving chances of getting ahead).

Here we identify one such governance mechanism in a collegial, "knowledge-intensive" organization (Lazega 1992b forthcoming; Starbuck 1992; Waters 1989). We describe a "locally multiplex" exchange system, with a specific pattern of *multiplex* ties among members, which suggests the presence of this mechanism that helps members both to encourage status auctions and keep them under control. In other words, it both cultivates and mitigates status competition among colleagues working together, thus solving a "too many cooks" problem. Technically, this notion of exchange pattern refers to dyadic, triadic, and higher-level substructures that reveal the social mechanism based on collective management of multiple resources.

Using a case study, a network study of a corporate law fir..
how three important production-related resources (co-workers ,
advice, and friendship) are transferred and exchanged by member.
cifically, we analyze the interlocking of ties among members and defi.
limited number of expected interdependencies among such ties. We argue
that regularities in these substructures contribute to the social capital of the
firm by creating typical transfers and exchanges and, as such, provide a
structural answer to the problem of their participation in collective action.
These regularities constitute a social mechanism that serves to control professional status auctions.

In order to appreciate the role of these substructures in the governance
mechanism, it is helpful to understand the work process typical of professional members in this organization, as well as the resources that interdependent individuals need to carry it out (Crozier & Friedberg 1977).
The firm is decomposed into small, flexible, and heterogeneous task
forces (Lazega 1992a) that must be able to cooperate quickly and effi-
ciently in order to react to complex nonstandardized problems. In this context, such temporary task forces composed of partners and associates (at
least one of each) are multifunctional and sometimes multidisciplinary
(litigation, corporate). The importance of cooperation in these task forces
to effective individual participation is evident from the fact that individual economic performance is positively and significantly associated with
task-force membership and constraint (Lazega 1999b). A specific aspect
of cooperation in such a collegial firm is that knowledge-intensive work
is inextricably mixed with status games (Bourricaud 1961). This type of
work in teams of partners and associates is very "deliberative": it encourages status competition in status auctions (Sutton & Hargadon 1996).
But at some point, there is a need for someone, usually the partner in
charge, to step in and stop the deliberation. This intervention of hierarchical authority can be damaging among professionals. There is also a
need for other members to help mitigate the negative effects of this intervention.

This picture of case-driven task forces thus illustrates why and how a
structural approach to cooperation should examine transfers and exchanges of resources central to the functioning of such groups. Here, p^*
models (Frank & Strauss 1986; Pattison & Wasserman 1999; Wasserman &
Pattison 1996; Robins, Pattison, & Wasserman 1999) are used to bring out
this mechanism by analyzing the interplay between the three social resources shaping cooperation among these professionals. After describing
the case study in more detail, we briefly describe the model, and then identify the specific local and multiplex exchange substructures that contribute
to the organization of this cooperation.

BRAINSTORMS AND STATUS AUCTIONS IN
A CORPORATE LAW FIRM

The case study used to establish this approach and describe the kind of relationships minimally involved in this type of cooperation among lawyers can be pictured by a short description of this organization and its functioning. The fieldwork was conducted in 1991 in a Northeastern corporate law firm, which will be called Spencer, Grace & Robbins (SG&R). The firm comprised 71 lawyers in three offices located in three different cities, and included 36 partners and 35 associates. All the lawyers in the firm were interviewed. In Nelson's (1988) terminology, this firm is a "traditional" one, without formally defined departments, as opposed to a more "bureaucratic" type. Interdependence among attorneys working together on a file may be strong for a few weeks, and then weak for months. As a client-oriented, knowledge-intensive organization, it tries to protect its human capital and social resources, such as its network of clients, through the usual policies of commingling partners' assets (clients, experience, innovations; see Gilson & Mnookin 1985) and by the maintenance of an ideology of collegiality. Informal networks of collaboration, advice, and "friendship" (socializing outside work) are key to the integration of the firm (Lazega 1992a).

It is a relatively decentralized organization, which grew out of a merger, but it has no formal and acknowledged distinctions between profit centers. Although not departmentalized, the firm breaks down into two general areas of practice: litigation (half the lawyers of the firm); and "corporate" (anything other than litigation). Sharing work and cross-selling among partners is done mostly on an informal basis. Given the classical stratification of such firms, work is supposed to be channeled to associates through specific partners, but this rule is only partly respected.

A weak administration provides information, but does not have many formal rules to enforce. The firm has an executive committee comprising a managing partner and two deputy managing partners; the executive is elected each year, renewable once, and is selected from partners who are prepared to perform administrative tasks and temporarily transfer some of their clients to other partners. This structure was adopted during the 1980s for more efficient day-to-day management and decision making. The current managing partner is not a "rainmaker" and does not concentrate strong powers in his hands. He is a day-to-day manager who makes recommendations to functional standing committees (finance, associate, marketing, recruitment, etc.) and to the partnership.

Partners' compensation is based exclusively on a seniority lockstep system without any direct link between contribution and returns. The firm goes to great lengths when selecting associates to become partners to take as few risks as possible and avoid selecting partners who will not "pull their weight." Partners may argue informally about what contribution might "fairly" match one's benefits, but the seniority system mechanically distributes the benefits to each once a year. Great managerial resources are devoted to measurement of each partner's performance (time sheets, billing, collecting, expenses, etc.), and this information is available to the whole partnership. A low performance cannot be hidden for long. Such firms usually make considerable profits, however, and this may help partners overlook the fact that some voluntary contributions to shared benefits may not always be consistent with the successful pursuit of narrow self-interest.

The firm does not have a formal peer review system which could provide an intermediate step between lateral control and formal court procedures. Before expulsion, partners have the power to "punish" each other seriously by preventing a partner from reaching the next seniority level in the compensation system. As mentioned above, a partner can be expelled only if there is near-unanimity against him/her. Buying out a partner is very difficult and costly. Therefore, despite the existence of direct financial controls, the firm does not have many formal ways of dealing with freeloading. The harm that a single partner can inflict on others might become very substantial in the long run. Conversely, partners can try to isolate one of their own informally by, at the very least, not referring clients, not "lending" associates, or not providing information and advice.

In this context, and as mentioned earlier, temporary partner-associate task forces constitute the core of multifunctional and sometimes multidisciplinary (litigation, corporate) teams. Activity is conducted in such temporary teams in which partners keep their autonomy in their negotiation of means and ends, and in which associates are often expected to brainstorm with higher-status members. This creates what Sutton and Hargadon (1996) call *status auctions*, as well as a pseudomarket for strong cooperation between members with similar and different hierarchical statuses. When deliberating about a case, associates and partners often play a temporarily collegial and egalitarian game in which all arguments have equal weight. At some point, however, partners' greater experience, greater skill and judgment, or responsibility to the client, becomes grounds for justifying stopping these exchanges and making a decision about how the case will be handled and how efforts will be allocated. This is often perceived to be autocratic behavior by partners imposing idiosyncratic standards of proper practice on frustrated associates, but the latter rarely say so. They hope to advance to the top of the associate pyramid and to make it to partnership. To partners, having the final word with associates seems an obvious duty as a service provider or as a professional educator. Differences among partners, however, can either be treated as differences in style or can trigger advice seeking outside the temporary task force; partners whose advice is sought are usually more senior (Lazega 1995; Lazega & Van Duijn 1997).

CULTIVATING AND MITIGATING STATUS COMPETITION

This form of status competition (among associates, between partners and associates, and among partners) is an efficient mechanism for motivating professionals at work. If receiving social approval from peers is one of Weberian value-oriented actors' goals, allocation of this approval through honors and recognition—along with the privileges of rank in the pecking order—is indeed a powerful motivation device. Status competition, however, can also get out of hand. Status can be endlessly challenged, especially on behalf of different conceptions of professionalism. In this firm, status games and conflicts can become personalized by partners puffing themselves up, thus creating a "too many cooks" problem. They can subsequently have negative or destructive effects on learning and the circulation of knowledge and experience (Lazega 1992b, 1995; Lazer & Katz, 2000). Of course, there are always moral exhortations to preserve consensus among peers, but these can remain artificial and rhetorical. Stimulating competition can easily get in the way of cooperation, and professionals know that they can lose control of this process. Status competition is thus a double-edged sword; it is both encouraged and contained.

Status competition creates management problems for professional organizations and firms, because it is always in danger of unraveling (Olson 1965). Economic approaches to labor markets (Frank 1985) assert that incentives such as specific compensation systems take care of the negative effects of status differences. Thus, low performers and low-status members tend to be overcompensated relative to the value they produce, whereas high performers and high-status members tend to be undercompensated relative to the value they produce: they pay a price for being recognized as high-status members. The firm's lockstep system can therefore be considered as a mitigation device for status competition among partners. A large majority of partners supports it because they believe it prevents yearly conflicts among themselves, especially about each member's value to the firm.

Since compensation in this firm is tied to seniority, and since each member's rank in the seniority scale is defined once and for all, status competition loses one of its most dangerous stakes: money. But it is thus refocused on other issues at stake, such as professional reputation and authority in workgroups. For example, partners can put down associates through associate reviews, which can also be considered humbling rituals, illustrating to associates that there are acceptable limits to challenges to partner status in the work process (Bosk 1979; Nelson 1988; Lazega 1993). The effects of these humbling rituals are softened by comparisons to other associates or by other members who indicate that they would have behaved or handled the case in another way. They nevertheless "underscore the status differences among their ranks" (Bosk 1979:143).

If knowledge-intensive work is inextricably mixed with status games, collegial organizations find themselves in a bind. Status auctions are double-edged. They can be destructive as well as constructive. Collegial firms, therefore, need both to cultivate and mitigate status competition among their professionals. Following Lazega and Van Duijn (1997; Van Duijn 1995; Van Duijn & Snijders 1995), where we were able to verify that status games are sometimes mitigated by friendship ties, we hypothesize that in such a situation, one would expect a social mechanism both to structure the "deliberative" work process and help mitigate such status-competition games. In the next section, we look at the social capital of this firm as a pattern of social ties and provide more specific and testable hypotheses regarding its functional dimension. Specifically, an analysis of the interlocking of ties among members is shown to provide a structural answer to this structural problem.

TOO MANY COOKS? HYPOTHESES ON A TWO-STEP MITIGATION MECHANISM

This picture of case-driven legal task forces suggests that a structural approach to participation in collective action should examine transfers and exchanges of resources central to the functioning of such workgroups and firms, including resources involved in the mitigation of status competition. This statement is consistent with previous literature on cooperation and exchange of various kinds of resources (Bearman 1997; Breiger & Ennis 1997; Burt 1982; Cook 1987, 1990; Coleman 1990; Crozier & Friedberg 1977; Ekeh 1974; Flap, Bulder, & Völker 1998; Galaskiewicz & Marsden 1978; Gouldner 1960; Han & Breiger 1999; Lazega 1994, 1999a; Lazega & Pattison 1999; Lin 1995; Lindenberg 1997; Levi-Strauss 1949). Here, we consider three types of such resources: co-workers' goodwill, advice, and "friendship." As in any organization, there is an unequal distribution of such resources among the members of this firm. Nevertheless, we contend that the interlocking of these resources is structured in such a way that it creates a mechanism for mitigating status competition. The structures can be construed as corporate social capital, contributing to the shaping of cooperation.

Co-workers' Goodwill, Advice, and "Friendship"

The first type of resource is co-workers' commitment to work, or goodwill related to cooperation. In view of the flexibility needed to accommodate clients' needs, given the size and complexity of some files, a good and committed co-worker is an important resource for individual attorneys. As mentioned above, formal structure imposes constraints on the work process. In general, a file (or case) is handled by two lawyers at least, one partner and one associate. Interdependence among attorneys working together on a file may be strong for a few weeks, and then weak for months. Access to work opportunities depends on intake and assignment policies, on which partners rely to try to prevent possible (ethical and business) conflicts among themselves.

Following the philosophy of apprenticeship in the legal profession, partners analyze and decompose a complex problem into several parts, and attribute to each associate working with them and observing this exercise a small part of the tasks they perform (Nelson 1988). Forced cooperation is nevertheless routine for many partners and most associates, but members also give themselves room to maneuver and be strategic in their choices of co-workers. In this structure, partners and associates need one another. In particular, partners may depend on each other for many reasons. They may have the same clients, represent large and complex files. The form of cooperation is thus dictated by the requirements of the market. In addition, one well-known way of keeping a client is to cross-sell services that can be provided by partners of different specialties. Thus, a client who initially needs advice for a specific problem, say buying a shopping mall, will also be offered tax and litigation services by the firm. This increases revenues and helps establish a relationship with the client. Sharing work and cross-selling among partners is done mostly on an informal basis, although less so among lawyers in general when including associates.

Under such organizational and professional rules, members of the firm have two preoccupations: finding interesting work; and getting cooperation from colleagues to carry it out, especially colleagues who are interested in a long term relationship, *and not in taking advantage of them.* Most members want shared work with reasonable people who pull their weight and do not grab all the credit for themselves, especially in successful cases. Thus, individual members' first preoccupation is with building strong, secure, and durable work relationships with others: partners want other well-connected partners and reliable associates; associates want rewarding partners. Strong work ties are a sort of insurance policy. They extend the horizon beyond short-term security.

The second type of resource is advice. SG&R organizes work among experts who often refer to abstract legal knowledge. The nature of knowledge-intensive work requires accumulation, transfer, and exchange of knowledge and experience. In this context, transfer and exchange of advice among members can be seen as vital, indeed as one of the main reasons for the existence of such knowledge-intensive firms. Members rely constantly on advice from others. Advice can be seen as a product of goodwill, but it is also different from goodwill in the sense that it can be provided by someone who is not a strong co-worker. In law firms of this type, advice is not billed to the advice-seeker. It does not show in lawyers' time sheets or in firm accounts. Advisors cannot claim credit in successful cases. Lawyers who are not assigned to a case may advise, but if they want to claim their share of the credit they would have to become official co-workers on the case. This is accepted only beyond a certain contribution and negotiated with the lawyers already in charge. It is difficult to predict unilaterally when providing advice may become collaboration. To seek advice in such a context of business, career, and symbolic competition is therefore sometimes a delicate operation. In a law firm that structures itself so as to protect and develop its human and social capital (Wilensky 1967; Smigel 1969; Gilson & Mnookin 1985; Nelson 1988), such a resource is particularly vital to individual members. Members see expertise as accumulated by the firm, and they rely constantly on advice from others. Without it, they cannot solve the usually complex legal problems that they handle (Lazega 1995). In sum, members sought out for advice can be considered to be members with high status (Blau 1964).

The third type of resource is friendship, or "role distance," a form of open-ended support that is not related to the tasks themselves. Rather it is a form of "backstage resource," to use Goffman's (1961) idea of a place where actors retreat to create some distance between themselves and their role.[2] We call this support "friendship," and understand it, in a nonromantic way, as a willingness to help in a difficult situation by providing different types of resources, such as socialization, emotional support, information, and a definition of the situation. A friend is considered as a potential source of many resources, for example, help in asserting or negotiating one's status, in carving out a place for oneself in the group. The importance of this definition of friendship is that it does not assume reciprocity and is not directly connected to the work process itself. Lawyers say that in law firms, such ties tend to be forged among associates of the same class or between associates who went together to the same law school, and last throughout their career.

It might be surprising that friendship ties are proposed as a third type of resource to be considered systematically in a competitive corporate environment. When speaking about the firm in general, many members perceive that there are not many bases other than business for building ties with others. This underlies discourse about the firm as an "almost exclusively" economic unit.[3] Friendship ties are not needed to drive the work process itself. Even if general discourse on present day collegiality often stresses the contrast between a business-oriented firm and an idealized collegial past, however, members do mix professional and social ties with some selected colleagues in the firm. The partners quoted here speak more of a general atmosphere, not of the existence of selected friendships and personalized relationships in the firm.[4] In general, they consider that, among business heads, sympathizing hearts also mean interference. Therefore, they tend to keep associates at arms' length, and friendship ties with most other partners are often uneasy. But the select few can help accept negative outcomes of status comparisons, and help deal with potential threats.[5]

A Two-Step Social Mechanism

Recall that in this firm, members work in temporary and flexible task forces, at least one partner and one associate form each team. The task force must deal with complicated and novel legal problems for corporate clients. Work is very intense, and interdependence among the members of the task force is very strong while the case is open. Then the team is dissolved, and the members form different task forces with other people to work on other cases. The partners are always in charge, but it is important to keep in mind that this kind of teamwork often requires that associates brainstorm with higher-status members in order to find innovative solutions to complicated legal problems. The interesting aspect of the work is that associates and partners often play a temporarily "collegial" and egalitarian game in which all arguments have equal weight. A form of professional status competition is deliberately used here to stimulate creativity because it is recognized as a powerful motivation device among professionals. Members seek some form of consensus about their strategy, but there is not always consensus and, at some point, partners stop this deliberation and make a decision about how the case will be handled, "the strategy," and how the efforts will be allocated. Stopping these deliberations without consensus is, however, tricky. Status competition is stimulating, but it can have negative effects. Associates are frustrated, even if they do not say so, and they may withdraw. Other partners, who are all formally equal, may either just grumble and defer to the partner in charge, or decide that there is a need to seek advice from more experienced or more senior partners outside the temporary task force. We understand that members resort to a third party, to an outside authority, as the first step in the mechanism of mitigation of status competition—the mechanism that is part of this firm's social capital. This use of third parties is similar to that of Coleman, Katz, and Menzel's physicians who, in a situation of uncertainty, turned to higher-status and authoritative colleagues for more information. This first step is already multiplex: members with work ties turn to someone with whom they have an advice tie. Therefore, if such a mechanism works in this firm, then work ties should be strongly interlocked with advice ties.

The second step in this mitigation process is due to the fact that, in a collegial and rather flat organization, members of the task force can easily turn to several different third parties for advice. In that case, without another step in the mechanism, the problems raised by status competition would simply be transferred to partners of higher status, with the danger of a domino effect. Therefore we argue that the second step of the mechanism consists in bringing in either only one advisor, or different advisors that are themselves connected by a third type of tie, a friendship tie as defined above. Why would status competition be tamed when advisors have a role distance tie with one another? Recall that in the second step of the mechanism, the two advisors are not involved in the case. They are usually higher-status partners in the first place (because one does not seek advice from people "below"), and it is easier for them to deal with status competition among themselves, to defer to one another so as not to jeopardize their valuable friendship ties. It is often said that higher-status members are under more pressure to be consensus-oriented than lower-status members. If this is an acceptable assumption, then advice ties and role distance ties should be strongly interlocked in this system. And in addition, if indeed this mechanism has two steps, then it should also be the case that work ties and role-distance ties are not strongly and directly interlocked. Work is work: among business heads, role-distance ties can mean interference, and many keep their colleagues at arm's length, particularly if they are of different status.

To summarize, with regard to the interlocking of the different types of resources, we can derive the following hypotheses from our previous argument. To structure the work process, interdependence between co-workers' ties and advice ties is expected to be strong in this exchange system. Specifically, members tend to mix work and advice ties so as to bring in status to control the deliberation process. In addition, to mitigate status competition, interdependence between advice ties and friendship ties is expected to be strong in this exchange system. In other words, members tend to mix advice and friendship ties so as to soften the potentially negative effects of status competition.

Finally, given that partners can always have the upper hand over associates in the same task force, and that partners in the same team seek out other, usually more senior, partners outside the task force to sort out status competition among themselves, we can also think that interdependence between co-workers' ties (often mixing partners and associates) and friendship ties is relatively unlikely: interdependence between strong co-workers' ties and friendship ties will be weak overall. In other words, members tend, in general, to sort their ties so as not to mix work and friendship directly. These expectations are evaluated using the p^* class of multivariate random graph models (Frank & Strauss 1986; Pattison & Wasserman 1999; Robins, Pattison, & Wasserman, 1999; Strauss & Ikeda 1990; Wasserman & Pattison 1996).

DATA AND ANALYSES

Based on this organizational analysis of resources associated with production, standard sociometric data were collected in the firm. The name generators used to conduct the network study are presented in Appendix A. As seen above, in this firm, such ties represent channels for various types of resources for each member. The first is the network of strong *work contacts;* close co-workers can be relied upon for their cooperation; they provide future work, more desirable work, or access to clients. The second is the network of *advisors;* advisors provide solutions to, or make final decisions in, complex problems in a knowledge-intensive organization handling sophisticated legal cases. In this law firm, the difference between advisors and co-workers is based on the fact that a partner can seek another partner's advice without including the advisor as a coworker in the file at hand (and thus sharing credit). The third network is the role-distance, or *friendship* network, identified as socializing outside work; friends provide many different resources associated with role distance, such as emotional and symbolic support, or a definition of the situation.

In order to evaluate the expectations derived above, it is necessary to formulate a model that permits dependencies among network ties. Such a model makes it possible to characterize the specific forms of interdependence among resources that help members solve the structural problem of collegial organizations, i.e., to mitigate status competition. The p^* class of models was developed specifically for the analysis of tie interdependencies. Models within the multivariate p^* class are probability models for multirelational networks (Wasserman & Pattison 1996; Pattison & Wasserman 1999). In their most general form, p^* models express the probability of an overall multirelational network structure in terms of parameters associated with particular network substructures. By *substructure*, we mean a specific hypothetical configuration of network ties linking a small set of network members—for instance, a pair of lawyers joined by mutual cowork ties, or a trio of lawyers, two of whom are linked by mutual advice ties and a third linked by friendship to one of these two. The substructures appearing in the model are determined by the independence assumptions that one makes: specifically, the substructures are defined by sets of possible ties, each pair of which is assumed to be conditionally dependent, given the remaining ties. (The number of possible ties in a particular substructure is termed the *level* of the substructure.) Pattison and Wasserman (1999) argued that the multivariate Markov assumption permits one to examine many of the forms of interdependence among ties that have been proposed in the network literature. These forms are associated with notions of role-set, exchange, path-dependence, structural position, and actor effects. The multivariate Markov assumption specifies that two possible network ties are conditionally independent, given all remaining ties, unless the pair of possible ties has a lawyer in common. The consequence of this assumption is that multiplex ties and multiplex dyadic and triadic configurations are all potentially critical in modeling the overall network structure.[6]

A presentation of model selection strategy and analyses of the data at the univariate level is presented in a more technical paper published elsewhere (Lazega & Pattison 1999).[7] Here we only present the final multivariate p^* model for the three network relations simultaneously. This model allows us to explore interdependencies among the three types of relations that can be evaluated at the level of ties, dyads, and triads. If a substructure has a large positive parameter in this p^* model, then the presence of the substructure enhances the likelihood of the overall network. This model is homogeneous in the sense of assuming that a relational substructure of a given form (e.g., a pair of reciprocal friendship ties, or some particular triadic structure) has a constant effect on the likelihood of the overall network structure and is not dependent on attributes of the participating nodes. As a result, the model has a single parameter corresponding to each possible substructure. Parameters are estimated using pseudolikelihood estimation (Strauss & Ikeda 1990; Pattison & Wasserman 1999). The approximate standard errors that accompany the pseudolikelihood estimates are given only for guidance as to likely order of magnitude.

THE COLLEGIAL BLEND OF RELATIONSHIPS: A TYPICAL PATTERN

The number of possible distinct dyadic and triadic substructures involving three relations is very large. As a result, the class of substructures used to define an initial multivariate p^* model was restricted to dyadic structures of level four or less; triadic structures of level three or less; and the level 4 triadic substructures identified in univariate analyses.[8] The pseudolikelihood estimates for parameters in the final model (following a hierarchical elimination) are presented in Table 1. The parameter labeling is indicated in Figure 1. The estimates are organized according to the types of tie in-

Table 1.   Parameter Estimates for Final Multivariate Model

Parameter	PLE	Parameter	PLE	Parameter	PLE
Co-work		Advice		Friendship	
τ_{15_W}	−3.49 (.25)	τ_{15_A}	−3.46 (.25)	τ_{15_F}	−4.65 (.29)
$\tau_{11\_W,W}$	4.45(.47)	$\tau_{11\_A,A}$	1.33 (.24)	$\tau_{11\_F,F}$	2.91 (.24)
$\tau_{12\_W,W}$	0.06 (.01)	$\tau_{12\_A,A}$	0.06 (.01)	$\tau_{12\_F,F}$	0.07 (.01)
$\tau_{13\_W,W}$	−0.04 (.02)	$\tau_{13\_A,A}$	−0.06 (.01)	$\tau_{13\_F,F}$	−0.06 (.02)
$\tau_{14\_W,W}$	0.10 (.02)	$\tau_{14\_A,A}$	0.06 (.01)	$\tau_{14\_F,F}$	0.03 (.02)
$\tau_{9\_W,W,W}$	−0.03 (.02)	$\tau_{9\_A,A,A}$	0.28 (.02)	$\tau_{9\_F,F,F}$	0.28 (.02)
$\tau_{10\_W,W,W}$	0.30 (.06)				
$\tau_{7\_W,W,W}$	−0.09 (.02)				
$\tau_{8\_W,W,W}$	−0.06 (.02)				
$\tau_{3\_W,W,W,W}$	−0.11 (.02)				
$\tau_{6\_W,W,W,W}$	0.21 (.04)				
Co-work and Advice		Co-work and Friendship		Advice and Friendship	
τ_{15_WA}	2.44 (.13)	τ_{15_WF}	0.96 (.17)	τ_{15_AF}	2.42 (.22)
$\tau_{11\_W,A}$	0.61 (.21)	$\tau_{22\_W,F}$	0.48 (.18)	$\tau_{11\_A,F}$	1.30 (.19)
$\tau_{12\_W,A}$	−0.01 (.01)				
$\tau_{13\_W,A}$	−0.03 (.01)	$\tau_{13\_F,W}$	0.01 (.01)	$\tau_{13\_A,F}$	−0.01 (.01)
$\tau_{13\_A,W}$	−0.04 (.01)	$\tau_{13\_W,F}$	−0.00 (.01)	$\tau_{13\_F,A}$	−0.03 (.01)
$\tau_{14\_A,W}$	−0.02 (.01)	$\tau_{14\_W,F}$	−0.01 (.01)	$\tau_{14\_A,F}$	−0.02 (.01)
$\tau_{11\_W,AW}$	−0.39 (.17)	$\tau_{11\_W,FW}$	−1.113 (.23)	$\tau_{11\_A,AF}$	−0.87 (.24)
$\tau_{11\_A,AW}$	−0.82 (.14)			$\tau_{11\_F,AF}$	−0.90 (.27)
$\tau_{9\_A,A,W}$	−0.08 (.02)				
$\tau_{9\_A,W,A}$	−0.10 (.02)			$\tau_{9\_A,F,A}$	0.07 (.02)
$\tau_{9\_W,A,A}$	−0.12 (.02)				
$\tau_{9\_A,W,W}$	0.13 (.02)				
$\tau_{9\_W,A,W}$	0.18 (.02)	$\tau_{9\_W,F,W}$	0.07 (.02)		
$\tau_{8\_W,W,A}$	0.03 (.01)				
		$\tau_{10\_F,F,W}$	−0.13 (.02)	$\tau_{10\_A,A,F}$	−0.15 (.02)
				$\tau_{13\_F,AF}$	−0.07 (.02)
				$\tau_{11\_AF,AF}$	1.55 (.45)
Co-work, Advice, and Friendship					
τ_{15_AFW}	−1.00 (.21)				
$\tau_{11\_W,AF}$	−0.30 (.24)				
$\tau_{11\_W,AFW}$	1.51 (.31)				

volved in the corresponding configurations. We focus discussion on the structures involving *combinations* of types of tie, noting the implications that they have for the form of interdependence of ties in the firm.[9]

The large number of parameters corresponding to configurations comprising both co-work and advice ties suggests that co-work and advice ties are distributed in a highly interdependent manner. We note first that the multiplexity parameter (lawyer *i* sends a duplex tie to lawyer *j*) is large and positive and suggests that the co-occurrence of the two types of tie is likely;

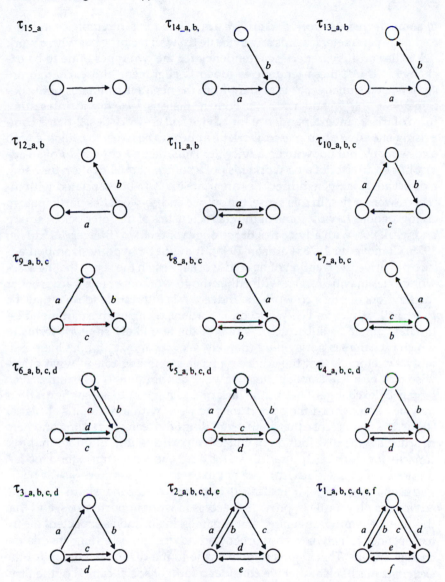

Figure 1.   Configurations corresponding to *p** model parameters. The symbols *a, b, c, d, e,* and *f* may refer to any of the uniplex or multiplex relations, namely W (co-work), A (advice), F (friendship), WA (co-work and advice), WF (co-work and friendship), AF (advice and friendship), WAF (co-work, advice, and friendship).

to some degree, co-work and advice are aligned in structure. Second, the exchange parameter (i sends an advice tie to j who reciprocates with a work tie) is also positive, reflecting a tendency for the two types of tie to be exchanged. Third, these tendencies towards alignment and exchange are somewhat disjunctive, as is evident from the negative estimates of the parameters $\tau_{11\_W,AW}$ and $\tau_{11\_A,AW}$. Fourth, there is a clear and interesting form of triadic interdependence for advice and co-work ties: 2-paths comprising one advice and one co-work tie appear to be likely to coincide with a co-work tie, but not with an advice tie. Thus, being a co-worker of an advisor or an advisor of a co-worker is not a sufficient qualification for being a direct advisor. Such indirect ties are more likely to be associated with direct co-worker ties. In this sense, the advice and co-work ties participate in configurations having some of the characteristics of the interlock of strong and weak ties, with advice ties the stronger of the two (Breiger & Pattison 1978; Granovetter 1973; Pattison 1993). It might be hypothesized that advice ties drive the creation of new co-worker ties, in the sense that new co-worker ties may be forged with either the co-workers of one's advisors or the advisors of one's co-workers. Indeed, it is interesting to note that the two triadic advice and co-work configurations with positive parameter estimates contain as substructures two of the few likely co-work forms in which exchange is not evident (namely, $\tau_{12\_W,W}$ and $\tau_{14\_W,W}$). One possibility, therefore, is that the advice tie has a stabilizing role in what otherwise may be a less stable pattern of work distribution in a system driven largely by exchange. That is, the lack of exchange in these configurations may be offset against the opportunity to work with individuals at higher status; it is in this sense that status-signaling advice ties are strong and help to articulate the distribution of collective participation. But note that this capacity for work ties to straddle status differences does not extend too far: the advisors of one's advisors are not likely to be co-workers (as the negative estimate for $\tau_{9\_A,A,W}$ indicates). Further, we note that status-signaling advice ties play a role in providing access to work opportunities, and that this may help mitigate against status games. In all, and as expected, the interdependence between co-worker and advice ties is strong in this exchange system. This begins to give shape to the distinctive nature of the exchange mechanism that we consider a form of social capital of the firm.

Advice and friendship ties also exhibit quite strong interdependence, with substantial multiplexity (i sends a duplex tie to j) and exchange (i sends an advice tie to j who reciprocates with a friendship tie) effects. In addition, the positive estimate for $\tau_{11\_AF,AF}$ indicates an enhanced reciprocity effect for one type of tie in the presence of a reciprocal tie of the other type; the enhancement is not observed, however, in the presence of an unreciprocated tie of the other type (as the negative estimates for $\tau_{11\_F,AF}$ and $\tau_{11\_A,AF}$ indicate). At the triadic level, the only positive estimate is associated with a triadic structure in which friendship links the advisors *j* and *k* of some lawyer *i*. Arguably, just as advice ties serve to articulate co-work relations, so friendship ties may serve a weak articulatory role with respect to advice ties (since configurations in which the friend of an advisor is also an advisor have a positive parameter estimate). Negative parameter estimates are associated with 3-cycles comprising two advice ties and a friendship tie (suggesting that even though the advisor of an advisor is a source of potential advice, such a person is unlikely to return a direct friendship tie). Thus, one might argue that the interdependence of advice and friendship ties can be described largely in the dyadic terms of a propensity for multiplexity and exchange, although there is also a weaker articulatory relationship between friendship and advice ties. These patterns of interdependence of friendship and advice ties can also be interpreted as suggesting that friendship "softens" the status differences inhering in advice ties, both directly (through multiplexity and exchange effects) and indirectly (by tending to link the advisors of an individual). Thus, these patterns are consistent with our general expectations regarding the role of role-distance ties in the mitigation of status competition.

As expected, the parameters for configurations involving co-work and friendship tend to be much weaker. The multiplexity and exchange parameters are weak but positive and, since the parameter for the configuration in which a mutual co-work tie occurs in the presence of an asymmetric friendship tie is large and negative, these effects appear to be disjunctive. At the triadic level, cycles comprising two friendship and one co-worker tie are unlikely and there is a weak tendency for friendship ties to link the two lawyers with whom a third claims co-work ties. This latter effect is similar to, but much weaker than, the pattern by which advice was claimed to help sustain one of the asymmetric co-work configurations. Thus, the members tend to sort their ties so as not to mix work and friendship too directly.

A very small number of dyadic configurations involving co-work, advice, and friendship have large estimated parameters. In particular, the triplex tie from *i* to *j* has a negative estimate, whereas the triplex tie accompanied by a reciprocal co-work tie has a positive estimate. This suggests that, even though pairs of lawyers may be linked by duplex ties more commonly than the overall frequency of individual ties would suggest, the observation of *all three* ties linking a pair is not a common structural form (unless also accompanied by a reciprocal co-work tie).

Finally, simple illustrative counts looking at the number of configurations with both partners and associates in each possible position in the elementary configurations of the auction process, are very helpful with respect to our main argument.[10] They confirm that the brainstorming overwhelmingly directs requests for advice toward partners (75 percent of cor-

responding triads), and that friendship ties in this context are mostly between advising partners (62 percent of corresponding triads). The status
competition process and its mitigation through a specific pattern blending
various sorts of ties among members are thus realistically anchored in the
established formal structure of the organization.

CONCLUSION

Cooperation between members of an organization can be seen as involving routine transfers or exchanges of various kinds of resources. Structural
analysis of cooperation and management of various types of social resources enhances understanding of effective participation in collective action by highlighting the relationship between choices of important sources
of resources in a specific type of organization. This approach helps identify generic social mechanisms that can be seen as constituting a form of
corporate social capital (Leenders & Gabbay 1999). In the case examined
here, the mechanism consists of encouraging then taming unbounded status auctions among peers. Using a network study of a corporate law firm,
we were able to reconstitute these structures in a specific work environment, one characterized by multifunctional and sometimes multidisciplinary task forces in which "status competition" is a particularly strong
motivation driving participation. Specific statistical tools, p^* models, were
used to analyze the interplay between the three social resources shaping
cooperation among these professionals, and then to identify the functional
role of this interplay in a mechanism dealing with this problem of status
competition. These models revealed insights about the intersection of networks (a key feature of this governance mechanism) at the substructural
level that would not have been apparent with less sophisticated data analysis methods. The importance of configurations reflecting the presence of
this social mechanism flesh out the form of collective social capital identified here.

In conclusion, this approach to social capital points out the importance
of considering organizations as sets of generic social mechanisms (Hedstrom & Swedberg 1998) attached to governance problems. These social
mechanisms are exemplified by this exchange system, and contribute to
corporate social capital by helping to provide structural solutions to col-
lective-action problems. Given that analyses were applied to a single case
study, we are in no position to generalize to other organizations based on
the findings reported. It remains to be seen whether this pattern has relevance for other types of collegial organizations or knowledge-intensive
firms, such as professional business partnerships in medicine, engineering,
accounting, scientific or R&D laboratories, and universities; in such orga-

nizations, the production process is difficult to routinize and professional expertise and advice cannot easily be standardized; as a result, "internal" transaction costs for the firm as a whole can be assumed to be a large part of the total costs of collective action. One might therefore expect to find a need to combine systematically several kinds of resources in order to make collective action possible. Thus, beyond our general statement regarding the connection between specific mechanisms as forms of social capital and members' participation in collective action or cooperation, more work needs to be done to extend such an approach to other types of mechanisms and organizations.

This conception of social capital is consistent with a general sociological tradition that focuses on social mechanisms supporting and enhancing economic performance, beginning with Durkheim (1893) and now strongly established (Burt 1992; Macaulay 1963; Bourdieu 1980; Coleman 1990; see Flap, Bulder, & Völker 1998, and Gabbay 1997 for a review). Here, maximizing performance not only means improving technology, product and organizational innovation, managerial coordination, or financial management. It also means maintaining the specific local constellations of relationships that are the basis of social mechanisms and that help organizations solve problems of coordination.

APPENDIX A: SOCIOMETRIC NAME GENERATORS USED TO ELICIT CO-WORKERS, ADVICE, AND ROLE-DISTANCE TIES

Here is the list of all the members of your firm.

Strong co-workers network: Because most firms like yours are also organized very informally, it is difficult to get a clear idea of how the members really work together. Think back over the past year, consider all the lawyers in your firm. Would you go through this list and check the names of those with whom you have worked with. [By "worked with" I mean that you have spent time together on at least one case, that you have been assigned to the same case, that they read or used your work product or that you have read or used their work product; this includes professional work done within the firm like bar association work, administration, etc.]

Basic advice network: Think back over the past year, consider all the lawyers in your firm. To whom did you go for basic professional advice? For instance, you want to make sure that you are handling a case right, making a proper decision, and you want to consult someone whose professional opinions are in general of great value to you. By advice I do not mean simply technical advice.

Friendship network: Would you go through this list, and check the names of those you socialize with outside work. You know their family, they know yours, for instance. I do not mean all the people you are simply on a friendly level with, or people you happen to meet at firm functions.

NOTES

We would like to thank Ron Burt for useful suggestions.

1. This term refers to Merton's (1959) observation on status segregation as a mechanism for managing role strain.

2. Goffman thought that constructing role distance was an individual activity, often a product of one's sense of humor. We think that it is a more relational activity; one needs others to construct this distance.

3. Listen, for example, to Partner 18: "*Our firm is almost exclusively a joint economic enterprise. If I were to pick up a paper tomorrow morning and learn that a lawyer was hit by a car, I would be concerned. If he is in my firm, I would be more concerned. But that marginal difference would not be that significant, unless I work with him, know his family and his children. There are lots of lawyers in the community that I care more about than for some of my partners. I see a partnership more like an economic unit. There is the economic sense of mutual obligation, of enhanced goodwill and cooperation. We help each other with work. I expect more goodwill from a partner than from a stranger, but that's all. 'I'll be glad to do that.' But my whole life does not revolve around my partners. When people are too close, it creates problems too. And it is not necessary for partnerships to survive. There is a leap of faith that's required that a partner would not seek a circumstance that is harmful to me. That may be naive. Our compensation system is a guarantee for that leap of faith. A change in that would undermine the sense of security that I feel with my partners.*"

4. This comes across in Partner 13's following observation: "*When the firm was small, among other things all partners had a good idea of what other partners were doing. There was a much greater level of social integration, I think, firm-wide, and a tendency to look much more inwardly toward the firm as sort of almost a family away from a family. In our instance, probably thirty years ago the partners in the firm tended to represent the most central social circle for themselves. When the firm gets to be this size there is still a tendency to look inwardly toward the firm but it's obviously no longer a closely knit family because there are lots of partners that you won't see for weeks at a time. And so there tends to be if anything a tendency for partners to start to look outward from the firm as opposed to inward to the firm. The closeness tends to be reduced. Now what you have are people whose predominant social circles may include other lawyers within the firm, but probably include many more people outside the firm. That's a healthy development, not an unhealthy development.*"

5. Overall densities for co-work, advice, and role-distance (or friendship) networks are respectively 0.22, 0.17, and 0.11.

6. In the case of a multirelational Markov assumption, the model for the network is expressed in relation to substructures of a multivariate triad, or of a multivariate *star* of order $n - 1$ (for a network of n nodes; see Pattison &

Wasserman, in press). We have not reported analyses of the role of higher-order stars of order three or more (that is, of substructures comprising three or more ties directed to or from a member of the firm), since preliminary investigations suggested that higher-order stars play a much less substantial role than the multivariate triadic configurations on which we focus here.

7. A hierarchical model elimination procedure was used: at any step, only those parameters corresponding to higher-order substructures were considered for elimination (i.e., setting to zero). Thus, if one substructure was a subset of another substructure in the model at any step, only the second was considered for elimination at that step.

8. Bivariate analyses confirmed that no additional level 4 triadic structures involving two relations made substantial contributions to model fit.

9. In Table 1, negative parameters for each type of tie signify that a tie between two actors is less likely than no tie (and the relative magnitudes of the parameters confirm, for example, that work ties are the most frequent and friendship ties are the least frequent).

10. For step 1 configurations (with a reciprocated work tie between i and j and an advice tie from i to k) and step 2 configurations (with an advice tie from i to j and from i to k, and a friendship tie from j to k):

Status of			Number of step 1	Number of step 2
i	j	k	configurations	configurations
A	A	A	508	503
A	P	A	1179	209
A	A	P	646	251
A	P	P	1470	693
P	A	A	456	57
P	P	A	535	105
P	A	P	2852	122
P	P	P	2921	1415

A: Associates; P: Partner

REFERENCES

Bearman, Peter. 1997. "Generalized Exchange." *American Journal of Sociology* 102:1383–1415.

Blau, Peter M. 1964. *Exchange and Power in Social Life.* New York: John Wiley.

Bosk, Charles. 1979. *Forgive and Remember.* Chicago: University of Chicago Press.

Bourdieu, Pierre. 1980. "Le Capital Social. Notes Provisoires." *Actes de la Recherche en Sciences Sociales* 3:2–3.

Bourricaud, François. 1961. *Esquisse d'une théorie de l'autorité.* Paris: Plon.

Breiger, Ronald L. 1974. "The Duality of Persons and Groups." *Social Forces* 53:181–90.

Breiger, Ronald L., and J. Ennis. 1997. "Generalized Exchange in Social Networks: Statistics and Structure." *L'Année Sociologique* 47:73–88.

Breiger, Ronald L., and Philippa E. Pattison. 1978. "The Joint Role Structure in Two Communities' Elites." *Sociological Methods & Research* 7:213–26.

Burt, Ronald S. 1982. *Toward A Structural Theory of Action*. New York: Academic Press.

———. 1992. *Structural Holes: The Social Structure of Competition*. Cambridge: Harvard University Press.

Coleman, James S. 1990. *Foundations of Social Theory*. Cambridge: Harvard University Press.

Coleman, James S., Elihu Katz, and Herbert Menzel. 1966. *Medical Innovation: A Diffusion Study*. Indianapolis: Bobbs-Merrill.

Cook, Karen S., ed. 1987. *Social Exchange Theory*. London: Sage.

———. 1990. "Linking Actors and Structures: An Exchange Network Perspective." In Calhoun, Meyer and Scott, eds.

Crozier, Michel, and Erhard Friedberg. 1977. *L'Acteur et le système*. Paris: Seuil.

Durkheim, Emile. 1893. *De la Division du Travail Social*. Paris: Presses Universitaires de France.

Ekeh, Peter. 1974. *Social Exchange Theory: The Two Traditions*. Cambridge: Harvard University Press.

Flap, Hendrik D., Bert Bulder, and Beate Völker. 1998. "Intra-organizational Networks and Performance: A Review." *Computational and Mathematical Organization Theory* 4:1–39.

Frank, Robert H. 1985. *Choosing the Right Pond: Human Behavior and the Quest for Status*. Oxford: Oxford University Press.

Frank, O., and D. Strauss. 1986. "Markov Graphs." *Journal of the American Statistical Association* 81:832–42.

Gabbay, Shaul M. 1997. *Social Capital in the Creation of Financial Capital: The Case of Network Marketing*. Champaign, IL: Stipes Publishing.

Galaskiewicz, Joseph, and Peter V. Marsden. 1978. "Interorganizational Resource Networks: Formal Patterns of Overlap." *Social Science Research* 7:89–107.

Gilson, Robert J., and Robert H. Mnookin. 1985. "Sharing among Human Capitalists: An Economic Inquiry into the Corporate Law Firm and How Partners Split Profits." *Stanford Law Review* 37:313–92.

Goffman, Erving. 1961. *Encounters: Two Studies in the Sociology of Interaction*. Indianapolis: Bobbs-Merrill.

Gouldner, Alvin. 1960. "The Norm of Reciprocity." *American Sociological Review* 25:161–78.

Granovetter, Marc. 1973. "The Strength of Weak Ties." *American Journal of Sociology* 78:1360–80.

Han, Shin Kap, and Ronald L. Breiger. 1999. "Dimensions of Corporate Social Capital: Towards Models and Measures." Working Paper in Networks and Interpretation, Department of Sociology, Cornell University, No. 97-2. Forthcoming in Leenders, R., and S. Gabbay, eds.

Hedstrom, Peter, and Richard Swedberg, eds. 1998. *Social Mechanisms: An Analytical Approach to Social Theory*. Cambridge: Cambridge University Press.

Lazega, Emmanuel. 1992a. "Analyse de réseaux d'une organisation collégiale: les avocats d'affaires." *Revue Française de Sociologie* 33:559–89.

———. 1992b. *The Micro-politics of Knowledge: Communication and Indirect Control in Workgroups*. New York: Aldine-de Gruyter.

————. 1993. "Bureaucratie et collégialité dans les firmes américaines d'avocats d'affaires." *Droit et Société* 23/24:15–40.

————. 1994. "Analyse de réseaux et sociologie des organisations." *Revue Française de Sociologie* 35:293–320.

————. 1995. "Concurrence, coopération et flux de conseils dans un cabinet américain d'avocats d'affaires: Les échanges d'idées entre collègues." *Revue Suisse de Sociologie* 21:61–84.

————. 1999a. "Generalized Exchange and Economic Performance: Multilevel Embeddedness of Labor Contracts in a Corporate Law Firm." In R. Leenders and S. Gabbay, eds. *Corporate Social Capital and Liabilities*. Boston: Kluwer.

————. 1999b. "Teaming Up and Out? Cooperation and Solidarity in a Collegial Organization." *European Sociological Review*. Forthcoming.

————. Forthcoming. *The Collegial Phenomenon: A Structural Theory of Collective Action Among Peers*. Oxford: Oxford University Press.

Lazega, Emmanuel, and Marijtje Van Duijn. 1997. "Position in Formal Structure, Personal Characteristics and Choices of Advisors in a Law Firm: A Logistic Regression Model for Dyadic Network Data." *Social Networks* 19:375–97.

Lazega, Emmanuel, and Philippa E. Pattison. 1999. "Multiplexity, Generalized Exchange and Cooperation in Organizations: A Case Study." *Social Networks* 21:67–90.

Lazer, David, and Nancy Katz. 2000. "Putting the Network into Teamwork." Paper presented at the Sunbelt INSNA Meeting, Vancouver, Canada.

Leenders, Roger, and Shaul Gabbay, eds. 1999. *Corporate Social Capital and Liability*. Boston: Kluwer.

Lévi-Strauss, Claude. 1949. *Les Formes élémentaires de la parenté*. Paris: Plon.

Lin, Nan. 1995. "Les Ressources sociales: une théorie du capital social." *Revue Française de Sociologie* 36:685–704.

Lindenberg, Siegwart. 1997. "Grounding Groups in Theory: Functional, Cognitive, and Structural Interdependencies." Vol. 14, pp. 281–331 in *Advances in Group Processes*. Greenwich, CT: JAI Press.

Macauley, S. 1963. "Non-Contractural Relations in Business." *American Sociological Review* 28:55–66.

Merton, Robert K. 1959. *Social Theory and Social Structure*. Glencoe: The Free Press.

Nelson, Robert. 1988. *Partners with Power: The Social Transformation of the Large Law Firm*. Berkeley: University of California Press.

Olson, Mancur. 1965. *The Logic of Collective Action*. Cambridge: Harvard University Press.

Pattison, Philippa E. 1993. *Algebraic models for social networks:* New York: Cambridge University Press.

Pattison, Philippa, and Stanley Wasserman. 1999. "Logit Models and Logistic Regressions for Social Networks: II. Multivariate Relations." *Journal of Mathematical and Statistical Psychology* 52:169–93.

Robins, Garry, Philippa Pattison, and Stanley Wasserman. 1999. "Logit Models and Logistic Regressions for Social Networks: III Valued Relations." *Psychometrika* 64:371–94.

Smigel, Erwin. 1969. *The Wall Street Lawyer: Professional Organizational Man?* 2nd ed. Bloomington: Indiana University Press.

Starbuck, William H. 1992. "Learning by Knowledge-Intensive Firms." *Journal of Management Studies* 29:713–40.

Stinchcombe, Arthur L. 1991. "The Conditions of Fruitfulness of Theorizing about Mechanisms in Social Science." *Philosophy of the Social Sciences* 21:367–88.

Strauss, D., and M. Ikeda. 1990. "Pseudolikelihood Estimation for Social Networks." *Journal of the American Statistical Association* 85:204–12.

Sutton, Robert I., and Andrew Hargadon. 1996. "Brainstorming Groups in Context: Effectiveness in a Product Design Firm." *Administrative Science Quarterly* 41:685–718.

Van Duijn, Marijtje. 1995. "Estimation of a Random Effects Model for Directed Graphs." In *Toeval zit Overall, Programmatuur voor Random-Coëfficiënt Modellen. Zevende Symposium Statistische Software*. Groningen: ProGAMMA.

Van Duijn, Marijtje, and Tom A. B. Snijders. 1995. "The P2 model." Internal publication, Department of Statistics, University of Groningen.

Wasserman, Stanley, and Katherin Faust. 1994. *Social Network Analysis: Methods and Applications*. Cambridge: Cambridge University Press.

Wasserman, Stanley, and Philippa Pattison. 1996. "Logit Models and Logistic Regressions for Social Networks: I. An Introduction to Markov Graphs and p*." *Psychometrika* 60:401–25.

Waters, Malcolm. 1989. "Collegiality, Bureaucratization, and Professionalization: A Weberian Analysis." *American Journal of Sociology* 94:945–72.

Wilensky, Harold L. 1967. *Organizational Intelligence*. New York: Basic Books.

9

Social Networks and Social Capital in Extreme Environments

Jeanne S. Hurlbert, John J. Beggs,
and Valerie A. Haines

Social capital has become a key concept in modern sociology. Despite that fact, its meaning remains the subject of an ongoing debate in both theoretical discussions and empirical applications. In this chapter, we draw on Bourdieu (1986:248) to define social capital as "the aggregate of the actual or potential resources which are linked to possession of a durable network of more or less institutionalized relationships of mutual acquaintance or recognition." As Portes (1998:1) points out, this definition "makes clear that social capital is decomposable into two elements: first, the social relationship itself that allows individuals to claim access to resources possessed by their associates [social networks and their constituent ties] and second, the amount and quality of those resources [social resources]." We use that definition to link our research on social networks and social resources in two extreme environments: Hurricane Andrew and the underclass.

Studies of the ways in which social networks and their constituent ties provide social capital have generally neglected an important context, extreme environments. Network studies of social support have focused on the association between the structure of routine interpersonal environments, or core networks, and the receipt of informal support, neglecting to ask how these environments allocate resources in nonroutine situations (but see Hurlbert, Haines, & Beggs 2000). Social-resources researchers have asked how ties drawn from social networks provide social capital (e.g., information and influence) in a nonroutine situation, job finding, but they have provided little information about how social networks constrain and facilitate the allocation of job-finding resources in low-income (particularly underclass) populations (for exceptions, see Fernandez & Harris 1992; Green, Tigges, & Browne 1995).

In this chapter, we consider these neglected contexts by asking how network structures and ties drawn from those structures facilitate and constrain access to social capital in two extreme environments: a hurricane and an underclass population. We begin our examination of the first context by reviewing our previous research on Hurricane Andrew, focusing on the types of networks that facilitate the reception of instrumental assistance. We then extend that research by exploring who has access to these networks, asking how positional characteristics (e.g., social statuses) and community integration (e.g., tenure in the area, participation in voluntary organizations) affect network structure.

Next, we shift our focus to the underclass context and review our argument that the network structure and network resources dimensions of social isolation must be examined separately in underclass populations. Using that distinction, we explore the prevalence and nature of informal job-finding methods in an underclass sample, addressing three questions. First, we explore whether the receipt of social capital from social-network ties in job finding is less prevalent among residents of underclass, as opposed to more affluent areas. Second, we ask whether, among individuals who received social capital from their social-network ties to find their current jobs, the nature of the searcher-contact ties and the characteristics of contacts and resources differ between residents of poorer and more affluent areas. Third, we explore the association between the nature of job-finding ties and the characteristics of contacts / resources, among residents of each type of area. In our conclusions, we consider how our analysis of this extreme environment could be extended by introducing the focus on the activation of network ties for social capital that we used in our study of the extreme environment of Hurricane Andrew.

SOCIAL NETWORKS AND SOCIAL CAPITAL IN HURRICANE ANDREW

Social Networks and Social Support

Our previous research on social-support transactions during Hurricane Andrew focused on the first element of social capital that Portes (1998) identified, asking what kinds of social networks provide access to social support in this extreme environment. We answered that question by examining how the structure of networks affected four support outcomes: receipt of informal support, receipt of formal support, provision of informal support, and the activation of core network ties for informal support. We developed our predictions by drawing on theoretical arguments and empirical findings from the social support and social resources streams of network analysis, and from research on helping behavior during natural disasters. For this discussion of our findings, we focus only on instrumental forms of social support that individuals received during the preparation and recovery phases of Hurricane Andrew.

Research outside the disaster context has established that access to informal support is associated with strong rather than weak and homophilous rather than heterophilous ties (Wellman & Frank this volume; Lin, Woelfel, & Light 1985), and with the dense and homogeneous networks in which these ties are likely to lie (Campbell, Marsden, & Hurlbert 1986; Fischer 1982; Haines & Hurlbert 1992). These kinds of ties and network structures characterize core networks (Bailey & Marsden 1999; Hammer 1983; Marsden 1987; Wellman et al. 1997). Therefore, core networks provided an appropriate arena for studying how embeddedness in different types of networks affected access to informal support. And, because informational advantages are key to the receipt of formal support, focusing on core networks also allowed us to examine the question of whether the network structures and ties that provide access to one resource (informal support) impede access to other resources (formal support) in the extreme environment of a natural disaster.

Our results for the first support outcome, the receipt of informal support, provided further evidence of its association with core network structure (Beggs, Haines, & Hurlbert 1996a; Haines, Beggs, & Hurlbert 2000). Density, size, and homogeneity (age and educational) served as social capital for victims of Hurricane Andrew. Individuals who were embedded in core networks with higher proportions of kin and higher proportions of less educated individuals also received more informal support. None of these results was surprising in the disaster context. Network density, homogeneity, and their dyadic counterparts, strong and homophilous ties, are associated with high levels of social integration (Marsden 1987; Pescosolido 1991); in core networks, network size also indicates this property (Marsden 1987; Pescosolido 1991). The sense of belonging and high degree of normative consensus associated with high levels of social integration reflect and contribute to the routinization of support exchanges among core network members (see Wellman & Frank this volume).

For individuals who are embedded in these environments, network ties that served as conduits of social support in the past should be dependable in the present, even if the present takes place in an extreme environment. That argument also finds support in our result for kin composition. Because they are governed by norms of obligation and responsibility, relations among kin serve as important sources of informal support (Haines & Hurlbert 1992). Finally, individuals with less education may be more likely to be in occupations that develop or use disaster-relevant skills (e.g., construction trades); therefore, our finding for educational composition is consistent with research on helping during natural disasters.

These effects of network composition and range on the receipt of informal support demonstrate that individuals who were embedded in core networks that had these characteristics gained access to support resources to a greater degree than individuals who were embedded in less typical core networks. Research on social capital outside the support context suggests that, where self-sufficiency is not an option, reduced access to forms of social capital that inhere in network structure may lead individuals to look to government agencies for social resources (Coleman 1990). To investigate that possibility in the extreme environment of a natural disaster, we explored the effect of network structure on aid from formal organizations.

To receive formal support during natural disasters, individuals must gain information about what is available and how to get it. For this resource, then, weak ties, heterophily, and range should serve as social capital (Lin, Ensel, & Vaughn 1981; Campbell et al. 1986). So should being embedded in networks with higher proportions of higher-status individuals (Lin & Dumin 1986). We tested these predictions for seven outcomes: the receipt of formal aid, the number of sources of formal aid, aid from the Federal Emergency Management Agency, aid from the Red Cross, aid from churches, aid from other organizations, and Food Stamps. Our results generally supported our predictions (Beggs et al. 1996a, 1996b). For receipt of Food Stamps, three of the four significant network effects involved network composition: Individuals embedded in networks of higher mean age, higher mean education, and higher-proportion men were less likely to receive Food Stamps than individuals embedded in networks that lacked these characteristics. For the other outcomes, network range proved more consequential than network composition. Being embedded in networks of greater size, lower density, and greater geographic range affected positively the receipt of formal support.

Our analyses of network determinants of informal and formal support strengthen the argument (e.g., by Coleman 1990; Podolny & Baron 1997; Portes 1998; Young 1999) that the forms of social capital that facilitate certain actions may prove useless or harmful for other actions: Embeddedness in more typical core networks facilitated receipt of informal but not formal support. Our results for informal support also resonate with arguments in the social capital literature that emphasize the role of trust, normative obligations, and expectations in ensuring that network members provide assistance when it is needed (see Coleman 1990; Wellman & Frank this volume). The operation of these processes may help explain why individuals who were embedded in more typical core networks enjoyed access to social capital that was less available to individuals embedded in less typical core networks. They may also help to explain why individuals embedded in these core networks activated a greater proportion of their core-network ties for informal support in the preparation and recovery phases of Hurricane Andrew.

Two predictions about resource allocation in extreme environments follow from this argument that an historical process of routine support transactions shapes perceptions of support availability in nonroutine situations. First, individuals who are embedded in the kinds of core networks that have been shown to facilitate support reception will activate a higher proportion of their core network ties than people who are embedded in core networks that lack these characteristics. Second, these individuals will receive a higher proportion of their informal support from individuals inside, rather than outside their core networks.

In the extreme environment of Hurricane Andrew, core-network structure affected both the proportion of core-network ties that individuals activated for informal support and the degree to which activated ties came from inside, rather than from outside the core network. Being embedded in core networks of greater density and gender diversity and that contained more men, kin, and younger individuals enhanced the activation of core-network ties. The effect of network size on the proportion of informal support providers who were core-network members was also positive (see Hurlbert et al. 2000).

Taken together, these analyses of how the structures of core networks affected the receipt of informal support, the receipt of formal support, and the activation of core-network ties for informal support suggest that embeddedness in more typical core networks provides social capital that is less available to individuals who are embedded in less typical core networks, and vice versa. The receipt of informal support and the activation of core-network ties for informal support were both enhanced by greater size, higher density, more educational and age homogeneity, more ties to kin, and more ties to individuals with less than high school education. But, despite the fact that these network structures and their constituent social ties enhanced transfers of informal support from core-network members, they impeded access to formal support and to informal support from individuals outside core networks. For individuals embedded in less typical core networks, then, the very network structures that precluded turning to core-network ties when responding to an extreme environment—weak ties and range—proved valuable because they provided information and because they may have linked disaster victims to individuals outside the core networks (see Beggs et al. 1996b; Hurlbert et al. 2000).

By establishing the beneficial consequences of different amounts and qualities of informal and formal support, researchers studying the support process inside and outside the disaster context have focused attention on the second element of social capital. Our study of the support process in the extreme environment of Hurricane Andrew suggests that studies of support outcomes must also consider the network structures and their constituent social ties that allow individuals to claim access to resources possessed by their associates. Shifting the focus from the former element of social capital to the latter entails asking what forms of social capital inhere in the structures of core networks (e.g., density for informal support and the activation of core-network ties for informal support; range for formal support and the activation of noncore ties for informal support)—a shift that, in turn, raises the question: Who has access to these forms of social capital?

We address that question here, focusing on the aspects of network composition and range that our analyses have shown to be consequential for support reception in the extreme environment of Hurricane Andrew. Specifically, we ask how positional characteristics (e.g., social statuses) and integration into the community affect access to the network structures that exhibit the compositional characteristics and the characteristics of the density, size, and diversity dimensions of network range that we found to be consequential in gaining access to informal support and in activating core-network ties for informal support in the hurricane context. We also ask whether network composition, as a form of social capital, affects the degree to which individuals' network structures exhibit the kinds of size, density, and diversity that promote the receipt of informal support and the activation of core-network ties for that support in this extreme environment.

DATA AND MEASURES—THE HURRICANE ANDREW SAMPLE

Data

Hurricane Andrew struck the Gulf coast of Louisiana in 1992. Our sample included residents of two adjacent southwestern Louisiana parishes that the Louisiana Office of Emergency Preparedness identified as most strongly affected by the storm. Because most residents maintained telephone service throughout the storm, we were able to use telephone interviews to collect data from residents of three towns in these parishes and the surrounding rural areas that share zip codes with the towns they adjoin. Chosen randomly from a list of telephone numbers, the 594 respondents who completed the interview represent 70 percent of screened eligible respondents (see Beggs et al. 1996a for further details on the sample).

Measures

Measures of Core Network Structure. The core networks that we examine include all nonredundant alters elicited by two name generators. The first, which tapped routine confidantes of respondents, modified the name-eliciting question that was used in the 1985 General Social Survey (Bailey & Marsden 1999; Marsden 1987). It asked respondents to name up to five individuals with whom they had discussed important matters in the six months prior to Hurricane Andrew. To tap the routine associates of respondents, we drew on Fischer (1982) and asked respondents to name up to five individuals with whom they had socialized in the six months prior to the storm.

Our name interpreter questions gathered information about the characteristics of the relationships among the alters, the characteristics of their relationships with the respondent, and the personal characteristics of the named alters (from respondents' reports). To measure the kin, gender, education, and age composition of respondents' networks, we use the proportion of alters who were kin (constructed from a variable contrasting kin [1] with non-kin [0]), the proportion of alters who were men (constructed from a variable contrasting men [1] with women [0]), the average education of alters (constructed from a measure of alters' education, in years), and the average age of alters (constructed from respondents' reports of alters' ages, in years). Because being embedded in networks of lower education and containing younger individuals increased access to informal support in our research, we multiplied the dependent variables tapping average education and average age of alters by −1, to ease the interpretation of coefficients.

Turning to network range, network size represents the total number of nonredundant alters elicited by our two name generators (maximum possible number is 10). To measure density, we constructed two measures. The first, a structural measure, taps the proportion of maximum-intensity ties among alters that were present in a network (constructed from respondents' reports of whether each pair of alters was especially close [1], neither close nor total strangers [.5], or total strangers [0] [Marsden 1987]). The second, the average closeness between the respondent and each alter, is constructed from a measure of whether the respondent felt especially close (1), somewhat close (.5), or not close at all (0) to each alter. Our first measure of the diversity dimension of range, gender heterophily, is the proportion of alters who were a different gender than the respondent. Age and educational homophily represent the average differences between the age and education, respectively, of the respondent and each alter, multiplied by −1.

Independent Variables: Positional Characteristics. Age is measured in years. Gender is coded male (1) and female (0) and race is coded white (1) and nonwhite (0). We measure respondent's education in years and family income in thousands of dollars.[1] To tap marital status, we construct two dummy variables. The first contrasts never married (1) with other (0) respondents; the second contrasts separated, widowed, and divorced (1) respondents with others (0). Married respondents serve as the reference category.

Independent Variables: Community Integration. We measure tenure in the area as the proportion of each respondent's life that he or she has lived in the local area. Participation in voluntary associations is the number of voluntary organizations to which a respondent belongs.

Control Variables. We control for whether (1) or not (0) respondents suffer from a chronic illness or disability.

RESULTS

Table 1 presents the results of our analysis of the factors that affect access to networks that facilitate reception of instrumental assistance in the extreme environment of Hurricane Andrew. Beginning with network composition (Table 1), we find that older individuals are less likely than younger to be embedded in networks of lower average education and lower average age. Because these aspects of network composition increase access to informal support in this context, older individuals have less access to these forms of social capital. In this extreme environment, men have greater access to some forms of network capital but not others. Men are significantly more likely than women to be embedded in networks of higher kin composition and networks containing more men, but they are less likely to participate in networks of lower average age. Race has only one significant effect on network composition: Whites have greater access to male-dominated networks than nonwhites do.

Higher education usually conveys greater access to resources. But our results suggest that is not the case in the hurricane context, because of the kinds of networks that are associated with the receipt of informal support. More educated individuals are less likely to participate in kin-dominated networks, networks of lower average education, and networks of lower average age. Having a higher income decreases access to networks containing less educated individuals. The significant effects of not being currently married on forms of social capital that inhere in core network composition are uniformly negative: Compared to their married counterparts, never married individuals and those who are separated, widowed, or divorced participate in networks of lower kin composition, a lower proportion of men, and higher average education. Overall, then, we find mixed effects of

Table 1. Structural Parameters of Network Characteristics

| | Composition | | | | Range | | | | | |
| | | | | | | Density | | Diversity | | |
	Kin (Hi)	Sex (Male)	Educ (Low)	Age (Low)	Size	Structural	Closeness	Sex (Het)	Age (Hom)	Educ (Hom)
Positional characteristics										
Age	.001	.000	−.022*	−.383**	.002	.003**	.001	.001	−.209**	−.019**
Sex (male)	.087**	.150**	.015	−1.602*	−.746**	.021	−.002	.038	.297	.100
Race (white)	.003	.054*	−.232	.178	.142	−.015	−.003	.067*	−.455	.471**
Education	−.013*	.001	−.257**	−.378*	.009	.000	−.002	.004	.131	.227**
Income	.000	−.001	−.020*	.021	.005	.000	−.000	.001	.017	−.010*
Never married	−.085*	−.123**	−.902**	−.393	−.226	−.007	.010	.012	−5.378**	−.208
Separated, widow, divorced	−.109**	−.077*	−.532*	.951	−.268	−.009	.003	−.048	−3.260**	−.233
Community integration										
Life in area (%)	.001*	.000	.005	−.037*	.007*	.001*	.000	−.000	.005	.000
Voluntary memberships	−.004	.011	−.184*	−.412	.247**	−.004	.002	−.001	.115	−.309
Network composition										
Kin (%)	—	—	—	—	−1.060**	.372**	.106**	.266**	−7.454**	−.200
Male (%)	—	—	—	—	.210	.035	−.017	.077	−1.946	−.108
Average age	—	—	—	—	−.017*	−.001	−.000	−.001	.050	−.013
Average education	—	—	—	—	−.020	−.004	−.001	.010	−.003	.037
Control										
Disability	.002	.046	.118	−.189	.418*	.026	.008	.047	−.127	−.489*
Intercept	.738	.343	−7.344	−19.391	4.754	.421	.883	−.065	−.968	−3.269
R²	.061	.102	.272	.305	.111	.324	.130	.135	.293	.247

*p < .05
**p < .01

217

social statuses on network composition and, therefore, on access to these forms of social capital in the extreme environment of Hurricane Andrew.

The effects of community integration are also mixed. Individuals who have spent a higher proportion of their lives in the local area are more likely than those who arrived more recently to participate in kin-dominated networks, but they are less likely to be connected to individuals of lower average age. Membership in a greater number of voluntary associations decreases access to networks of lower average education.

Turning to network range, we find that older individuals are more likely than younger to have access to the dense networks that facilitate both the receipt of informal support and the activation of core network ties for informal support in the hurricane context. They are less likely, though, to be embedded in networks of higher age or educational homophily. We find only one significant gender effect on network range: Men are embedded in smaller networks than women are. Whites have greater access than nonwhites to the networks of higher gender heterophily and educational homophily that are associated with the activation of core-network ties for informal support and the receipt of informal support, respectively. More educated individuals have greater access to networks of higher educational homophily but individuals with higher incomes have less access to them. Never married individuals and individuals who are separated, widowed, or divorced enjoy less access to age-homophilous networks than currently married individuals do. Both indicators of community integration exert positive effects on network size and having spent a higher proportion of one's life in the area has a positive effect on network density.

Turning to the examination of the effects of network composition on network range, we find that kin composition has the most widespread effects. Being embedded in a network of higher kin composition decreases access to two aspects of network range that are associated with the receipt of informal support: size and age homophily. But it increases access to networks of higher density (both measures) and gender heterophily. Being embedded in a network of higher average age has a negative effect on network size.

In the extreme environment of a natural disaster, social capital can take various forms. Where most support researchers focus exclusively on the amount and quality of support resources, our examination of social networks and social capital in Hurricane Andrew demonstrated the importance of considering social capital that inheres in network structure and the factors that affect access to that social capital. Our analyses of these factors in this chapter show that positional and community integration variables affect access to forms of social capital that inhere in the composition and range of core networks and that kin composition and age composition affect access to other forms of network social capital. Acknowledging both the forms of social capital that inhere in network structure and the complexity of their determinants is necessary to explain how social networks and their constituent ties allow individuals to claim access to resources possessed by their associates in the extreme environment of a hurricane. To examine the question of whether these conclusions also hold for the second element of social capital, the amount and quality of resources, we turn to our research on social networks and social capital in the underclass.

SOCIAL NETWORKS AND SOCIAL CAPITAL IN THE UNDERCLASS

Social Capital and Social Isolation

As sociologists have renewed their focus on the underclass, they have begun to ask what role network structures play in perpetuating poverty (see Fernandez & Harris 1992; Hurlbert, Beggs, & Haines 1998; Tigges, Browne, & Green 1998; Stanton-Salazar 1997; Wacquant & Wilson 1989). The impetus for this research comes primarily from Wilson's (1987, 1991; Wacquant & Wilson 1989) and Granovetter's (1982) discussions of the structure and dynamics of social isolation and its relationship to poverty. Wilson (1987, 1991) argued that poor populations are socially isolated, where social isolation conveys a lack of connection to mainstream individuals and institutions that results in separation from job networks and resources that would help poor individuals escape poverty. Social isolation, he contends, is inextricably linked to economic isolation—poverty and welfare dependence, loss of economic capital, and high rates of unemployment and underemployment. Social isolation reflects a lack of social capital (Wacquant & Wilson 1989) and is linked to a lack of economic capital. Underlying this social and economic isolation are macrolevel demographic and economic shifts that have transformed the inner city. Following mainstream norms (Singh 1991), middle-class blacks have migrated out of center cities toward more affluent areas, depriving inner-city areas of key social and economic resources (Wilson 1987; Wacquant & Wilson 1989). Economic shifts have reduced the availability of inner-city jobs.

Because the concept of social isolation is inherently relational, this thesis clearly demands a network approach to understanding social isolation and its obverse, access to social capital, in the underclass. That approach is beginning to emerge (see, e.g., Fernandez & Harris 1992; Hurlbert et al. 1998; Oliver 1988; Tigges et al. 1998; Stanton-Salazar 1997). But the development of that approach has been limited by the failure of many studies (see, e.g., Fernandez & Harris 1992; Tigges et al. 1998) to recognize that the concept of social isolation, like the concept of social capital (Portes 1998), is decomposable into two dimensions: network structure, illustrated by Wilson's identification of the geographic restriction of underclass residents' networks, and network resources, which, as Wilson (1987, 1991) argues, entails a lack of connection to "mainstream" individuals and institutions, job networks, and the information and influence that these networks can provide. Granovetter's (1982:116–17) discussion of poverty points to the same two dimensions: He suggests that one factor perpetuating poverty is poor individuals' lack of weak ties and network range (network structure dimension) that would increase their access to instrumental resources (network resources dimension).

To explore these arguments about social isolation and social capital fully, two types of analysis are necessary. First, researchers must examine (a) the structure of the routine networks in which individuals are embedded (e.g., density, range), and (b) the potential resources contained in these networks (e.g., employed individuals, communication/transportation resources). Second, they must examine the activated resources to which those networks grant access by comparing, between underclass and other populations: (a) the prevalence of resource transfers through activated network ties, and (b) the nature of those ties and resources.

Beginning with the first type of analysis, Fernandez and Harris (1992) did operationalize the concept of social isolation in network terms, but they failed to distinguish between its network structure and network resources dimensions. Their ability to assess social isolation was also impeded by the fact that the only name generator in the data that they used (the University of Chicago's Urban Poverty and Family Structure Project) tends to tap strong ties. The Multi-City Study of Urban Inequality (MCSUI) data, used by Green and his colleagues (Green et al. 1995; Tigges et al. 1998; Green, Tigges, & Diaz 1999) provide a restricted range of measures of each dimension of social isolation, which limited their ability to measure the construct. Particularly problematic in both studies was the fact that neither could assess a key aspect of Wilson's and Granovetter's arguments about the network structure dimension of social isolation, the argument that residents of underclass areas lack access to weak ties.

In earlier work (Hurlbert et al. 1998), we used data that included an expanded range of name generators and name interpreters to examine the relationship between the two dimensions of social isolation. Treating these dimensions as conceptually and empirically distinct, we asked whether the structures of social networks of underclass individuals in our sample differed from those of residents of more affluent areas in the ways that Wilson's (1987) and Granovetter's (1982) arguments predict. Then, focusing on residents of an underclass area, we asked what kinds of network structures and ties yielded access to social resources, or social capital, in that population. In doing so, we explored not only the aspects of network structure that Wilson (1987) and Granovetter (1982) suggested are consequential, but also aspects of network structure that social resources studies have shown to affect access to social capital (see, for example, Lin et al. 1981).

We began by using the two dimensions of social isolation to compare residents of a "core" underclass area to (a) residents of the transitional "ring" that surrounds it, and (b) residents of nearby middle-class areas. We did find some differences on the network-structure dimension between the "core" and the two comparison areas, including the surprising finding that residents of the underclass sample had higher, rather than lower proportions of weak ties in their networks. But our results show that the core is more distinct on the network-resources dimension than on the network-structure dimension of social isolation. For example, residents of the core had less access to educated individuals and to communication and transportation resources than either of the two comparison groups did.

In our exploration of how the network-structure dimension of social isolation affected the network-resources dimension among residents of the core underclass area, we found that geographic concentration of network members constrained access to some job-finding resources and network diversity increased it; sharing voluntary organization memberships with network members increased access to employment and transportation resources; and network size increased access to employment resources. But the effects of tie strength were mixed: Weak ties appeared to increase access to some types of resources, but not others.

These findings provide information about the structure of routine networks in the underclass and about what kinds of networks yield access to "potential" or "latent" social capital in that extreme environment. In the analyses that follow, we shift the focus to activated ties to ask how the prevalence and nature of the use of informal job-finding contacts and resources varies between residents of underclass areas and residents of more affluent areas.

Our first question is whether employed individuals who reside in underclass areas are less likely than their counterparts in more affluent (i.e., middle-class) areas to have found out about the jobs they currently hold through social contacts. By definition, if individuals found out about their current jobs through contacts, then those contacts provided social capital; we compare the prevalence of this form of social capital between residents of the two types of areas.[2] We then compare the nature of the ties that transferred job-finding resources (their strength and their gender composition) and the characteristics of the contact and the resources (whether the contact was employed at the destination firm and whether the contact provided influence) between the two groups. Finally, we examine the association between (a) the characteristics of searcher-contact ties and (b) characteristics of contacts and resources between the two comparison groups.

Wilson's (1987, 1991) and Granovetter's (1982) arguments predict that the receipt of social capital from job-finding contacts should be less common among residents of underclass areas than among residents of more affluent areas. Because Wilson (1987) and Granovetter (1982) contend that lack of access to weak ties is a key aspect of the network-structure dimension of social isolation, their arguments predict that residents of underclass areas are less likely than their more affluent counterparts to have used weak ties to find jobs. We note, though, that our earlier analyses suggest that this prediction may not be supported in these data. Given the argument that underclass residents' networks have lower range and are less likely to convey access to higher-status individuals, we expect a higher proportion of searcher-contact ties in underclass areas to be gender-homophilous and to connect searchers to women. Finally, underclass-area residents who found jobs through network ties should be less likely than their more affluent counterparts to have used contacts who were connected to the destination firm and who exerted influence on their behalf.

Green et al. (1995) explored similar issues with the Atlanta sample of the MCSUI data. They found that, of the individuals in their sample who used personal contacts to find jobs, the poor were significantly more likely than the nonpoor to use relatives. They also found that a significantly lower proportion of poor than nonpoor respondents found their jobs through contacts who were connected to destination firms. They did not, however, find significant differences in the proportions whose contacts hired them or whose contacts talked to the employers about them.

At the same time that our analyses provide a comparison in a mid-sized Southern city, they extend the work of Green and his colleagues in three ways. First, drawing upon the distinction between the network-structure and network-resources dimensions of social isolation, we explore the association between characteristics of the searcher / contact tie and the nature of the social capital that the contact provided. Second, we provide a better measure of tie strength: Rather than tapping the role relation between the searcher and contact, our measure taps the emotional closeness between them (see Marsden & Campbell 1984). Third, in considering the network-structure dimension, we measure not only the strength of the searcher-contact tie but also its gender composition and gender homophily.[3]

DATA AND MEASURES—THE UNDERCLASS SAMPLE

Data

The data we use to test these arguments come from a 1995 study of residents of a mid-sized Southern city in the United States. The characteristics of the areas from which our underclass sample is drawn correspond to conventional definitions of the underclass: high rates of poverty, unemployment, and underemployment. We compare residents of these poor areas to residents of middle-class areas that surround these communities. We collected data through telephone interviews with residents of these areas, using random-digit dialing to select the sample (see Hurlbert et al. 1998 for more details on the characteristics of the sample). Because census data indicated that as many as 30 percent of households in the core underclass study area lacked telephones, we constructed a supplemental sample of these households, selected through randomization techniques from blocks in which the proportion of households without a working telephone was high. Interviews with residents of sampled nontelephone households were conducted by cellular telephones, provided by field contacts.

Measures

In order to assess the extent to which our respondents used social capital that inheres in network structure to find their current jobs, we first asked employed respondents how they found the jobs that they currently held. Our classification contrasts those who used informal methods (e.g., ties drawn from social networks) with those who did not (e.g., who used formal methods [employment agencies, newspaper ads] and direct application). We then asked respondents who used informal methods a series of questions about the contact who provided information about their current jobs. To measure the strength of the searcher-contact tie, we asked each respondent whether he or she was very close (1), somewhat close (.5), or not close at all (0) to the contact. We use two versions of this measure in our analyses. The first, "strong tie," compares very close (1) ties to those who were either somewhat close or not close at all (0); the second, "closeness," uses all three categories. Using information on the gender of the search contact and the respondent, we created a measure of gender homophily that taps whether the search contact was the same (1) or a different (0) gender than the respondent. We asked respondents whether (1) or not (0), at the time of the search, the contact was employed at the destination firm. Finally, we asked whether (1) or not (0) respondents perceived that the contacts used influence on their behalf.

Because the case bases for our analyses are small, we cannot control for job tenure. Although we are not predicting search outcomes, the issue of tenure becomes important in considering the time at which the job search took place: Because some respondents may have found their current jobs 5 years ago and others 15 years ago, they may have faced very different labor-market conditions. The average tenure among residents of underclass areas is 5.26 years; among residents of middle-class areas, it is 6.18. The difference between them is not statistically significant.

RESULTS

We begin our exploration of differences between residents of underclass and more affluent areas in the use of network social capital for job finding by comparing the job-finding methods of the two groups. The first line of Table 2, Panel A shows a statistically significant difference between residents of underclass and more affluent areas in the proportions of individuals who used informal methods: Contrary to predictions drawn from Wilson's (1987, 1991) and Granovetter's (1982) work, a larger proportion of residents of poorer, as opposed to more affluent areas used this form of social capital to find their current jobs. This finding is particularly surprising in light of the fact that the work histories of residents of the underclass areas are poorer (e.g., they have longer spells of unemployment, less work experience) than those of residents of more affluent areas. Consistent with that pattern, we find significantly greater use of personal contacts among individuals with poorer work histories (results available upon request).

Turning to our comparisons for people who used informal methods (contacts) in their job searches, we explore (a) the characteristics of the searcher-contact ties (Table 2, Panel A), (b) the characteristics of search contacts and the resources that they provided (Panel A), and (c) the association between (a) and (b) (Panels B–E). Beginning with the characteristics of searcher-contact ties, we find no significant difference in the proportions of residents of underclass and more affluent areas who found their jobs through weak ties, on either tie-strength measure. These results contradict the predictions drawn from Wilson (1987) and Granovetter (1982), who cite the absence of weak ties as a defining characteristic of social isolation in the underclass. Gender homophily of the contact also fails to differentiate residents of underclass areas from residents of more affluent areas.

When we examine the nature of the network social capital used to find jobs among residents of the two types of areas, we find no significant difference in the proportions of job-finding contacts who were employed at the destination firm or in the proportions of contacts who were perceived to exert influence. These results suggest that some residents of underclass areas may have better access to network social capital for job finding than social-isolation arguments predict. That suggestion finds support in the fact that, among employed residents of underclass areas who found their jobs through personal contacts, nearly 71 percent found them through contacts who were employed at the destination firm and over 57 percent found them through contacts who were perceived to exert influence.

To extend these analyses, we combined these two measures to compare individuals who used contacts who were either employed at the destination firm or used influence on the searcher's behalf to those whose contacts provided only information. We found that a significantly higher propor-

Table 2. Social Capital and the Underclass: Mean Differences

A. One-Way Comparisons	Underclass	Middle Class	t-Test
Person contact	.550 (129)	.446 (121)	+
Strong tie	.463 (54)	.525 (40)	
Closeness	.639 (54)	.675 (40)	
Gender homophily	.763 (59)	.675 (40)	
Contact employee	.709 (55)	.568 (44)	
Contact influence	.571 (55)	.568 (44)	
Influence or employee	.855 (55)	.682 (44)	*

B. Tie Strength	Strong	Weak	t-Test
Contact employee	.630 (46)	.608 (46)	
Underclass	.680 (25)	.704 (27)	
Middle class	.571 (21)	.474 (19)	
Contact influence	.587 (46)	.511 (47)	
Underclass	.600 (25)	.536 (28)	
Middle class	.571 (21)	.474 (19)	
Influence or employee	.804 (46)	.717 (46)	
Underclass	.880 (25)	.814 (27)	
Middle class	.714 (21)	.579 (19)	
Gender homophily	.652 (46)	.813 (48)	+
Underclass	.720 (25)	.828 (29)	
Middle class	.571 (21)	.789 (19)	

C. Gender Homophily	Homophilous	Heterophilous	t-Test
Strong tie	.435 (69)	.640 (25)	+
Female contact	.514 (72)	.148 (27)	**
Underclass	.533 (45)	.143 (14)	**
Middle class	.481 (27)	.154 (13)	*
Contact employee	.582 (67)	.731 (26)	
Underclass	.625 (40)	.923 (13)	**
Middle class	.519 (27)	.538 (13)	
Contact influence	.618 (68)	.385 (26)	*
Underclass	.610 (41)	.462 (13)	
Middle class	.629 (27)	.308 (13)	*
Influence or employee	.761 (67)	.769 (26)	
Underclass	.800 (40)	1.000 (13)	*
Middle class	.704 (27)	.538 (13)	

D. Contact Gender	Male	Female	t-Test
Contact homophily	.603 (58)	.902 (41)	**
Underclass	.636 (33)	.923 (26)	**
Middle class	.560 (25)	.867 (15)	*

continued

Table 2.   (continued)

E. Respondent Gender	Male	Female	t-Test
Contact homophily	.897 (39)	.617 (60)	**
Underclass	.913 (23)	.667 (36)	**
Middle class	.875 (16)	.542 (24)	*
Contact influence	.692 (39)	.492 (61)	*
Underclass	.609 (23)	.545 (33)	
Middle class	.812 (16)	.429 (28)	*

+$p < .10$.
*$p < .05$.
**$p < .01$.
N for each group appears in parentheses.

tion of residents of underclass, as opposed to more affluent areas, found their jobs through contacts who were either employed at the destination firm or used influence on their behalf. These findings differ from the predictions of the social-isolation literature and the findings of Green et al. (1995).

Finally, we asked whether an association existed between the nature of the searcher-contact tie and the characteristics of contacts and resources, among residents of each type of area. Because our case base is small, we interpret these comparisons cautiously. We found no significant differences in the degree to which strong, as opposed to weak ties were associated with access to employed contacts or contacts who used influence on behalf of the searcher, among residents of either type of area (Table 2, Panel B). Among employed residents of both areas who found their jobs informally, gender-homophilous ties were significantly more likely than gender-heterophilous ties to connect the searcher to female job-finding contacts (Panel C). A significant, positive association exists between the gender homophily of the tie and the nature of the social capital provided. Among residents of underclass areas, gender-heterophilous contacts are significantly more likely to have been employed at the destination firm. We also found a significant, positive association between gender heterophily of the job-finding contact and the variable that taps whether the contact either used influence on the searcher's behalf or was employed at the destination firm, among residents of underclass areas. Conversely, among residents of more affluent areas, gender-homophilous contacts were significantly more likely to have used influence on the searcher's behalf. Thus, gender heterophily seems to have served as social capital for residents of underclass areas, whereas gender homophily proved beneficial for residents of more affluent areas.

The last two panels of Table 2 explore further the gender structure of searcher-contact ties. These panels suggest three things. First, female contacts are used almost exclusively by female searchers, among residents of both areas; conversely, male contacts are used by both male and female searchers (Panel D). Second, among residents of both areas, male job searchers are more likely than female searchers to have found their jobs through gender-homophilous contacts (Panel E). Third, among residents of more affluent areas, male searchers are significantly more likely than female searchers to have received influence from the contact. But the pattern does not hold for residents of underclass areas: There, male searchers do not appear to have received significantly more of this form of social capital.

The results of Table 2, Panels D and E, can inform the interpretation of the effects in Panel C. For example, among residents of underclass areas, the significant difference between heterophilous and homophilous ties, in the proportion of contacts who were employed at the destination firm (Panel C), needs to be interpreted in light of the fact that nearly all gender heterophilous ties connected female searchers to male contacts (Panels D and E). Among residents of middle-class areas, the significant difference, between heterophilous and homophilous ties, in connecting the searcher to a contact who used influence needs to be interpreted in light of the fact that male residents of middle-class areas are significantly more likely than their female counterparts to have used a contact who provided influence.

Among employed residents of underclass areas, then, we find more extensive receipt of job-finding social capital from network ties than the social-isolation literature predicts. We find no significant differences between residents of the two types of areas in the characteristics of ties, contacts, or resources, with one exception: A significantly higher proportion of underclass residents found their current jobs through contacts who were either connected to the destination firm or used influence on their behalf; this finding is primarily a function of contacts' connections to the destination firm. These results are inconsistent with predictions drawn from the social-isolation literature. We find some differences between residents of the two areas in the association between the nature of searcher-contact ties and the resources that they provided. Chief among these is the finding that gender-heterophilous ties are more likely than gender homophilous ties to have provided social capital to residents of underclass areas, but the reverse is true for residents of more affluent areas.

CONCLUSIONS

Our analyses of social networks and social capital in the extreme environments of a natural disaster and an underclass population underscore the importance of recognizing the social-network and social-resources elements of social capital and the relationship between them. Taken together, they show that, for both elements, forms of social capital that are valuable in one environment may be useless or even harmful in another. For example, although more educated individuals typically enjoy greater access to social capital, they may have less access to the kinds of network structures that facilitate reception of informal support in the hurricane context. Our analyses of social capital among residents of underclass areas suggest that gender-heterophilous ties provide resources for residents of underclass areas, whereas gender-homophilous ties are more likely to benefit residents of more affluent areas. Just as Erickson (this volume) argues that forms of useful social capital may be labor-market specific, so too can they be specific to broader social contexts. We note that gender-heterophilous ties are used primarily by women. It is possible that, among residents of middle-class areas, gender-homophilous ties are beneficial because a majority of individuals are locating sex-segregated jobs. Conversely, if residents of underclass areas are finding employment in less sex-segregated jobs, then the range indicated by gender-heterophilous ties may be more beneficial.

Our analyses of the ways in which social networks and their constituent ties provide social capital in extreme environments also underscore the need to consider the relationship between potential and activated forms of social capital (see Erickson, this volume). The analyses we present in this chapter explore the prevalence and nature of activated social capital. But we focus only on employed individuals; as our earlier analyses (Hurlbert et al. 1998) of potential resources in the underclass suggest, the social-isolation argument may portray more accurately the potential resources available to the portion of the underclass population that is not employed. Exploring the social-isolation argument fully will require both types of analyses. It will also require exploration of the processes by which potential resources become actual resources in underclass populations. One strategy for doing so is to follow the approach that we developed in our study of Hurricane Andrew and ask what kinds of core networks are activated for social capital in underclass populations (the link between core networks and activated ties) with what results (linking activated ties and outcomes).

These kinds of studies are more difficult to craft in an underclass population: Unlike the general population, residents of these areas function routinely in an extreme environment. Thus, it becomes more difficult to identify a situation in which a large number of residents, at any time, activate network ties for a given resource. Events like those that surround the current welfare reform in the United States may provide an opportunity for such analyses. As individuals who have been forced off welfare rolls move into job-training programs and attempt the transition into the labor force, exploring the activation process may help us to understand better how their networks constrain and facilitate access to social capital.

NOTES

1. We asked respondents to place their income in one of seven categories. We recoded the first six categories to their midpoints and the seventh to $85,000. We developed a prediction equation to estimate family income for the 59 respondents who failed to report it. Details are available from the first author upon request.
2. Thus, we do not consider the utility of these methods or of contact / tie characteristics. We also note that we make only one comparison here, between residents of underclass and middle-class areas.
3. Tigges et al. (1998) used a measure of contact gender in examining the utility of social resources, but did not compare the prevalence of gender-homophilous contacts between poorer and more affluent individuals.

REFERENCES

Bailey, Stefanie, and Peter V. Marsden. 1999. "Interpretation and Interview Context: Examining the General Social Survey Name Generator Using Cognitive Methods." *Social Networks* 21:287–309.

Beggs, John J., Valerie A. Haines, and Jeanne S. Hurlbert. 1996a. "Situational Contingencies Surrounding the Receipt of Social Support." *Social Forces* 75:201–22.

———. 1996b. "The Effects of Personal Network and Local Community Contexts on the Receipt of Formal Aid During Disaster Recovery." *International Journal of Mass Emergencies and Disasters* 14:57–78.

Bourdieu, Pierre. 1986. "The Forms of Capital." Pp. 241–58 in *Handbook of Theory and Research for the Sociology of Education*, edited by John G. Richardson. New York: Greenwood Press.

Campbell, Karen E., Peter V. Marsden, and Jeanne S. Hurlbert. 1986. "Social Resources and Socioeconomic Status." *Social Networks* 8:87–117.

Coleman, James S. 1990. *Foundations of Social Theory*. Cambridge: Harvard.

Erickson, Bonnie. 2001. "Good Networks and Good Jobs: The Value of Social Capital to Employers and Employees." In *Social Capital: Theory and Research*, edited by Nan Lin, Karen Cook, and Ronald S. Burt. New York: Aldine de Gruyter.

Fernandez, Roberto M., and David Harris. 1992. "Social Isolation and the Underclass." Pp. 257–93 in *Drugs, Crime, and Social Isolation*, edited by Adel Harrell and George Peterson. Washington, DC: The Urban Institute.

Fischer, Claude S. 1982. *To Dwell Among Friends: Personal Networks in Town and City*. Chicago: University of Chicago Press.

Granovetter, Mark S. 1982. "The Strength of Weak Ties: A Network Theory Revisited." Pp. 105–30 in *Social Structure and Network Analysis*, edited by Peter V. Marsden and Nan Lin. Beverly Hills: Sage.

Green, Gary P., Leann M. Tigges, and Irene Browne. 1995. "Social Resources, Job Search, and Poverty in Atlanta." *Research in Community Sociology* 5:161–82.

Green, Gary Paul, Leann M. Tigges, and Daniel Diaz. 1999. "Racial and Ethnic Differences in Job Search Strategies in Atlanta, Boston and Los Angeles." *Social Science Quarterly* 80:263–78.

Haines, Valerie A., and Jeanne S. Hurlbert. 1992. "Network Range and Health." *Journal of Health and Social Behavior* 33:254–66.

Haines, Valerie A., John J. Beggs, and Jeanne S. Hurlbert. Forthcoming. "Exploring the Structural Contexts of the Support Process: Social Networks, Social Statuses, Social Support, and Psychological Distress." *Advances in Medical Sociology*.

Hammer, Muriel. 1983. "'Core' and 'Extended' Social Networks in Relation to Health and Illness." *Social Science and Medicine* 17:405–11.

Hurlbert, Jeanne S., Valerie A. Haines, and John J. Beggs. 2000. "Core Networks and the Activation of Ties: What Kinds of Routine Social Networks Allocate Resources in Nonroutine Situations?" *American Sociological Review* 65:598–618.

Hurlbert, Jeanne S., John J. Beggs, and Valerie A. Haines. 1998. "Exploring the Relationship Between the Network Structure and Network Resources Dimensions of Social Isolation: What Kinds of Networks Allocate Resources in the Underclass?" Presented at the International Conference on Social Networks and Social Capital, Duke University, November 1998.

Lin, Nan, and Mary Dumin. 1986. "Access to Occupations Through Social Ties." *Social Networks* 8:393–405.

Lin, Nan, Walter M. Ensel, and John C. Vaughn. 1981. "Social Resources and Strength of Ties: Structural Factors in Occupational Status Attainment." *American Sociological Review* 46:393–405.

Lin, Nan, Mary W. Woelfel, and Stephen C. Light. 1985. "The Buffering Effect of Social Support Subsequent to an Important Life Event." *Journal of Health and Social Behavior* 26:247–63.

Marsden, Peter V. 1987. "Core Discussion Networks of Americans." *American Sociological Review* 52:122–31.

Marsden, Peter V., and Karen E. Campbell. 1984. "Measuring Tie Strength." *Social Forces* 63:482–501.

Oliver, Melvin L. 1988. "The Urban Black Community as Network: Toward a Social Network Perspective." *The Sociological Quarterly* 29:623–45.

Pescosolido, Bernice A. 1991. "Illness Careers and Network Ties: A Conceptual Model of Utilization and Compliance." Pp. 161–84 *Advances in Medical Sociology*, edited by Gary Albrecht and Judith Levy. Greenwich, CT: JAI.

Podolny, Joel M., and James N. Baron. 1997. "Resources and Relationships: Social Networks and Mobility in the Workplace." *American Sociological Review* 62:673–93.

Portes, Alejandro. 1998. "Social Capital: Its Origins and Applications in Modern Sociology." *Annual Review of Sociology* 24:1–24.

Singh, Vijai P. 1991. "The Underclass in the United States: Some Correlates of Economic Change." *Sociological Inquiry* 61:505–21.

Stanton-Salazar, Ricardo D. 1997. "A Social Capital Framework for Understanding the Socialization of Racial Minority Children and Youths." *Harvard Educational Review* 67:1–39.

Tigges, Leann M., Irene Browne, and Gary P. Green. 1998. "Social Isolation of the

Urban Poor: Race, Class, and Neighborhood Effects on Social Resources." *Sociological Quarterly* 39:53–77.

Wacquant, Loïc J. D., and William Julius Wilson. 1989. "The Cost of Racial and Class Exclusion in the Inner City." *Annals of the American Academy of Political and Social Science* 501:8–25.

Wellman, Barry, Renita Yuklin Wong, David Tindall, and Nancy Nazer. 1997. "A Decade of Network Change: Turnover, Persistence, and Stability in Personal Communities." *Social Networks* 19:27–50.

Wellman, Barry, and Kenneth Frank. Forthcoming. "Network Capital in a Multi-Level World: Getting Support from Personal Communities." In *Social Capital: Theory and Research*, edited by Nan Lin, Karen Cook, and Ronald S. Burt. New York: Aldine de Gruyter.

Wilson, William Julius. 1987. *The Truly Disadvantaged: The Inner City, the Underclass, and Public Policy*. Chicago: University of Chicago.

———. 1991. "Public Policy Research and the Truly Disadvantaged." Pp. 460–81 in *The Urban Underclass*, edited by Christopher Jencks and Paul E. Teterson. Washington, DC: Brookings Institution.

Young, Alford A., Jr. 1999. "The (Non)Accumulation of Capital: Explicating the Relationship of Structure and Agency in the Lives of Poor Black Men." *Sociological Theory* 17:201–27.

10

Network Capital in a Multilevel World: Getting Support from Personal Communities

Barry Wellman and Kenneth A. Frank

TIES AND NETWORKS

When people need help, they can either buy it, trade for it, steal it, get it from governments and charities, or obtain it through their *"personal community networks"*—supportive ties with friends, relatives, neighbors and workmates. Such ties supply *"network capital,"* the form of "social capital" that makes resources available through interpersonal ties. It is widely available, usually specialized, and unevenly distributed among people, ties, and networks. Network members provide emotional aid, material aid, information, companionship, and a sense of belonging. Their *"social support"* is one of the main ways that households obtain resources to deal with daily life, seize opportunities, and reduce uncertainties.

These are not trivial pursuits for people or society. For people, personal community networks are flexible, efficient, available, and custom-tailored sources of social capital that are low in financial cost. They may strengthen bonds while providing needed resources (Fischer 1982; Wellman 1999; Schweizer et al. 1998). For society, network capital conveys resources, confirms identity, influences behavior, and reinforces integrative links between individuals, households, and groups (Durkheim 1893; Espinoza 1999; Ferrand, Mounier, & Degenne 1999). The nature of network capital affects the quality, quantity, novelty, and availability of resources (Popielarz 2000). The loosely coupled, networked nature of contemporary societies means that social capital comes contingently from a variety of persons, ties, and networks, rather than stably from a single, solidary group (Wellman 1999, 2001).

Bases of Support

Where does network capital come from? The explanation for who gives what to whom may be in the nature of the giver and receiver, the relationship, or in the composition and structure of the network in which people and ties are embedded. When people need assistance, they often want to know which *relationship* is likely to help them. They wonder:

- Will my brother or my mother lend me money to buy my dream house?
- Will my best friend or my sister be more understanding of my marital problems?
- Who is the best person to ask to babysit tomorrow night?

Such questions provide the basis for our investigation of network capital:

- Is it the *social characteristics of the people* involved, as when a rich man gives money or information to a poor woman (Lin & Dumin 1986)?[2]
- Is it the nature of the *tie*, as when close friends are more supportive than acquaintances (Wellman & Wortley 1990)?
- Is it a network phenomenon, such as the network's *composition:* For example, does a network filled with close friends impel each of them to be extraordinarily supportive?
- Perhaps it is the network's *structure*, with densely knit networks communicating about needs, enforcing norms of supportiveness, and coordinating deliveries of support (Burt 1992; Cook & Whitmeyer 1992; Lin 2001).

When people ponder these kinds of questions, they are analyzing their relationships with different kinds of network members. Because personal communities rarely operate as solidarities, people cannot count on all the people in their network to leap in and provide needed help. Nor is all help actively sought (Wellman 1982; Pescosolido 1992). Hence the provision of network capital depends on the social characteristics of each network member (or *alter*) and the *relational characteristics* of each *tie* with a network member. With respect to the *social characteristics of network members*, support may be a function of the characteristics of *egos* who may receive support or of *alters* who may provide support. For example, women are more likely to receive support, and parents and adult children are more likely to provide support.

People who provide support are not homogeneous grains of sand nor are their ties unstructured heaps of pick-up sticks. When analyses of *social characteristics* look only at the attributes of what aggregated heaps of individuals "possess," they neglect variation in which kinds of alters provide support. On the other hand, analyses at the *tie level*, of the providers and receivers of support, treat each tie as a discrete dyad and ignore the network context of supportive ties. They do not take into consideration how variation in network composition and structure might affect the provision of social support through ties (see the reviews in Gottlieb & Selby 1990; House, Landis, & Umberson 1988; Wellman 1992a).

Sociologically informed analyses of ties within networks have investigated whether the attributes of ties (such as tie strength or frequency of contact) are linked to support or information obtained through these ties. Mark Granovetter has argued that weak ties with socially heterogeneous alters provide more diverse information (1982); our group's research has shown that strong, intimate ties provide more emotional support and companionship (Wellman 1979; Wellman & Wortley 1990), and Haythornthwaite and Wellman (1998) have shown that co-workers who are friends exchange more email. But such analyses have examined effects at the tie level without accounting for the supportive effects of variations in the kinds of people involved and the networks within which they interact.

Support Comes from Ties and Networks

There is more to interpersonal life than just individuals and ties. People are often immersed in milieus filled with companionship, emotional support, or caring for others whose dynamics go beyond the level of the individual alter or tie. The compositional and structural characteristics of *networks* must be taken into account (Hogan & Eggbeen 1995; Wellman & Gulia 1999b). People wonder:

> Where can I get help from? Is my network large enough, coordinated enough, and containing enough of the right kinds of people to give me someone—or perhaps, several people—who can babysit, lend me money, provide marital understanding, or help when I am ill?

Network capital works differently than dyadic capital because in a network there may be group pressures to provide support. The biblical tale of Cain and Abel describes the sanctions that will be imposed on those who act against group members. Those who are disconnected, who are not "their brother's keepers," will find themselves "a fugitive and a wanderer" (*Genesis* 4:12). God serves as the Simmelian third party who can punish transgression in the dyad (Simmel 1922).

Therefore, at the *network level* of analysis, researchers look at the *composition* of the networks (e.g., network size, network heterogeneity, mean frequency of contact, the percent of contacts who are friends) and the *structure* of these networks (e.g., density of *links* among alters). Such analyses seek to understand how the properties of networks affect what happens in them (and to them). Which attributes of networks tend to occur together? For example, are densely knit networks more supportive, more controlling, or both? The size and heterogeneity of a network (its "range") affect its members' access to resources (Haines & Hurlbert 1992; Burt 1983, 1992), and networks with more socioeconomic resources better mobilize supportive network capital (Lin 2001).

Some theories of network capital directly link the provision of support to the social structure in which a person or a tie is embedded. H. G. Wells (1913) wondered if "in the country of the blind" (but nowhere else) would a one-eyed man be king. Portes and Sensenbrenner (1993:1325) describe *enforceable trust* as occurring in networks, when an "actor's behavior is not oriented to a particular other but to the web of social networks." (See also Weber 1922 on "particularistic obligations.") In our biblical example, Abel should have been able to enforce the trust of Cain due to their mutual obligation to the network that includes God. We have the moral in terms of sanctions imposed for violated trust. By contrast, other forms of network capital such as *specific exchanges, generalized reciprocity* (Sahlins 1965), and *altruistic value introjection* may depend on the specific circumstances of the tie, if they are not embedded in a densely knit network.

Nor is it only a question of whether the characteristics of the network *or* the tie *or* the alter independently affect the availability of network capital. The story of Cain and Abel illustrates how the effects of ties may be contingent on the types of networks in which they are situated. As in biblical times, kin may be called on for support when they are enmeshed in networks, and adult sons are more likely to aid their elderly parents when there are not any adult daughters available (Stone, Rosenthal, & Connidis 1998). People navigate nimbly through partial involvements in multiple networks; as members of these networks they are subject to the networks' constraints and opportunities. The helpfulness of ties is enhanced by being in a resource-rich network (Lai, Lin, & Leung 1998).

How are the propensity of alters and ties to be supportive affected by the kinds of networks in which they are embedded? At this *interactive level* of analysis, we wonder if being in a network composed of similar others will foster a greater tendency to supportiveness. For example, are kin more apt to be supportive when the tie is embedded in a network filled with kin.

This would be a potentiating interaction effect. But there could be suppressive interactions as well. Consider the folk saying, "quantity doesn't equal quality," which argues that intimates are less likely to be supportive in large networks.

Network capital thus operates through many aspects of interpersonal life that make resources available:[3]

1. Ego's Social Characteristics: The needs and resources that a person already possesses, including his/her ability to attract social support.
2. Network Size: The number of ties that a person ("ego") has in his/her personal network.
3. Resource Possession: The resources that these network members ("alters") possess.
4. Ego-Alter Similarity: The similarity of ego's and alters' social characteristics.
5. Resource Availability: The willingness of alters to provide these resources to ego.
6. Resource Delivery: The ability of alters to deliver these resources to ego.
7. Support History: The support that alters have already given to egos, short-term and long-term.
8. Reciprocity: The history of support that egos have given to alters.
9. Network Composition: The characteristics of all alters in a network, both:
   a. *Similarity:* The tendency of similar alters to facilitate each other's delivery of resources.
   b. *Dissimilarity:* The diversity of alters in a network.
10. Network Structure: The structure of interpersonal relations that:
    a. *Information Flows:* Disseminate knowledge about ego's needs and resources.
    b. *Social Control:* Facilitate or constrain the provision of resources.
11. Indirect Ties: Ties to people outside the network that provide access to additional resources.

The Usefulness of a Multilevel Approach

Until recently, studies of network capital have been constrained by their methodological inability to integrate analytic levels into a comprehensive analysis. Methodological weakness has led to constrained analysis. Technical incompatibilities (and disciplinary preoccupations; see Milardo & Wellman 1992) have largely led individual, tie, network, and interactive analyses to develop separately until now. Quantitative analysts have examined separately the effects of *either* individual characteristics, ties, *or* the ego-centered, personal community networks in which they are embedded. Little quantitative analysis has been done of interactive effects.

Because many statistical techniques assume independence between units of analysis, they cannot focus simultaneously on different units of analysis. Yet the availability of network capital may well be affected by individual "agency" (self-organized actions on one's own behalf), ties dancing interpersonal duets, *and* the constraints and opportunities provided by networks with different sorts of structure and composition.[4] Not only do people need—and want—to know which kinds of people (an *individual-level analysis*) and relationships (a *tie-level analysis*) are apt to provide different kinds of support, they also need and want to know the extent to which their social networks as a whole can support them (a *network-level analysis*).

Although scholars "know" that individuals and ties are affected by their environing networks, and "know" that the effects of networks occur through the behavior of individual actors in specific interpersonal ties, it is one thing to state this knowledge metaphorically and quite another to specify how the contingent effects of individual, tie, and network characteristics actually play out. There is the danger of reification: seeing findings at only one analytic level—individual, tie or network—as the only truth rather than taking into account the comprehensive interplay of multiple levels.[5]

MULTILEVEL MODELS FOR TIES NESTED IN EGO-CENTERED NETWORKS

Research Approach

This chapter goes beyond an *either/or* analysis to a form of *multilevel analysis* (Bryk & Raudenbush 1992; DiPrete & Forristal 1994; Longford 1995; Snijders & Bosker 1999; Snijders, Spreen, & Zwaagstra 1995). Multilevel analysis is just starting to be used in sociology to integrate "nested data" into a single statistical model, such as occurs with residents in neighborhoods, children in schools, nation-states in world systems, or, as here, individuals and ties in personal networks (e.g., Sampson, Morenoff, & Earls 1999; Thomése & van Tilburg 1998, 2000; van Duijn, van Busschbach, & Snijders 1999). As van Duijn, van Busschbach, and Snijders (1999) state:

> Multilevel or hierarchical linear models explicitly take into account the nested data and the related dependency structure by incorporating unexplained variables between ties . . . and also between egos (van Duijn [p. 188]). Ignoring the nested structure of the data can lead to two kinds of analysis.

> First, ignoring the nesting completely by treating the data as independent observations [as earlier tie-level analyses had done]. Second, eliminating the dependency by averaging [tie data in each personal network]. The first method . . . [produces] biased standard errors, underestimation of standard errors, and possibly . . . false conclusions. The second method is statistically correct, but suffers from loss of information [and lessened analytic power]. (p. 205)

Along with van Duijn, van Busschbach, and Snijders, we pioneer here the integration of individual, tie, and network-level analyses in a single statistical model to see how the provision of support in ties is a joint product of the characteristics of people, ties, and networks. Each tie and the person (or "alter") at the end of that tie is nested in each personal network and the person (or "ego") to which that network belongs. The nature of ego-centered networks means that we take individual-level analyses into account in two ways. First, because each ego possesses a personal community network, for the purposes of empirical analysis there is a 1:1 mapping between egos and such networks. An individual-level social characteristic, such as the ego's gender, is as much a property of the network as is the density or size of this network, or if you like, the density of the network is a property of the ego. This means that network and ego characteristics can be analyzed at the same network level of analysis. Second, there is a similar mapping between the characteristics of ties (e.g., tie strength, provision of social support) and the characteristics of alters (e.g., gender, marital status) at the other ends of these ties with egos. For example, an alter's gender is as much a property of the tie as is the strength of the tie. This means that the characteristics of ties and alters can be analyzed at the same tie level of analysis.

As we go beyond a single focus on the effects of either individual, tie, *or* network properties on behavior, we encounter the basic social scientific question of *emergent properties*. We ask if the provision of support is related only to the characteristics of individuals or ties, or is it also related to the characteristics of the personal networks in which they are embedded? Does one also have to take into account the characteristics of all network members—will women be more supportive in networks filled with women?—and the social structures in which their ties are embedded—will people be more supportive in densely knit networks? We suspect that all levels of analysis are contingently important. If so, multilevel analysis can contribute to theory, as well as to method and substance.

In particular, we tease out the extent to which the provision of social support is associated with the effects of the following:

1. The social characteristics of the ego who receives support (e.g., the gender of the individual);

2. The ego's personal network (e.g., the size of the network; the general level of access ego has to alters);
3. The social characteristics of the alters in these networks (e.g., the gender of the alter);
4. The characteristics of the ties that connect egos and alters (e.g., membership in a common organization);
5. Combinations of ego and alter characteristics that characterize the tie (e.g., the access of the alter);
6. Interactions of ego/network characteristics with alter/tie characteristics.

This multilevel approach has two advantages. First, it provides estimates of the effects of variables at the individual, tie, and network levels while controlling for effects at the other levels. Where it had been easy to misattribute tie effects to network effects (and vice versa), the multilevel approach enables us to identify the relative strength of individual, tie, and network effects on the provision of social support.

Second, it captures elusive interactive effects of network capital by examining how the composition and structure of networks affect individual and tie supportiveness. This test for emergent properties is captured in multilevel analysis by crossing tie-level effects (the characteristics of the tie) and network-level effects (of the composition and structure of the network). Moreover, multilevel statistical models can be more carefully specified by aligning the tie- and network-level effects to be crossed. For example, the effects of network capital among kin can be observed by crossing the parent/child effect with the extent to which ego's network generally contains kin.

To assess the analytic power of our approach, we compare our results to earlier baseline analyses of the same data that analyzed individual, tie, and network characteristics separately: Effects 1 and 2 are at the ego/network level, effects 3, 4, and 5 are at the alter/tie level, and effect 6 is a cross of ego/network and alter/tie levels.

We define a basic model specified at the level of the dyadic tie comparable to the model estimated by Wellman (1979)—whose data we use. For example, define *everyday support*$_{ij}$ to take a value of 1 if person j receives everyday support from her ith tie, and 0 if person j does not receive support from her ith tie. As in Wellman and Wortley (1990), we employ the logistic transformation of the probability that a dichotomous outcome takes a value of 1 or 0 (this defines a logit model). In this example, our model includes effects of the characteristic of the jth alter (e.g., *alter's gender*$_{ij}$), and two characteristics of the tie (e.g., the tie's access—*access*$_{ij}$—and if the tie is a parent/adult child relationship—*parent/child*$_{ij}$):

$$\log\left[\frac{P(Everyday\ Support_{ij} = 1)}{1 - P(Everyday\ Support_{ij} = 1)}\right] = \beta_0 + \beta_1\ alter's\ gender_{ij} + \beta_2\ access_{ij}$$

$$+ \beta_3\ parent/child_{ij} \tag{1}$$

Model 1 does not account for the unique effects of individual egos. That is, there may be some people who are particularly likely to engender support. If such people are also likely to have ties with women, parents, and children, or to have highly accessible ties, we will not be able to differentiate the effect of the person from the effects of the types of ties.

Therefore, we extend 1 by incorporating the unique effect of each ego, assigning the subscript j to β_0:

$$\log\left[\frac{P(Everyday\ Support_{ij} = 1)}{1 - P(Everyday\ Support_{ij} = 1)}\right] = \beta_{0j} + \beta_1\ alter's\ gender_{ij} + \beta_2\ access_{ij}$$

$$+ \beta_3\ parent/child_{ij} \tag{2}$$

Here the subscript j indicates that there is one β_0 that accounts for each ego j's effect on the likelihood of receiving support. While we could obtain estimates of each of the J egos using a fixed-effects model (such as through the use of dummy variables or an ANOVA-like framework), this would tax our degrees of freedom, distracting from the focus of the model. Moreover, the egos are merely a sample from a larger set of persons. Therefore, we treat the β_{0j} as random effects, distributed normally, with variance σ^2. Thus we need only estimate one extra parameter, σ^2, which represents the variation in ego's tendencies to attract support.

Further, we might hypothesize that the extent to which a given person is supported is a function of some characteristics of the ego such as his/her age or gender. In order to estimate the effect of an ego's gender on everyday support we model the term β_{0j}, which represents the baseline extent to which ego j receives support. This is the key to multilevel models (Burnstein 1980), as β_{0j} is used as an outcome in a "level two" model:

$$\beta_{0j} = \gamma_{00} + \gamma_{01}ego's\ gender_j + u_{0j} \tag{3}$$

This model can be reinterpreted as a typical regression model. There is an outcome representing the extent to which a given ego is likely to receive support from a given tie (β_{0j}), an intercept (γ_{00}), an effect of the ego's gender (γ_{01}), and an error term (u_{0j}).[6]

Without the multilevel model defined by 2 and 3, we fail to account for effects of each ego and network on the multiple ties in which each ego engages. That is, there are dependencies among the observations of the multiple ties nested within each ego. If ignored, these dependencies have negative implications for statistical estimation and hypothesis testing (Bryk & Raudenbush 1992). By contrast, the multilevel model captures the sampling design of the data, namely the nesting of ties within egos. Therefore we observe at the first level effects of the alter and tie—such as the effect of *access*, and we observe at the second level effects of the ego or network—such as the effect of *ego's gender*.

The multilevel model also facilitates the differentiation of effects at the tie level from corresponding effects based on aggregate characteristics at the ego/network level. For example, although we hypothesize that people may be more likely to receive support from more accessible ties, there may also be a compositional effect. Egos who in general have more accessible ties may receive more support. To differentiate the two effects of tie and ego/network, we first "center" the tie level (level one) predictor, $access_{ij}$, around the mean level of accessibility of ego's ties (this is accomplished by creating a new predictor: $access^*_{ij} = access_{ij} - access_{.j}$). This new term captures the accessibility of a tie *relative to* the general level of accessibility of ego's ties. Next, we include the general level of the accessibility of ego's ties in the ego level (level two) model:

$$\beta_{0j} = \gamma_{00} + \gamma_{01}\overline{access}_j + u_{0j} \tag{4}$$

Thus γ_{01} represents the compositional effect of ego's general access to ties.

Multilevel models also facilitate specification of effects produced by crossing characteristics at each level. In particular, the theory of network capital suggests that those ties that are embedded in homophilous networks (containing ties and alters with similar characteristics) are more likely to be supportive than those that are not (Lazarsfeld & Merton 1954; Marsden 1988; Wellman & Gulia 1999b). In our case, this can be tested by assessing the effect of ego's mean access on β_2, the effect of access at the tie level. We expect that ties who have high access to ego will be more likely to be supportive if ego in general has high access to ties, because in such a case the accessible alter is committed not only to ego, but to the accessible network of ties in which ego and alter are both embedded. This effect can be tested by modeling β_{2j}, the effect of the accessibility of the tie on the likelihood of support for ego j, as a function of the general level of accessibility of the ties of ego j:

$$\beta_{2j} = \gamma_{20} + \gamma_{21}\overline{access}_j + u_{2j} \tag{5}$$

Here, γ_{21} represents the extent to which the effect of access to a particular tie is accentuated (or attenuated) when ego's ties generally tend to be accessible. Technically, the effect associated with γ_{21} is an interaction effect, resulting from the multiplication of the level 1 ($access_{ij}$) and level 2 ($access_j$) predictors.[7]

The differences in the effects associated with γ_{01}, γ_{20}, and γ_{21} are represented in the two hypothetical networks shown in Figure 1. The distance between ego and alter represents accessibility, and a line connects the two if the tie is supportive. The effect of the tie level is shown as: for each ego, the closer the tie (relative to ego's other ties), the more likely the tie is to provide support (the effect associated with γ_{20}). Also, the effect at the network level is shown as: ego A, who has more close ties, in general receives more support than ego B. (This effect is associated with γ_{01}). But note that the effect of the tie accessibility is greater for ego A than for ego B. The more accessible alters for ego A are 200 percent more likely to offer support than the less accessible alters (all six of the more accessible alters offer support whereas only three of the less accessible alters offer support). By contrast, the more accessible alters for ego B are only 50 percent more likely to offer support as the less accessible alters (three versus two). This interaction effect is associated with γ_{21}.

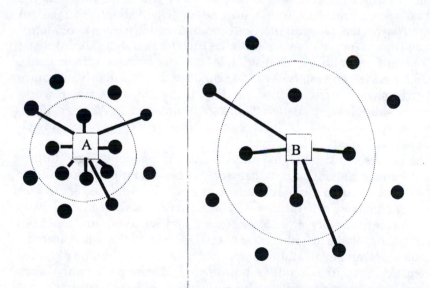

Figure 1.   Effects of accessibility on support in a multilevel framework. Egos are in squares, alters are represented by circles. Distance between ego and alter indicates accessibility. A line that indicates alter supports ego.

We can explore similar effects with regard to a tie being with a parent or an adult child. The main effect of a *parent/child* tie may be that such ties are more supportive at the tie level. At the network level there may be an additional effect of egos who have many ties with parents and adult children. But without testing the interaction effect we do not know if the extra support for such egos actually comes from the parents and children. By estimating a parameter similar to γ_{21} for the *parent/child* effect we can learn whether the effect of parent/child ties is heightened when ego is embedded in a network with several parent/child alters. If such were true it would suggest that the commitment of the parent/child tie is accentuated when embedded in a familial context. This would be consistent with the argument that the commitment is as much to the family as to the individual.

STUDYING THE NETWORK SOURCES OF SUPPORT

Data Collection

Our data come from a random sample survey of 845 adult (18+) Torontonians residing in the Borough of East York in 1968, conducted supplemented by lengthy interviews a decade later with a small subsample of the original respondents. East York, with a population of about 100,000, is an integral part of the transportation and communication networks of Metropolitan Toronto (population = 3 million +). It is located about six miles east of Toronto's central business district, a half-hour subway ride or drive. When the survey and interviews were conducted, its small private homes and apartments housed a settled, predominantly British-Canadian working- to middle-class population (Gillies & Wellman 1968; Wellman 1982). East York has had a long tradition of active social service agencies and voluntary organizations.

The in-person, closed-ended survey asked respondents/egos to provide information about each of their socially closest, intimate ties outside of their household up to a maximum of six ties.[8] They reported about a total of 3,930 intimate ties (mean = 4.7). Most networks were a low-density mixture (mean density = 0.33) of friends and relatives, and most ties stretched beyond the neighborhood to elsewhere in Metropolitan Toronto. One-quarter were beyond the metropolitan boundaries. The data provided systematic information about each intimate and information about each network's composition and structure. Thus our study provides information about the strong ties that supply much social support and ignores the many weaker ties important for acquaintanceship, obtaining information, and integrating social systems. Despite the vintage of the data, its findings have proven consistent with more contemporary studies (Wellman 1999).

Independent Variables

For reliability and comparability, our variable definitions are based on previous tie and network-level analyses of these data. We provide more rationale in this section for those constructs that are relatively new.[9]

Tie Strength: Are Stronger Ties More Likely to Be Supportive? Egos/respondents' ranking of the *strength* of their ties with three to six *alters* to whom they feel close.[10] Such *"intimate"* ties usually provide much of the support in a network (Erickson, Radkewycz, & Nosanchuk 1988).

Work and Organizational Ties: Are Socially Close Workmates and Fellow Organization Members More Likely to Be Supportive? "Modernization" arguments suggest a shift from kinship and neighborhood-based ties to those based on working together or participating in voluntary organizations (e.g., Parsons 1943; Inkeles & Smith 1974; Wireman 1984). We use a dichotomous variable at the tie level to represent whether ego and alter are socially close at work or in voluntary organizations.

Mutual Ties: Are Members of Transitive Triads More Likely to Be Supportive? Our Simmelian (1922) argument suggests that those alters who are tied to many of ego's other alters would be more likely to be supportive. Hence we measure the number of mutual ties shared by ego and alter.[11]

Accessibility: Are Accessible Ties in Accessible Networks More Likely to Be Supportive? Our measure of accessibility derives from three equally weighted, correlated, log-transformed, and standardized variables: Frequency of Face-to-Face Contact, Frequency of Telephone Contact, and Residential Distance. These three variables are combined with the percentage of alters who live in Metropolitan Toronto to form a single accessibility measure.[12]

Kinship: Are Immediate Kin More Likely to Be Supportive? Many scholars have found kin more likely to be supportive, especially parents, adult children, and siblings, however, some scholars, have found ties with extended kin—cousins, aunts, uncles, and grandparents—to be less supportive than other network ties.[13] We use three dichotomous variables to explore the three types of kin: parents/adult children, siblings, and extended kin. We report only on effects for parents/children as there were no significant effects for siblings or extended kin.

Reciprocity: Are Alters More Likely to Provide Support to Egos Who Have Helped Them? Support may be given as part of tit-for-tat *reciprocity transactions* (Portes & Sensenbrenner 1993). Egos reported dichotomously if they had provided emergency support to each alter. (Alas, a similar question about everyday support was not asked.)

Network Size: Are Alters in Larger Networks More Likely to Be Supportive? The size of a network may affect its members' access to resources (Haines & Hulbert 1992; Burt 1983, 1992). Size was measured as the number of alters in the network.[14]

Gender of Ego and Alter: Are Women More Likely to Give and Receive Support? Earlier analyses of our data as well as other research have shown that women are more apt to provide support to others.[15] Women often bear a *"triple-load"* of domestic work, paid work and supportive *"net work."* Their *"network-keeping"* is an extension of their historic role as the kin-keepers of western society (Rosenthal 1985). Women may also receive more support than men, as women's everyday practices have become the focus of privatized, domesticated networks. We code female *egos* and *alters* as 1 and males as 0.

Aggregate of Tie/Alter Level Measures: Does Network Composition Affect Extent of Support Provided? For each tie/alter level characteristic, we calculated the mean of the characteristic across all alters for each ego. This provides measures of mean tie strength, mean access to alters, and percentages of each of the dichotomous variables, such as the percentage of women in each network.

Interaction of Tie and Network Characteristics: Are Ties Embedded in a Network of Ties with Similar Characteristics More Likely to Be Supportive? Are the tie-level effects of parent/child and accessible relationships accentuated if an ego is embedded in a network in which such ties predominate? When the tie is embedded in a network of similar ties the support coming from the tie is likely to be stronger because of commitment to the network of ties as much as to the specific ego. Exploring a similar argument, we also test the interaction of *reciprocity* in emergency support with each ego's general level of supporting alters in emergencies. We wonder if tie-level reciprocity would be less important in dense networks of support. These cross-level interaction effects are represented in multilevel analysis by using a characteristic of the ego/network level to model the *effect of* a characteristic at the tie/alter level (see model 5).

Measuring Social Support

As this survey was one of the earliest to inquire about social support (Wellman 1979, 1982), the differentiated nature of social support was not appreciated at that time. Respondents/egos were asked only two broad questions about whether each person they felt socially close to provided social support. The "yes/no" answers to these questions are our dependent variables, and their dichotomous nature calls for logistic regression in tie-level analyses.

- *Which of these do you rely on for help in everyday matters?* Respondents/
  egos report that 23 percent of their socially close, intimate ties provide such everyday support.
- *Which of these do you rely on for help in an emergency?* Respondents/

egos report that 30 percent of their socially close, intimate ties provide such emergency support.

These two forms of support differentiate effects that require the large and immediate contribution of resources in emergencies from smaller, frequent, less immediate acts of everyday support. Thus, the different forms of support tap different levels of commitment and processes. Although the percentages for each form of support are small, 60 percent of egos indicate that they can draw on at least one intimate for everyday support, and 80 percent indicate that they can draw on at least one intimate for emergency support. From the perspective of most egos, their *networks* typically provide support.

Not all people need the same amount of support, and not all forms of support are equally variable across people. The multilevel approach allows us to account for variation in the odds that egos receive support from a given alter. (The estimate of this variation is referred to as $\hat{\sigma}^2$ and is defined by the variation of the u_{0j} in a level 2 model that contains only intercepts in the level 1 and level 2 models.) Egos vary more in the extent to which they received everyday support from an alter ($\hat{\sigma}^2 = 1.69$) than in the extent to which they received emergency support ($\hat{\sigma}^2 = .74$). The relative lack of variation in the provision of emergency support reflects both floor and ceiling effects:

Floor: There is more of an interpersonal and humanitarian obligation to provide emergency support when needed.
Ceiling: Emergency support is rarely needed and can be demanding to provide.

WHICH CHARACTERISTICS OF TIES AND NETWORKS AFFECT SUPPORT

By taking into account the clustering of alters/ties into personal networks, multilevel models integrate the analysis of how both tie and network characteristics affect the provision of social support. In practice, this statistically more appropriate approach generally confirms the robustness of earlier single-level analyses that had looked separately at tie/alter and network/ego characteristics. We are gratified that more than thirty years of analyzing the Toronto data have not been wasted.

Our multilevel results go beyond previous findings. Integration into a single statistical multilevel model:

1. Disentangles identification of what are truly the effects of tie characteristics, network characteristics, or both. For example, if larger networks are more supportive, is this because they are just an aggregation of larger numbers of supportive ties or is there something

about larger networks, *sui generis*, that is associated with more support?

2. Allows the comparative weighing of tie, network and interaction effects. For example, which is more important for the provision of support, a kinship relationship, or having any sort of relationship in a network composed predominantly of kin?

3. Shows the interaction of tie and network characteristics. By computing statistics that cross levels, we identify interactions between individual, tie, and network characteristics. For example, while alters who are in frequent contact tend to be supportive, are they especially supportive when they are in networks where most people are in frequent contact?[16]

We present our findings here, based on the statistics reported in Table 1, as supplemented by information gathered in detailed interviews. Column 1a presents the main effects of tie and network characteristics for *everyday support*, and column 2a presents the main effects for *emergency support*. Columns 1b and 2b include effects generated by crossing variables from the tie and network levels. We follow Bryk and Raudenbush's (1992) convention for presenting multilevel models. We present effects on the intercept at the ego level ("level 2" in multilevel analysis terms) at the top of the table. Terms in bold below represent alter (level 1) slopes. Italicized terms represent cross-level effects. The final multilevel models for everyday and emergency support are presented in a Technical Appendix at the end of this chapter.

Tie Effects (Only)

Tie Strength.   Although we only examine socially close, strong ties here, some ties are closer than others. The data show that the stronger the tie, the more likely is a network member to provide everyday and emergency support. (The reverse is also true: Supportive ties are apt to become stronger over time [Wellman et al. 1997]). This replicates the findings of the first and second studies that tie strength is associated with providing a wide variety of support. Because tie strength is measured relative to ego's other alters, is defined as a tie-level phenomenon only. Multilevel analysis shows that network characteristics do not affect the relationship of tie strength to support. In the loosely coupled world of contemporary personal communities, strong ties function somewhat independently of the networks in which they are embedded.

Workmate Ties.   The only other supportive phenomenon that is purely a tie characteristic is relationships with coworkers. The East Yorkers we studied rarely have socially close ties with co-workers, but when they do, such "workmates" are especially apt to provide more everyday support (but not emergency support). They are in almost daily physical contact,

Table 1. Multilevel Effects on Everyday and Emergency Support

Variables[a]	Everyday Support (1a)	Everyday with Cross-Level Effects (1b)	Emergency Support (2a)	Emergency with Cross-Level Effects (2b)
Intercept	−1.458***	−1.463***	−.341	−.358
	(.372)	(.382)	(.250)	(.252)
Parents/Children	−.260	−.350	−.034	−.041
in the Network (%)	(.403)	(.410)	(.241)	(.244)
Mean Access to	1.077***	1.257***	.379***	.419***
Alters	(.180)	(.185)	(.117)	(.118)
Alters Who Are	1.272***	1.278***	.944***	.955***
Women (%)	(.341)	(.348)	(.229)	(.231)
Ego Is a Woman	.450**	.380*	.282**	.286**
	(.212)	(.216)	(.143)	(.144)
Network Size	−.193***	−.199***	−.224***	−.227***
	(.071)	(.072)	(.046)	(.046)
Alters to Whom Ego Has			2.536***	2.589***
Provided Emergency			(.154)	(.157)
Support (%)				
Alter Is a Parent/Child	.713***	.315	.654***	.204
	(.145)	(.232)	(.134)	(.220)
Parents/Children in		2.460**		2.826**
the Network (%)		(1.102)		(1.099)
Extent of Access to Alter	1.372***	1.411***	.791***	.794***
	(.096)	(.099)	(.084)	(.085)
Mean Access to Alters		1.083***		.592***
		(.220)		(.194)
Alter Is a Woman	.196	.165	.905***	.885***
	(.121)	(.123)	(.111)	(.111)
Strength of Tie	.462***	.396***	.333***	.338***
	(.037)	(.052)	(.031)	(.031)
Ego Is a Woman		−.148***		
		(.065)		
Number of Mutual Ties	.139***	.147***	.071*	.077*
between Ego and Alter	(.050)	(.050)	(.037)	(.038)
Alter Is a Workmate	1.300***	1.302***		
	(.196)	(.199)		
Ego Provided Emergency			1.642***	1.603***
Support to Alter			(.101)	(.104)
Alters to Whom Ego				−1.578**
Provided Emergency				(.618)
Support (%)				

*p ≤ .10.
**p ≤ .05.
***p ≤ .01.
[a]Network/ego predictors are in ordinary font; **tie/alter** predictors are in bold;
cross-level predictors are in italic.

and are well-placed to learn about needs and provide help. Multilevel analysis demonstrates—in a way that earlier single-level analyses did not—that the everyday supportiveness of workmates goes beyond that of other accessible ties. The interviews show that not only do workmates jointly cope with problems on the job, but their proximity and collaboration provide occasions for helping each other in routine ways outside of work, such as lending small amounts of money or discussing problems.

The everyday supportiveness of workmates is more an outcome of their socially close interpersonal relationship than a function of their common involvement in the same work organization. We infer this because socially close members of the same voluntary organizations are not especially supportive. The few intimate ties with members of the same voluntary organizations (who are neither friends, kin, nor workmates) tend to be relatively weak and to have a narrow focus that does not extend to domestic or community concerns (see also Wireman 1984). Although theories of social capital suggest a link between organizational membership and active ties (Putnam 2000), this may be more true at the macrosocial level than in personal networks.

Network Effects (Only)

Mutual Ties.   Pioneer network analyst John Barnes observed: "To discover how A, who is in touch with B and C, is affected by the relation between B and C . . . demands the use of the network concept" (1972:3). Therefore, although we define *mutual ties* at the tie level, we interpret them as a network-level phenomenon. Barnes' observation is borne out by the presence of network effects showing that a tie's supportiveness depends on more than the characteristics of the ego-alter tie alone. The data show that an alter who has many ties with other members of an ego's network is considerably more likely to provide everyday support to this ego and marginally more likely to provide emergency support.[17] The Simmelian (1908) argument applies: those that are connected to common others feel more of a bond to ego, and therefore are more likely to be supportive. This is a local phenomenon—ego-alter ties embedded in densely knit clusters of ties—and not an outcome of whether an entire network is densely knit.

Network Size.   As the size of a personal network increases, so does the number of alters who *might* give support. If the percentage of *actual* support providers does not vary with the size of the network, there would only be an effect of aggregating ties in larger or small networks. An independent network-size effect would occur only if the percentage of supporters varies with different sizes of networks.

The data show a network effect that is consistent with earlier network-only analyses. Egos who have a small number of intimates are more likely to receive both everyday and emergency support from each intimate. This suggests that for the two to six intimates at the heart of a person's networks, quality compensates for quantity. Persons with smaller intimate networks may have more time to attend to each alter and might be more able to evoke support from each of them.

We emphasize here that these findings refer only to intimates. The dynamics of support from intimates may be different from nonintimates. The second interview-based study, which analyzed both intimates and somewhat weaker *"active"* ties, found that active alters were more likely to be supportive when they were in networks containing many other active alters. It is possible that egos with more social skills are able to maintain nonintimate networks that are both larger and more supportive (see also Moore 1990; Parks & Eggert 1991; Riggio & Zimmerman 1991).

Tie Effects, Network Effects, and Cross-Level Interactive Effects

Kinship.   Although exactly half of all intimate ties are with kin, kinship is no longer a particularly supportive system. With one important exception, ties between kin are no more likely to be supportive than ties between unrelated people.

The exception is that the ties between parents and adult children (including in-laws) are especially likely to provide everyday and emergency support. We see remnants of the systemic nature of kinship in the 15 percent of all ties that are parent-child. The presence of more than one parent or adult child in the network makes it more likely that *each* tie between parent and adult children will be supportive (see the cross-level columns 1b and 2b of Table 1). The results are dramatic: The probability of each parent or adult child providing everyday support increases by about 60 percent if there is another parent or child in the network. While about 34 percent of parents and adult children provide everyday support, if there is an additional parent or adult child in the network, the probability of support from *each* parent or child increases to 54 percent.[18] Because each parent or adult child is more likely to be supportive in a network containing more than one parent or adult child, there is a high probability of getting support in such a network from at least one parent or adult child. Support is both a product of parent-child ties and a product of the composition of the networks in which these ties are embedded.

Accessibility.   The impact of accessibility on support is *both* a tie and network phenomenon. Accessible alters (in frequent contact or living nearby) provide more everyday and emergency support. For example, although 23 percent of all ties provide everyday support, 37 percent of *moderately accessible* ties provide everyday support. (We define "moderately accessible" as one standard deviation above average.) This *tie-level* finding supports analysts' contentions that the more contact, the more supportive the relationship. Frequent contact fosters shared values, increases mutual aware-ness of needs and resources, mitigates feelings of loneliness, encourages reciprocal exchanges, and facilities the delivery of aid.[19]

Interviews suggest that the effect of accessibility is specialized. The co-efficients in Table 1 show that accessibility is more important for everyday support. The heavier demands of emergency support partially override the handy availability of help from accessible alters. Frequent contact—or even just being physically available for contact—is vital for the delivery of goods and services such as child minding or the lending of household goods (see also Marsden & Campbell 1984; Espinoza 1999). Accessibility may also make it easier for people to deliver services when their relation-ships are not strong. The interviews show that even nonintimate neighbors exchange services.

More accessible *networks*, containing a high number of accessible ties, are more apt to provide everyday and emergency support. Each tie in a generally accessible network is more likely to be supportive—even those ties that are not themselves accessible. Although this network effect of ac-cessibility is not as strong as the tie-level effect, the high level of contact and supportiveness in accessible networks apparently increases the sup-portiveness of even the less accessible ties in these networks.

The likelihood that an accessible tie will be supportive is higher when it is in an accessible network. This is a potentiating, cross-level effect, sim-ilar to the one described above for ties between parents and adult children. In terms of parameter estimates, while only 23 percent of all alters provide everyday support, a substantially higher percentage (37 percent) of those alters who are moderately accessible provide everyday support. (We de-fine "moderately accessible" as one standard deviation above average.) However, if the *network* (as well the alter) is moderately more accessible than average, the probability of everyday support from a moderately ac-cessible alter in a moderately accessible network rises to 54 percent–more than double the 23 percent baseline probability. Of course, the probability of at least one alter giving support is high in such an accessible network, filled as it is with accessible alters.[20]

Gender of Alter and Ego.   For both egos and alters, gender is the only in-dividual characteristic we studied that is related to the provision of sup-port.[21] Women are more involved in exchanges of social support: female *alters* are more likely to provide emergency support, and female *egos* are more likely to receive everyday and emergency support from their net-works. Multilevel analysis shows that *networks* with a high percentage of women are especially likely to provide everyday and emergency support. It appears that a high percentage of women in a network potentiates the entire network to be more supportive. Or, perhaps egos at the center of such networks have consciously organized their networks to provide more support.

The second East York study suggests that it is *emotional support* that women are especially likely to provide (Wellman & Wortley 1990; Wellman 1992a). There is also a cross-level effect: stronger ties are even more likely to provide everyday support if ego is a man. In other words, not only do women get more everyday support from intimates, this support is likely to come without regard to the strength of the intimate tie. By contrast, men receive their support disproportionately from their very closest intimates.[22] Our findings are basically congruent with the hypothesis *cum* empirical generalization that "women express, men repress," with women interacting "face-to-face" by exchanging emotional support while men interact "side by side" by exchanging goods and services (Perlman & Fehr 1987:21; see also Moore 1990; Wright 1989).

Reciprocity. Egos are likely to receive emergency support from *alters* to whom they have provided emergency support. This is a *tie-level* manifestation of the Matthew (25:29) effect: those who have given also receive. When we interviewed egos a decade after the original survey, we found that those alters who had provided support were more likely to continue as active network members (Wellman et al. 1997).

Reciprocity operates as a network process even more than as a tie process. Egos who have provided emergency support to many alters are more likely to receive emergency support from a given alter. This may represent an effect in which egos and alters contribute to the general group, with reciprocity being from the group instead of from the individual. In fact, the *cross-level interaction* effect of ego's general level of providing emergency support attenuates the reciprocity effect considerably. This suggests that reciprocity transactions between ties and enforceable trust in networks are interrelated forms of network capital that need not be employed concurrently (Portes & Sensenbrenner 1993; Frank & Yasumoto 1998). Where there is a commitment to a larger network, actors need not draw their network capital primarily in the form of tie-level reciprocity transactions. When the network owes support to ego, ego need not depend on ties with specific alters who owe reciprocity.

TOWARD A MULTILEVEL THEORY OF NETWORK CAPITAL

Comparing Multilevel with Single-Level Findings

Just as the nature of social support is diversified, so are the processes that supply it:

- Attenuated Primordial Norms: Kinship, but only between Parent and Adult Child
- Sociobiological Forces: Women

- Handiness: Accessibility through In-Person and Phone Contact
- Structural Imperatives: Mutual Ties
- Self-Interested Politeness: Reciprocity/Social Capital

It is gratifying to veteran researchers to discover that thirty-plus years of single-level analyses are robust enough to hold up in multilevel models (Table 2). As before, we find that strong ties and central ties are more likely to provide most forms of support; parents and children are most likely to provide all forms of support except emotional support; and accessible ties

Table 2. Comparison of Estimates from Multilevel and Single-Level Models

Variables[a]	Everyday Support[b]		Emergency Support[b]	
	Tie Level	Multilevel	Tie Level	Multilevel
Parents/Children in the Network (%)	NC	0	NC	0
Mean Access to Alters	NC	+	NC	+
Alters Who Are Women (%)	NC	+	NC	+
Ego Is a Woman	NC	+	NC	+
Network Size	NC	−	NC	−
Alters to whom Ego has Provided Emergency Support (%)	0	0	NC	+
Alter Is a Parent/Child	Indirect effect	+	+	+
Parents/Children in the Network (%)	NC	+	NC	+
Extent of Access to Alter	+	+	+	+
Mean Access to Alters	NC	+	NC	+
Alter Is a Female	0	+	0	+
Strength of Tie with Alter	+	+	+	+
Ego Is a Woman	NC	−	0	0
Number of Mutual Ties between Ego and Alter	NC	+	NC	+[†]
Alter Is a Workmate	Indirect effect	−	0	0
Ego Provided Emergency Support to Alter	0	0	0	+
Alters to Whom Ego Provided Emergency Support (%)	0	0	NC	−

Source: Tie level data from Wellman (1979).

[a]**Tie or alter** predictors are in bold; network or ego predictors are in ordinary font; *cross-level* predictors in italic.

[b]+ indicates positive effect; − indicates negative effect; 0 indicates effect not significantly different from zero;

[†] indicates effect significant at $p \leq .10$.

NC = not considered when only tie level models were employed. Although such effects could have been specified in a single level framework, they are more likely to emerge when one considers a multilevel model.

are the preeminent providers of small services. Our findings are also consistent with previous network-level analyses that larger, more accessible networks, and networks with a higher percentage of women provide more support.

Yet the multilevel approach is more than a fancier way to confirm what we already know. It affords several distinct advantages that allow us to go beyond earlier analyses:

1. We can estimate the effects of variables at the tie and network levels more clearly and confidently, because the multilevel approach controls for effects at the other level and obtains more correct standard errors at each level. This enables us to discuss tie-level effects without the nagging suspicion that the nonrandom clustering of ties may have distorted analysis. It makes us more confident that the effects of tie strength and workmate relationships occur independently of any possible effects of the composition and structure of the networks in which the ties are situated.

2. It also allows us to discuss network-level effects without the nagging suspicion that they are only a pseudo-outcome of the aggregation of tie-level effects in each network. Highly accessible networks are more likely to provide support over and above the propensity of each accessible alter in the network to be supportive. Networks containing many women are more likely to provide support over and above the likelihood of each individual woman in that network to be supportive. Small networks have more ties that are apt to provide everyday support.

3. We can specify a wider range of models that represent and extend existing theory. This allows us to decompose effects previously conceptualized at the tie level into an effect of the tie and an effect of the aggregate of the tie characteristic. For example, the effect of accessibility is stronger at the tie level than at the network level for both everyday and emergency forms of support. This means that the supportiveness of accessibility is primarily an interpersonal, ego-alter, process that is heightened when accessible ties are in a network with other accessible ties.

4. We can examine interactive effects between tie/alter and network/ego characteristics. Many aggregate and all cross-level effects had not even been considered in previous analyses, although they may have been hinted at in theory. For example, when we cross tie/alter and network/ego predictors we find that the already high likelihood of accessible alters to be supportive is greatly increased when they are members of especially accessible networks. Similarly, parent-child ties are more likely to be supportive when there is more than one parent-child tie in the network.

Capitalizing on Networks

Multilevel analysis has enabled us to elucidate the interplay between individual agency, dyadic dancing, and network facilitation. The characteristics of egos, ties, and alters clearly affect the extent of support. But so does network composition, network structure, and the cross-level effects of composition and tie/alter characteristics. These are network capital in a deeper sense: It is the nature of the network that facilitates capitalizing on potentially supportive ties.

Consider the effect of mutual ties: When alter and ego are tied to common others, the alter is more likely than other alters to provide support. Technically this is a dyadic effect, but it corresponds to standard sociological interpretations suggesting that the better norms, communication, and coordination of densely knit, kin-dominated *networks* make them more supportive (Durkheim 1897; Bott 1957; Kadushin 1983; Fischer 1982; Thoits 1982; Marsden & Hurlbert 1988; Pescosolido & Georgiana 1989).

A second form of network capital appears when particular types of ties operate in networks heavily composed of such ties. This is manifest in the effects of parent/child ties and accessible ties, the vestigial remnants of traditional kinship and neighborhood solidarities. Parents and adult children (including in-laws) are especially likely to provide support in networks composed of a relatively high number of parents and children, and accessible ties are especially apt to provide support when they are in networks filled with accessible ties. These effects cannot be attributed to the number of mutual ties between alter and ego, because we controlled for this. We believe that they are effects of the potentiating capacity of network capital, indicating that a particular tie is more likely to be activated when embedded in a network of similar ties. In such homophilous situations, a tie-level commitment between an ego and an alter is increased by the commitment of many similar alters in the network. There are several reasons why this may be so. For example, people with atypically high needs for support may have networks especially filled with immediate kin. These immediate kin may accentuate the norm of intrafamily supportiveness. In the case of accessibility, there may be a shared skill in cultivating accessible ties and cultivating support. Or, those who need support may attract support providers to live near them or move to live near those likely to provide support.[23]

A third form of network capital pertains to reciprocity. An ego is likely to receive support reciprocally from an alter whom this ego has previously supported. Although this support may come through obligations that occur in networks with strong ties or with parent-child bonds, it may also come with the obligation of reciprocity that operates independently of tie strength or immediate kinship. Ego may call on emergency support for this year's financial crisis from the intimates whom ego has supported through a previous emergency. But the tie-level effect of reciprocity is reduced when ego has contributed extensive emergency support to a number of alters. Under these conditions, tie-level dynamics apparently are superseded by network-level dynamics: Ego need not turn to a specific alter whom one supported last year because ego can rely on the network. Ego may draw on network capital from the specific alter *and* from the network.

Dyadic Duets and Emergent Structural Properties

That a social network is more than the sum of its ties has been a fact since Cain dealt with both Abel and God, and a central assertion of social-network analysis for at least thirty years. But the debate about the existence of emergent structural properties goes beyond social-network analysis. It has been a longstanding core sociological controversy which we personify as a heavyweight match between George Homans (1961)—who argued that social phenomena were nothing more than the sum of two-person ties and Georg Simmel (1908)—who argued that the presence of third parties inherently affects the operation of two-person ties.

The struggle between Homans and Simmel is a toss-up in our analysis. Favoring Homans is that tie dynamics predominate. Certain types of ties—strong ones, parent-child ones—are apt to be supportive regardless of what network they are in. Another argument for the primacy of tie-level dynamics is the relative supportiveness of ties deriving from direct interactions between egos and alters, as compared to the relative unsupportiveness of ties whose existence derives from environing social systems. These include ties with workmates, fellow members of voluntary organizations, and extended kin (uncles, nieces, grandparents, etc.). The case of extended kin is particularly instructive. If kinship were a strong system, then all types of kin should be supportive. In fact, only immediate kin are especially supportive, operating as dyads or as members of quite small social systems.

Yet the data also support a Simmelian assertion of the importance of networks that cannot be reduced to a mere summation of two-person relationships. The structural effect standardly applied to "density of a network" appears in our models in the form of the tie-level effect of mutual ties between alter and ego. Emergent properties are important for obtaining network capital, although the emergent properties come from the composition of the networks rather than their structures: the percentage of parents and children in the networks, mean access to alters, reciprocal ties, and female alters. Cross-level effects show the oversimplified fallaciousness of ascribing support to only the tie or the network. Take the case of reciprocity. Small acts provided by immediate alters are likely to be reciprocated quickly. In the event of failed reciprocity, the losses are minimal. However, larger forms of support may not be directly or immediately reciprocated. They occur in a context where the commitment is to the network—or some component of it—and the likely eventual benefit is derived through the network rather than through specific reciprocal acts between ego and alter. Thus, immediate family members provide multiple forms of support through a commitment to the family that is beyond a commitment to ego.

Living Networked in a Networked World

Since the 1950s, there has been a practical and analytic shift from seeing community as kinship or neighborhood solidarity to seeing it as a personal community network (Wellman 1999). The shift in perspective from a solidarity to a network view has probably lagged the shift in social structure. Although almost all people possess community ties of sociability and support, many of these ties are only weakly connected. They function as dyads and small clusters, and not as densely knit groups. The tie, not the network, may be the most important determinant of network capital. As the network is dominated by the tie, the individual persona becomes an even more active player of the network capital game, rather than sitting back passively and letting social support come from a group (Burt 1992; Wellman 2001). It is only at home that a person can expect a wide range of support to be provided (Wellman & Wellman 1992), and home—and the marital couple—are where the network capital game is played—obtaining support tie-by-tie.

Instead of total involvement in a single solidarity community, the personal mobility and connectivity that are the hallmarks of the industrial and information ages have replaced solidarity with *networked individualism* (Wellman 2001). People move through partial, specialized involvements with multiple sets of network members. Interactions with network members are principally in duets, two couples, and informal get-togethers of friends and relatives. These are not simple, homogeneous strictures but complex compositions and sparsely knit structures. Most interactions are not in public places, but tucked away in private homes or telecommunications. Relationships are not permanent: Even socially close ties are often replaced within a decade. Rather than each network member providing a broad spectrum of support, people get specialized support from a variety of ties.[24]

This means that within networks there is much possibility for individual *agency* and *autonomously acting ties* (White 1992; Emirbayer and Goodwin 1994). People and ties are affected by their networks, but only partially so. People maneuver to form relationships and find support from them, ties often operate without much constraint from their environing networks, and clusters of ties within networks operate privately in domestic spaces rather than collectively in public places (Oldenburg 1989; Lofland 1998). Husbands and wives spend evenings together. Couples operate their personal networks jointly, with wives more active in determining network membership and setting agendas (Wellman 1992a). The characteristics of individuals, ties, and networks all affect the supply of supportive resources.

Even though people no longer inhabit solidarity groups, they do not function alone. Even though personal networks are fragmentary and loosely coupled, support is given to clusters within a network as well as to an ego. Ties do not operate in isolation. They contribute to networks; networks encourage and potentiate ties. The supportive relationship is social in another sense. Support is often given for the general benefit of a household or a network rather than for the specific benefit of the individual (Wellman & Wellman 1992).

Just as investment is not only zero-sum but also builds a fund of capital, one person's support of another may also contribute to the network of which both are members. The network's provision of supportive resources adds to the fund of network capital circulating in a community as well as benefiting the individual. Social support is rarely a zero-sum game. Companionship is usually a mutual benefit, while helping others increases one's own standing in the community. It gives the giver the *naches* of seeing oneself as a worthwhile contributor, and raises the level of overall supportiveness (Schweizer & White 1998). For example, providing others with emotional support often increases happiness and decreases stress levels (Pennebaker 1990). Not only does "it takes a village to raise a child" (Clinton 1996), the support provided increases the village's overall level of social capital and civic trust.

In such personal communities, network capital is inherently multilevel. It is affected by individual agency and specific ties as well as by the organizational and normative effects of the networks in which individuals and ties are linked. While people dance to their own tunes and in step with their alters, their movements take place within the network ensemble. The structure of the networks is important as a background factor, for its sparse interconnections allow people to participate in many worlds. In these communities of shared interest, networks provide contexts for similar people to act similarly and observe each other acting similarly. It is the composition of these networks that is important, often connecting similar alters who have experienced similar life events and have similar interests (see also Suitor, Pillemer, & Bohanon 1993). The *"cultural convoys"* of similar network members potentiate the supportiveness that any one tie can provide.

It is time to stop trying to view the present through the lens of the past. It is time to stop seeing networks as nascent groups. The pervasiveness of ties and the ability of such ties to link distinct social circles provide abundant network capital (Laumann 1973; Granovetter 1982, 1995; Ferrand,

Mounier, & Degenne 1999). The interplay of tie, network, and individual characteristics strongly affects where such network capital will flow. At a larger scale, the transformation of national and global societies into "network societies" (Wellman 1988, 1997; Castells 1996) suggests the usefulness of thinking of social capital as a product of personal community networks as well as of formally institutionalized groups.

We have reversed the precept of Research Design 100: We have gone from method toward theory by way of substance. As van Duijn et al. (1999) noted, multilevel models provide a powerful new way to study ties and networks (or other nested phenomena). We have also drawn on the fact that multilevel models are an epistemologically more accurate way of representing the contemporary network world in which phenomena are inherently multilevel. Our findings fit the nature of loosely coupled "liberated" communities (and possibly organizations with similar characteristics). Such communities are not enveloping, binding solidarities. People are members of multiple networks, and they enact specific ties and networks on an hourly, daily, monthly, and yearly basis. They can—and do—change ties and networks in response to opportunities, difficulties, and changes in their personal and household situations (Wellman et al. 1997). Under these circumstances, network phenomena can only be facilitating and partially constraining—and rarely dominating or controlling. To understand the place of network capital more fully, we need to know more about how people think about and operate their networks:

1. Can we move beyond regression coefficients and understand how the multilevel potentiation of ties by networks actually works?
2. The handful of strong alters/ties we have studied are only the core constellation in a person's network universe, typically containing more than 1,000 alters. Do the many other weaker ties exhibit the same tendencies we have discovered here? As weaker ties may be less densely connected by mutual ties to the egos at the centers of these universes, this might lead to more individual-agency and independent tie dynamics in the behavior of each ego and alter. Yet this same weakness in the ties may require the structuring and potentiating capacity of densely knit clusters of ties to transmute the ordinary behavior of ego and alter into truly supportive exchanges.
3. How do compositional effects work as network processes? If many network members do not know each other, are similarities in their supportiveness the consequence of status similarity or of assortative mating (Smith & Stevens 1999): "belonging" to the same ego who may have gathered a particular set of alters through force of circumstance or planning?
4. Under what circumstances do people think and act in relational,

network, or group terms (Freeman 1992; White 1992)? Can there be a collective group identity and individual sense of belonging if people are heavily involved in individual agency and dancing dyadic duets rather than nesting in encompassing networks?

5. To what extent is network capital an outcome of a normative, reference-group process or an outcome of information flows and structural coordination?

6. Is the network potentiation of supportive ties, so apparent for parent-child and accessible relationships, in part a result of people consciously constructing their networks to fit their needs? What is the empirical reality of "networking"? Are people "cultural dopes" in Harold Garfinkel's sense (1967): passively allowing ties, networks and support to happen to them? Or are they steely-eyed practitioners of Ron Burt's craft (1992): actively amassing network capital by forging (and dropping) their ties and (re)shaping their networks?

TECHNICAL APPENDIX

The final multilevel model for everyday support for alter i for ego j is

Level 1 [Tie/Alter level]:

$$\log\left[\frac{P(Everyday\,Support_{ij} = 1)}{1 - P(Everyday\,Support_{ij} = 1)}\right] = \beta_{0j} + \beta_{1j}\,Alter\,Is\,a\,Parent/Child_{ij}$$
$$+ \beta_{2j}\,Extent\,of\,Access\,to\,Alter_{ij}$$
$$+ \beta_{3j}\,Alter\,Is\,a\,Woman_{ij}$$
$$+ \beta_{4j}\,Strength\,of\,Tie_{ij}$$
$$+ \beta_{5j}\,Number\,of\,Mutual\,Ties\,between$$
$$i\,and\,j$$
$$+ \beta_{6j}\,Alter\,Is\,a\,Workmate_{ij}$$

Level 2 [Ego/Network level]:

[Overall Support intercept] $\quad \beta_{0j} = \gamma_{00} + \gamma_{01}\,\%Parents/Children\,in\,the\,Network_j$
$$+ \gamma_{02}\,Mean\,Access\,to\,Alters_j$$
$$+ \gamma_{03}\,\%Alters\,Who\,Are\,Women_j$$
$$+ \gamma_{04}\,Ego\,Is\,a\,Woman_j$$
$$+ \gamma_{05}\,Network\,Size_j + u_{0j}$$

[Parent/Child slope] $\beta_{1j} = \gamma_{10} + \gamma_{11}$ *%Parents/Children in the Network$_j$,*

[Extent of Access slope] $\beta_{2j} = \gamma_{20} + \gamma_{21}$ *Mean Access to Alters$_j$,*

[Alter Is a Woman slope] $\beta_{3j} = \gamma_{30}$,

[Strength of Tie slope] $\beta_{4j} = \gamma_{40} + \gamma_{41}$ *Ego Is a Woman$_j$,*

[Number Mutual Ties slope] $\beta_{5j} = \gamma_{50}$, *and*

[Alter Is a Workmate slope] $\beta_{6j} = \gamma_{60}$.

Level 1 [Tie/Alter level]:

$$\log\left[\frac{P(Everyday\,Support_{ij} = 1)}{1 - P(Everyday\,Support_{ij} = 1)}\right] = \beta_{0j} + \beta_{1j}\,Alter\,Is\,a\,Parent/Child_{ij}$$
$$+ \beta_{2j}\,Extent\,of\,Access\,to\,Alter_{ij}$$
$$+ \beta_{3j}\,Alter\,Is\,a\,Woman_{ij}$$
$$+ \beta_{4}\,Strength\,of\,Tie_{ij}$$
$$+ \beta_{5j}\,Number\,of\,Mutual\,Ties\,Between$$
$$i\,and\,j$$
$$+ \beta_{6j}\,Ego\,Provided\,Emergency\,Support\,to\,Alter_{ij}$$

Level 2 [Ego/Network level]:

[Overall Support intercept] $\beta_{0j} = \gamma_{00} + \gamma_{01}$ *%Parents/Children in the Network$_j$*
$$+ \gamma_{02}\,Mean\,Access\,to\,Alters_j$$
$$+ \gamma_{03}\,\%Alters\,Who\,Are\,Women_j$$
$$+ \gamma_{04}\,Ego\,Is\,a\,Woman_j$$
$$+ \gamma_{05}\,Network\,Size_j$$
$$+ \gamma_{06}\,\%Alters\,to\,Whom\,Ego\,Has\,Provided$$
$$Emergency\,Support_j + u_{0j}$$

[Parent/Child slope] $\qquad \beta_{1j} = \gamma_{10} + \gamma_{11}$ *%Parents/Children in the Network$_j$,*

[Extent of Access slope] $\qquad \beta_{2j} = \gamma_{20} + \gamma_{21}$ *Mean Access to Alters$_j$,*

[Alter Is Woman slope] $\qquad \beta_{3j} = \gamma_{30}$,

[Strength of Tie slope] $\qquad \beta_{4j} = \gamma_{40}$,

[Number Mutual Ties slope] $\beta_{5j} = \gamma_{50}$, *and*

[Ego Provided Support slope] $\beta_{6j} = \gamma_{60} + \gamma_{61}$ *%Alters to Whom Ego Has*

$$\textit{Provided Emergency Support}_j.$$

All tie / alter level 1 predictors were centered around their group means except for *Number of Mutual Ties*. Thus if this were a linear model β_{0j} would represent the predicted value for an average alter with whom ego has zero mutual ties. The interpretation is not as exact for nonlinear models, such as in the logistic regression at level 1.

All ego / network level 2 predictors were centered around their grand means except for *Ego Is a Woman* and *Network Size*. Note that only the intercept is associated with a random term; the residual variances of all other level 1 slopes are set to zero, as these were not the focus of our models.

NOTES

We are grateful to earlier collaborators in East York personal community research for the foundation laid for this study, to the Rockefeller Foundation for providing Wellman with a month's stay to complete this work at the Bellagio (Italy) Center for Study and Conferences, and to the University of Toronto's Centre for Urban and Community Studies for its thirty years of being an eminently supportive research base. The contributions of Milena Gulia, Catherine Kaukinen, Stephanie Potter, and Scot Wortley have been especially important for our work here, as have been the comments of Dean Behrens, Bonnie Erickson, Vicente Espinoza, Nan Lin, Uwe Matzat, Pamela Popielarz, Ray Reagans, Fleur Thomése, Charles Tilly, Beverly Wellman, and the members of the "Socnet" electronic mail discussion list. Earlier versions of this paper were presented to the Duke University Social Networks and Social Capital Conference (1998), the American Sociological Association (1999, 2000) and the International Sunbelt Social Network Conference (1999, 2000). Our research has been supported by grants to Barry Wellman from the Bell Canada University Laboratories, and the Social Science and Humanities Research Council of Canada. This chapter is dedicated to Natalie Sherban and Joan Harvey, founding stalwarts of East York's Neighbourhood Information Centre, who have demonstrated for thirty years that an organization can provide social capital and foster supportive networks.

1. Network capital is a form of "social capital." Social capital is a sprawling term, ranging from an individualistic framework that emphasizes the advantages that individuals can gain through their personal networks to a collective perspective that emphasizes the advantages of volunteerism to a community (Coleman 1988; Paxton 1999; Putnam 2000; Lin 2001). For further discussions of social support, see Erickson, Radkewycz, and Nosanchuk (1988); Gottlieb and Selby (1990); Kadushin (1981); Lin, Dean, and Ensel (1986); Wellman (1999). Two other means of obtaining resources, less prevalent in industrialized countries, are *self-provisioning* (Pahl 1984) and *coercive appropriation* (such as robbery, theft, and extortion (Dickens 1838; Pileggi 1985; Turnbull 1972).

2. We ignore here personal characteristics, such as intelligence, health, and attractiveness.

3. Although we have tried to produce an inclusive list of the aspects of network capital, our analysis does not dwell equally on all of them.

4. There are also the effects of the environing society, but that is beyond our analytic scope here.

5. Like the chicken and egg, it is not clear which came first, ties or networks. To be sure, ties constitute a network, and on that grounds, one might give ties precedence. But as Simmel (1908) pointed out, networks can endure while ties come and go within them. So a network may have precedence over any tie currently in it.

6. Note that now it is the *errors* in 3, the u_{0j}, that are assumed normally distributed (with variance σ^2). In estimating σ^2, multilevel software accounts for unreliability in the estimation of each β_{0j} due to small and varying sample sizes. In particular, the estimates are "shrunk" to a conditional mean (based on the characteristics of ego modeled at level 2) using an Empirical Bayes approach. While these procedures have been available for over a decade (see Raudenbush & Bryk 1986), they have only recently been extended to models with dichotomous outcomes (Raudenbush 1995). Such models pose special difficulties for obtaining maximum likelihood estimates. We use here Yang's (1998) extension of the penalized-quasi-likelihood to obtain estimates based on an extremely precise approximation to the likelihood.

7. When we report main effects at the network or tie level we do so based on models that do not include these interaction terms. We then estimate separate models that include the interaction terms.

8. The question was "I'd like to ask you a few questions about the people outside your home that you feel closest to; these could be friends, neighbors, or relatives."

9. Individual characteristics are analyzed in Wellman (1985, 1992a); Wellman and Wellman (1992); tie characteristics in Wellman (1979, 1996); Wellman, Carrington, and Hall (1988); Wellman and Wortley (1989, 1990); and network characteristics in Wellman, Carrington, and Hall (1988); Wellman and Gulia (1999b); Wellman and Potter (1999b).

10. Rank = 6 for the highest-ranked (strongest) tie; Rank = 1 for the lowest-ranked tie.

11. Data on ties between alters were based on reports from egos. Network analysts and graph theorists often refer to the number of mutual ties as "degree centrality" (Wasserman & Faust 1994), and this independent variable would be part of the set in recent p^* models (Wasserman & Pattison 1996).

12. We logged$_{10}$ contact and distance data because, for example, a one-day increase of contact at higher values (e.g., from 364 to 365 days) is less socially meaningful than an increase at lower values (e.g., from 1 to 2 days). We used percentage living in Metropolitan Toronto rather than the percentage living in the same neighborhood, because previous research has shown that alters living outside the neighborhood but elsewhere in Metropolitan Toronto have about as frequent contact and are as supportive as those living locally (Wellman & Tindall 1993; Wellman & Wortley 1990).

13. E.g., Allan (1979); Cicirelli (1995); Farber (1981); Goetting (1986); Schneider (1984); Willmott (1986); Beverly Wellman (2001). Information about extended kin are in Stokowski and Lee (1991); Degenne, Lebeaux, and Lemel (1998); Wellman and Wortley (1989).

14. As preliminary analyses did not show any association between support and network density, heterogeneity or range, they were removed from the final models. Although network density was found to be significant in an earlier study that looked only at the network level (Wellman & Gulia 1999b), the multilevel approach used here removes the impact of possibly confounding tie-level phenomena from our analyses here. For example, it enables us to answer the question of whether a high level of parent-child support is based on their bond or on the kinds of densely-knit networks in which such supportive parent-child ties reside. The answer, as we shall see, is that it is the parent-child tie, and not the densely-knit network, that facilitates the provision of support.

15. E.g., Vaux (1985); Cancian (1987); Perlman and Fehr (1987); Sherrod (1989); Wright (1989); Wellman and Wortley (1990); Bly (1990); Wellman (1992a); Canary and Emmers-Sommer (1997).

16. In general, the partitioning of variances between levels is an important aspect of multilevel models. But in this case our level 1 model (the tie/alter level) is based on a logistic regression. As such, we do not estimate a variance at level 1 or discuss variance explained at level 1, nor do we partition variances between level 1 and level 2.

17. Although statistical analysis of mutual ties is done at the tie level, the substantive effect is at the network level. The reciprocity effect may also be caused by the number of mutual ties—the more mutual ties, the more ego is likely to be supportive of an alter. Therefore it may not make sense to control for reciprocity before assessing the effect of mutual ties. The effect of mutual ties prior to controlling for reciprocity was stronger and significant at $p \leq .05$.

18. The overall probability of a parent-child tie providing support, 0.34, is associated with an odds ratio of .51. This means that the chance that a parent or adult child is supportive is about half the chance that the parent or adult child is not supportive. The odds that a parent or child provides everyday

support increases by $e^{2.46 \times \%parents/children \times alter \text{ is parent or child}}$ or about 11 as networks increase from containing no (0 percent) parents or adult children to containing all (100 percent) parents or children in the network. This translates to an increase in odds (or chances of support versus nonsupport) of about 2/3 for each additional parent or child in ego's network. Starting with an odds of support of .51 for the average parent/child, the odds increases by 2/3 to .85 for the addition of one parent or child in ego's network, making the probability of support equal to .45. The effect is slightly stronger for emergency support.

19. See Homans (1950, 1961); Clark and Gordon (1979); Galaskiewicz (1985); Connidis (1989); Bumpass (1990); Wellman (1999).

20. The 23 percent of alters who provide everyday support are associated with an odds of 0.30. If the alter is moderately accessible (0.49 above the mean), the odds double ($e^{1.4 \times .49} = 2$) to .6, which is associated with a probability of 0.37. If, in addition, the network is moderately more accessible than average (one standard deviation, or .73, above the mean), the odds double again ($e^{1.083 \times .73} = 2.2$) to 1.2, associated with a probability of 0.54. The effect on the odds ratios is halved for emergency support.

21. Preliminary analyses found that egos' and alters' socioeconomic status, age, and family status were *not* associated with the provision of support at the tie or network levels.

22. Reading the coefficients in Table 1 is a bit tricky here. The basic gender effects for egos receiving support and alters providing support can be found in columns 1a and 2a. The cross-level effect is found in column 1b, but one should not use the estimates from columns 1b and 2b to described gender effects since these models contain cross-level interaction terms regarding gender.

23. By contrast, a Dutch study of the elderly finds the opposite: The greater availability of nearby ties decreases the instrumental support received from any given tie (Thomése & von Tilburg 1998, 2000). There may be a different dynamic working for the provision of support to those with high needs for assistance. In fact, the effect of mean access is reduced for our older respondents, but the trend is not statistically significant.

24. For documentation and amplification, see Castells (1996); Craven and Wellman (1973); Fischer (1982, 1984); Hampton and Wellman (1999); Putnam (2000); Simmel (1922); Suitor, Wellman, and Morgan (1997); Wellman (1990, 1992a, 1992b, 1999, 2001); Wellman and Gulia (1999a); Wellman and Leighton (1979); Wellman and Potter (1999); Wellman and Tindall (1993); Wellman et al. (1997).

REFERENCES

Allan, Graham. 1979. *A Sociology of Friendship and Kinship*. London: Allen & Unwin.
Barnes, J. A. 1972. *Social Networks*. Reading, MA: Addison-Wesley.
Bly, Robert. 1990. *Iron John: A Book about Men*. Reading, MA: Addison-Wesley.
Bott, Elizabeth. 1957. *Family and Social Network*. London: Tavistock.

Bryk, Anthony, and Stephen Raudenbush. 1992. *Hierarchical Linear Models: Applications and Data Analysis Methods*. Newbury Park, CA: Sage.

Bumpass, Larry. 1990. "A Comparative Analysis of Coresidence and Contact with Parents in Japan and the United States." Working Paper. Center for Demography and Ecology, University of Wisconsin.

Burnstein, Leigh. 1980. "The Analysis of Multilevel Data in Educational Research and Evaluation." *Review of Research in Education* 8:158–233.

Burt, Ronald. 1983. "Range." Pp. 176–94 in *Applied Network Analysis*, edited by Ronald Burt and Michael Minor. Beverly Hills, CA: Sage.

———. 1992. *Structural Holes*. Chicago: University of Chicago Press.

Canary, Daniel J., and Tara M. Emmers-Sommer. 1997. *Sex and Gender Differences in Personal Relationships*. New York: Guilford Press.

Cancian, Francesca. 1987. *Love in America: Gender and Self-Development*. Cambridge: Cambridge University Press.

Castells, Manuel. 1996. *The Rise of the Network Society*. Malden, MA: Blackwell.

Cicirelli, Victor G. 1995. *Sibling Relationships Across the Life Span*. New York: Plenum Press.

Clark, William, and Michael Gordon. 1979. "Distance, Closeness and Recency of Kin Contact in Urban Ireland." *Journal of Comparative Family Studies* 10:271–75.

Clinton, Hilary Rodham. 1996. *It Takes a Village: And Other Lessons Children Teach Us*. New York: Simon and Schuster.

Coleman, James. 1988. "Social Capital in the Creation of Human Capital." *American Journal of Sociology* 94:S95—S120.

Connidis, Ingrid. 1989. *Family Ties and Aging*. Toronto: Butterworth.

Cook, Karen, and J. M. Whitmeyer. 1992. "Two Approaches to Social Structure: Exchange Theory and Network Analysis." *Annual Review of Sociology* 18:109–27.

Craven, Paul, and Barry Wellman. 1973. "The Network City." *Sociological Inquiry* 43 (1):57–88.

Degenne, Alain, Marie-Odile Lebeaux, and Yannick Lemel. 1998. "Social Capital in Everyday Life." Working Paper No. 9827. Malakoff, France: Centre de Recherche en Économie et Statistique, Institut National de la Statistique et des Études Économiques.

Dickens, Charles. 1838 [1998]. *Oliver Twist*. Oxford: Oxford University Press.

DiPrete, Thomas, and Jerry Forristal. 1994. "Multilevel Models: Methods and Substance." *Annual Review of Sociology* 20:331–57.

Durkheim, Émile. 1893. *The Division of Labor in Society*. New York: Macmillan.

———. 1897. *Suicide*. Glencoe, IL: Free Press.

Emirbayer, Mustafa, and Jeff Goodwin. 1994. "Network Analysis, Culture, and the Problem of Agency." *American Journal of Sociology* 99 (6):1411–54.

Erickson, Bonnie, Alexandra Radkewycz, and Terence Nosanchuk. 1988. "Helping Hands." Centre for Urban and Community Studies, University of Toronto.

Espinoza, Vicente. 1999. "Social Networks among the Urban Poor: Inequality and Integration in a Latin American City." Pp. 147–84 in *Networks in the Global Village*, edited by Barry Wellman. Boulder, CO: Westview Press.

Farber, Bernard. 1981. *Conceptions of Kinship*. New York: Elsevier North Holland.

Ferrand, Alexis, Lise Mounier, and Alain Degenne. 1999. "The Diversity of Personal Networks in France: Social Stratification and Relational Structures." Pp. 185–

224 in *Networks in the Global Village,* edited by Barry Wellman. Boulder, CO: Westview Press.

Fischer, Claude. 1982. *To Dwell Among Friends.* Berkeley, CA: University of California Press.

———. 1984. *The Urban Experience.* 2nd ed. Orlando, FL: Harcourt Brace Jovanovich.

Frank, Kenneth A., and Jeffrey Yasumoto. 1998. "Linking Action to Social Structure within a System: Social Capital Within and Between Subgroups." *American Journal of Sociology* 104 (3):642–86.

Freeman, Linton. 1992. "The Sociological Concept of Group: An Empirical Test of Two Models." *American Journal of Sociology* 98:152–66.

Galaskiewicz, Joseph. 1985. "Professional Networks and the Institutionalization of a Single Mind Set." *American Sociological Review* 50:639–58.

Garfinkel, Harold. 1967. *Studies in Ethnomethodology.* Englewood Cliffs, NJ: Prentice-Hall.

Gillies, Marion, and Barry Wellman. 1968. "East York: A Profile." Report to Community Studies Section, Clarke Institute of Psychiatry.

Goetting, Ann. 1986. "The Developmental Tasks of Siblingship over the Life Cycle." *Journal of Marriage and the Family* 48 (November): 703–14.

Gottlieb, Benjamin, and Peter Selby. 1990. *Social Support and Mental Health: A Review of the Literature.* Department of Psychology, University of Guelph, Canada.

Granovetter, Mark. 1982. "The Strength of Weak Ties: A Network Theory Revisited." Pp. 105–30 in *Social Structure and Network Analysis,* edited by Peter Marsden and Nan Lin. Beverly Hills, CA: Sage.

———. 1995. *Getting a Job: A Study of Contacts and Careers.* 2nd ed. Chicago: University of Chicago Press.

Haines, Valerie, and Jeanne Hurlbert. 1992. "Network Range and Health." *Journal of Health and Social Behavior* 33:254–66.

Hampton, Keith N., and Barry Wellman. 1999. "Netville On-Line and Off-Line." *American Behavioral Scientist* 43 (3):478–95.

Haythornthwaite, Caroline, and Barry Wellman. 1998. "Work, Friendship and Media Use for Information Exchange in a Networked Organization." *Journal of the American Society for Information Science* 49 (12):1101–14.

Hogan, Dennis P., and David J. Eggbeen. 1995. "Sources of Emergency Help and Routine Assistance in Old Age." *Social Forces* 73 (3):917–36.

Homans, George. 1950. *The Human Group.* New York: Harcourt, Brace & World.

———. 1961. *Social Behavior: Its Elementary Forms.* New York: Harcourt Brace Jovanovich.

House, James, Karl Landis, and Debra Umberson. 1988. "Social Relationships and Health." *Science* 241:540–45.

Inkeles, Alex, and David Smith. 1974. *Becoming Modern: Individual Change in Six Developing Countries.* Cambridge, MA: Harvard University Press.

Kadushin, Charles. 1981. "Notes on Expectations of Reward in N-person Networks." Pp. 235–54 in *Continuities in Structural Inquiry,* edited by Peter Blau and Robert Merton. Beverly Hills, CA: Sage.

———. 1983. "Mental Health and the Interpersonal Environment." *American Sociological Review* 48 (2):199–210.

Lai, Gina, Nan Lin, and Shu-Yin Leung. 1998. "Network Resources, Contact Resources, and Status Attainment." *Social Networks* 20:159–78.

Laumann, Edward O. 1973. *Bonds of Pluralism: The Forms and Substance of Urban Social Networks.* New York: Wiley.

Lazarsfeld, Paul, and Robert Merton. 1954. "Friendship as Social Process." Pp. 18–66 in *Freedom and Control in Modern Society,* edited by Morroe Berger, Theodore Abel, and Charles Page. New York: Octagon.

Lin, Nan. 2001. *Social Capital: A Theory of Social Structure and Action.* Cambridge: Cambridge University Press.

Lin, Nan, Alfred Dean, and Walter Ensel. 1986. *Social Support, Life Events and Depression.* Orlando FL: Academic Press.

Lin, Nan, and Mary Dumin. 1986. "Access to Occupations through Social Ties." *Social Networks* 8:365–83.

Lofland, Lyn H. 1998. *The Public Realm: Exploring the City's Quintessential Social Territory.* Hawthorne, NY: Aldine de Gruyter.

Longford, Nicholas. 1995. *Random Coefficient Models.* Oxford: Clarendon Press.

Marsden, Peter. 1988. "Homogeneity in Confiding Relations." *Social Networks* 10:57–76.

Marsden, Peter, and Karen E Campbell. 1984. "Measuring Tie Strength." *Social Forces* 63:482–501.

Marsden, Peter, and Jeanne Hurlbert. 1988. "Social Resources and Mobility Outcomes." *Social Forces* 66:1038–59.

Milardo, Robert, and Barry Wellman. 1992. "The Personal is Social." *Journal of Social and Personal Relationships* 9 (3):339–42.

Moore, Gwen. 1990. "Structural Determinants of Men's and Women's Personal Networks." *American Sociological Review* 55 (October):726–35.

Oldenburg, Ray. 1989. *The Great Good Place: Cafes, Coffee Shops, Community Centers, Beauty Parlors, General Stores, Bars, Hangouts, and How They Get You Through the Day.* New York: Paragon House.

Pahl, Ray E. 1984. *Divisions of Labour.* Oxford: Basil Blackwell.

Parks, Malcolm, and Leona Eggert. 1991. "The Role of Social Context in the Dynamics of Personal Relationships." *Advances in Personal Relationships* 2:1–34.

Parsons, Talcott. 1943. "The Kinship System of the Contemporary United States." *American Anthropologist* 22–38.

Paxton, Pamela. 1999. "Is Social Capital Declining in the United States? A Multiple Indicator Assessment." *American Journal of Sociology* 105 (1):88–127.

Pennebaker, James W. 1990. *Opening Up: The Healing Power of Expressing Emotions.* New York: Guilford Press.

Perlman, Daniel, and Beverley Fehr. 1987. "The Development of Intimate Relationships." Pp. 13–42 in *Intimate Relationships,* edited by Daniel Perlman and Steve Duck. Newbury Park, CA: Sage.

Pescosolido, Bernice. 1992. "Beyond Rational Choice: The Social Dynamics of How People Seek Help." *American Journal of Sociology* 97:1096–1138.

Pescosolido, Bernice, and Sharon Georgianna. 1989. "Durkheim, Suicide, and Religion: Toward a Network Theory of Suicide." *American Sociological Review* 54:33–48.

Pileggi, Nicholas. 1985. *Wiseguy.* New York: Simon and Schuster.

Popielarz, Pamela. 2000. "Connecting Structure and Content: Shaping Social Capital Early in Life." Presented to the American Sociological Association, Washington, August.

Portes, Alejandro, and Julia Sensenbrenner. 1993. "Embeddedness and Immigration: Notes on the Social Determinants of Economic Action." *American Journal of Sociology* 98 (6):1320–50.

Putnam, Robert. 2000. *Bowling Alone.* New York: Simon and Schuster.

Raudenbush, Stephen. 1995. "Posterior Model Estimation for Hierarchical Generalized Linear Models with Application to Dichotomous and Count Data." Unpublished manuscript, Michigan State University, College of Education.

Raudenbush, Stephen, and Anthony Bryk. 1986. "A Hierarchical Model for Studying School Effects." *Sociology of Education* 59:1–17.

Riggio, Ronald, and Judy Zimmerman. 1991. "Social Skills and Interpersonal Relationships: Influences on Social Support and Support Seeking." *Advances in Personal Relationships* 2:133–55.

Rosenthal, Carolyn. 1985. "Kinkeeping in the Familial Division of Labor." *Journal of Marriage and the Family* 47:965–74.

Sahlins, Marshall. 1965. "On the Sociology of Primitive Exchange." Pp. 139–236 in *The Relevance of Models for Social Anthropology*, edited by Michael Banton. London: Tavistock.

Sampson, Robert, Jeffrey Morenoff, and Felton Earls. 1999. "Beyond Social Capital: Spatial Dynamics of Collective Efficacy for Children." *American Sociological Review* 64 (Oct.):633–60.

Schneider, David. 1984. *A Critique of the Study of Kinship.* Ann Arbor: University of Michigan Press.

Schweizer, Thomas, Michael Schnegg, and Susanne Berzborn. 1998. "Personal Networks and Social Support in a Multiethnic Community of Southern California." *Social Networks* 20:1–21.

Schweizer, Thomas, and Douglas R. White, eds. 1998. *Kinship, Networks, and Exchange.* Cambridge: Cambridge University Press.

Sherrod, Drury. 1989. "The Influence of Gender on Same-Sex Friendships." Pp. 164–86 in *Close Relationships*, edited by Clyde Hendrick. Newbury Park, CA: Sage.

Simmel, Georg. 1908 [1971]. "Group Expansion and the Development of Individuality." Pp. 251–93 in *Georg Simmel: On Individuality and Social Forms*, edited by Donald Levine. Chicago: University of Chicago Press.

———. 1922 [1955]. "The Web of Group Affiliations." Pp. 125–95 in *Conflict and the Web of Group Affiliations*, edited by Kurt Wolff. Glencoe, IL: Free Press.

Smith, Thomas, and Gregory Stevens. 1999. "The Architecture of Small Networks: Strong Interaction and Dynamic Organization in Small Social Systems." *American Sociological Review* 64 (June):403–20.

Snijders, Tom, and Roel J. Bosker. 1999. *Introduction to Multilevel Analysis.* London: Sage.

Snijders, Tom, Marinus Spreen, and Ronald Zwaagstra. 1995. "The Use of Multilevel Modeling for Analysis of Personal Networks: Networks of Cocaine Users in an Urban Area." *Journal of Quantitative Anthropology* 5:85–105.

Stokowski, Patricia, and Robert Lee. 1991. "The Influence of Social Network Ties on Recreation and Leisure." *Journal of Leisure Research* 23 (2):95–113.

Stone, Leroy O., Carolyn J. Rosenthal, and Ingrid Arnet Connidis. 1998. *Parent-Child Exchanges of Support and Intergenerational Equity.* Ottawa: Statistics Canada.

Suitor, J. Jill, Karl Pillemer, and Shirley Keeton Bohanon. 1993. "Sources of Support and Interpersonal Stress for Women's Midlife Transitions: The Case of Returning Students and Family Caregivers." Presented at Sunbelt Social Network Conference, Tampa, February.

Suitor, J. Jill , Barry Wellman, and David L. Morgan, eds. 1997. "It's About Time: Introduction to a Special Issue on How, Why and When Networks Change." *Social Networks* 19 (1):1–8.

Thoits, Peggy. 1982. "Life Stress, Social Support, and Psychological Vulnerability." *Journal of Community Psychology* 10:341–62.

Thomése, Fleur, and Theo van Tilburg. 1998. "The Importance of Being Close Together: Contextual Effects of Neighbouring Networks on the Exchange of Instrumental Support Between Older Adults and Their Proximate Network Members in the Netherlands." Working Paper. Department of Sociology, Free University of Amsterdam, April.

———. 2000. "Neighbouring Networks and Environmental Dependency: Differential Effects of Neighbourhood Characteristics on the Relative Size and Composition of Neighbouring Networks of Older Adults in the Netherlands." *Ageing and Society* 20 (1):55–74.

Turnbull, Colin. 1972. *The Mountain People.* New York: Simon and Schuster.

van Duijn, Marijtje, Jooske van Busschbach, and Tom Snijders. 1999. "Multilevel Analysis of Personal Networks as Dependent Variables." *Social Networks* 21 (2):187–209.

Vaux, Alan. 1985. "Variations in Social Support Associated with Gender, Ethnicity and Age." *Social Issues* 41 (1):89–110.

Wasserman, Stanley, and Katherine Faust. 1994. *Social Network Analysis: Methods and Applications.* Cambridge: Cambridge University Press.

Wasserman, Stanley, & Phillipa Pattison. 1996. "Logit Models and Logistic Regressions for Univariate and Bivariate Social Networks: I. An Introduction to Markov Graphs." *Psychometrika* 61(3):401–26.

Weber, Max. 1922 [1947]. *The Theory of Social and Economic Organization.* New York: Free Press.

Wellman, Barry. 1979. "The Community Question." *American Journal of Sociology* 84:1201–31.

———. 1982. "Studying Personal Communities." Pp. 61–80 in *Social Structure and Network Analysis,* edited by Peter Marsden and Nan Lin. Beverly Hills, CA: Sage.

———. 1985. "Domestic Work, Paid Work and Net Work." Pp. 159–91 in *Understanding Personal Relationships,* edited by Steve Duck and Daniel Perlman. London: Sage.

———. 1988. "Structural Analysis: From Method and Metaphor to Theory and Substance." Pp. 19–61 in *Social Structures: A Network Approach,* edited by Barry Wellman and S. D. Berkowitz. Cambridge: Cambridge University Press.

——— 1990. "The Place of Kinfolk in Community Networks." *Marriage and Family Review* 15:195–228.

——— 1992a. "Men in Networks." Pp. 74–114 in *Men's Friendships,* edited by Peter Nardi. Newbury Park, CA: Sage.

———— 1992b. "Which Types of Ties and Networks Give What Kinds of Social Support?" *Advances in Group Processes* 9:207–35.

————. 1996. "Are Personal Communities Local? A Dumptarian Reconsideration." *Social Networks* 18:347–54.

————. 1997. "An Electronic Group is Virtually a Social Network." Pp. 179–205 in *Culture of the Internet*, edited by Sara Kiesler. Mahwah, NJ: Lawrence Erlbaum.

————. 1999. "The Network Community." Pp. 1–48 in *Networks in the Global Village*, edited by Barry Wellman. Boulder, CO: Westview.

————. 2001. "Physical Place and Cyber Place: The Rise of Networked Individualism." *International Journal of Urban and Regional Relationships* 25: forthcoming.

Wellman, Barry, Peter Carrington, and Alan Hall. 1988. "Networks as Personal Communities." Pp. 130–84 in *Social Structures: A Network Approach*, edited by Barry Wellman and S. D. Berkowitz. Cambridge: Cambridge University Press.

Wellman, Barry, and Milena Gulia. 1999a. "Net Surfers Don't Ride Alone." Pp. 331–66 in *Networks in the Global Village*, edited by Barry Wellman. Boulder, CO: Westview Press.

————. 1999b. "The Network Basis of Social Support: A Network is More than the Sum of its Ties." Pp. 83–118 in *Networks in the Global Village*, edited by Barry Wellman. Boulder, CO: Westview Press.

Wellman, Barry, and Barry Leighton. 1979. "Networks, Neighborhoods and Communities." *Urban Affairs Quarterly* 14:363–90.

Wellman, Barry, and Stephanie Potter. 1999. "The Elements of Personal Communities." Pp. 49–82 in *Networks in the Global Village*, edited by Barry Wellman. Boulder, CO: Westview.

Wellman, Barry, and David Tindall. 1993. "Reach out and Touch Some Bodies: How Telephone Networks Connect Social Networks." *Progress in Communication Science* 12:63–94.

Wellman, Barry, Renita Wong, David Tindall, and Nancy Nazer. 1997. "A Decade of Network Change: Turnover, Mobility and Stability." *Social Networks* 19 (1):27–51.

Wellman, Barry, and Scot Wortley. 1989. "Brothers' Keepers: Situating Kinship Relations in Broader Networks of Social Support." *Sociological Perspectives* 32: 273–306.

————. 1990. "Different Strokes From Different Folks: Community Ties and Social Support." *American Journal of Sociology* 96:558–88.

Wellman, Beverly. 2001. "Partners in Illness: Who Helps When You are Sick?" Pp. 143–61 in *Complementary and Alternative Medicine: Challenge and Change*, edited by Merrijoy Kelner, Beverly Wellman, Mike Saks, and Bernice Pescosolido. Reading, UK: Gordon and Breach.

Wellman, Beverly, and Barry Wellman. 1992. "Domestic Affairs and Network Relations." *Journal of Social and Personal Relationships* 9:385–409.

Wells, H. G. 1913. "The Country of the Blind." In *Short Stories of H. G. Wells*, edited by H. G. Wells. London: Thomas Nelson.

White, Harrison. 1992. *Identity and Control*. Princeton, NJ: Princeton University Press.

Willmott, Peter. 1986. *Social Networks, Informal Care and Public Policy.* London: Policy Studies Institute.
Wireman, Peggy. 1984. *Urban Neighborhoods, Networks, and Families.* Lexington, MA: Lexington Books.
Wright, Paul. 1989. "Gender Differences in Adults' Same- and Cross-Gender Friendships." Pp. 197–221 in *Older Adult Friendship*, edited by Rebecca Adams and Rosemary Blieszner. Newbury Park, CA: Sage.
Yang, Megli. 1998. "Increasing the Efficiency in Estimating Multilevel Bernoulli Models." Doctoral dissertation, Michigan State University.

11

Guanxi Capital and Social Eating in Chinese Cities: Theoretical Models and Empirical Analyses

Yanjie Bian

In Chinese society, *guanxi,* or interpersonal connections that facilitate favor exchanges, is developed and maintained through social eating: eating a meal with other people. For instance, the popular phrase "drinking and eating buddies" (*jiu rou peng you*) denotes that friends among the Chinese are those who repeatedly offer meals to each other. I will review three theoretical models about the nature of *guanxi*, each having different implications for the relational bases of *guanxi*, sources and forms of *guanxi* capital, and strategies of accumulating *guanxi* capital, or the capacity to mobilize social resources through network ties to others. Then I will analyze some empirical implications of these models for social eating, using data from a 1998 urban consumer project in Chinese cities.

THREE MODELS OF *GUANXI* CAPITAL

Guanxi *as the Web of Extended Familial Obligations*

This school of thought argues that the family is the core of the social structure and the original source of social relations in Chinese society. Consequently, *guanxi* is understood as the web of extended familial ties and familial obligations. Proponents of this conception include, in the Chinese-language literature, such influential scholars as Liang (1986 [1949]), Fei (1992 [1949]), and Ambrose King (1985, 1988), and, in English, Morton H. Fried (1969 [1953]) and C. K. Yang (1965 [1959]).

Liang began by recognizing that each person is born into complex relationships with parents and other family members. He argued that in China these relations are ethical in nature, combining both sentiment (*qing*) and obligation (*yi*). In interaction among family members, sentiments and obligations complement and reinforce each other, creating a harmonious structure that resists confrontation and encourages cooperation within the family. Because group life based on individual interests never became a mode of social organization in China, argued Liang, the ethical relations of familial sentiments and obligations were extended from the family into society, becoming characteristic of Chinese culture. Liang thus termed Chinese culture and society ethics-centered (*lun li ben wei*). Fei emphasized that the ethical relations of familial sentiments and obligations are egocentric; therefore, the farther one gets from family, the wider the range of ties to alters and the lower the degree of ego's sentiments and obligations to alters. Fei called this tendency the structure of differentiation (*cha xu ge ju*). King argued that Liang's and Fei's theories, though developed in the 1940s, can explain behavioral patterns of Chinese individuals in post-World War II Hong Kong, Taiwan, and Mao's mainland China. He points to the persistence of *guanxi* in shaping social life among the Chinese across political regimes.

In Liang's and Fei's theories, the relational bases of *guanxi* are family, kinship, and the communities extended from the family and kinship. Fried's study of a county seat in Anhui province before 1949 confirms that the web of familial and kinship obligations indeed extended into and became the "fabric" of the economic, political, and social organizations of the county seat before the 1949 Communist revolution. And C. K. Yang's research on postrevolution Chinese families in Guangdong indicates that agricultural collectivization did not greatly alter this structure, because the unofficial, informal networks of familial and kinship obligations provided the social-support mechanisms through which peasant families survived in the economy of transition and hardships. Because familial obligations and sentiments shape the communities extended from the family and kinship, Lin (1989, 1998a) has conceptualized these communities as "pseudofamilies."

According to Lin, pseudofamily ties refer to *intimate* friendships. These ties, however, may come about in different ways in traditional and modern societies. In Yang's village and Fried's county seat, intimate social and economic relations were normatively restricted to the family, and the pseudofamily tie was a "social fiction" to widen the boundaries. In broader and more complex urban societies, such ties develop from diverse social relations, namely, classmates, roommates, army comrades, neighbors, co-workers, business partners, and patron-client relations. While frequent interactions and mutual exchanges are objective conditions under which these social relations may transform into ties of high intimacy, key to a pseudofamily tie is the intimate friends' subjective recognition of such a tie. One general indication is that the pseudofamily tie links persons who normally call each other brothers or sisters and kids normatively call their parents' friends aunts or uncles.

From Liang and Fei to Fried and Yang, no researcher has used the term "*guanxi* capital." Nevertheless, all of them have implied that the capacity to mobilize social resources from *guanxi* networks lies in ego's reputation for fulfilling moral and ethical obligations to one's family and pseudo-families. In both popular and scholarly discourses, this kind of reputation has been termed "face" (*mian zi*) (King 1985, 1988). For example, in Yang's village or Fried's county seat, the men who fulfilled these obligations earned respect from villagers or neighbors, who in turn gave face to these men. Face giving from villagers and neighbors was important when the men had to rely on popular support for carrying out their duties in public domains. Face giving of this sort was also important when the men tried to mobilize tangible resources (e.g., temporary labor hires, money loans, donations, etc.) from the villagers and neighbors on behalf of their families or pseudofamilies. In urban China in the 1980s, this kind of "face work" was found to operate in business circles (Cheng & Rosett 1989). In this sense, having face means having *guanxi* capital, or the capacity to mobilize social resources from *guanxi* networks; and losing face means lacking *guanxi* capital, or the incapacity to mobilize resources through *guanxi* networks. Thus, in the Chinese context, face work is about *guanxi* capital accumulation.

Face is relational, for it lies in how ego is evaluated by the members of one's *guanxi* networks. In his theory of structural differentiation, Fei maintains that face is based on sentiments and closeness between face givers and face receivers. According to him, face is greatly ensured from social circles close to ego's family, but less so from the circles that are farther away. Therefore, the face work that everyone must do is to maintain social relations in the farther and wider circles by the standard of familial sentiments and obligations. Liang believed that the web of extended familial sentiments and obligations reflected the nature of the classless social structure of China. In this structure, rational persons must extend ties of familial sentiments and obligations to as many people around them as possible.

In summary, given the definition that *guanxi* is the web of extended familial obligations, proponents of this view shared the consensus that the relational bases of *guanxi* are family and pseudo-families. Moreover, the sources of *guanxi* capital lie in ego's reputation for fulfilling the moral obligations to family and pseudo-families. Third, *guanxi* capital is understood in terms of face, and ego earns face from alter because of high sentiment and closeness between ego and alter. Finally, the strategy of accumulating *guanxi* capital is to extend the ties of familial sentiments and obligations to all social relations.

Guanxi *as Exchange Networks of Particular Instrumental Ties*

Unlike early writers on *guanxi*, researchers of contemporary urban Chinese society have suggested that *guanxi* refers to exchange networks of particular instrumental ties (Jacobs 1979; Chiao 1982; Walder 1986; Hwang 1987; Yang 1994). This view does not automatically reject the idea that *guanxi* is a web of extended familial obligations; here, instead, the defining character of *guanxi* is the instrumentality of particular ties (familial ties included) that facilitate favor exchanges. The shift in emphasis to particular instrumental ties points to a different set of implications for the relational bases of *guanxi*, sources and bases of *guanxi* capital, and strategies of *guanxi* capital accumulation in Chinese society.

When *guanxi* is defined as particular instrumental ties, the relational bases of *guanxi* are no longer limited to family and pseudofamilies, but also include a broad range of social and work-related connections. Walder (1986) found in Mao's China three kinds of particular instrumental ties that shaped work life. The first was between state planners and factory directors. Under the soft budget constraint (Kornai 1986), all factory directors demanded economic resources from state planners, but those who established particularistic ties with state planners were better able to extract government resources. The second type of tie was between party officials and political activists in the workplace. In the political culture of party clientelism, the best strategy for getting ahead was to show personal loyalty to the party secretaries who provided career mobility opportunities. The third tie was between shop-floor supervisors and ordinary workers. In this relationship, the former operated day-to-day production through a network of loyal workers, who received favorable work assignments, performance evaluations, and bonuses and prizes from their supervisors. The defining character of these various particular ties was instrumental, argued Walder, because favor exchange was both the motivation and the anticipated outcome of them.

In the exchange networks of particular instrumental ties, the key source of *guanxi* capital lies in one's reputation for keeping promises to provide and return favors to the members of one's *guanxi* networks. In other words, the rule of the game is reciprocity. Yang (1994) observed that in post-Mao

China, indebtedness and the obligation to reciprocate are the binding power of social relations. Hwang (1987) argued that for all Chinese societies, reciprocity is the basis of face, because face is based less on the degree of sentiment of a tie than on the mutual trust and loyalty between the parties engaged in favor exchanges. This point was used to examine the utility of strong ties in job searches in China (Bian 1997, 1999) and Singapore (Bian & Ang 1997). Consequently, the goals of networking have shifted from extending ties of familial sentiments and obligations to cultivating ties of diverse resources for mutual favor exchanges.

Guanxi *as Social-Exchange Networks of Asymmetric Transactions*

Recently Nan Lin (1998a) has provided both a critical review of the *guanxi* literature and a new conceptual model about the nature and operating mechanisms of *guanxi* networks. Recognizing the different emphases on the sentimental basis and instrumental uses of *guanxi* by previous researchers of China, he argues that both of these characterize *guanxi* when it is defined in the broad context of social-exchange networks of asymmetric transaction.

Lin distinguishes between economic exchanges of symmetric transaction and social exchanges of asymmetric transaction. The rationale of *economic exchanges* is to focus on short-term transactions of valued resources and the relative gain to loss in the resources transacted between the parties involved. In contrast, the rationale of *social exchanges* shifts the focus to long-term commitment to maintaining relationships in which resources are embedded. In social exchanges, transactions of resources are asymmetric in that resources flow from favor giver to favor receiver, and this is also true when the resource flow in social networks is access to other ties (in this case, favor giver performs as a network bridge). But the favor giver does gain—by being recognized as resourceful. The spread of recognition in social networks enhances the reputation of the favor giver, thus helping him/her maintain and strengthen his/her network centrality.

Lin classifies *guanxi* as a type of social exchange, permitting instrumental uses and favor-seeking purposes to characterize *guanxi* networks. He argues, however, that "it is the relationship that is valued and must be maintained, not the value of the favor transacted per se"; thus, "instrumental action becomes the means and *guanxi* [building] becomes the end" (p. 22). It is in this sense that Lin also emphasizes the sentimental basis of *guanxi*.

In Lin's conceptualization, the relational bases of *guanxi* become very broad, including all kinds of kin and nonkin relations. The key source of *guanxi* capital is neither the reputation of fulfilling moral obligations to

Table 1.   Models of *Guanxi* and Some Implications for Social Eating

	Model I	Model II	Model III
Definition of *guanxi*	Web of extended familial obligations	Exchange networks of particular-instrumental ties	Social exchange networks of asymmetric transaction
Relational bases	Family, kinship, community	Family, kinship, community, work	All kinds of kin and nonkin relations
Sources of *guanxi* capital	Reputation for fulfilling moral obligations to family and pseudofamilies	Reputation for keeping promises of providing and returning favors	Reputation for being network bridges to resourceful ties
Bases of *guanxi* capital	Face based on sentiment and closeness	Face based on mutual trust and loyalty	Face based on repeated asymmetric transaction
Strategies of *guanxi* capital accumulation	To extend ties of familial sentiments and obligations	To cultivate ties of diverse resources for favor exchanges	To increase network centrality for more network ties
Who to invite	Family and pseudo family connections	*Guanxi* connections with resource diversity	*Guanxi* connections with network diversity
Purposes	Predominantly expressive	Predominantly instrumental	Equally expressive and instrumental
Payment	One eating partner pays	Instrumental: favor seeker pays Expressive: eating partners share	Mostly favor seeker pays Favor giver may pay

family and pseudofamilies, nor the reputation for keeping promises in favor exchanges; after all, resource transactions in social exchanges are asymmetric. Instead, *guanxi* capital lies in one's reputation as a generous favor giver and a network bridge to resourceful ties. In this context, face—the Chinese version of social capital—can be reinterpreted: Face giving means lending access to connections, and face receiving means getting access to connections. Predictably, granting favors (access to connections) is the best strategy to maintain one's networks and enhance one's capacity for accumulating *guanxi* capital. Table 1 displays the key points of the three models just reviewed.

EMPIRICAL IMPLICATIONS OF SOCIAL EATING

It is well known that banquets are popular and used as an important social venue through which Chinese people network (Yang 1994). In the United States, the term "banquet" generally connotes a fairly large, formal gathering or a rather elegant, elaborate party on a formal occasion (wedding, retirement, etc). For Chinese society and in following Yang, I use the term to include a wider range of gatherings of relatives, friends, and acquaintances that involve social eating. In a *guanxi* society, when a person receives an invitation to a banquet hosted by one's *guanxi*, the invitee is seen as having face. If the person turns down the invitation, then the host loses his / her face. And if the invitee accepts the invitation and attends the banquet, this is interpreted as giving face to the host (Yan 1996). The operation of such face work means that banqueting is a deliberate social process involving network strategies. Many banquets in China may appear to be less deliberate and more informal and spontaneous. But then, many of these occasions do involve considerable calculations about whom to invite, whom to pay, and what to talk about during the course of a meal. What clues can we learn from the three theoretical models of *guanxi* to these networking processes?

Expectations of Model I

According to Model I, *guanxi* is the web of extended familial obligations; *guanxi* capital accumulates when one invests time and energy to extend the ties of familial sentiments and obligations. This model implies that family and pseudofamily connections are more highly represented in eating-partner networks than are other kinds of connections. Furthermore, within the circles of family and kinship connections, banquets are initiated for expressing hosts' familial sentiments and emotional attachments to relatives; and relatives are expected to have the same expressive purposes in mind when attending the banquets. In less formal and more spontaneous occasions, meal costs are not shared but paid for by a self-offered host; it would cause damage to the familial sentiment if the meal costs were split among relatives engaging in social eating. If *guanxi* connections are defined as family and pseudofamily connections, then social eating is intended more for expressive than for instrumental purposes, and meals are expected to be paid for by a host, rather than shared by all eating partners.

Expectations of Model II

Model II implies different expectations about patterns of social eating. According to this model, *guanxi* refers to exchange networks of particular instrumental ties. This notion of *guanxi* makes it explicit that reciprocity is the guiding principle of *guanxi* networking. It means that if a person wants to accumulate *guanxi* capital through social eating, he or she tends to engage in it with persons who have a lot of resources at their disposal. Under this circumstance, the occasions of social eating are then used to hint, initiate, or complete a course of favor exchange. At the aggregate level, the model makes no assumption about relational bases of eating-partner networks, but it points to the tendency that social eating is arranged more frequently among people who have many different kinds of resources to trade than among those with a small number of resources to trade. Second, social eating is intended more for instrumental purposes than for expressive purposes. Finally, the favor seeker is expected to pay the bill. When social eating is indeed for social, expressive purposes (rather than instrumental purposes), however, it is understood that the cost would be shared among eating partners.

Expectations of Model III

Model III projects *guanxi* as a type of social-exchange network of asymmetric transaction. The model assumes that *guanxi* building is an everyday phenomenon in Chinese society, that favor seeking and favor giving are typical of *guanxi* building, and that a favor seeker and favor giver both benefit, though in different ways, from each transaction. This model has the following implications for social eating. First, freely chosen eating partners come from all kinds of connections, especially from those with high network diversity, because the higher such diversity, the greater the potential for network bridging. Second, since *guanxi* building aims to maintain social relations through favor seeking and favor giving, any occasion of social eating should have a mixture of instrumental and expressive purposes. Thus, Model III makes no expectation that either kind of purpose will dominate social eating. Finally, according to this model *guanxi* networking is asymmetric in nature. This implies that the favor seeker should pay the cost of social eating. However, the relational rationale postulated by Model III indicates that the favor giver may pay the bill. The two possibilities combined indicate that social eating is a hosted setting, either by a favor seeker or favor giver.

ANALYSES

My data come from an urban consumer project conducted in several Chinese cities in 1998 and 1999. Four waves of data were collected over more than a year; in this chapter I analyze part of the data from the first two waves. In the first, 401 households participated in the project, and data collection focused on social networking during the Spring Festival (the New Year celebration in the lunar calendar) in February. The second wave, in May, focused on social eating, with 351 households remaining in the project and five new households added. In each wave, data were collected through a face-to-face interview using a structured questionnaire. In addition, a book of diary forms was left so that each participating household could record a week's consumption and networking activities by the household head, spouse, and up to four more household members. My analysis here will be limited to household heads, who were the respondents in the questionnaire survey. For convenience of presentation, I term a respondent "ego" and his/her eating partners, whether one or more on each occasion, "alter."

Perceptions about Banquets

I begin by describing how banquets (*qing ke chi fan*) are perceived by respondents. As revealed in the first section of Table 2, 75 percent of the respondents agreed with the statement that banquets are designed not solely for eating meals but for providing a good environment for conversation with others. A similarly large majority agreed that banquets are necessary for maintaining social relations (70 percent), but are not intended as a means to return favors to helpers (68 percent). Although a minority of respondents disagreed with each statement, variation in response is not associated with any of the stratification variables considered (class, employment status, employer type, home ownership, and income). As can be seen in the second section of Table 2, none of the null hypotheses can be rejected. These results indicate that there is a shared value system among

Table 2. Social Values about Banquets

Value Items	N	Agree (%)	Disagree (%)	No Opinion (%)
1. Banquets are not meant to eat meals, but to have a good environment for conversations	326	75	11	14
2. Banquets are necessary for maintaining social relations	326	70	14	17
3. Banquets are not intended as a means to return favors to helpers	313	68	13	19

	F-texts from ANOVA: p value and d.f.			
Respondent's attributes	Value Item 1	Value Item 2	Value Item 3	d.f.
Occupational class (10 categories)	.947	.200	.697	9
Employment status (11 categories)	.370	.908	.942	10
Type of employer (9 categories)	.524	.809	.255	8
Home ownership (3 categories)	.294	.785	.201	2
Income ranking (16 categories)	.613	.340	.771	15

Chinese urbanites about banquets: they are a means of maintaining social relations. In the Chinese context this means maintaining *guanxi* networks. Who, then, from an ego's network is invited to a banquet?

Core-**Guanxi** *Networks and Eating-Partner Networks*

Is social eating more likely among family and pseudofamily ties (Model I)? Or, does social eating frequently go beyond the network circles of families and pseudofamilies to occur among particular-instrumental ties (Model II)? Or, does it more frequently occur among persons who have more diverse network connections than just family and pseudofamily ties (Model III)? To analyze these questions, a referent point about a person's core *guanxi* network is needed. Such a network is the *network structure* from which the network of eating-partners emerges.

It is well known that people's social networks are multidimensional in both Chinese and non-Chinese societies (Ruan et al. 1997), and that *guanxi* networks are dynamic, evolving, and probably without boundary (Liang 1949; King 1985, 1988). This makes it difficult to measure accurately a person's core *guanxi* network through the standard techniques of name generator and position generator (Lin 1999). I measure the core *guanxi* network as confined to "greeters" during the week of the Spring Festival for two reasons. First, *guanxi* connections traditionally greet each other through home visits and, increasingly, telephone calls during the period. Second, this gives us the opportunity to take an accurate reading of the number and relational types of greeters to the households used in our project. This task was completed during the first wave of the 1998 urban consumer project.

The recording was limited to the eve and the first five days of the New Year, the period of the holiday. Some households ($N = 23$) were away from home during the entire six days; the remaining households ($N = 378$) reported a total of 7,436 greeters to their homes, averaging about 20 greeters per household. For my analysis, these greeters form the core *guanxi* networks of my respondents. Data about eating-partner networks were collected from a separate recording during a week in May, in the second wave. Although breakfasts were recorded, my analysis is confined to lunches, dinners, and night snacks, where social eating is concentrated. Table 3 reports aggregate data about the relational compositions, class compositions, and network diversities of respondents' core *guanxi* networks and eating-partner networks.

According to Model I, a person's kin ties and pseudofamily ties would be more likely to be involved in social eating than are their other ties. This expectation is partially supported by the data: Although 39 percent of ties from core *guanxi* networks are pseudofamily ties, these ties have a 45 per-

Table 3. Compositions of Core-*Guanxi* Network and Eating-Partner Network

Variables	Core-Guanxi Network[a] (1)	Eating-Partner Network (2)	(2) − (1)	(2) − (1) Hypothesized by Models
Relational composition (%)				Model I
Kin ties	36	19	−17*	(2) > (1)
Pseudofamily ties[b]	39	45	6*	(2) > (1)
Other ties[c]	25	36	11*	(2) < (1)
Class composition[d] (%)				Model II
Same as egos	52	60	8*	(2) < (1)
Different than egos	48	40	−8*	(2) > (1)
Network diversity[e]				Model III
Average number of types of ties[f]	4.89	5.86	0.97*	(2) > (1)
Average number of job positions[g]	4.86	5.17	0.31	(2) > (1)
Average number of types of units[h]	3.26	3.68	0.42*	(2) > (1)

*Two-tailed *t*-test significant at the .05 level.
[a]Defined as greeters during the holiday of Spring Festival in February 1998. A total of 7,436 greeters were reported by 378 households.
[b]These include guests of the family, villagers, classmates, army-comrades, teachers, students or apprentices, neighbors, and friends.
[c]These include superiors and subordinates at work, work colleagues of the same rank, other work-related contacts, and business partners and contacts.
[d]A three-class scheme is used here, including cadre class, professional-technical class, and working class.
[e]The averages reported here are adjusted under an equal occurrence assumption for greeting activities during the Spring Festival and eating arrangements recorded separately.
[f]Out of a maximum of 14 different types of ties.
[g]Out of a maximum of 20 different occupational positions.
[h]Out of a maximum of 12 different employer types.

cent representation in eating-partner networks. Kin ties, however, have a lower representation and other ties have a higher representation in eating-partner networks than in core *guanxi* networks. This result is contrary to the expectations of Model I.

Model II predicts that eating-partner networks are used to mobilize resources for favor exchanges. This model implies that ties in eating-partner networks may be more resourceful than ties in core *guanxi* networks. Recent stratification research of urban China (Lin & Bian 1991; Walder 1992, 1995; Bian 1994; Bian & Logan 1996; Zhou et al. 1996, 1997) revealed that occupational classes vary considerably and increasingly in such resources as power, prestige, income, and redistributive benefits (housing, medical care, etc.). I use a class composition (cadre, professional, and worker) to

measure the probability that an ego can mobilize different kinds of resources from his/her eating-partner network. If eating partners share the
same class as egos, the probability is low, otherwise it is high. The data
show that 48 percent of the ties in core *guanxi* networks are from different
class categories from the respondent's, but the percentage is lower (40 percent) for ties in eating-partner networks. This finding contradicts the prediction of Model II.

There is some evidence from Table 3 to support the prediction of Model
III: greater network diversity for ties in eating-partner networks than for
ties from core *guanxi* networks. Table 3 shows that the average number of
types of ties (out of a maximum of 14) is significantly larger for the eating-
partners network than for the core *guanxi* network. Second, the average
number of types of employers (a maximum of 12) is also significantly
larger for the eating-partner network than for the core *guanxi* network. Finally, a similar tendency is revealed for diversities of job types between the
eating-partner network and core *guanxi* network, but the differential is
small and statistically insignificant.

Who Pays and for What Purposes?

Table 4 tests the implications of the three models for payment arrangements and intentions of social eating. During the week of data collection
in May 1998, the 356 respondents had a total of 5,054 lunches, dinners, and
night snacks. Of these, 19 percent were eaten alone by respondents, 60 percent with the family, and 21 percent with "others." This last category meets
the requirement of social eating, so it is further analyzed in Table 4.

All three models expect, though for different reasons, a joint payment
arrangement to be significantly less likely than an arrangement in which ego
or alter pays. This expectation is supported by the data: 53 percent of meals
were paid by either ego or alter, compared with 20 percent of meals paid
jointly by ego and alter. The other 27 percent of meals were paid through
"other arrangement," a predesigned response. The wording ("other arrangement") was chosen to avoid the more natural, but probably unwise,
response category of "paid by employer" or "paid by public funds," which
would give respondents an impression of corruption and thus possibly dis-
tort the reliability of their answers. My theoretical interest is in the choice
between the first two responses.

Models I and II go in opposite directions in predicting the purposes of
banquets. Model I predicts that banquets would be used predominantly
for expressive purposes, and significantly less for instrumental purposes.
Model II predicts the opposite. The data indicate a clear tendency in support of the prediction of Model I: 63 percent of the 1,086 meals were "just
for a conversation" (*sui bian liao liao*), compared with 28 percent for the purpose of having "a business to talk over" (*you shi yao tan*).

Table 4. Features of Social Eating in a Week in May 1998 (*N* = 356)

Variables	%	Model I	Model II	Model III
		Hypothesized Direction by		
Total meals eaten (*N* = 5,054)				
Eat alone	19			
Eat with family	60			
Eat with others	21			
Eating with others (*N* = 1,086)				
Who pays?				
Ego or alter pays	53	Predominant	Predominant	Predominant
Ego and alter jointly pay	20			
Other arrangement	27			
What for?				
Just for a conversation	63	Predominant		
Talk about business	28		Predominant	
For other purposes	9			
Just for a conversation (*N* = 608)				
Ego or alter pays	45		Greatly less	Greatly more
Ego and alter jointly pay	19		Greatly more	Greatly less
Other arrangement	37			
Talk about business (*N* = 274)				
Ego or alter pays	85		Greatly more	Greatly more
Ego and alter jointly pay	9		Greatly less	Greatly less
Other arrangement	6			

After the purpose of the meal is considered, Models II and III make different predictions about payment arrangements. When a meal is for an expressive purpose, Model II—under the assumption that reciprocity rules *guanxi* networking—predicts that the bill is more likely to be shared by ego and alter than to be paid for by either party. The data do not support this prediction: 45 percent of meals were paid for by either ego or alter, and only 19 percent paid for jointly by ego and alter. This finding supports the expectation of Model III, which implies that a hosted banquet, rather than a shared arrangement, is typical of social eating in a *guanxi* society. Of banquets arranged for instrumental purposes, 85 percent are paid for by either ego or alter, as is expected by both Models II and III.

Banquet Guest, Banquet Host, and Banquet Attendee

The aggregate analyses presented so far reveal to us a macropicture about Chinese network patterns in the context of social eating. I now turn to the question of network effects on individuals' engagement in banquets. To what extent is one's engagement in banquets due to one's political influence and economic ability, and to what extent is it due to one's network advantage and disadvantage? Table 5 suggests answers to these questions.

A respondent's engagement in banquets is measured by the frequencies of being (1) a banquet guest, (2) a banquet host, and (3) a banquet attendee during the week of data recording in May. The last category is the combination of the first two plus the frequency of ego's presence to banquets as invitees' "escorts" (in popular discourse this role is called *pei chi*, or "escort eater"). Regression analyses of these three dependent variables are reported in Table 5. The results indicate that personal economic strengths (as measured by income) increase the frequency of one's being a banquet guest, a banquet host, and a banquet attendee. Moreover, if the respondent is a Communist party member (a measure of political influence), he or she

Table 5. Factory and Regression Analyses of Network Effects on Banqueting Frequencies

Factor Analysis			Regression Analysis: Standardized Coefficients[a]		
			Frequency of Being a Banquet	Frequency of Being a Banquet	Frequency of Being a Banquet
Measures	Factor Loading	Predictors	Guest	Host	Attendee
		(1) Network size	−.011	.020	−.006
Kin	.736	(2)			
Pseudofamily	.871	Relational	.262***	.189***	.267***
Other	.613	composition			
Tie diversity	.902				
Job diversity	.946	Network	.129***	.120!	.140**
Unit diversity	.927	diversity			
Cadre	.818				
Professional	.852	Class	.103!	−.078	−.023
Worker	.762	composition			
		(3)			
Variance explained (%)		Respondent party member	.111**	.074	.114**
Relational composition (58%)		Income	.355***	.300***	.384***
Network diversity (86%)		Constant	1.534***	2.925***	4.472***
		$R^2_{(1)}$	.012	.010	.011
		$R^2_{(1+2)}$	.240	.109	.202
Class composition (66%)		$R^2_{(1+2+3)}$	.266	.196	.348
		N	332	335	331

[a]Two-tailed significant tests: $p < .10$.
**$p < .01$.
***$p < .001$.

is a frequent banquet guest and attendee, but not a frequent banquet host. Although one might consider other personal attributes (e.g., gender, age, education, and cadre or professional class), none of these variables survives the significant tests in an initial analysis (not shown), so they have been removed from the model reported in Table 5. Confined to the effects of income and party membership on one's engagement in banquets, the regression results suggest that banqueting is an economic and political process in Chinese cities.

Nevertheless, banqueting is also a social-networking process. I consider four network variables as predictors of one's engagement in banquets. Of these, network size (as measured by the total number of greeters during the Spring Festival) has a marginal value in predicting one's being a banquet guest, host, or attendee, but it fails to survive the statistical test when other predictors are included in the regression equations. Note that network size reduces only 1 percent of variation in each of the three dependent variables (see R squared (1) in each equation).

The relational composition of respondents' networks is a significant predictor and produces a positive Beta coefficient in all three equations. This predictor is a factor of three measures: frequencies of interaction with (1) a kin tie, (2) a pseudofamily tie, and (3) a tie of "other type." All of these measures are confined to the core-*guanxi* network of greeters, as reported in Table 3. Exceedingly high intercorrelations among the three measures prevent them from being included simultaneously in any regression equation, but the factor generated can do just as well in reducing variances of the dependent variables (result not shown). The significant Beta coefficients indicate that the more frequent interactions one has with the three different kinds of ties, the more likely one is to be a frequent banquet guest, host, and attendee. The factor loadings suggest that pseudofamily ties (.871) are most important, and that kin ties (.736) are more important than other ties (.613) for increasing one's chances of banquet engagements. These findings lend partial support to Model I, which predicts that banquets are more frequently offered among family and pseudofamily connections.

Furthermore, network diversity also significantly increases the frequency of one's being a banquet guest, host, or attendee. Like relational composition, network diversity is also a factor, generated from the three measures of tie diversity, job diversity, and unit diversity, whose measurements are described in Table 3. These are confined to the core-*guanxi* networks of greeters. The positive Beta coefficients indicate that the more diverse one's network is, the more likely one is to be a banquet guest, host, or attendee. The large and similar magnitudes of factor loadings for the three diversity measures indicate that tie diversity, job diversity, and unit diversity are about equally important for increasing one's banquet engagements. These findings support the prediction of Model III: Persons with high network diversity are more likely to give and receive favors, and thus to engage in banquets more frequently than persons with less diverse networks.

The final network measure is class composition, a factor considering class backgrounds of persons with whom the respondents had social eating during the week of May, 1998, in which data on social eating were recorded on a meal-by-meal basis. Three classes (cadre, professional, and worker) were identified, and each class was used as a dummy variable (1 = yes, 0 = no). The high factor loadings for all three variables indicate high intercorrelation (thus, persons who had a meal with a cadre are more likely than not to have a meal with a professional or worker). The resulting factor shows, in the regression analysis, a moderate effect on the frequency of one's being a banquet guest, but not a banquet host or addendee. A casual observation is that in the 1990s cadres and high professionals are frequent attendants to banquets that are paid for by public funds. This likely reduces the probability that cadres and high professionals attend privately hosted banquets. It is quite possible, however, that banquets privately hosted to cadres and high professionals are underreported because of the implication of "pooling a relation" (la *guanxi*) with the powerful or the resourceful.

SUMMARY AND DISCUSSION

The 1998–99 urban consumer project shows that Chinese urbanites have great consensus about banqueting. A great majority of respondents perceive banquets to be a way to maintain social relations. This perception cuts across social and economic boundaries measured by respondents' class, employment status, occupation, employer type, home ownership, and income. These findings provide an empirical validity for analyzing patterns and processes of *guanxi* networking in the context of banquets or social eating in Chinese cities.

Scholars differ in their definitions of *guanxi*. A traditional view defines *guanxi* as the web of extended familial obligations and sentiments. A more recent view emphasizes the instrumentality of *guanxi* in facilitating favor exchanges. And a most recent advancement synthesizes *guanxi* as driven by relational rationality. These views inform different models about relational bases of *guanxi*, sources and forms of *guanxi* capital, and strategies used to accumulate *guanxi* capital. Although data analyses have tested the implications of these models for social eating, some findings are open for more interpretations than provided. Here I revisit some of these findings and attempt to discuss them in the broad context of social capital.

From Guanxi *Network to* Guanxi *Capital*

Portes (1995) defines social capital as "the capacity of individuals to command scarce means by virtue of their membership in networks or broader social structures" (p. 12). This refers to a process of resource mobilization from one's networks. For Lin (1998b), this is a two-step process: First, individuals access social resources embedded in their networks. Second, they mobilize and convert accessed social resources into social capital for goal attainment. If the first step is more a network constraint, the second reflects a rational choice: Individuals will rationally network with some people more frequently than with others within and beyond their networks. My findings provide clues to how these two steps of networking are correlated with one another in a *guanxi* society.

In China, although the *guanxi* network is multidimensional and evolving, it is well understood that those connected by *guanxi* normally greet each other on the important holiday of the Spring Festival. I therefore measure a Chinese person's core *guanxi* network by his/her Spring Festival greeters. The relational and class compositions and network diversities of these greeters are measured and can be interpreted as indicators of resources *accessed* by individuals in their core *guanxi* networks. Social eating, on the other hand, gives a Chinese person a choice scenario, because people can choose to eat meals with some connections more frequently than with other connections. Relational and class compositions and network diversities of eating-partner networks then can be seen as indicators of resources *mobilized* from one's *guanxi* network.

Table 2 shows that kin ties are highly represented in core networks (36 percent). Kin ties, however, are underrepresented in eating-partner networks (19 percent), which contradicts the expectation of the traditional model of extended familial obligations and sentiments. Pseudofamily ties are more highly represented in eating-partner networks than in core *guanxi* networks (39 percent versus 45 percent), and this is also true for other types of ties (25 percent versus 36 percent). The growth of these two types of ties from core *guanxi* networks to eating-partner networks does not seem to be driven by a search for eating partners of greater class differences, a hypothesis that is implied by the model of instrumental-particular ties. It is motivated, instead, by greater network diversity, a hypothesis derived from and confirmed for the model of social exchange networks of asymmetric transaction. I find that eating partners are more diversified by types of dyadic ties and types of employers than are greeters at Spring Festival. Job diversity is also greater for the former than for the latter, although the differential is not statistically significant.

These findings have important implications about the mobilization of *guanxi* capital in China. First, *guanxi* resources are more highly embedded in pseudofamily ties than in kin ties or any other types of ties. Work colleagues and business partners are included in the "other types of ties" category. Although these ties are most available in everyday interaction outside the family, they have a low representation in core *guanxi* networks (25 percent), and they are not as highly represented in eating-partner networks as are pseudofamily ties (36 percent and 45 percent, respectively). Second, eating partners tend to associate with one other within the social class boundaries of cadres, professionals, and workers. One may argue that the broad class categories would artificially make in-class connections a major type of network; however, interclass connections are substantially reduced from core *guanxi* network to eating-partner network. This implies that in China *guanxi* resources are less likely to be mobilized across class boundaries than within. Third, eating-partner networks are more diversified than are core *guanxi* networks, suggesting that network bridging and relational transfers, rather than the transfers of tangible resources, are the main mechanisms through which *guanxi* capital is accumulated. This conclusion about the mobilization of *guanxi* capital in China in the 1990s supports Lin's social-network model of relational rationality and asymmetric transaction.

Face as Social Capital

Two findings are seemingly confusing. On one hand, social eating is highly motivated for expressive purposes (63 percent of meals eaten with others are "just for a conversation," compared to 28 percent for talking about "a business"). On the other hand, it is also highly likely to be a hosted banquet (53 percent of the meals are paid for by ego or alter, compared to 20 percent paid jointly by ego and alter). Even for the meals designed for expressive purposes only, payment by ego or alter is more common than joint payment by both parties (45 percent, as compared to 19 percent). These findings can be understood with reference to face, the Chinese form of social capital.

In the context of banqueting, a person is considered to have received face if he/she receives an expected invitation to a banquet from a *guanxi* connection. This demonstrates the invitee's social recognition and potential to mobilize *guanxi* resources. On the other hand, one is seen as losing face if an expected invitation does not materialize. This failure indicates the individual's inability to maintain *guanxi* and mobilize *guanxi* resources. If the invitee accepts the invitation and attends the banquet, this points to two capacities: the capacity of the banquet host to maintain *guanxi* and to commend *guanxi* resources from the invitee later, and the capacity of the invitee to maintain and extend *guanxi* networks (getting the opportunity to develop potential *guanxi* connections through banqueting). Therefore, the frequency of being a banquet guest, host, or attendee is a sensible measure of social capital in the Chinese context.

The individual-level analyses presented in Table 5 suggest that the rich and the politically powerful have greater social capital than the poor and the politically weak. These are expected by both stratification and network researchers, but this is not the end of the story. Of special interest in this paper is that a Chinese person's social capital is also strongly affected by his/her network positions. First, to increase one's social capital one must have a mixed relational composition containing kin ties, pseudofamily ties, and other types of ties. Second, network diversity is very important. Specifically, in China, not only must a person have diversified relational types, but, significantly, this person must also have contacts who work with different types of employers and in different kinds of jobs. Network size does not automatically increase social capital, unless large networks contain ties that offer these kinds of relational and positional diversities, but not necessarily placed in different social classes. All these findings support the expectations of Lin's model about social-exchange networks of relational rationality.

NOTE

I thank Deborah Davis, Jeff Broadbent, Joe Galaskiewicz, Nan Lin, Jeylan Mortimer, and Jiping Zuo for their helpful comments on an earlier version. It was presented at the conference "Social Capital and Social Networks," Duke University, October 30–November 1, 1998, and the workshops "Social Capital in China" and "East Asian Culture," University of Minnesota, September 18 and December 2, 1999, respectively.

REFERENCES

Bian, Yanjie. 1994. *Work and Inequality in Urban China.* Albany, NY: State University of New York Press.
———. 1997. "Bringing Strong Ties Back In: Indirect Connection, Bridges, and Job Search in China." *American Sociological Review* 62:266–85.
Bian, Yanjie, and John R. Logan. 1996. "Market Transition and the Persistence of Power: The Changing Stratification System in Urban China." *American Sociological Review* 61:739–58.
Cheng, Lucie, and Arthur Rosett. 1989. "Contract with a Chinese Face: Socially Embedded Factors in the Transformation from Hierarchy to market, 1978–1989." *Journal of Chinese Law* 5 (No. 2):143–244.
Chiao, Chien. 1982. "*Guanxi:* A Preliminary Conceptualization." Pp. 345–60 in *The*

Sinicization of Social and Behavioral Science Research in China, edited by Kuo-shu Yang and Chong-yi Wen. Taipei, Taiwan: Academia Sinica.

Fei, Xiaotong. [1949] 1992. *From the Soil, the Foundations of Chinese Society.* Berkeley, CA: University of California Press.

Fried, Morton H. 1969 [1953]. *Fabric of Chinese Society: A Study of the Social Life in a Chinese County Seat.* New York: Octagon Books.

Hwang, Kwang-kuo. 1987. "Face and Favor: The Chinese Power Game." *American Journal of Sociology* 92(4):944–74, 4.

Jacobs, J. Bruce. 1979. "A Preliminary Model of Particularistic Ties in Chinese Political Alliances: Kan-Ch'ing and Kuan-Hsi in a Rural Taiwanese Township." *China Quarterly* 78:237–73.

King, Ambrose Y. C. 1985. "The Individual and Group in Confucianism: A Relational Perspective." Pp. 57–70 in *Individualism and Holism: Studies in Confucian and Taoist Values,* edited by Donald J. Munro. Ann Arbor: Center for Chinese Studies, University of Michigan.

———. 1988. "Analysis of *Renqing* in Interpersonal Relations (Renqi *Guanxi* Zhong Renqing Zhi Fensi)." Pp. 319–45 in *Psychology of the Chinese (Zhongguoren de Xinli),* edited by Kuo-shu Yang. Taipei, Taiwan: Guiguan Press.

Kornai, Janos. 1986. *Contradictions and Dilemmas: Studies on the Socialist Economy and Society.* Cambridge, MA: MIT Press.

Liang, Shuming. [1949] 1986. *The Essential Meanings of Chinese Culture.* Hong Kong: Zheng Zhong Press.

Lin, Nan. 1989. "Chinese Family Structure and Chinese Society." *Bulletin of the Institute of Ethnology* 65:382–99.

———. 1998a. "*Guanxi:* A Conceputal Analysis." Chapter for *The Chinese Triangle of Mainland, Taiwan, and Hong Kong: Comparative Institutional Analysis,* edited by Alvin So, Nan Lin, and Dudly Poston. Westport, CT: Greenwood (in press).

———. 1998b. "Social Exchange: Its Relational Basis." Paper read at the Sunbelt XVIII International Social Network Conference, May 28–31, Sitges, Spain.

———. 1999. "Social Networks and Status Attainment." *Annual Review of Sociology* 25:467–87.

Lin, Nan, and Yanjie Bian. 1991. "Getting Ahead in Urban China." *American Journal of Sociology* 97:657–88.

Portes, Alejandro. 1995. "Economic Sociology and the Sociology of Immigration: A Conceputal Overview." Pp. 1–41 in *The Economic Sociology of Immigration: Essays on Networks, Ethnicity, and Entrepreneurship,* edited by Alejandro Portes. New York: Russell Sage Foundation.

Ruan, Danching, Linton C. Freeman, Xinyuan Dai, Yunkang Pan, and Wenhong Zhang. 1997. "On the changing structure of social networks in urban China." *Social Networks* 19:75–89.

Walder, Andrew G. 1986. *Communist Neo-Traditionalism: Work and Authority in Chinese Industry.* Berkeley, CA: University of California Press.

———. 1992. "Property Rights and Stratification in Socialist Redistributive Economies." *American Sociological Review* 57:524–39.

———. 1995. "Career Mobility and the Communist Political Order." *American Sociological Review* 60:309–28.

Yan, Yunxiang. 1996. *The Flow of Gifts Reciprocity and Social Networks in a Chinese Village*. Stanford: Stanford University Press.

Yang, C. K. 1965 [1959]. *Chinese Communist Society: the Family and the Village*. Cambridge, MA: MIT Press.

Yang, Mayfair Mei-hui. 1994. *Gifts, Favors, and Banquets: The Art of Social Relationships in China*. Ithaca, NY: Cornell University Press.

Zhou, Xueguang, Nancy Brandon Tuma, and Phyllis Moen. 1996. "Stratification Dynamics under State Socialism." *Social Forces* 28:440–68.

———. 1997. "Institutional Change and Job-Shift Patterns in Urban China." *American Sociological Review* 62:339–65.

12

Change and Stability in Social Network Resources: The Case of Hungary under Transformation

Róbert Angelusz and Róbert Tardos

PREVIOUS APPROACHES, RELATED RESEARCH

The Hungarian Scene

Recently, interest in social-network resources has increased in Hungarian social research. This heightened attention has historical and political, as well as scientific motives. As to the former, we may primarily refer to the features of Hungarian developments, which created a special role for informality, or the personal handling of matters in late Kadarite society. Undoubtedly, the importance of nexus or multilayered contacts surfaced conspicuously in a world characterized by the generic feature of a shortage economy and the reciprocal networks of under-the-counter goods and services. Since the seventies, dualistic models based on the hidden networks of intertwined formal and informal relations have moved to the forefront of social research.

Systemic changes and the targeted transition to a market economy shed new light on these phenomena. The question arose whether the primacy of market relations and the virtual end of the shortage economy have led to the diminished role of informal behavior patterns and thus of personal nexus. Researchers who focused on this question, both Sík (1994) and Czakó (1994) emphasize path-dependent features. The former author in particular made a salient statement when he predicted that after the transition period, following the systemic changes, the role of networks and social capital would increase, side by side with the survival of nonmarket mechanisms in the economy. In addition to an expansive nexus system, Sík also attributed growing importance to defensive (mainly family or kinship) contacts in the period of economic hardship, fast-changing world events, increasing unemployment, and inflation.

In addition to these features, Sík and Wellman (1998) emphasized the protective role of people's social bonds in their struggle against state intrusion under the old system, while pointing to the survival (the growth, perhaps) of informal ties of a somewhat changed character even under the new conditions of high uncertainty.

The recent wave of literature on social stratification or restratification and on the emergence of an elite leading the systemic changes has also highlighted the role of networking, even raising it to the rank of paradigmatic status. Böröcz and Southworth (1995), Szelényi and Szelényi (1995), and Róna-Tas (1994) examined the relative role of network resources with respect to income- and career-related status attainment, while Lengyel (1998) focused on the effect of social capital on the development and success of enterprises.

Another important aspect of this topic is the changes reshaping the organizational structure of the economy, i.e., the network-driven devolution and restructuring of traditional state property. Stark (1996) outlined the development of a recombined type of property, a characteristic form of the region that may prevail in the long term. The traditional division between public and private ownership is blurred here, just as the borders of organizations become more "porous" when the informal network becomes predominant and organizational elements acquire a high degree of both external and internal variability. Increased attention to network relations and the system of organizational contacts within the business sector is also reflected by Hungarian research on overlapping and merged managerial positions (see, for example, Vedres 1997).

Conceptual Issues

In the past decade, a conceptual shift has occurred in this field of research, reflected by new trends in international literature. The increasing popularity of the "social network" approach, popular since the 1970s, and the spread of sociological theories of capital over the past two decades have resulted in the widespread application of the "social capital" concept. It is to a certain extent a fad, no doubt, where it is often hard to distinguish metaphorical and rhetorical devices from scientific ones. But even within the scientific approach, one may discern a number of different directions in interpretation according to the level of analysis or range of focus. (For a review of these see Tardos [1996]; for a tentative scheme see Table 1.) The

Table 1. A Tentative Scheme of Three Lines of Interpretation of the Social Capital (SC) Concept

	SCI1	SCI2	SCI3
Short notation of the related approach	The **symbolic** approach	The **network** approach	The **normative** approach
Main topics	Group belonging, "good name," prestige, embeddedness in "high society"	Good connections, help through nexus; range, variety, strength of ties, broker position, structural holes	Social integration, mutual obligations, trust, civic engagement
Level of analysis	1. Group 2. Individual	**Individual**	**Group** level
Character of resources	Symbolic	**Instrumental**	Normative-expressive
Source of availability of SC	1. **Ascribed** (derived from group membership, family origin, media salience, etc.) 2. Achieved	**Achieved**	"By-product" of other types of activities
Specific benefits related to SC	Reputation, honor	Help, advice, extra information	Confidence, mutual support
Origin of resources	One's **status** group	One's **acquaintance** ties, friends, relations	The **community** (group, family, etc.) as a whole
Capital accumulation issues	Reconversion strategies, **legitimization** struggles around symbolic positions	**Investment** in contacts for status attainment, costs/benefits	Public good aspects, free-rider problems
Lead concerns	Differential **access** to SC	Role of social vs. human capital in **status attainment**	Maintenance of **cooperation**
Typical loci of studies	The European (French) scene	The American and European scene	Cross-cultural and intracultural (longitudinal) perspectives
Characteristic target populations	Elite studies	General population	Community
Degree of operationalization of the SC concept	Low (highly metaphoric)	High (through the social network apparatus)	Moderate
Network aspects as SC features	(Low emphasis on network features)	**Range, variety** of contacts, heterophily, **bridging** ties, **low structural constraint**	**Dense** ties, **closure**, group cohesion
(Potential) methodology, variables in focus	Direct **background** variables; (position generator data related to high status positions)	**Name generator** and **position generator** techniques	**Density** indices through name generator techniques; **statistics** of memberships

fact that clear terminology is still to be developed apparently has not diminished the popularity of this concept and its multiple layers may attract even greater attention.[1]

We find it appropriate to tackle this problem with a degree of caution. Generally, when discussing various kinds of contacts, we use the term "social-network resources," which is somewhat more neutral and theoretically less biased. As for the concept of social capital, we would bring its application closer to the original definition of capital in the economic sense (with the related concepts of investment, yield, exchange, and accumulation). Through this approach we can get closer to those instrumental types of network resources that may contribute in some fashion to the elevation of one's social status. Undoubtedly, an adequate operationalization along this line is a daunting task and we are not prepared to make a definite attempt at it, although some of our survey findings point in the direction of this interpretation. As to its overall character, our instrumental focus appears to agree with authors like Burt or Lin, who sharply delineate the scope of the concept (see, e.g., Burt 1992; Lin 1995). However, it is far from us to contest the rich heuristic potential of other lines of interpretation of this term such as suggested by Coleman (1988) or Putnam (1995) or, to mention one more characteristic direction, its distinction from other types of capital by Bourdieu (1983).

Examining the central themes of Hungarian research, it appears as a question of utmost importance how the change of system has affected the relative roles of various capital types and, more particularly, how the relative significance of social or interpersonal network capital has been modified. Theoretically, we should also know how the social distributions of different types of network resources have changed in the past decade, how social inequalities changed in various aspects, whether and how the weight of various structuring factors and the relative significance of basic (cultural, economic, and political) factors have been affected. Drawing conclusions that go beyond hypotheses and can are supported by empirical evidence is strongly restricted by the fact that there are still few research findings from the period preceding and following the systemic changes which might serve as the direct basis of comparison.

Bases of Comparison

Some of the most comprehensive research findings are available from the second half of the 1980s, part of which provide an opportunity to carry out cross-national comparisons. According to the conclusions of the ISSP "social network survey" carried out in 1986 (Utasi 1991), family and kinship ties were more crucial and the choice-based contacts within the support networks generally carried less weight in Hungary than in Western countries that participated in the project. Our own study, more exactly a survey of social-network resources in the cultural stratification of Hungary in the second half of the 1980s, led to similar conclusions in this respect.[2] An adaptation of the ZUMA (Mannheim) version relying on the Fischer—McAllister multiple-situation name-generator technique was chosen as the basic network element of our survey, which allowed us to compare it to the German survey carried out a short time before. In this case we were also in a position to record a greater proportion of family and kinship ties under Hungarian circumstances. In other relationships we have observed a greater proportion of work-related, and a lesser proportion of extrainstitutional friend / acquaintance-type contacts (Angelusz & Tardos 1988). While these aspects could be derived from the prevalence of more traditional elements in the structure of Hungarian society, the signs of mobility and the manifestations of status enhancing nexus-seeking could be discerned in the relatively high frequency of contacts directed upward toward others of higher education and occupation. (In fact, we can find more choices of this type than among the corresponding data of the Mannheim survey.) Similarly, we found tendencies to intentionally shape the character of contacts and the predominance of such contact-oriented skills among knowledge styles (the other pillar of our stratification study in the second half of the eighties). For the higher status segments of younger professionals who started their careers in the seventies and eighties, skills of self-presentation and networking clearly gained dominance over both cognitive-instrumental and authoritative-representative skills, which played dominant roles in older age groups (Angelusz & Tardos 1990).

The still sparse longitudinal survey data, which cover the whole period following the systemic change, nevertheless suggest the changing character of the social networks. According to the results of the 1986 survey repeated in 1993 (Utasi 1996), the role of network resources had generally increased in various areas of access to information and goods, while the role of friendship contacts involving intimate and emotional ties had decreased. The cross-national comparison in 1986 had already shown that, except in the younger age groups, intimate contacts of this type were less frequent in Hungary than in Western societies, which served as the basis of comparison. By 1993, this tendency had gained more strength to the extent that the proportion of these more spiritual friendship contacts in the younger age groups by and large fell back to the formerly low values of the older age groups. Data drawn from the set of answers concerning friendship contacts within the Panel Study of Hungarian Households (Albert 1998) in recent years, specifically 1993 and 1997, seem interesting in this respect. It is certainly remarkable that the number of friends reported in this questionnaire decreased from 7.1 to 4.5 and the proportion of respondents who said they had no friends increased from 20 to 30 percent during these four years. Further studies are needed to determine whether this result corresponds to the tendency described above—i.e., to the instrumentalization of contacts and the weakening of emotional ties, if it is a hallmark of a general deprivation in personal contacts and the impoverishment of certain strata as to their networks—or whether we should further expand the series of possible explanations.

Variety of Contexts—Substantive and Methodological Problems

Based on the findings above and on more general concerns, the strong-weak scheme introduced by Granovetter, which gained paradigmatic importance in social-network literature, offers a useful frame of reference. The validity of "the strength of weak ties" thesis can mainly apply to pluralistic societies where different segments of society are not separated by rigid boundaries and an acquaintance nexus reaching beyond strata limits, thus exhibiting features of heterophily rather than homophily, can establish contacts between relatively distant social regions. Contacts based on market transactions and information exchange are the privileged areas of such a nexus. Several theoretical considerations support the view that a social transition to market relations increases the significance of the weaker, looser, acquaintance-type contacts. Granovetter's original research (1974) was directed toward labor-market relations and mechanisms of finding employment. This aspect is also relevant under the circumstances of transition when the structure of employment radically changed and, for broad social groups, it became a challenge to get and keep not just a better but *any* job. We could go on listing relevant areas. To name but a few, creating and maintaining enterprises, "sniffing out" privatization opportunities, and carrying off favorable securities transactions all require access to a wide range of information and the utilization of the potentially widest range of social contacts. If resources available for making and maintaining contacts are scarce, a shift of emphasis from strong ties to weak ones may occur in this period (and, to continue with the ideas introduced above, from the noncapital network resources to those of a capital nature).

Again, care should be taken when studying the general theoretical concerns of this paradigmatic framework and distinguishing strong and weak ties. This is a further case of a serious operationalization problem with respect to empirical study. It would be a mistake to automatically assign the place of certain types of contacts at one or the other extreme. On the one hand, we should think along a continuum rather than in a rigid dichotomy (where strong and weak ties are represented by separate dimensions); on the other hand, various types of questions require various types of operationalization, when, for example, more distant kinship or closer acquaintance links can be accounted for, on one side, in certain cases and, on the other side, in other cases. The result of our survey, conducted back in the late eighties, has already warned us against drawing hasty conclusions (Angelusz & Tardos 1991). In this survey we found that contacts of strong and weak ties typically occur in correlating pairs when either an abundance or the scarcity of contacts manifest themselves. Furthermore, certain theoretical considerations also warn us to avoid indulging in abstractions. Feld's (1981) influential article emphasized that the locus or the roots of contacts in social groups and institutions should always be kept in sight, and it is prudent for us as well to make these sources the starting point of our more specific investigations. If we look first at the institution of the family which, as we have already noted, is a highlighted locus of contacts in international comparison, we are likely to see contradictory developments. It is known from related statistics that partly with an increase in education and also because of economic hardships facing those trying to establish a family, the typical age of first marriage has increased considerably, and remarriage has become less frequent. Even within the time span of a decade, the number of couples living in traditional marriage settings decreased by a remarkable 10 percent, leaving this number at 55 to 60 percent, as shown by current data. Nevertheless, certain tendencies point to an increased utilization of family network resources. In the absence of other resources, in times of economic hardship it is generally the family that provides the best line of defense against unfavorable external circumstances. International experience shows that the utilization of family resources is also important for the creation and success of small enterprises and the instrumentalization of contacts outside the home, and can in itself increase the significance of emotional and similar strong ties provided by the family.

If economic and political processes have contradictory effects on the development of the network role of the family, we can discover a more unequivocal tendency with respect to work-related and co-worker contacts. In the last decade it was not only the occupational structure that went through a considerable change in the course of economic restructuring, but the number of jobs has also decreased almost by a third. While formerly about 60 percent of the adult population had jobs, by recent years this proportion has fallen to 40–45 percent.[3] This result is partly due to the increase in the number of students in the nineties, while most of it is due to the increase in the proportion of the unemployed, of people living on disability compensation, and of homemakers (the last two, in many cases, are hidden forms of unemployment). As a result of the increase in the number of small individual and family enterprises employing only a few people, the proportion of active earners who rely on work-related contacts has also decreased. These contacts, even if accompanied by paternalistic features, had provided a safety net and a source of integration for large social groups. The significance of these protective networks has diminished during the transition, when the workplace itself became more functional.

In Hungary, unions, clubs, and voluntary associations, which are important forums for network development in regions of a more advanced civil society, provided network resources only for a limited segment of the population in the past decades. Although we saw a revival of these institutions in the period preceding the systemic change, the demand for cadres in the new political system and in the parties siphoned off most of the still-meager resources of these associations. In fact, no serious impulses toward change in network structures can be expected from these quarters.

As for those elements of social networks that are least related to institutions and formal settings, even friendships and close acquaintance contacts have probably not been unaffected by the above-mentioned tendencies toward instrumentalization. Economic and social aspects such as the material conditions of keeping contacts (e.g., the increased costs of social events, gatherings, parties, or even meeting in public places) can have a direct impact, accompanied by the increased focus on material parity among the criteria of social contacts under circumstances of economic polarization. Former contacts between individuals and families who have been split into "winners" and "losers" are not likely to prevail. The political aspect of the systemic change itself can also have certain implications. In several cases, political affinity or similar party affiliations entered the list of important selection criteria, weakening the intensity of former friendship contacts, or abolishing them permanently, often the case among the intelligentsia. There is less evidence, however, that these new contacts, based on political allegiance, became the source of closer friendship contacts (obviously, the typically instrumental nature of such links is not likely to allow this).

All of these speculations would be hard to verify empirically as they entail details not covered by the surveys carried out in the eighties. Besides, to describe the nature of these processes accurately, survey findings from the initial period of the systemic change would be necessary. Although comprehensive bases of comparison covering several details and an adequate time span are scarcely available, existing partial data sets can be included within the outlined frames of interpretation. In addition to the surveys mentioned above, we can refer to our own survey, particularly to the one from late 1997. To account for social network resources, we could apply a set of questions from the "omnibus" survey carried out on a national representative sample and part of the Research Group of Communication Studies working under the auspices of the Hungarian Academy of Sciences and Eötvös Lóránd University.

ANALYTIC ISSUES

Measurement

Limited space (one questionnaire block at our disposal) did not allow us to repeat the entire social network module of the 1987/88 survey; in particular, we could not replicate the most time-intensive Fischer technique in the same form. However, we insisted on maintaining a variety of approaches and methods. Since experience shows that none of the routinely used techniques can be applied to mapping network resources entirely, it is extremely important to rely on different methods and techniques simultaneously.[4] During the 1987/88 survey we included an adaptation of the Lin—Dumin position generator to approach a wider range of looser links, in addition to the Fischer—McAllister technique, which afforded us a better grasp of family and friendship/acquaintance links with strong and mid-strength ties. Based on a rather extensive list of occupations (including 20, and in the second wave 23, items in our survey),[5] we attempted, by the use of the former technique, to measure the extent of the social field that can be approached by each individual, and the range of acquaintances covered by existing contacts represented by occupations of high and low prestige. (For possible extension of this method toward class nexus and network variety, see Erickson [1996] and for hints at a novel, more generalized approach to social categories based on various kinds of position generators see Lin [1998a, 1998b].) Moreover, as a supplementary method, to characterize the broader contact circle, we also examined the custom of sending Christmas and New Year's greeting cards and the usual number of these cards, as well as the number of union and society memberships.

During a late 1997 survey, within a more limited framework, we used similar approaches as a basis, and aimed to use more or less equivalent, if not identical, indices. The greatest modification was carried out on the Fischer-type name generator. We reduced the number of situations, while somewhat altering their content, from eight to three so that they would still reflect the essential characteristics of contacts. Generally, the most important aspects of personal contacts include the intimate discussion of important matters, asking for help to sort things out around the family, as well as keeping in touch through shared leisure activities and programs. For the first mentioned situation, the basic question of the 1985 U.S. General Social Survey (GSS) was adopted with the same text (see Burt 1984; Marsden 1987), which also allows us to make certain comparisons. While the employment of these three situations as name generators amounted to a certain combination of the GSS and the Fischer technique, and thus to the introduction of a more or less new method, the repetition of the wider ranging Lin—Dumin technique in a similar, though not identical, form yielded some more direct opportunities for comparison. (For this technique, the following modifications were also made during our recent survey: The list applied was adjusted to the change in the occupational structure, and newly emerged occupations, particularly from the entrepreneurial and financial sectors, were included. And to measure the significance of nexus, the simple categorization of acquaintances was replaced by the question whether specific contacts could also be used to move matters along and ask favors.[6])

The question about sending Christmas and New Year's cards provided the most direct possibility of comparison. The formerly open question concerning unions and associations was changed into a closed-item series by including a wide range of society and club types, as well as interest groups.

In addition to the above, the range of approaches applied to characterize contacts was complemented with a block concerning kinship patronage contacts through roles such as that of a wedding witness or a godparent. These relationships, hardly discussed in the social-network literature, gain added significance in more traditional societies and social settings, thus holding these positions in such settings is an important network resource.

The Development of Scales

In the end, we have four pairs of more or less corresponding indicators of various social network resources from 1987 and 1997. We have a better handle on strong ties through the 1987 name-generator and the 1997 combined Fischer—GSS techniques, and on the resources of weaker ties through approaches based on the occupational roster, greeting cards and the number of union members. Theoretically, the indicator of kinship patron role from the 1997 survey can be placed between these two indicators. While correspondence between individual indicators moves within narrower or broader limits, generally the combined indices constructed for each point of time covered by our project to characterize the development of social network resources in a global way, present a more perfect match. The construction of these global indices was grounded in a relatively high correlation between their components. For both years, we have the first component of the principal component analysis and the factor scores based on this component. (Due to their strong correlation and good fit, the components could be arranged into a single principal component in both 1987 and 1997.[7])

When creating the index, two theoretical problems had to be considered. One of these dilemmas revolves around the question whether components included in the index should be weighted, and whether theoretical considerations like the 'proportionate' representation of various contact types or the content-related significance of some primary indices should be taken into account. This matter was settled partly by the fact that it would have been hard to attach preliminary weights to components based on exact criteria, (in fact, none of the basic indices could be assigned to one or the other contact type exclusively), and partly by the fact that in both cases components fitted well to the principal components providing the basis of the global index.

The other problem for the later survey was posed by the inclusion of components providing the basis, where a new aspect, the kinship patron role, was added to former factors. Our analysis shows that this factor fits, although less closely than the other components, basically well with the principal component which was created through its addition, and that the content aspect of representing a certain contact type also supported its inclusion into the global index. However, the concern that global indices should be comparable over time supported the omission of this factor. Finally, for 1997, the index was created in both versions, and certain analyses were performed using these alternatives. Since differences between their results were not really considerable, the more comprehensive index including the kinship patron role was used in further analyses.

Frames of Analysis: A Review of Basic Data

Our aim here is to shed light on factors affecting the differentiation of social network resources from as many sides as possible, including the recent tendencies related to socioeconomic transformation, using possible comparisons over time. In addition to global associations, results by contact type are also considered. Due to the nature of our survey and the present stage of processing, we do not discuss the effect of network resources as an independent variable on other phenomena. The focus of our attention in the present phase of our study concerns access in the first place, while mobilization aspects may be treated in a later stage.[8]

First, analyses of resource types from 1987 and 1997 are presented. The analyses cover four components for 1987 and five components for 1997, while the aforesaid global resource index enters as the fifth and sixth factor, respectively. Before we present the results of regression analyses revealing underlying factors, it will be useful to treat briefly the basic variables and the respective data themselves.

Among the components we introduce in the first place is the range of all contacts reported for all situations, based on the Fischer method in 1987, and on the combined GGS—Fischer method in 1997. It is a more complex index than the number of social-network members reported since it also includes the degree of multiplicity in contacts made with various individuals—which itself can be considered a resource. (In fact, the application of one or the other index makes little difference since the correlation between the two is remarkably high.) While direct temporal comparison is ruled out in this case, a cross-cultural data pair presents itself for observation. The first situation of the technique used in 1997, "discussing important matters during the past six months," can be compared to the 1985 U.S. data (refer to Marsden 1987). Data concerning contacts reported are here available for comparison. An average of three people were mentioned in response to this question during the American survey which was carried out roughly ten years before our Hungarian survey, where this number hardly exceeded two (2.23). It shows an important difference and also signals the persistence of certain traditional patterns that, compared to the essentially equal distribution of kinship and nonkinship contacts in the American population, Hungarian respondents reported nearly three times as many kinship than nonkinship contacts.

When our analyses are based on the results derived from all three situations, the inclusion of the two additional situations (getting help and shared leisure activities) somewhat modifies the above picture. The proportion of nonkinship contacts will be somewhat higher (from 25 to 30 percent). Generally, an average of 3.5 people were reported on these questions (remember that the eight situations resulted in 6.1 people reported ten years before).

There are more possibilities of direct comparison in the case of the position-generator technique, based on the occupational list, where some of the basic data can be juxtaposed with data collected ten years earlier. While the number of total cases reported shows little change, we can discern certain typical modifications. Generally, acquaintance with certain traditionally blue-collar occupations (e.g., factory or railway worker) considerably decreased, that with traditionally white-collar and service occupations remained more or less the same, while that with groups falling into the entrepreneurial sphere (e.g., boutique owners), which had appeared on the list used ten years earlier, increased significantly.

Questions concerning contact through correspondence (i.e., greeting cards) provide the most direct basis of comparison since they had the same form in both surveys. The changes observed correspond to other data concerning the loosening of certain contacts and their deterioration, at least in the deprived social strata. The average number of Christmas and New Year's greeting cards decreased from 9.0 in 1987 to 5.8 in 1997, while the number of those who did not send such cards increased from 15 to 30 percent. Obviously, this result can also be attributed to material circumstances such as the significant increase in postal charges; this, however, cannot be considered a specific factor—as will be seen later, material factors exerted great influence on all contacts.[9]

As to union and organizational memberships, a third of those interviewed reported membership in 1997, and a total average frequency of 0.44 was recorded. It is much lower than values measured in the United States in the nineties, which was an average of 1.5 memberships per respondent (Putnam 1995). Although the difference between the earlier open and the current closed versions restricts comparison over time, findings show that no remarkable change occurred in this field, i.e., willingness to associate did not increase considerably in the last decade.[10]

MAJOR FINDINGS

Determining Factors of Access

As indicated above, the focus of our analysis in the present stage of the study concerns those factors that have a considerable effect on social differences in access to social network resources in the two years (or at least one of them) covered by the survey, based on the results of the performed regression analyses. Tables 2, 3, and 4 contain only independent variables proving to have significant influence on the social distribution of network assets on the basis of preliminary analyses. Tables 2 and 3 summarize the results from 1987 and 1997, while Table 4 allows direct comparison between the change in the predictors of the global index reflecting the most general associations in the two years. Since, as mentioned above, we should ask whether the inclusion of the new factor, kinship patron role, in 1997 had a more significant influence on comparability, the third table presents the results of regression analyses for both 1997 versions (the one including this factor and the other, which does not).

Among the independent variables, the measurement of two, economic and political resources (wealth and political involvement), deserve special attention. The wealth factor was measured through an inventory of household durables (the frequency of about a dozen household and entertainment appliances) in both years. Although a richer repertory of assets was available when we developed the index for the first survey, the two kinds of indices can be considered more or less equivalent. It is also true for the indicator of political involvement, whose basis was a simple item selected from the variables of the given survey in both years. We used the frequency of political discussions in 1987 and self-categorization on a scale of five of interest in political issues in 1997, respectively. The two indices cover essentially similar contents, which is also reflected in the results below.

For three indices, relative distribution is also presented to illustrate the distribution of the given characteristics within the population (low frequency did not allow us to determine relative distribution for union and club membership). As noted above, all associations shown in Tables 2–4

Table 2. Predictors of Personal Network Resources in Hungary, 1987 (OLS Regression, Beta Coefficients)

	1 Range of Ties (Fischer Technique)	2 Range of "Useful Contacts" (Lin–Dumin Occupational Position Generator)	3 "Mail Networking" (Sending Christmas and New Year Cards, Number)	4 Membership in Voluntary Associations (Number)	5 Index of Combined (1–4) Network Resources (PCA Scores)
Wealth (household assets)	.14	.11	.11	.11	.18
Political involvement	.21	.16	.11	.09	.24
Education	.05	.05	.10	.12	.13
Work activity	.05	.09	.15		
Age	−.25				−.04
Sex (female: +)	.04	−.04	.07	−.12	.06
Family status (married: +)	−.05	.09	.10		
Locality (rural: +)		.16		.04	
Parents' land ownership					
Region (West Hungary: +)		.06	.10	.05	.10
Self-employed, entrepreneur			.08		
Manager, supervisor				.10	.09
Ex-membership in HSWP[a]		.05		.10	.06
R²	.22	.12	.09	.14	.28
Relative variance	.64	.63	.92		

Source: Angelusz–Tardos project on cultural-interactional stratification, 1987, implemented by TÁRKI, Budapest (sample representative of adult population, n = 2982).
[a]Hungarian Socialist Workers' Party before 1989.

Table 3. Predictors of Personal Network Resources in Hungary, 1997 (OLS Regression, Beta Coefficients)

	1 Range of Ties (Fischer Technique)	2 Range of "Useful Contacts" (Lin–Dumin Occupational Position Generator)	3 "Mail Networking" (Sending Christmas and New Year Cards, Number)	4 Membership in Voluntary Associations (Number)	5 Kinship Patron Roles (Wedding Witness, Godparent, Number)	6 Index of Combined (1–4) Network Resources (PCA Scores)
Wealth (household assets)	.27	.19	.16	.10	.09	.26
Political involvement	.24	.22	.13	.12		.27
Education		.11	.12	.14		.14
Work activity	.09	.11		.13		.14
Age	−.07		.13	.08	.29	.09
Sex (female: +)	.12			−.10	−.11	
Family status (married: +)		.07			.17	.09
Locality (rural: +)		.14		.09		
Land ownership	.07	.12			.08	.09
Region (West Hungary: +)		.07	.12			.07
Self-employed, entrepreneur		.07				
Manager, supervisor			.11			.06
Membership in former HSWP[a]		.07			.10	
R²	.21	.25	.11	.15	.18	.36
Relative variance	.60	.78	1.18			

Source: Omnibus survey of the Research Group of Communication Studies, Budapest, November–December, 1997 (sample representative of adult population, n = 995).
Hungarian Socialist Workers Party before 1989.

Table 4. Comparison of Predictors of Overall Personal Network Resources in Hungary, 1987 and 1997 (OLS Regression, Beta Coefficients; Dependent Variable: Unrotated Principal Component from Components 1–4 and 1–5)

	1987	1997	
		Based on Components	
	1–4	*1–4*	*1–5*
Wealth (household assets)	.18	.27	.26
Political involvement	.24	.27	.27
Education	.13	.17	.14
Work activity		.12	.14
Age	−.04		.09
Family status (married: +)	.06	.06	.09
Locality (rural: +)		.10	
(Parents') land ownership		.08	.09
Region (West Hungary: +)	.10	.08	.07
Self-employed, entrepreneur	.04		
Manager, supervisor	.06		
Membership in former HSWP[a]	.06		.06
R²	.28	.36	.36

[a]Hungarian Socialist Workers Party before 1989.

and Figures 1 and 2 are significant (with the empty cells indicating negligible values).

Results (Figures 1 and 2) indicate a simultaneous stability and change in the social differentiation of personal network resources. We can speak of stability to the extent that the overall explanation of various factors outlines an essentially similar pattern, and that political involvement and

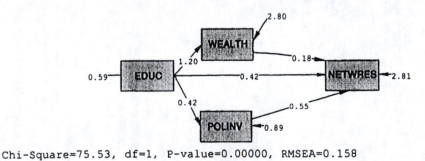

Chi-Square=75.53, df=1, P-value=0.00000, RMSEA=0.158

Figure 1. A path model of prediction of personal network resources in Hungary, 1987 (LIREL 8.30, standardized coefficients).

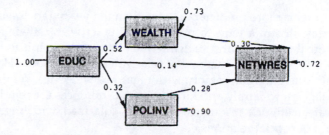

Chi-Square=39.77, df=1, P-value=0.00000, RMSEA=0.114

Figure 2. A path model of prediction of personal network resources in Hungary, 1997 (LIREL 8.30, standardized coefficients).

wealth can be considered the main predictors in both years. As for other factors, education, managerial position, family status, and region, they retained their significant role in the explanation of differences.

Manifestations of Stability and Change

These results are by no means self-evident. To begin with, take the role of political involvement that in 1987 proved to be the main predictor of personal-network resources (according to both individual and combined indices). Here the assumed direction of the correlation itself should be reconsidered since in pluralistic political settings and at a certain degree of differentiation among various social spheres the possession of network resources as a whole can just as well be an antecedent of involvement in politics as a consequence of it. We think that for the Hungary of 1987, where political resources were highly integrated with other resources and played a major role in creating these syndromes, the assumption of this model of variables is justified. This line of interpretation is also supported by the fact that former party membership exerted a considerable influence on social-network resources at that time. It is a matter of further research to find out why political involvement as seen in the 1997 model was given a role similar to that in the first survey.[11] This question deserves attention also because the close integration of political involvement with other kinds of capital, whether we consider it an antecedent or a consequence, may be considered a paradoxical feature of democratic settings.

When discussing the factors of change, first we should point out that for some components, primarily for the occupational nexus as well as for the global index, explanation for social differentiation increased. To go into specific detail concerning the former issue, based on the social-demographic factors included in our recent survey, whether the respondent is acquainted with a lawyer, a secondary-school teacher, or an unskilled worker is more predictable today than ten years ago. Results indicate that today all strata tend to move and interact within their own boundaries more than earlier, and such internal networking points toward a class-specific isolation. The increase of relative variance values also shows increasing differentiation mainly with regard to weak ties. While in aspects that fall closer to family and kinship links differences are relatively more moderate, network resources are more polarized with regard to assets of broader social relations.

The increased role of economic resources and wealth in the social differentiation of network resources points to a similar direction. Its influence has strengthened in almost all aspects and it has become one of the leading predictors, its weight being essentially identical to that of political involvement. The role of wealth increased in establishing looser contacts and nexus, as well as in the conditioning of family and kinship contacts. More detailed analyses show that, in light of the range of kinship links, the influence of wealth resources within the personal network significantly increased between 1987 and 1997 (respective beta coefficients are 0.04 and 0.20). It is probably due not just to the fact that maintaining and keeping even these contacts requires increased assets, but also that kinship reciprocity demands a certain level of material conditions for all parties. In younger age groups, it can be attributed to the factor that establishing one's own family requires increasingly substantial, previously accumulated wealth.

Education appears in the series of moderately strong variables in both cases; this, however, does not mean that it is not one of the most influential factors. Its indirect role approaches its direct role, primarily through its association with wealth, but also partly with political involvement. According to the data, it is clear, however, that the realization of cultural resources in improving personal network positions assumed a significant degree of material and political mediation in the period surveyed, while less mediation is required in the reverse direction (for instance, wealth itself provides for the development of proper nexus).

An important lesson of the 1997 survey to be further analyzed in more detail is that personal networks became more homophilious and generally more closed with respect to education and occupation. Based on the results of the multiple-situation name-generator technique, we can conclude that fewer people with higher social status were chosen, and the educational and occupational status of respondents and their contacts became generally more similar, representing a shift toward the "like attracts like" pattern of social relationships. A more detailed breakdown of data shows that contacts initiated from below (mainly from respondents who completed secondary school) became more closed mainly toward diploma holders.

The Role of Wealth, Culture, and Political Involvement

The changes in the relative predictive strengths of the three primary resources above are, compared to Tables 2–4, reflected in a more clear-cut way by the results of the regression analyses, which included only these three basic factors, and their prediction was not influenced by less relevant factors. They show that before the systemic change, in addition to the outstanding role of political involvement, the direct roles of wealth and education corresponded to each other. By the second half of the 1990s, the influence of wealth had significantly increased, while the direct effect of education fell back to the third position in the rank order of compared factors (Table 5).

At first sight, one might interpret these findings as a sign of decreased significance of the role of education as compared to resources directly related to the market. It would be mistake, however, to totally discount the cultural factor in conditioning the range of personal network assets. Starting from a comprehensive view of education as a background factor behind both one's material status and access to the political sphere one can arrive at a more complex conclusion.[12] The four-variable LISREL path model based on this premise for both 1987 and 1997 yields an output manifesting this double role of cultural background.

Taking the direct and indirect effects, mediated through wealth and political involvement, as a whole, the role of education tends to converge with those of the other two variables included in the explanation of the variance of personal network resources. While the direct effect diminished somewhat between 1987 and 1997, the indirect one grew as mediated through the material factor with increased strength of explanation.

On the whole, one can at the same time observe a picture of striking stability in the chain of interrelationships. The size of the coefficients remained almost unchanged in all but some cases, not to speak of the signs.

Table 5. Comparison of Predictors of Overall Personal Network Resources in Hungary, Short Model, 1987 and 1997 (OLS Regression, Beta Coefficients)

	1987	1997
Wealth (household assets)	.17	.31
Political involvement	.28	.28
Education	.18	.12
R^2	.23	.29

Given this pattern of overall permanence, the increased role of wealth in the wake of system change in access to network resources is all the more remarkable.[13]

Some Specific Effects: Regional and Cohort Characteristics

Returning to the wider set of factors included in the models of Tables 2–4, the result related to the role of land ownership points to an interesting development clearly having to do with the transformations of the last decade. The fact that it has also appeared in the series of significant predictors of social network resources underlines the increased role of wealth-related factors. However, the finding is of interest on its own as well, for it shows that land possession began to reconquer its traditional role in the prestige order of rural localities.

Similarly, the increased role of activity or working status can be related to the consequences of economic transition. It reflects the social impoverishment that comes with a pensioner existence, as well as that having a job became an important division within younger and middle-aged generations under the new circumstances. The sidelined, by losing their important network resource, were also devalued as potential partners (obviously, it is not only that the unemployed generally have less cultural and material resources available, since this effect, when the above factors are accounted for, can be solely attributed to work activity). The data indicating the minimum of network resources suggest that members of this group are hardly able to compensate for the lack of contacts from within their own circles through mutual support. The correlation observed indicates a downward spiral running along long-term unemployment, which can contribute to its reproduction.

Among the stable background variables of social-network resources, in addition to managerial and supervisor jobs and family status (which points to the social resources of married people), the regional factor, also of long-term effect, deserves attention. Although differences by settlement type are vague—and even if we can discern some tendency, it shows that people living in villages or small towns have a social background that is socially more heterogeneous or more embedded in locality—settlements in West Hungary show a richer population network. These values were the highest in the northwest region of the country, which is the most developed in many respects, followed by the southwest in both years. Since, again, it cannot be considered the aggregate effect of the higher education and wealth status of people living in these regions, we can obviously find a contextual effect which may be related to the urban traditions of these areas, to the smoother development of local societies and perhaps to the fact that because they are more frequently visited tourist spots, they provide a wider access to nonlocal, external contacts.

Regional differences also deserve attention from another aspect. If the divide between western and eastern areas (or, first, between the capital and the country) is really significant, then we can assume a different pattern of the social differentiation of network resources, and from an additional longitudinal perspective we can have an insight into certain development trends. Focusing on essential aspects of the short model, we compared the predictors of network resources, measured on the basis of the global index at the two survey dates, in various regions. (To have a better overview, regions were divided into three parts only: the capital, West Hungary, and East Hungary.)

While practically no time-specific changes were discerned in the influence of relationships to politics, definite regional differences could be observed in the relative role of cultural and material resources in addition to the era-specific features discussed above. Material resources in West Hungary played a more significant role in differentiating social relations than in other regions, while cultural resources tended to have a dominant influence in East Hungary during the first survey. After the systemic change, the economic aspect became still more prominent and the cultural one fell back conspicuously in West Hungary. The increase in the influence of the wealth factor is also conspicuous in the capital. These findings suggest that the discussed restructuring of network resources along class lines occurred mainly in regions close to the center, in the capital and West Hungary, while features of traditional status-order social organization, related to the dominance of political and cultural aspects, were more resistant to change in East Hungary.

As an additional direction of our analyses, period effects and the trend of overall change have been approached from one more angle by means of contrasting various age-groups/cohorts of the population (through a filtering).[14] While available data do not permit a cohort analysis proper, we must remind ourselves that we had data from only two times. This problem is lessened to the extent that it is not so much cohort but period effects that are of most interest in this context. It has seemed sufficient to discern three groups for this purpose: those under 35 (at the time of the 1997 survey those starting their adult careers around the systemic change), the middle (35–54) and the older (above 55) age groups. As for the variables included, we have employed the module of the short model again.

While the pattern of determinants remained almost unchanged among the older population (those above 55, mostly inactive in Hungary in the economic sphere), likely related to the fact that they have shaped the main features of their social bonds in earlier stages of their life-paths (that is in periods prior to the transformations of the last decade), members of younger age groups still advancing along their careers seem to be better adapted to the changed circumstances. It is these contexts where the growing influence of material assets manifests itself most saliently in shaping the access to network resources, pointing to new patterns of capital conversion in the wake of advancing market forces in Hungary.[15]

CONCLUSION

Systemic change and the targeted transition to a market economy raised the question whether the primacy of market relations and the disappearance of shortages has led to a decreased role for informal behavior patterns and personal nexus. Or whether, for other reasons and in some altered form, nonmarket mechanisms in the economy, intertwined with informal means in polity, have survived, strengthening traditional features of the social fabric.

With the transition still under way, we need a broader time perspective. Also, to date there is a paucity of evidence on these issues based on empirical research. Existing data sets, however, such as survey data from 1987 and 1997 on the development of social network resources, can be included in the given context. The findings suggest the existence of both stability and change in the pattern of the social distribution of network resources. The two strongest explanatory variables remained the same as in the past: political involvement and wealth. Though obviously with a shift in character, political involvement has kept its leading role in shaping network resources. The finding points to the strong interdependence of political and social capital even under the present circumstances, revealing a problematic feature of the transformation process.

One can observe, on the other hand, a rearrangement in the influence of components of the social scale. The most salient change is related to the material dimension. Though even earlier an important factor, the significance of wealth has increased in almost all respects under study. The role of education has become, on the other hand, more indirect, mediated by the factors above. This new pattern manifests itself most saliently with the younger age groups and the Western regions of the country closer to the central areas of Europe.

Some new factors surfaced as important predictors, emphasizing the increased role of economic factors. Work activity (earning status, job security) has become more influential across most aspects and the overall resources, too. Following the privatization process, land ownership has become a new component on its own. An additional element, clearly a result of the transition, the range of network resources available to entrepreneurs and the self-employed has joined that of managers and professionals.

While the worth of weak ties instrumental in acquiring patronage and scarce information in business life and elsewhere has increased in all probability, one can observe growing inequality in the access to these types of network resources. At the same time, the exchange value of contacts with representatives of some traditional occupations (not to speak of the broadened inactive population) has depreciated. Nonfamily, nonkin resources have become scarce for a large segment in the lower strata of the population.

NOTES

The article is a revised version of the authors' paper for the Social Networks and Social Capital Conference at Duke University in 1998. The project has been supported by two consecutive OTKA grants (National Research Fund) for research on civic participation, social integration, and the sociocultural context.

1. Van Meter's paper on the use of the concept of "social capital" is a richly documented review of the fragmented character of the various approaches applying to this catchall term before 1995. Since the period covered, one can see certain signs of a theoretical elaboration of the concept, the conference at Durham representing an important stage. Nan Lin's (1998b) distinction of the structure, and action-oriented, macro-, mezzo-, and microlevel interpretations of the concept (corresponding respectively to its embeddedness, access, and mobilization aspects) is a significant step in the direction of clarification. Hardin's treatise yields some interesting distinctions of interpersonal and institutional capital beside Becker's specific usage of the term SC (implying the enhancement of consumption value owing to one's social milieu) from a utilitarian point of view. Also, Burt's differentiation between three (entrepreneurial, clique, and hierarchical) network forms of social capital provides a more subtle view of one subdomain of the concept in question.

2. Our approach of stratification emphasized cultural and interactional aspects. It was based on two conceptual pillars: social network resources (as outlined below in more detail) and types of knowledge based on the distinction of three types of skills: cognitive-instrumental; contact-oriented, self-presentational; and symbolic-representative, all of which were approached by various sets of empirical indicators.

3. Our references in this respect include both statistical and survey research data. To start with to the former, in the 1980s the number of active employed adult population moved around 4.8–5 million people. By 1997 the correspondent figure among the age 15–74 population dropped to 3.6 million (Statistical Yearbook of Hungary 1987, 1998). As to the latter we can refer both to the surveys covered by this study and, with regard to the last period, the 1997–1998 preelection surveys of Szonda Ipsos Institute based on a 6000-person national sample (all of these covering the adult popula-

tion over 18). While according to our 1987 survey (carried out by TARKI) 62 percent of the respondents proved to be actively employed earners, this proportion decreased to 44 percent on the basis of our 1997 survey (carried out by the Research Group for Communication Studies, Budapest). The corresponding proportion was similarly even, 43 percent according to the Szonda Ipsos preelection survey of 1997–98 based on a larger sample. To point to some salient differences in some demographic categories: in 1987 the proportion of active earners amounted to 94 percent of the age 41–50, and 73 percent of the age 51–60 male population. By the 1997–98 survey, these figures dropped to 70 percent and 50 percent, respectively, in the sim-ilar male age groups (well below the normal retirement threshold in Hun-gary, earlier at the age of 60, and at the age of 62 from the end of the 1990s).

4. It seems to us that position-generator techniques may be more closer to the study of the macrolevel structural embeddedness (and partly access), while name-generator techniques are more appropriate to the microlevel mobilization aspects of social capital.

5. The selection of occupations was led by several criteria. On one hand we wanted to ensure a degree of correspondence with the original source (see Lin & Dumin 1986), and include a variety of job types representing high- and low-status positions. Our more specific objective, on the other hand, had to do with the topic of our cultural and interactional stratification sur-vey: distinct types of skills. The occupations selected could be more or less adjusted to our starting typology distinguishing three kinds of knowledge: cognitive-instrumental, self-presentation and contact-creation, and sym-bolic-representative.

6. It is worth noting that during a recent omnibus survey of the Research Group for Communication Studies, carried out at early October 1998, a fur-ther 800 respondents were added to our social network data set from 1997. Only one subquestion of the position-generator technique was changed. Instead of the question about how many (1–2 or more) persons one knows within a given occupation, a new question was included inquiring whether one addresses the respective persons in the informal or the more formal manner (a specific feature of linguistic and sociocultural settings in Hun-gary).

7. Within the principal component that served as a basis, weights of various factors were the following in the two years, respectively: 1987—total num-ber of contacts reported (Fischer) 0.63, occupational nexus 0.60, union membership 0.61, number of greeting cards sent 0.55; 1997—occupational nexus 0.73, total contacts reported (combined GSS—Fischer) 0.69, union membership 0.58, number of greeting cards 0.53, kinship patron role (fac-tor score) 0.37. (When we omitted the last factor, weights changed moder-ately, and factors were 0.75, 0.72, 0.59, and 0.53, respectively.) Generally, factor structure can be considered relatively stable between the two survey dates, although the indices somewhat changed. The most notable change is that the two components that may be considered the central elements of our approach, i.e. the weights of the GSS—Fischer and the Lin—Dumin indices were somewhat greater at the time of the second survey.

8. It deserves mentioning at this point that the central theme of our present topic had to do with political and civic participation and social integration, rather than aspects of individual status attainment.

9. It should be noted, on the other hand, that at the time of the survey (and even now, more or less) Internet contact was available for only a small segment of the population.

10. Twenty percent of respondents reported such membership in 1987, which yielded an average value of 0.27. It should be noted that trade union membership, which was still more or less compulsory at that time, was ignored in 1987, but it was accounted for during the latter survey. If we account for these two factors in current data, then we find that only 23 percent of this population indicated some kind of membership, and the average value fell to 0.33. If we also control for the somewhat more imperative nature of the closed form, no considerable change between 1987 and 1997 can be reported.

11. A problem emphasized by Professor Erickson concerning our findings at the Sunbelt Conference, Sitges.

12. We hereby express our thanks to Professors Burt and Lin for raising the question of direct and indirect effects of education and the need of further analyses in this respect at the Durham Conference.

13. It is certainly debatable whether we have been right to base our model on the same chain of paths in both cases. While the placement of education as a background factor concerning both wealth and political involvement may be more or less generally shared, there may be more disagreement, a question already raised above, about assuming an unchanged path of interrelationship in the model between political and network resources. While the statistical technique employed is of little help in making this decision, it is the authors' conception of the overall web of factors that is to be referred to when keeping with the initial pattern of dependent and independent (or endogenous) variables.

14. With these analyses we have been greatly stimulated by Professor Fernandez's suggestions raised concerning our paper at the Social Networks and Social Capital Conference.

15. More specifically, the regression coefficients related to wealth more than doubled in these younger age groups, jumping to first place among the three independent variables.

REFERENCES

Albert, F. 1998. "Friendships and the Transition in Hungary." Paper presented at the INSNASunbelt Conference paper, Sitges, Spain.

Angelusz, R., and R. Tardos. 1988. "A magyarországi kapcsolathálózatok néhány sajátossága" (Some characteristics of social networks in Hungary). *Szociológiai Szemle* (2):185–204.

———. 1990. "Basic Data of the Social Distribution of Knowledge Styles in Hungary in the Eighties. Pp. 230–49 in *Social Report 1990*, edited by R. Andorka, T. Kolosi, and Gy. Vukovich. Budapest: TÁRKI.

———. 1991. "A gyenge kötések ereje és gyengesége" (The strength and weakness of "weak ties"). Pp. 40–59 in *Társas kapcsolatok* (Social relations), edited by Á. Utasi.Budapest: Gondolat.

Bourdieu, P. 1983. Ökonomisches Kapital, kulturelles Kapital, soziales Kapital. Pp. 183–98 in *Soziale Ungleichheiten*, edited by R. Kreckel. Soziale Welt Sonderband. Göttingen: Otto Schwartz.

Böröcz, J., and C. Southworth. 1995. "Kapcsolatok és jövedelem. Magyarország 1986–87" (Contacts and income. Hungary, 1986–87). *Szociológiai Szemle* (2): 25–48.

Burt, R. S. 1984. "Network Items and the General Social Survey." *Social Networks* 293–339.

———. 1992. *Structural Holes*. Cambridge, MA: Harvard University Press.

———. 1998. "The Network Structure of Social Capital." Paper for the "Social Networks and Social Capital" Conference at Duke University, Durham, NC.

Coleman, J. 1988. "Social Capital in the Creation of Social Capital." *American Journal of Sociology* 94:95–120.

Czakó, Á. 1994. "Kapcsolathálózatok szerepe a magyar gazdaságban" (The role of social networks in Hungarian economy). Manuscript, Budapest.

Erickson, B. 1996. "Culture, Class, Connections." *American Journal of Sociology* 102:217–51.

Fischer, C., and L. McAllister. 1978. "A Procedure for Surveying Personal Networks." *Sociological Methods and Research* 7:131–48.

Granovetter, M. S. 1974. *Getting a Job*. Cambridge, MA: Harvard University Press.

Hardin, R. 1998. "Social Capital." Paper for the "Social Networks and Social Capital" Conference at Duke University, Durham, NC.

Lengyel, Gy. 1998. "Megszûnés, bõvülés, kapcsolat: A kisvállalkozások helyzete 1993–1996" (Abolition, extension, and relations: The situation of small enterprises between 1993 and 1996). Manuscript.

Lin, N. 1995. Les ressource social: Une theorie de capital social. *Revue Francaise de Sociologie* 36:685–704.

———. 1998a. "Social Networks and Status Attainment." *Annual Review of Sociology* 25.

———. 1998b. "The Position Generator: A Measurement for Social Capital." Paper for the "Social Networks and Social Capital" Conference at Duke University, Durham, NC.

Lin, N., and M. Dumin. 1986. "Access to Occupations through Social Ties." *Social Networks* 8:365–86.

Marsden, P. V. 1987. "Core Discussion Networks of Americans." *American Sociological Review* 52:122–31.

Putnam, R. 1995. "Tuning In, Turning Out: The Strange Disappearance of Social Capital in America." *Political Science and Politics* 28:664–83.

Róna-Tas, Á. 1994. "The First Shall Be the Last?" *American Journal of Sociology* 100:40–69.

Sík, E. 1994. "Network Capital in Capitalist, Communist and Post-Communist Societies." *International Contributions to Labor Studies* 4:73–93.

Sík, E., and B.Wellman. 1998. "Network Capital in Capitalist, Communist and Post-communist Countries." In *Networks in the Global Village*, edited by B.Wellman. Boulder, CO: Westview Press.

Stark, D. 1996. "Recombinant Property in East European Capitalism." *American Journal ofSociology* 101:993–1027.

Statistical Yearbook of Hungary, 1987. Bp.KSH 1988.

———. 1998. Bp.KSH 1999.

Szelényi, I., and Sz. Szelényi. 1995. "Circulation or Reproduction of Elites During Post-Communist Transformation in Eastern Europe." *Theory and Society* (Oct.).

Tardos, R. 1996. "Some Remarks on the Interpretation and Possible Uses of the Social Capital Concept with Special Regard to the Hungarian Case." *Bulletin de Methodologie Sociologique* 53:52–62.

Utasi, Á. 1991. "Az interperszonális kapcsolatok néhány nemzeti sajátossága" (Some nationalcharacteristics of interpersonal relations). Pp. 169–93 in *Társas kapcsolatok* (Social relations), edited by Á. Utasi. Budapest: Gondolat.

———. 1996. "Hungarian Peculiarities in the Choice of Friends." Paper for the Conference of International Network on Personal Relationship, Seattle, WA.

Van Meter, K. 1998. "Social Capital Research Literature." Paper for the XVIII Sunbelt Conference. Sitges, Spain.

Vedres, B. 1997. "Bank és hatalom" (Banks and power). *Szociológiai Szemle* (2):101–24.

INDEX